Criminalising Coercive Control

Marilyn McMahon · Paul McGorrery
Editors

Criminalising Coercive Control

Family Violence and the Criminal Law

Springer

Editors
Marilyn McMahon
School of Law
Deakin University
Burwood, VIC, Australia

Paul McGorrery
School of Law
Deakin University
Burwood, VIC, Australia

ISBN 978-981-15-0655-0   ISBN 978-981-15-0653-6 (eBook)
https://doi.org/10.1007/978-981-15-0653-6

© Springer Nature Singapore Pte Ltd. 2020

This work is subject to copyright. All rights are reserved by the Publisher, whether the whole or part of the material is concerned, specifically the rights of translation, reprinting, reuse of illustrations, recitation, broadcasting, reproduction on microfilms or in any other physical way, and transmission or information storage and retrieval, electronic adaptation, computer software, or by similar or dissimilar methodology now known or hereafter developed.

The use of general descriptive names, registered names, trademarks, service marks, etc. in this publication does not imply, even in the absence of a specific statement, that such names are exempt from the relevant protective laws and regulations and therefore free for general use.

The publisher, the authors and the editors are safe to assume that the advice and information in this book are believed to be true and accurate at the date of publication. Neither the publisher nor the authors or the editors give a warranty, expressed or implied, with respect to the material contained herein or for any errors or omissions that may have been made. The publisher remains neutral with regard to jurisdictional claims in published maps and institutional affiliations.

This Springer imprint is published by the registered company Springer Nature Singapore Pte Ltd.
The registered company address is: 152 Beach Road, #21-01/04 Gateway East, Singapore 189721, Singapore

Foreword

The Honourable Professor Marcia Neave AO FASSA

This interesting collection of essays examines whether the criminal law should punish a family member who systematically controls and dominates another member of their family. The contributors are experts in criminal law, criminology, family violence, sociology and feminist legal theory.

The book focuses on intimate partner violence in heterosexual relationships, where one member of the couple (more commonly the man) exercises coercive control over his female partner ('domestic violence'). However much of the discussion is also relevant to coercive control exercised in other family relationships ('family violence'), for example, violence between gay couples, and violence by adult children against elderly parents.

The expression coercive control recognises that family violence is not limited to physical assault and threats. As State intervention/protection order legislation acknowledges, it often includes psychological or emotional abuse such as demeaning the victim by constantly telling them they are stupid, incompetent and ugly, manipulating the victim so that they distrust their own sanity (sometimes called 'gaslighting') and preventing the victim seeing their own friends or family. Coercive control may take the form of economic abuse, for example stopping a partner from working outside the home, depriving them of money or forcing them to guarantee a loan or to borrow money for the perpetrator. It may include bombarding the victim with messages or threats, which keep them in a constant state of fear. Technological abuse can involve using phones, computers and other devices to keep the victim under surveillance. In one case described to the Victorian Royal Commission into Family Violence, a woman's former partner kept her under surveillance by concealing a tracking device in her child's teddy bear.

The central question canvassed by this edited collection is whether the various forms of non-physical abuse of family members should be criminalised and, if so, what forms of behaviour should be punished? So far, Tasmania is the only Australian State to create offences of economic and emotional abuse. Legislation which criminalises various forms of coercive control has also recently been enacted in England, Scotland, Wales and Ireland. Discussion of jurisdictional differences and of the different costs and benefits of criminalisation will provide an excellent guide to policymakers.

The Victorian Royal Commission into Family Violence was told by survivors of non-physical forms of family violence that it could take longer to get over the effects of sustained emotional or financial abuse than to recover from a physical assault. Some survivors even said that they would have preferred to have been physically injured because even when they realised that non-physical abuse was a form of family violence, and reported it to family members, doctors or the police, they might not be believed. But although the Commission recognised that coercive control is a central feature of family violence, and particularly violence directed at intimate partners, it did not recommend that new offences be introduced to punish coercive control or specific aspects of such control, for example, emotional or economic abuse.

Criminalising the horrific forms of cruelty and abuse which are used by some perpetrators is immediately appealing. Introducing offences to cover these forms of domestic terrorism would acknowledge the long-lasting harm suffered by victims of coercive control. Applying criminal sanctions to non-physical abuse would condemn abusive behaviour and deter those who might be inclined to rely on it. But in my view, it would be premature to introduce such offences. There are practical difficulties in ensuring that these offences actually help victims of family violence. Some police are still reluctant to investigate physical assaults, and investigating allegations of non-physical abuse is likely to be particularly difficult. Except in extreme cases, which are likely to involve physical abuse as well, victims may be reluctant to give evidence or unable to describe accurately what happened to them. We know there are difficulties in prosecuting alleged offenders for behaviour which takes place over a significant period, rather than in one or more separate incidents. These difficulties already arise in prosecuting continuing sexual offending against children, where justice to alleged offenders requires that they understand the behaviour for which they are being prosecuted and victims often have difficulty in describing or are unable to recall examples of the prohibited behaviour. Widespread change is required to ensure that perpetrators of physical violence are effectively prosecuted and that prosecutors do not accept guilty pleas to lesser assault charges, rather than persisting with prosecutions for non-physical abuse. In my view we should be satisfied that police, prosecutors and courts have changed their practices, before we widen the criminal justice response to cover emotional or financial abuse. There is also a concern that introducing a coercive control offence might unfairly differentiate between the situation where egregious bullying and abusive behaviour occurring inside a family is criminalised, but long-standing similar behaviour in work, school or institutional settings is not.

It was for these reasons that the Victorian Royal Commission into Family Violence decided not to recommend the adoption of an offence of the kind that now exists in Scotland under the *Domestic Abuse (Scotland) Act 2018*. The concerns about criminalisation that I have expressed may prove wrong in the future, but the value of this approach has not yet been fully demonstrated. We need more evidence on the success of introducing criminal offences of this kind in other jurisdictions.

Despite my reservations about the criminalisation of coercive control, I applaud the editors and authors for their deft and comprehensive contribution to this debate. All of us share the goal of reducing all forms of family violence including the cruelty of non-physical abuse, which injures and blights the lives of all those subjected to it. This book makes an important contribution to that goal.

The Hon Professor Marcia Neave AO
Faculty of Law, Monash University
VIC, Australia

Preface

On 29 December 2015, the British Parliament did something extraordinary. It brought into law a new offence that recognised non-physical domestic abuse as criminal. Only once before (in Tasmania, Australia) had a common law jurisdiction enacted such an offence. Traditionally, the criminal law has been exclusively concerned with physical violence committed by one partner (usually a male) against another (usually a female). This narrow construction of family violence meant that the criminal law has been incapable of responding to what most family violence victims describe as the 'worst part': the emotional and psychological abuse, the economic abuse, and the deprivation of liberty, autonomy and identity.

That is no longer the case. With the offence of controlling or coercive behaviour now in operation in England and Wales and related offences enacted in Tasmania, Scotland and Ireland, criminal justice systems are recognising and responding to a much broader range of harms. Early cases in England reveal that offenders who have been convicted of the offence of controlling or coercive behaviour have: threatened to publicly share explicit photographs of their partners or ex-partners; prevented their partner from ending the relationship by threatening to, or actually, engaging in self-harm; isolated their partners by confiscating or destroying their mobile phones and deleting all male contacts on their social media; demanded that their partners eat certain foods, sleep in certain places and exercise daily; prohibited their partners from engaging in employment; conducted regular inspections of their partner's home and body for any evidence of infidelity; and a myriad of other behaviours, all of which were connected by the singular goal of exerting dominance, coercion and control over another human being.

Other jurisdictions are now considering whether to implement similar offences. As these jurisdictions decide whether, and how, to criminalise non-physical abuse, the need for careful and considered policy and lawmaking in this area is critical. It is to those matters that this edited volume is directed. The book originated from a roundtable that we hosted in Melbourne, Australia in November 2017. We invited noted academics and criminal justice practitioners from Australia, the United Kingdom and the United States to discuss key issues involved in criminalising coercive control. Many of the people who attended and presented at the roundtable have contributed to this book.

Part I of this book outlines the harms and wrongs of non-physical abuse. Chapter 1 locates the new domestic abuse offences within contemporary developments in the criminal law and argues that they reflect the growing impact of human rights considerations as well as an increasing recognition of the serious harms caused by this abuse. In Chap. 2, Evan Stark, whose work has been credited as the inspiration for the offence in England and Wales, clarifies his definition of coercive control and outlines a 'constellation of factors' that he believes will determine the efficacy, or otherwise, of any new offence. In Chap. 3, Supriyah Singh explains economic abuse through the lens of her own qualitative research comparing the experiences of Anglo-Celtic and Indian women in Australia and concludes that this particular form of abuse must be included within any offence that purports to criminalise non-physical abuse. More generally, Danielle Tyson (Chap. 4) outlines the important role of coercive control in domestic violence (and particularly intimate partner homicide) and outlines how the recognition of coercive control could inform claims of self-defence for women who kill their abusive partners.

Part II of the book is then directed at the notion that there is a 'gap' in the current law which a new offence might fill. We, along with Kelley Burton (Chap. 5), consider whether a new offence is even necessary or whether extant stalking laws might already be capable of capturing non-physical abuse between intimate partners. We conclude that while stalking laws are technically capable of applying in those contexts, limitations in community and expert understandings of stalking restrict the effective operation of those laws. In Chap. 6, Julia Quilter applies a new processes and modalities approach to understanding criminalisation and considers the challenges that must be addressed when attempting to transpose a new criminal offence from one jurisdiction to another. She concludes that despite the inherent problems of criminalisation through 'gap-filling', the time for a new family violence offence is 'now'.

Part III of this book is an analysis of the offences that have been introduced in Tasmania, England and Wales, and Scotland. While the English and Welsh offence has received a considerable amount of attention in both the media and scholarly circles, it is perhaps less well known that the Australian State of Tasmania introduced similar offences of 'economic abuse' and 'emotional abuse and intimidation' over a decade earlier in 2005. Along with police prosecutor Kerryne Barwick, we discuss the Tasmanian offences, focusing on difficulties in their construction that likely contributed to the scarcity of prosecutions (Chap. 7). In Chap. 8, Cassandra Wiener traces how Evan Stark's sociological construct of 'coercive control' was transformed into a legal (and policy) concept in England and Wales, and identifies a number of successes and problems that occurred during that translation. And in Chap. 9, Marsha Scott outlines the new Scottish offence of domestic abuse, an offence that is acclaimed by many as 'the new gold standard'. As CEO of *Women's Aid Scotland*, Scott is in the unique position of being able to outline how victim-survivors and their advocates contributed to the development and enactment of the Scottish offence, and how critical it is for policymakers to engage with them during the reform process.

Finally, in Part IV of this book, the authors consider ways of moving forward. In Chap. 10, Vanessa Bettinson presents a comprehensive overview of the various offences in Tasmania, England and Wales, Ireland and Scotland and a comparative analysis of those offences. She identifies considerable variations, with different approaches to, for example, who the victims may be (partners, ex-partners, other family members), maximum penalties for the offences, and whether an offender will only be liable if they actually caused the victim significant harm of some sort. In Chap. 11, Jane Wangmann argues that while a new offence could potentially be a positive development, the true value of 'coercive control' lies in it informing understandings of domestic abuse throughout justice systems. And finally, in Chap. 12, Heather Douglas offers an alternative approach, suggesting that the formulation of crimes such as 'torture' (introduced in Queensland, Australia in 1997) could be used more frequently to prosecute non-physical abuse and could be modified (with a lesser offence of 'cruelty') to address a range of domestic abuse.

As readers progress through the book they will be exposed to varying viewpoints. Our particular contributions reveal that we favour introducing a new offence that broadens the range of harms captured by the criminal law in relation to family violence. We don't identify a model offence; on this, readers will no doubt benefit from the descriptions and evaluations provided by other contributors. Our aim is to engage in further discussion and debate about the optimal form such an offence might take, its likely impact, and issues in relation to operationalisation. We think that criminalisation is warranted because the harms experienced by victims are considerable and the human rights abuse significant. To fail to criminalise relevant abuse means that it will continue to be borne by victim-survivors as a private burden.

We know that some think otherwise and are yet to be convinced that criminalising non-physical abuse is a positive step. They argue, *inter alia*, that there is a risk that such an offence could further disenfranchise those it is designed to protect, and that introducing a new offence could distract attention from other vital reforms. These are valid concerns. But they are inherent challenges to address in the process of reform, not reasons to avoid it altogether.

Melbourne, Australia
Marilyn McMahon
Paul McGorrery

Contents

Part I The Harms and Wrongs of Non-Physical Abuse

1 Criminalising Coercive Control: An Introduction 3
   Marilyn McMahon and Paul McGorrery

2 The 'Coercive Control Framework': Making Law Work
   for Women 33
   Evan Stark

3 Economic Abuse and Family Violence Across Cultures:
   Gendering Money and Assets Through Coercive Control 51
   Supriya Singh

4 Coercive Control and Intimate Partner Homicide 73
   Danielle Tyson

Part II Fixing a 'Gap' in the Law?

5 An Alternative Means of Prosecuting Non-Physical Domestic
   Abuse: Are Stalking Laws an Under-Utilised Resource? 93
   Marilyn McMahon, Paul McGorrery and Kelley Burton

6 Evaluating Criminalisation as a Strategy in Relation
   to Non-Physical Family Violence 111
   Julia Quilter

Part III New Initiatives

7 Ahead of Their Time? The Offences of Economic and Emotional
   Abuse in Tasmania, Australia 135
   Kerryne Barwick, Paul McGorrery and Marilyn McMahon

8 From Social Construct to Legal Innovation: The Offence
   of Controlling or Coercive Behaviour in England and Wales 159
   Cassandra Wiener

9	The Making of the New 'Gold Standard': The *Domestic Abuse (Scotland) Act 2018* 177
	Marsha Scott

Part IV A Way Forward?

10	A Comparative Evaluation of Offences: Criminalising Abusive Behaviour in England, Wales, Scotland, Ireland and Tasmania 197
	Vanessa Bettinson
11	Coercive Control as the Context for Intimate Partner Violence: The Challenge for the Legal System 219
	Jane Wangmann
12	Alternative Constructions of a Family Violence Offence 243
	Heather Douglas

Contributors

Kerryne Barwick Prosecution Services, Tasmania Police, TAS, Australia

Vanessa Bettinson School of Law, De Montfort University, Leicester, UK

Kelley Burton School of Law and Criminology, University of the Sunshine Coast, QLD, Australia

Heather Douglas TC Beirne School of Law, University of Queensland, QLD, Australia

Paul McGorrery School of Law, Deakin University, VIC, Australia

Marilyn McMahon School of Law, Deakin University, VIC, Australia

Julia Quilter School of Law, University of Wollongong, NSW, Australia

Marsha Scott Scottish Women's Aid, Edinburgh, Scotland

Supriya Singh Graduate School of Business and Law, RMIT University, VIC, Australia

Evan Stark School of Public Affairs and Administration, Rutgers University, NJ, USA

Danielle Tyson School of Humanities and Social Sciences, Deakin University, VIC, Australia

Jane Wangmann Faculty of Law, University of Technology Sydney, NSW, Australia

Cassandra Wiener School of Law, Politics & Sociology, University of Sussex, Brighton, UK

Part I
The Harms and Wrongs of Non-Physical Abuse

Chapter 1
Criminalising Coercive Control: An Introduction

Marilyn McMahon and Paul McGorrery

Abstract Novel criminal offences introduced in England and Wales in 2015, and in Scotland and Ireland in 2018, criminalise non-physical abuse in the context of family relationships in distinctive ways: they criminalise conduct that causes, or is intended to cause, psychological or economic harm without necessarily requiring that a victim sustain physical injury or fear death or serious physical harm. In Tasmania (Australia) related offences had been introduced a decade earlier. These significant and distinctive extensions of the criminal law apply to certain current or past familial relationships and supplement other criminal legislation that penalises physical assault, stalking or other offending against intimate partners or other family members. The new offences were designed to protect human rights by addressing gaps in the criminal law, gaps which permitted significant harmful activities to previously go unpunished. In the context of the ongoing debate about how best to tackle the problem of family violence, these developments raise significant legal issues—theoretical and practical—in relation to how best to protect victims. This chapter presents an overview of the offences, locates them within contemporary developments in the criminal law and identifies key matters that must be taken into account when evaluating them.

Keywords Non-physical abuse · Coercive control · Domestic violence · Human rights · Criminal law

1.1 Introduction

Since the 1970s, a great deal of research, policymaking and legal reform concerning domestic violence has focused on the compelling issue of physical violence in intimate relationships. Considerable attention has been directed to protecting victims through developing more effective police responses, improving the experi-

---

M. McMahon (✉) · P. McGorrery
School of Law, Deakin University, VIC, Australia
e-mail: Marilyn.mcmahon@deakin.edu.au

© Springer Nature Singapore Pte Ltd. 2020
M. McMahon and P. McGorrery (eds.), *Criminalising Coercive Control*,
https://doi.org/10.1007/978-981-15-0653-6_1

ences of victims in their contacts with criminal justice systems and more appropriate sentencing of offenders. Legislation in many common law countries has also introduced a range of civil orders (family intervention orders, protection orders, harassment orders or similar) that aim to protect victims from anticipated future violence.

There has also been an equally long-standing but perhaps less visible concern about non-physical aspects of domestic violence (Dobash and Dobash 1979). Feminist researchers identified that physical violence constitutes a significant, but neither exclusive nor necessarily dominant, aspect of domestic abuse (e.g. Johnson and Ferraro 2000), and that there are other, often more serious, forms of abuse, including psychological, emotional and economic abuse (collectively referred to in this chapter as non-physical abuse). Much of the attention in this area has focused on psychological abuse, which includes verbal abuse (ridicule, harassment, name-calling, etc.), isolation, jealousy, possessiveness and threats or abuse to a victim's children, friends, pets or possessions (Crowell and Burgess 1996).

Non-physical forms of domestic abuse have been analysed through the perspectives of public health and human rights law. The myriad negative health consequences of this form of abuse have now been clearly established (e.g. Garcia-Moreno et al. 2006). Significantly, policymakers and academics have also emphasised the human rights abuse inherent in the intimidation and control of a spouse, restricting their freedom of movement, limiting their access to other family members or curtailing their social activities (Crown Prosecution Service 2015; Stark 2009). Increasingly, the 'public' language of human rights has been employed to analyse the 'private' harms produced by domestic violence (Libal and Parekh 2009).

Models of domestic abuse developed by Michael Johnson (1995, 2006) ('intimate terrorism') and Evan Stark (2007) ('coercive control') have been particularly influential in framing the harms associated with non-physical abuse. These researchers go beyond merely cataloguing a diverse range of psychologically and economically abusive behaviours, and have developed models of abuse that use the core concepts of control and coercion to link a wide range of behaviours, analysing their function and identifying the key motivation of the men who engage in this gendered form of abuse. Their models emphasise that the severity of abuse cannot be measured simply by aggregating physical harms, and reject 'incident-based' explanations of domestic violence. Moreover, they acknowledge that coercive and controlling behaviours are not categorically different from ordinary gendered behaviour; they occur at the extreme end of the spectrum of power relations that exist in ordinary heterosexual intimate partner relationships. Distinguishing tolerable (normative) from abusive conduct in intimate relationships, therefore, creates challenges (Hoffman 1984; O'Leary 1999). Consequently, criminalising coercive and controlling behaviour requires distinguishing conventional (albeit perhaps dysfunctional) intimate and family relationships from those which are 'controlling and coercive' and warrant legal proscription.

Nevertheless, broad definitions of domestic abuse, encompassing a wide range of harms, have been increasingly incorporated in government policies and have impacted on the civil law. But until recently these expanded understandings of domestic abuse have had little impact on the criminal law. Several common law jurisdictions have now addressed this 'gap' by introducing 'standalone' family violence offences that criminalise non-physical abuse of family members, particularly intimate partners. In 2004, the State of Tasmania in Australia created the offences of emotional abuse or intimidation and economic abuse (*Family Violence Act 2004* (Tas) ss 8–9). In England and Wales 'coercive or controlling behaviour' was criminalised in 2015 (*Serious Crime Act 2015* (E&W) s 76), with Ireland adopting a similar offence of 'coercive control' in 2018 (*Domestic Violence Act 2018* (IR) s 33), and Scotland enacting a related offence of 'domestic abuse' in 2018 (*Domestic Abuse (Scotland) Act 2018* (Scot) s 1). These developments have been lauded for criminalising the coercive and controlling behaviour which is 'at the heart of domestic abuse' (Neate 2015). They have also been criticised for being difficult to operationalise, dissipating limited resources and placing too much faith in the power of the criminal law (Fitz-Gibbon and Walklate 2018; Walklate et al. 2018). These issues are explored in this book. In this introductory chapter, we chart the introduction of these new offences and locate them within public health concerns and an emerging engagement of the criminal law with human rights. We identify some of the key features of these offences as well as common concerns expressed about their construction and operation. The authors in this book outline the key concept of coercive control (Stark, Chap. 2), as well as its centrality to domestic violence (Tyson, Chap. 4) and economic abuse (Singh, Chap. 3). They identify the distinctive characteristics of the new offences in England (Wiener, Chap. 8), Scotland (Scott, Chap. 9) and Tasmania (Barwick et al., Chap. 7) and provide a comparative analysis of their construction (Bettinson, Chap. 10). Alternative formulations of offences that might capture non-physical forms of domestic abuse are outlined (Douglas, Chap. 12), as well as the possibility of using coercive control to inform other aspects of the operation of criminal justice systems (Wangmann, Chap. 11).

Before moving to detailed consideration of these issues, we establish a framework for these considerations, identifying the wrongdoing that the new offences are designed to remedy, the distinctive (and different) forms of the offences, and the general issues raised by introducing this novel type of offence into the criminal law.

1.2 The Lacuna: Liability at Common Law for Causing Non-Physical Harm

Traditionally, the criminal law proscribed activity which resulted in physical injury (or the threat of physical injury) to another. For instance, the common law offences of assault and battery clearly require physical contact or the threat thereof. (Of course, although the criminal law protected the physical integrity of persons, it did not do so consistently. The historical reluctance of the criminal law to acknowledge as criminal physical violence against a female domestic partner has been well established: Pleck 1987; Schelong 1994; Siegal 1995). But in relation to circumstances where there was no actual violence but simply a threat made, it is noteworthy that common law assault required a threat of imminent and unlawful violence (*Knight v R* (1988)). From at least the last quarter of the nineteenth century, it is clear that there was a requirement of a threat to do a 'corporal hurt' to another (Sheridan and Bakewell 1879, p. 181). This requirement is often echoed in modern formulations of statutory offences of assault (e.g. *Criminal Justice Act 1988* (UK) s 39; *Summary Offences Act 1986* (Vic) s 23) as well as the offences of threatening to kill or threatening to cause serious injury—which usually require a threat to inflict physical harm of some sort (e.g. *Offences Against the Person Act 1861* (UK) s 16; *Crimes Act 1958* (Vic) ss 20–21; *Criminal Law Consolidation Act 1935* (SA) s 19).

Other forms of harm experienced by victims of domestic abuse—in particular psychological abuse and economic abuse—were recognised to some degree in the defences of duress and marital coercion, but the conduct of the abuser did not constitute an offence per se: it was beyond the ambit of laws governing assault and battery. Thus, commonplace aspects of domestic abuse—such as chronic verbal abuse and humiliation of a person by their spouse, or preventing a person from accessing jointly acquired assets or income (O'Leary 1999; Dobash and Dobash 1998)—could cause considerable harm to victims, but such behaviour was not easily captured by the criminal law (if at all). Consequently, many contemporary commentators and reformers identified a 'gap' in the criminal law that permitted significant abuse within domestic relationships to go unpunished (e.g. Bettinson and Bishop 2015; Bishop and Bettinson 2017; Home Office 2014; Scottish Government 2018a, para [1.1]; Quilter, Chap. 6). This lacuna, in conjunction with a growing recognition of the significant harms associated with non-physical abuse, underpinned calls for the introduction of novel, standalone domestic violence offences which would criminalise conduct that caused (or was intended to cause) psychological and other non-physical harms to an intimate partner or other family member (e.g. Special Taskforce on Domestic and Family Violence in Queensland ('Special Taskforce') 2015).

1.3 Contemporary Offences Involving Non-Physical Harms

Although distinctive, the new offences that criminalise non-physical abuse are not totally unprecedented. They can be located within broader developments in criminal law that occurred in the last quarter of the twentieth century. During this period, in some jurisdictions, the law of assault evolved or was statutorily modified to recognise some forms of psychological harm. In addition, the modern statutory offences of stalking and/or harassment penalised some non-physical forms of abuse.

And in relation to domestic abuse, civil laws governing protective, restraining, intervention orders indirectly criminalised a wider range of abusive behaviours than was directly prohibited by the criminal law by imposing criminal sanctions for breaches of those orders.

1.3.1 Assault

Modern laws governing assault have sometimes evolved to include non-physical harm experienced by victims. This occurred either through changes in interpretations of offence requirements or amendments to statutory definitions. For instance, in England and Wales and New South Wales, Australia, offences of assault causing 'actual bodily harm' are now interpreted to include psychological harm within the meaning of 'bodily harm'. Thus, the Crown Prosecution Service (CPS) for England and Wales advises that—

> Psychological harm that involves more than mere emotions such as fear, distress or panic can amount to [actual bodily harm]'. (CPS, n.d.)

In these circumstances in England and Wales, expert psychiatric evidence must be called (*R v Chan-Fook* [1994]); in practice, this means that for the purposes of prosecuting this type of assault, the psychological injury experienced by the victim must amount to a recognised psychiatric illness. Similarly, in New South Wales, Australia a very serious psychological injury going beyond mere transient emotions, feelings and states of mind (NSW) may constitute actual bodily harm (*Shu Qiang Li v R* [2005] at [45]).

In other jurisdictions, legislative definitions in assault offences have allowed non-physical harms to meet statutory definitions of injury. For example, in Queensland, Australia the definition of 'injury' in s 663A of the Criminal Code includes psychiatric injury as 'bodily injury' within the meaning of that section; consequently, it is possible to commit assault by causing another person to experience a psychiatric injury, such as posttraumatic stress disorder (*R v Beaton; ex parte Smee* [1997]). Similarly, in Victoria, Australia from 1985 until 1 July 2013, some statutory assaults could be prosecuted where the victim experienced a particular form of mental harm (hysteria). Thus, under ss 16–18 of the *Crimes Act 1958* (Vic) it was theoretically possible to prosecute a person who intentionally or recklessly caused 'hysteria' to another. The curious and archaic reference to hysteria—a term that is not used as a specific diagnosis in modern taxonomies of psychiatric disorder (North 2015) and was most frequently employed in psychoanalysis to refer to the conversion of a psychic injury to a physical injury—would seem to have permitted prosecution for an assault that resulted in purely non-physical (mental) harm. Since 2013, the Victorian definition of injury has been replaced by an even more expansive definition that includes temporary or permanent 'harm to mental health' (which includes psychological harm but does not include an emotional reaction such as distress, grief, fear or anger unless it results in psychological harm: *Crimes Amendment (Gross Violence Offences) Act 2013* (Vic) s 3). Interestingly, neither definition appears to have generated prosecutions based on mental harm *simpliciter*. There does not appear to be a single reported case of a successful prosecution (or unsuccessful for that matter) under these provisions for an assault resulting in purely psychological injury. Consequently, despite these shifts in definitions of 'injury' and 'actual bodily harm' in the laws of assault, the impact has been minimal.

The lingering reluctance of the criminal law to recognise those who experience non-physical harms as victims of criminal wrongdoing was recently confirmed by an appellate court in Tasmania; the court restricted crimes compensation to victims of actual or threatened physical violence, thereby excluding offences that involve coercion and intimidation, emotional abuse and intimidation or economic abuse (*Attorney-General (Tas) v CL* [2018]).

1.3.2 Stalking and Harassment

Laws developed in the 1990s relating to stalking and harassment gave tangible recognition to non-physical (psychological, mental or emotional) harm. These laws generally prohibit behaviour that is repeated and constitutes a course of conduct—an important prelude to the new family violence offences.

The introduction of stalking offences, initially enacted in the United States and then quickly adopted in England and Wales, Scotland, New Zealand and Australia, was a bold development that proscribed certain conduct performed with the intent to cause, *inter alia*, certain forms of non-physical harm to victims. In England, stalking involving harassment or 'serious alarm or distress' for the victim is an offence (*Protection from Harassment Act 1997* (E&W) ss 2A(1), 4A(1)(b)(ii)). In Scotland, stalking that is likely to cause 'fear or alarm' is prohibited (*Criminal Justice & Licensing (Scotland) Act 2010* (Scot) s 39). And in Australia, stalking statutes commonly prohibit causing mental harm, which can include 'psychological harm' and suicidal thoughts (*Crimes Act 1958* (Vic) s 21A(8)). Under all these statutes it is not necessary to establish that the victim experienced a medically diagnosed, or diagnosable, condition; victims who report lesser or more transient disturbances (e.g. 'shattered', 'visibly distressed', 'tearful') might satisfy a requirement of 'serious alarm or distress' or 'psychological harm' (*RR v The Queen* [2013]). Indeed in some jurisdictions, it is not necessary to establish any harm at all to the victim, so long as the offender intended or was reckless about causing mental harm and a reasonable person would have foreseen such harm as likely (e.g. *Crimes Act 1958* (Vic) s 21A(2)(g)).

In relation to the application of stalking laws, while courts have demonstrated a willingness to interpret stalking laws relatively expansively when the relationship between the parties is that of strangers or ex-partners, these laws have not generally been applied to behaviour that occurs while a marital, de facto or other intimate relationship is ongoing (see McMahon et al., Chap. 5). While courts, prosecutors and police now acknowledge that many activities that could constitute stalking occur within abusive ongoing intimate relationships, there remains an enduring reluctance to identify stalking that occurs in a relationship where the parties were cohabiting at the time of the relevant behaviour.

1.3.3 Restraining/Protection/Family Violence Orders

In the absence of laws that can readily and specifically be used to prohibit non-physical abuse, perhaps the most commonly utilised legal strategy to protect victims from this form of abuse has been through the use of protection orders. Variously known as restraining, protection, family violence, intervention, or apprehended violence orders, these civil orders are intended to be preventive and protective; they can be taken out by victims to protect themselves from future, anticipated violence by an intimate partner or family member.

Definitions of what constitutes 'family violence' or 'domestic violence' for the purpose of these orders differ in various jurisdictions. In Australia, the definitions of family violence are generally expansive and include emotional, psychological and economic abuse; sometimes they also specifically include coercive and controlling behaviour. For instance, in family violence legislation in Victoria, Australia 'family violence' is defined to include behaviour by a person towards a family member that—

(i) is physically or sexually abusive; or

(ii) is emotionally or psychologically abusive; or

(iii) is economically abusive; or

(iv) is threatening; or

(v) is coercive; or

(vi) in any other way controls or dominates the family member and causes that family member to feel fear for the safety or wellbeing of that family member or another person (*Family Violence Protection Act 2008* (Vic) s 5).

(See also, England and Wales: *Protection From Harassment Act 1997* (E&W) s 5 (not limited to domestic relations); Australia: *Restraining Orders Act 1997* (WA) s 5A; *Intervention Orders (Prevention of Abuse) Act 2009* (SA) s 8; *Domestic and Family Violence Protection Act 2012* (Qld) ss 8, 11–12; *Domestic and Family Violence Act 2007* (NT) ss 5, 8. The remaining Australian jurisdictions do not yet define family violence to include economic and emotional abuse: *Crimes (Domestic and Personal Violence) Act 2007* (NSW); *Domestic Violence and Protection Orders Act 2008* (ACT) s 13 (though the ACT legislation does include causing nervous shock as a form of domestic violence)).

The more expansive definitions adopt a human rights perspective, expressly noting that 'family violence is a fundamental violation of human rights' (*Family Violence Protection Act 2008* (Vic) Preamble (b)) and sometimes specifying that family violence includes preventing a person from doing something that the person is lawfully entitled to do (or hindering the person from doing the act) and/or compelling the person to do something that the person is lawfully entitled to abstain from doing (*Criminal Code Act Consolidation Act 1913* (WA) s 388D(1) definition of 'intimidate').

The purpose of these orders is distinctive. In England, their function is preventative and protective rather than punitive (Crown Prosecution Service, n.d.). In Australia, the New South Wales Court of Appeal noted the distinctive protective function of these orders, not just in relation to protecting the physical integrity of victims but also their human rights:

> Apprehended Violence Orders constitute the primary means in this State of asserting the fundamental right to freedom from fear. The objects served by such orders are quite distinct from those that are served by civil adversarial proceedings or proceedings in which an arm of the State seeks to enforce the criminal law. (*John Fairfax Publications Pty Ltd v Ryde Local Court* [2005] at [20]).

These civil orders link to the criminal law through sanctions for their breach. Respondents who breach civil orders (including by engaging in emotionally or psychologically abusive behaviours) commit a criminal offence: (e.g. *Protection From Harassment Act 1997* (E&W) s 5(5); *Family Violence Protection Act 2008* (Vic) ss 37–37A, 123—123A and 125A). The criminalisation of the causing of psychological or emotional harm only occurs where the relevant conduct occurs after a relevant order is already in place (making such an order/notice a required precondition for prosecution). Thus, the abusive behaviour is only indirectly criminally proscribed; the proscribed non-physical abuse only has criminal consequences when the intervention order is breached. A question that arises is why the human rights of victims should only be indirectly protected by the criminal law when a court order is in place? The issue becomes particularly pressing as not only does this suggest that the wrongfulness lies in the breach of a court order as opposed to the abuse itself (Douglas 2015, p. 438, 2007), but there is a significant reason to doubt the effectiveness of these orders.

Multiple studies have identified inconsistencies in responses by police (Douglas and Stark 2010; Robertson et al. 2007), which suggests that only a minority of breaches are prosecuted (Bagshaw et al. 2010), and that there is little understanding of the psychological and emotional abuse that occurs (Bagshaw et al. 2010). Moreover, critics point to the relatively light sentences imposed when breaches are prosecuted (Sentencing Advisory Council (Vic) 2009, pp. 133–134). And while a meta-analysis of relevant international studies concluded that these orders 'are associated with a small but significant reduction in domestic violence' (Dowling et al. 2018, p. 1), it also noted that about half of victims who obtained a protection order would experience some form of re-victimisation (Dowling et al. 2018, p. 7). In essence, these orders are of limited value in keeping victims safe.

In the light of the aforementioned limitations, and in the context of contemporary discussions of family violence, governments, activists and academics have identified a 'gap' in the criminal law that permitted (and in many jurisdictions, continues to permit) non-physical abuse to go unpunished (e.g. Home Office 2014; Bettinson and Bishop 2015; Bishop and Bettinson 2017). Although there are perils associated with 'gap-filling' lawmaking (see Quilter, Chap. 6; Wiener, Chap. 8), this lacuna provided a powerful underpinning for the introduction of the new standalone family violence offences that criminalise non-physical abuse. The issue of whether such offences should be introduced in more common law jurisdictions is also being debated (Whiting 2014). These developments were the catalyst for this book.

1.4 Coercive Control, Human Rights Abuse and Liberty Crimes

It is against the background of the traditional limits of the criminal law that standalone offences that directly criminalise non-physical abuse of family members were introduced. In 2004 Tasmania, Australia, introduced an offence prohibiting emotional abuse or intimidation and another offence of economic abuse (*Family Violence Act 2004* (Tas) ss 8–9). These offences were justified by reference to the work of Dr. Lenore Walker, a pioneer in the study of domestic violence and the developer of 'battered woman syndrome'. Walker had observed that most abused women experienced multiple forms of abuse and they—

> describe[d] incidents involving psychological humiliation and verbal harassment as their worst battering experiences, whether or not they ha[d] been physically abused (Walker 1979, p. xv).

For a decade, the Tasmanian offences were unique in common law countries. However, the development of policy relating to family violence and the enactment of the offence of controlling or coercive behaviour in England and Wales in 2015, and the offences of domestic abuse in Scotland and coercive control in Ireland in 2018, were underpinned by another advance in the understanding of domestic abuse: the role of coercion and control in abusive relationships. Developed to address perceived inaccuracies, reductionism and demeaning aspects of earlier approaches to family violence (Stark 1995, p. 975), influential models of abuse incorporating notions of coercion and control were developed by Michael Johnson (2006) and Evan Stark (2007), while others employed these concepts to outline the strategies used by abusive men (e.g. Dutton and Goodman 2005). While differing, these approaches shared a reframing of domestic abuse as more than 'the number of hits' (O'Leary 1999; Dobash and Dobash 1998), and identified coercive control as a highly gendered pattern of male domination, power and control that characterised severely abusive relationships but which did not necessarily involve high levels of physical violence.

Ultimately, the most influential model of psychological and physical abuse and economic oppression was Stark's (2007) concept of 'coercive control'. This model provides a framework to explain the ongoing control and coercion inherent in the micro-management of controlling a woman's activities, stopping or changing the way she socialises, limiting her access to family and friends, controlling her finances, monitoring her via online communication tools, and repeatedly 'putting her down' (e.g. telling her she is worthless), humiliating and embarrassing her. The model explains how this conduct undermines a victim's capacity for independent decision-making and inhibits effective resistance to, and escape from, the abusive relationship (Stark 2012).

Significantly, Stark frames abuse involving coercive control as a crime against liberty and equality (Stark 2012); domestic violence is analysed as a form of human rights abuse. Stark eschews conventional terms such as 'psychological abuse' as limited, incomplete and misleading, and prefers to speak of 'liberty harms' (Stark 2007, p. 397). Abuse based on coercive control is a 'liberty crime' (Williamson 2010). In relation to victims, Stark has observed that—

> what is done to them is less important than what their partners have prevented them from doing for themselves by appropriating their resources; undermining their social support; subverting their rights to privacy, self-respect, and autonomy; and depriving them of substantive equality (Stark 2009, p. 13).

This approach is distinctive because it shifts the discussion of family violence away from a focus on physical aggression, rejects a public/private dichotomy, and explicitly reframes domestic violence as a violation of the human rights of victims, perpetrated by private individuals (rather than the state) (Pogge 2001). In this framework, domestic abuse is not simply private, abusive conduct perpetrated by pathological men; it involves a complex interplay of physical and non-physical abuse that violates victims' rights to liberty, security, freedom from torture, and freedom of thought, conscience, and religion by subjecting them to a pattern of intimidation, isolation, manipulation, physical violence, threats of physical harm, stalking, destruction of personal property and restrictions on their movement. In this context, Stark (2006, p. 1019) also reframes physical violence: it is not simply an assault and battery, but a form of achieving subordination.

Stark favours criminalising coercive control as 'liberty crimes' (Stark 2009) and has described the Scottish offence of domestic abuse as the 'new gold standard' for criminalising this conduct (Brooks 2018). However, he emphasises that simply expanding the range of abusive behaviours which are subject to criminal sanctions is not the solution to domestic abuse; these reforms should incorporate an affirmative concept of freedom and must be embedded within broader policy and social reforms that work to eliminate coercive control and the gendered discrimination and power imbalance that creates the conditions in which this form of gendered abuse occurs (Stark, Chap. 2). In this respect, Stark's model of criminalisation carries on the work of feminists such as Turkheimer (2004) and Burke (2007), who promoted the development of a new standalone domestic violence offence that would criminalise coercive control and complement existing assault laws (Turkheimer 2004, pp. 1019–1020; Burke 2007, pp. 601–602).

Those scholars noted the potential impact of an offence that criminalised coercive control model. As Stark observed:

1 Criminalising Coercive Control: An Introduction

Although some of the tactics deployed in coercive control are already illegal, such as stalking, others, such as taking a woman's money, confining her in the house, or continually demeaning or harassing her, rarely prompt outside intervention when they occur in relationships, although they would be illegal if committed against a stranger (Stark 2012, p. 31).

The implications of the increasing recognition of coercive control in intimate partner relationships for developing new domestic abuse offences are manifold:

- Consistent with feminist theorising over many years, the coercive control model recognises that domestic abuse is not an 'incident' but is constituted by a pattern of behaviours. The model emphasises that abuse is ongoing and chronic, and that the harm sustained is cumulative.
- The coercive control model emphasises that physical violence is only one constitutive element (an important element, but just one nevertheless) of a complex pattern of abusive conduct. Physical violence can be isolated and severe, routine and minor, or almost entirely absent in abusive relationships. Thus, this approach recognises that it is possible to have situations of extreme domestic abuse where there are high levels of fear and entrapment but low levels of physical injury.
- New laws should not simply protect victims from economic, psychological or emotional harms but should embody an affirmative concept of freedom that protects human rights.
- If new criminal laws are to be consistent with the model of coercive control, behaviours that were not previously criminalised will now fall within the ambit of proscribed conduct.
- Recognising that separation is a process rather than an event, and that separating from an abusive partner does not bring safety but is likely to result in an escalation in violence, means that any new, relevant offences should not be limited to abusive relationships where the parties were cohabitating at the relevant time but should also include both past intimate relationships as well as 'on-again-off-again' relationships.
- Children who observe domestic abuse are not merely 'witnesses' but are victims themselves.

To varying degrees, the new standalone domestic abuse offences incorporate these characteristics. They criminalise non-physical abuse of family members thereby giving effect to expansive approaches to family violence that address what most researchers and activists have argued for many years—that the infliction of psychological harm and economic restrictions are core aspects of family violence. The conversion of this recognition into criminal offences was underpinned by two major developments: the increasing recognition of domestic violence as a public health problem, and the emerging impact of human rights considerations on the criminal law.

1.4.1 Domestic Abuse: A Public Health Perspective

A consolidating body of research has confirmed the negative impact of non-physical forms of domestic abuse. Most victims experience both physical and psychological abuse (Street and Arias 2001), with a small proportion of victims experiencing psychological abuse only. For instance, a study of more than one thousand women in the United States reported that 54% had experienced abuse from their partner; 40% experienced both physical and psychological abuse, and 14% experienced psychological abuse only (Coker et al. 2000). But the absence of physical violence does not bring lesser sequelae; those who experience only psychological abuse are as likely to report adverse health outcomes as those exposed to physical abuse (Coker et al. 2000; Follingstad 2009).

The outcomes of long-term non-physical abuse are significant: elevated levels of substance abuse (Straight et al. 2003), depression (VicHealth 2004), anxiety (VicHealth 2004), posttraumatic stress disorder (Mechanic et al. 2008), suicide attempts (Devries et al. 2011), homelessness (Australian Institute of Health and Welfare 2014), chronic stress, hypertension and a range of other physical ailments (Coker et al. 2000; Sackett and Saunders 1999; Follingstad et al. 1990). Indeed, some studies have reported that psychological abuse is a stronger contributor to the development of several of these disorders than physical abuse (Arias and Pape 1999; Baldry 2003). This finding is consistent with reports from victims, who typically rate psychological abuse as having a more negative impact than all but the most extreme levels of physical violence (Folingstad et al. 1990; Stark 2007, p. 278; Tolman 1992; Walker 1979, p. xv). In the words of one victim, 'It's the emotional scars that scar the worst, more so than physical violence' (quoted in Bolger 2015).

Consequently, physical violence constitutes a significant, but neither exclusive nor necessarily dominant, part of the experience of family violence (Johnson and Ferraro 2000; Stark 2007). The psychological abuse that typically accompanies physical violence can itself also have profound consequences, and constitutes a significant public health problem. This point was made by Alison Saunders, the former Director of Public Prosecutions in England, when she was explaining the reason for the introduction of the controlling or coercive behaviour offence:

> Being subjected to repeated humiliation, intimidation or subordination can be as harmful as physical abuse, with many victims stating that trauma from psychological abuse had a more lasting impact than physical abuse (Crown Prosecution Service 2015).

1.4.2 Human Rights Abuse and the New Offences

In addition to accumulating knowledge about the public health consequences of non-physical domestic abuse, a further catalyst to the development of the new offences was the increasing framing of domestic violence as an abuse of the human rights of victims. This is directly reflected in the construction of the offences—they do not simply protect the physical, psychological and economic integrity of victims, but do so within a human rights framework, distinctively constructing non-physical harms as breaches of freedom from fear and torture, freedom of movement, thought, etc.

Although the antecedents of this approach can be found in the work of nineteenth-century feminists such as Frances Cobbe (1878, p. 72) and a smattering of contemporary legal scholars (e.g. Hogg 2017; McQuigg 2011; Tadros 2005), the recent catalyst came from international obligations and treaties that increasingly recognised violence against woman as a human rights issue. For instance, the *Convention on Preventing and Combating Violence Against Women and Domestic Violence* (the Istanbul Convention) categorises violence against women as a violation of human rights and a form of discrimination (art 3(b)). Article 3(a) expansively defines violence against women as—

> all acts of gender-based violence that result in, or are likely to result in, physical, sexual, psychological or economic harm or suffering to women, including threats of such acts, coercion or arbitrary deprivation of liberty, whether occurring in public or private life.

Significantly, the Istanbul Convention requires that states criminalise psychological violence where the conduct is intentional, seriously impairs the psychological integrity of the victim, and takes place through coercion or threats (art 33). The Explanatory Report accompanying the Convention indicates that psychological violence refers to a course of conduct rather than a single event, and is intended to capture an abusive pattern of behaviour occurring over time—the similarities to the standalone offences are clear.

The Istanbul Convention is a recent (albeit direct and expansive) expression of a fundamental individual, civil and constitutional rights that were previously established under earlier international treaties and conventions such as the *International Covenant on Civil and Political Rights* and the *Convention on the Elimination of all Forms of Discrimination against Women*. Although the United Kingdom has not yet ratified the Istanbul Convention (and countries which are not members of the Council of Europe are not eligible to do so), it has established a powerful benchmark against which laws, policies and practices can be evaluated and explored. There have also been more local attempts to give effect to specific rights via a legislative framework (e.g. *Human Rights Act 1998* (UK); *Charter of Human Rights and Responsibilities Act 2006* (Vic); *Human Rights Act 2004* (ACT); *Human Rights Act 2019* (Qld); Chalmers 2014, pp. 491–492; Griffin 2008).

Governments and their agencies in common law countries are increasingly acknowledging their obligations under these instruments when developing policy and law in relation to domestic abuse. For instance, the Scottish Government noted its obligations to protect the right to life and to prohibit torture or inhuman or degrading treatment or punishment under the *European Convention on Human Rights* (ECHR), acknowledging that the Convention imposed 'an overarching duty… to put in place mechanisms to protect the life and well-being of a person who is at risk of domestic abuse' (Scottish Government 2018a, para [1.11]). In England and Wales, the CPS similarly observes that the offence of controlling or coercive behaviour (and other domestic violence prosecutions) must be addressed within the framework of government policy on violence towards women 'and human rights' (CPS 2017). It is within this framework that the standalone domestic abuse offences were enacted in England, Scotland and Ireland. The offences recognise, either directly or indirectly, that domestic abuse can violate victims' rights to liberty, security, education, work, freedom of thought, conscience and religion, freedom from torture and other cruel, inhuman or degrading treatment or punishment by subjecting them to patterns of coercive control.

Constructing domestic abuse as a human rights issue has not only helped to generate a distinctive, expansive legal conception of abuse but also transforms victims into rights-bearing subjects (Merry 2003, p. 344), thereby providing an alternative to a clinical (psychologised, individualised, pathologised) model for the abuse (Stark 1995, p. 975; cf. Walklate et al. 2018). Stark, for example, is notably hostile towards terms such as 'psychological abuse' and 'trauma', and legal terms such as 'harms' (Stark 2016), regarding them as limited, incomplete and misleading; he prefers to construct domestic violence as a 'liberty crime' (Williamson 2010). In this approach domestic violence is not simply private, abusive conduct perpetrated by pathological men; it is a form of gender discrimination facilitated by structural and cultural factors with the abuse building on gendered power imbalances and tasks (Pogge 2001).

The ramifications of constructing domestic abuse as human rights abuse extend beyond enacting standalone domestic abuse crimes. The rise of due diligence in international law has expanded notions of state responsibility based on an omission or failure to act, prevent, investigate or punish violations in breach of its international obligations, even where private persons commit those violations (Hessbruegge 2004). This development challenges the traditional doctrine of state responsibility, which holds that states can only be held responsible for human rights violations perpetrated by the state and its agents against its citizens (e.g., Pogge 2001; Marshall 2008, p. 147).

Of course, this approach to domestic violence is not uncontested. Some fear that it provides a mechanism for increased intrusion of the state into women's lives (e.g. Römkens 2001) and that it is an example of carceral feminism (Polavarapu 2018, p. 9) (carceral feminism describes 'the 'commitment of abolitionist feminist activists to a law and order agenda', viewing the state (particularly its criminal justice arm) as a key, or *the* key, actor in the protection of women against gendered violence (Bernstein 2007, p. 143)). Additionally, constructing domestic abuse as human rights abuse challenges political and conceptual analyses which view the 'public' language of human rights as inapplicable to the domestic space and which regard it as inappropriate to impose liability on governments for human rights violations perpetrated by private citizens.

1.5 Models for Criminalising the Causing of Psychological Harm

If it is accepted that victims of domestic abuse should be protected by the criminal law against some non-physical harms, the key issue then becomes how to formulate an appropriate offence. As the following outline of models of criminalisation demonstrates, different approaches have been employed in England and Wales, Ireland, Scotland and Tasmania, Australia. (Each of these offences is subject to more detailed exposition, analysis and comparison in Chaps. 7–10; the aim here is to present a broad, introductory overview of some of their shared and distinctive features).

The most notable shared feature of these offences is that they protect victims from certain forms of continuing or repeated behaviours, where those behaviours exert (or are intended to exert) psychological and/or economic pressure without necessarily requiring that the victim experience physical violence, or fear such violence. All the offences require more than a single, discrete act of abuse; they require persistent behaviour (*Domestic Violence Act 2018* (IR) s 39); *Family Violence Act 2004* (Tas); *Domestic Abuse (Scotland) Act 2018* (Scot) s 1; *Serious Crime Act 2015* (E&W) s 76(1)(a)). By capturing the harms experienced by victims through a course or pattern of behaviour, these offences criminalise conduct that would have been difficult or impossible to prosecute before their enactment. This is especially important when individual incidents of abuse may themselves appear to be relatively minor and transient in impact. Employing this approach acknowledges that the context of the offending behaviours is critical.

Although specifically developed with female victims in mind, the offences are gender neutral. Each of the offences requires a particular intimate or familial relationship between perpetrator and victim; there is no offence if the victim does not fall within the specified category of persons. Current intimate partners are included in all offences and ex-intimate partners are also included, however in England and Wales a previous partner will only satisfy the relationship requirement if they were living with the victim at the time of the offending (*Serious Crime Act 2015* (E&W) ss 76(2), (6)). amended

All of the offences acknowledge that the core nature of much domestic abuse is constituted by the cumulative effect of intimidating, coercive and controlling behaviour rather than by physical abuse. Interestingly, legislation that creates these offences has uniformly failed to define key terms; thus, there are no statutory definitions of 'emotional or economic abuse', 'controlling or coercive behaviour' or 'domestic abuse'. Guidance may sometimes be found in government policies and documents but these instruments do not have the force of law. However, the offences appear to criminalise a wide range of behaviours and capture a wide variety of harms. For instance, the offence of 'controlling or coercive behaviour' can be committed (all other elements being satisfied) where the offender's conduct has a 'serious effect' on the victim, causing them 'serious alarm or distress which has a serious adverse effect on [their] usual day-to-day activities' (*Serious Crime*

Act 2015 (E&W) s 76(4)(b)). Similarly, the Scottish offence of 'domestic abuse' includes circumstances where an offender intends their behaviour to, or should know it will likely have the effect of, isolating or making their victim dependent, limiting their freedom of action, controlling, regulating or monitoring their daily activities, isolating them or frightening, humiliating, degrading or punishing them (*Domestic Abuse (Scotland) Act 2018* (Scot) s 2).

The offences are not intended to capture trivial conduct; they exclude it by requiring that the abusive conduct has a 'serious effect' on the victim (*Serious Crime Act 2015* (E&W) s 76); *Domestic Violence Act 2018* (IR) s 39) and/or that the behaviour is not reasonable. Statutory provisions in Tasmania and Scotland (and in England, in relation only to the limb involving the causing of serious alarm or distress to the victim) use a 'reasonable person' standard, either requiring that the relevant behaviour was unreasonably controlling or unreasonably intimidating (*Family Violence Act 2004* (Vic) ss 8–9), that a 'reasonable person' would consider the course of abusive behaviour to be likely to cause the victim to suffer physical or psychological harm (*Domestic Abuse (Scotland) Act 2018* (Scot) s 2(b)(ii)) or (as a defence) that the accused believed that their behaviour was, in all the circumstances, reasonable and that they were acting in the victim's best interests (*Serious Crime Act 2015* (E&W) s 76).

Significant differences also exist between the offences. In relation to the *mens rea* requirement, some offences require that the perpetrator knew about the likely effect of their conduct, whereas the Scottish offence requires an intention to cause, or recklessness about causing, physical or psychological harm. Another notable point of difference is whether the prosecution must establish that the victim actually experienced the proscribed harm. The Tasmanian and Scottish offences do not require that the victims actually experienced psychological, economic or other harm; the requirement is simply that the accused intended or was reckless or should have known that the conduct would have that effect. On the other hand, the English, Welsh and Irish offences require that the prosecution establish that the offender's conduct actually caused the victim to suffer harm ('has a serious effect': *Serious Crime Act 2015* (E&W) s 76(c); *Domestic Abuse Act 2018* (IR) s 39(b)). Of course, as a practical and evidentiary matter, a prosecution would be unlikely to succeed in the absence of such an effect. Nevertheless, the different formulations mean that the Tasmanian and Scottish offences are more likely to focus on the abuse itself, rather than how it affected the victim.

A further major difference between the offences is whether the prohibited behaviours include physical violence. The Tasmanian offences of emotional abuse or intimidation and economic abuse, and the offences of controlling or coercive behaviour in England and Wales and Ireland, do not include physical violence within their scope. Only the Scottish offence of domestic abuse encompasses physical violence (the relevant behaviour must be likely to cause the victim 'physical or psychological harm': *Domestic Abuse (Scotland) Act 2018* (Scot) s 1). As previously noted, many victims experience multiple forms of domestic abuse (e.g. Coker et al. 2000). When physical violence is not covered by the offence but is part of the overall pattern of abuse, the simultaneous charging of conventional assaults would appear to be necessary in order for the criminal law to fully capture the entirety of the abuse. Finally, the offences also vary considerably in the maximum penalty that can be imposed. In Tasmania, the offences of economic abuse and psychological or emotional abuse are summary offences that carry a maximum penalty of a fine or imprisonment for 2 years (*Family Violence Act 2004* (Tas) ss 8–9). In England, Scotland and Ireland the relevant offences may be prosecuted as either summary or indictable offences. When prosecuted as a summary offence, the maximum penalty is imprisonment for 12 months or less, or a fine or both; when prosecuted as an indictable offence, the maximum penalty is a term of imprisonment for no more than 5 years in England, Wales and Ireland (*Serious Crime Act 2015* (E&W) s 76; *Domestic Abuse Act 2018* (IR) s 39), whereas in Scotland the maximum term of imprisonment is 14 years (*Domestic Abuse (Scotland) Act 2018* (Scot) s 1).

1.6 Concerns

Numerous concerns have been expressed about the introduction of the standalone offences, including that they may constitute overcriminalisation, that they will be impossible or undesirable to implement, and that they are a misguided product of carceral feminism. Any evaluation of them should take into account the following matters.

1.6.1 *What Interests Should the Criminal Law Protect?*

The new domestic abuse offences significantly extend the ambit of the criminal law. The intentional infliction of emotional (psychological) harm was previously addressed in the civil law (Garfield 2009); other limited protections from non-physical harms came from stalking laws and (indirectly) through criminal sanctions for breaches of civil protection orders. Early attempts to rationalise the introduction of a criminal offence based on non-physical harms were predicated on a claimed link between verbal assaults and physical pain, and a belief that the intentional infliction of psychological harm was rare (Garfield 2009, p. 40). However, the domestic abuse offences address conduct which is not uncommon and are not restricted to intentional behaviour. They unmoor criminalisation from the infliction (or threat) of physical injury and allow for prosecution on the basis of purely psychological harm (isolation, humiliation, monitoring, etc.). Consequently, evaluating them requires consideration of more fundamental issues than likely problems with implementation and enforcement; their introduction raises the fundamental issue of what interests (or *rechtsugt*: Ambos 2015) the criminal law should protect (a matter which is central to concerns about overcriminalisation).

In the absence of the new offences, there is no relevant law that directly protects victims from non-physical abuse by family members and the human rights abuses and psychological and other harms must be borne by victims as private injuries. Conversely, with limited exceptions, non-physical harms have been traditionally beyond the ambit of the criminal law because the harm is difficult to prove, easy to fabricate, and viewed as less significant than physical integrity. Yet harms are not immutable; they are a historically contingent construction of the criminal law (Lacey and Zedner 2012). Jurisdictions that have enacted the domestic abuse offences have clearly recalibrated notions of harm, injury and abuse within the crucible of contemporary concerns for violence against women, psychological well-being and respect for human rights.

1.6.2 Can the Offence Be Embedded Within Existing Socio-Political Frameworks?

It is uniformly acknowledged that the new offences must be embedded within supportive and complimentary existing socio-political frameworks if they are to be effective (see Stark, Chap. 2); as a corollary, it cannot be assumed that particular laws developed in one jurisdiction can be readily transposed elsewhere. Nor can a new offence ever constitute a panacea to gendered abuse. The impact and effectiveness of the offences will be dependent on their congruence with other policies, practices and strategic aims within a comprehensive policy framework.

Governments that have enacted these offences have been cognisant of this and have invariably introduced them as part of 'whole of government' reform packages rather than as isolated discrete initiatives. For instance, in Tasmania, the offences of emotional abuse or intimidation and economic abuse were included in the Safety First program adopted by the State government (Department of Justice and Industrial Relations (Tas) 2003). Similarly, in England and Wales, the concept of coercive control had been adopted in multiple policy documents and guiding initiatives since 2011 as part of the government's action plan to end gendered violence (Home Office 2010). Indeed, when the Home Secretary launched a public consultation about domestic violence and criminal justice in 2014 she pointed out that the purpose of the review was to determine whether a new offence should be introduced that was 'in line with the Government's non-statutory definition of domestic abuse' (Home Office 2015, p. 5). In Scotland, the offence of domestic abuse gave statutory form to an approach to domestic violence that had been embedded in government policies for more than a decade and was incorporated into the Equally Safe initiative (see Scott, Chap. 9; Scottish Government 2014, 2015, 2018b). Moreover, the offence was introduced as just one part of the '4Ps' guiding Scottish government policy in relation to domestic abuse: it was an element of the government's protection policies (legal remedies), and was supplemented by strategies aimed at the provision of effective services, the prevention of domestic abuse (and the reduction of re-offending) and the participation of victims in all processes (see Scott, Chap. 9).

Even then, congruence with existing socio-political frameworks is a necessary, but not sufficient condition. New laws require substantial commitments by the government to resources, education, training and the dissemination of information about their operation. With only a minority of forces in England and Wales receiving specialised training thus far, significant deficiencies in practice already exist (Wiener, Chap. 8). Thus, despite the fact that the offences have been enacted as part of broader government initiatives, emerging research on the operationalisation of the offences of emotional abuse or intimidation in Tasmania (McMahon and McGorrery 2016) and controlling or coercive behaviour in England (Wiener, Chap. 8) has already identified significant limitations in the introduction of the new offences.

1.6.3 Will There Be a Mistaken Charging of Victims?

There are concerns that the new offences may result in the mistaken charging of victims (particularly in light of recent findings in Victoria, Australia, that police are prone to misidentifying the primary aggressor: Women's Legal Service (Vic) 2018). Relying on matters as diverse as the frequency of cross-application in protection order applications, and cultural tropes of the 'nagging wife', critics have warned that the offence may be particularly dangerous for women (Walklate et al. 2018; Tolmie 2018), especially indigenous or marginalised women (Special Taskforce 2015, p. 301). Initial analyses of the operation of the offence of controlling or coercive behaviour in England have not, however, supported this claim (Barlow et al. 2018; McGorrery and McMahon 2018) and further research will indicate whether charging continues to accurately reflect the gendered nature of the abuse.

1.6.4 Will These Offences Compound the Investigation, Prosecution and Evidentiary Challenges Associated with Domestic Violence?

Predictably, the enactment of the domestic abuse offences will increase the number of criminal investigations and prosecutions. Clearly, the intended consequence of the new offences is that previously lawful behaviour will be criminalised and the criminal net will widen. Indeed, commentators have warned that it would be unwise to make it 'a crime to cause … emotional harm without restriction' because this would 'open the floodgates' to prosecutions (Stannard 2010, p. 555). However, available evidence from Tasmania and England does not substantiate this concern.

In addition to there having been so few prosecutions under the new offences in Tasmania that police have been criticised for under-utilising them (McMahon and McGorrery 2016), the empirical evidence from England and Wales in relation to the offence of controlling or coercive behaviour thus far paints a very similar picture of a relatively small number of prosecutions (Hill 2016; McGorrery and McMahon 2018).

Nevertheless, offences addressing non-physical abuse are likely to be harder to investigate and prosecute (and meet with more resistance from police and other law enforcement bodies) than conduct which results in physical injuries—tangible injuries that are more readily susceptible to proof and more commonly the subject of the criminal law. As Simester and colleagues warned in relation to the expansion of the law of assault, 'A more expansive approach to the question of harm … would entail considerable difficulties of definition and proof in cases of non-corporeal bodily harm' (Simester et al. 2010, p. 437).

In addition, the prosecution of these offences is likely to be more challenging than physical assault because it is probable that it will require more collaboration and engagement with victims. It has been suggested that trials of these offences will involve an increased likelihood of a complainant/witness being declared hostile (Special Taskforce 2015, p. 301). This raises the long-standing issue of the desirability of mandatory criminal justice interventions in circumstances of domestic violence. Initiatives from mandatory arrest to prosecutions that occur without the support of the victims of the alleged offence attract the criticism that they destroy the autonomy of victims; that is, by allowing prosecutors and courts to decide that victims have been subject to criminal wrongdoing (in this case, non-physical abuse) they paternalistically strip victims of their autonomy and decision-making power (e.g. see Hirschel and Hutchison 2003). In the present discussion, this issue crystallises on whether people should be free to put themselves into abusive, damaging relationships and whether victim consent should be a defence to the non-physical abuse offences? Of course, underpinning this issue is the difficulty of constructing 'autonomy' for persons who have been in coercive and controlling relationships where a predictable outcome is impaired decision-making and independence of the victim (Stark 2007).

A further problematic issue that has been identified in the prosecution of these offences is that they are likely to disproportionately rely on mechanisms such as the exception to the hearsay rule where the maker of a statement is not available (for instance, due to fear), rather than rely on the live testimony of the complainant as the only or principal evidence (Bishop and Bettinson 2017, p. 11). As with the preceding criticisms, ongoing empirical evaluation of prosecutions for these charges will provide valuable evidence about the validity of these concerns.

1.6.5 Domestic Abuse as a Problem of Law

The introduction of the new offences addressing non-physical abuse has enlivened ongoing debates about law, policy and practice in relation to domestic abuse with key concerns relating to the role of law in regulating abuse, the desirability of a standalone offence and the dissipation of resources.

1.6.5.1 The Role of Law in Regulating Domestic Abuse

What is at issue here is the role of law in bringing about broader social and cultural changes, a topic that has long exercised the minds of feminists and other reformers. Critics have long argued that the criminal law is problematic as a means of dealing with violence against women (e.g. Martin 1998; Snider 1998). The new offences are similarly criticised for placing too much reliance on law as an agent of social change (see Wangmann, Chap. 11). Conversely, those who favour the enactment of new offences recognise that law reform by itself is insufficient, but endorse Piet Van Hempen's (2014, p. xii) view that 'human rights … can only be effective within the structure of a comprehensive criminal justice system'. In essence, laws are located in particular social and cultural conditions, but can contribute to social and cultural change. Law reformers emphasise the latter, while those who are pessimistic about the role of law often ground their criticism in the former.

1.6.5.2 Do We Need a 'Standalone' Domestic Abuse Offence?

The new offences are based on the foundation that intimate, familial relationships provide a particular context for a wide range of gendered, repeated, controlling or coercive behaviours resulting in distinctive non-physical harms. However, some commentators suggest that domestic violence is not so different from other forms of violence that it needs separate concepts and laws (e.g. Walby and Towers 2018, p. 8). A close examination of this argument is warranted. For instance, Walby and Tower's (2018) rejection of the need for a standalone offence is based on their exclusion of non-physical harms from their consideration of violent crimes. Thus, threats of violence—physical or sexual—and non-violent coercion, such as stalking or harassment, are not included in their analysis. By defining violent crime in this restrictive manner it is easy to see why they concluded that 'Domestic violent crime is a subset of violent crime, not a separate type of crime' (Walby and Towers 2018, p. 12); indeed, it is arguable that the conclusion is simply an artefact of their analysis. But if non-physical aspects of domestic abuse (psychological harms, economic harms, etc.), as well as its repeated and cumulative nature, are included, then their conclusion is undermined. Consequently, it appears that intimate familial relationships can provide the context for distinctive harmful behaviours which are not captured by the traditional criminal law. How the criminal law should recognise different forms of abuse according to the context in which they are perpetrated is complex and requires careful consideration (see Burman and Brooks-Hay 2018, p. 71).

1.6.5.3 Dissipating Resources

Discussion of the new offences also raises a pragmatic issue: laws dealing with physical violence are not being adequately resourced and implemented, and it is, therefore, arguable that we should ensure that existing laws are properly enforced, rather than focusing on creating new laws that will redistribute available financial and other resources (Padfied 2016; Travis 2014; Walklate et al. 2018, p. 5). Indeed, feminist criticisms of the offences or controlling or coercive behaviour have overwhelmingly focused on implementation and impact issues (e.g. Walklate et al. 2018; Tolmie 2018). Women's limited access to justice has been identified at each stage of the criminal justice processing of domestic violence cases, including the reluctance of abused women to involve police (Walklate et al. 2018, p. 7), the trial process and the adversarial system of justice (Tolmie 2018), and sentencing (Special Taskforce 2015, pp. 301–305). This concern has been influential in jurisdictions that have chosen not to enact similar, specific domestic abuse offences (e.g. Special Taskforce 2015, p. 301; Royal Commission into Family Violence 2016, pp. 211–213, 224).

Close examination of this concern unearths many issues. It expressly adopts a 'hierarchy of harms' that has been rejected by advocates of the new offences (see Scott, Chap. 9). And it may underestimate the pragmatic value of identifying and prosecuting non-physical abuse as an 'early intervention' strategy to disrupt the escalation of abuse. Nearly 40 years ago, Del Martin (1982, p.xviii) warned that 'In many cases … psychological abuse is a prelude to physical violence' and recent research has empirically confirmed a relationship between coercive control, stalking and intimate partner homicide (Monckton-Smith et al. 2017; Tyson, Chap. 4).

1.6.5.4 Are the New Offences Undesirable Instances of Carceral Feminism?

Another concern that may be raised in relation to the new offences is that by further criminalising domestic abuse they simply replicate conventional law-and-order responses to gendered violence and fail to engage with critiques of the criminal punishment system ('feminism as crime control': Bernstein 2012, p. 251).

The anti-carceral critique raises key issues in relation to conventional legal responses to gendered violence. While originally focused on female offenders (e.g. Chesney-Lind 1991), the critique now frequently focuses on the position of male offenders (Gottschalk 2015, p. 199), and posits that conventional legal responses not only fail victims (especially marginalised women: Polavarapu 2018), but routinely exacerbate their distress (e.g. Hudson 1998). Additionally, the critique identifies that conventional criminal justice responses disregard rehabilitation and reintegration, involve inhuman prison conditions, fail to protect the community, and are excessively costly (e.g. see Taylor 2018).

There are multiple points at which the critique could be directed at the standalone domestic abuse offences—their creation, their enforcement by police, their processing in the courts, and the punishments imposed. For instance, in Australia there is evidence that indigenous women are more likely to be victims of violence (including domestic and family violence) than non-indigenous women, and that indigenous male offenders are more likely to be sentenced to prison for domestic violence than other offenders—yet imprisonment 'is not a sanction that deters or rehabilitates Indigenous offenders' (Cunneen 2010, p. 14).

Consequently, the critique presents significant challenges. However, countervailing considerations, such as the expressive value of identification and prosecution of non-physical harms as criminal wrongs (e.g. Chalmers and Leverick 2008) and the continuing effect of failing to have state-sponsored criminal justice responses to these harms, must also be taken into account. The long history of the failure of the criminal law to be utilised to protect women because of the 'privatised' nature of domestic violence should not be replicated through ignoring established harms or adopting alternative justice mechanisms which actually perpetuate gender inequalities and structures that permit violence (Stubbs 2002, pp. 52–53).

1.7 Conclusion

Few issues have generated more concern in recent years than domestic abuse. Among the multiple and varied government initiatives seeking to reduce and punish this type of conduct, the introduction of 'standalone' criminal offences based on notions of coercive control has been distinctive. These offences address a core but hitherto non-criminalised aspect of domestic abuse: non-physical harms. They prohibit forms of abuse that can result in a wide range of adverse psychological, economic and physical harms and human rights abuses. They provide an alternative to the indirect criminalisation—first, a court order, second, a breach, and third, a prosecution—that has previously (and ineffectively) been utilised.

These offences have generated much controversy. Such a significant development in the criminal law clearly requires detailed consideration of the rights of victims, an evaluation of the proper scope of the offences, of their likely impact and effectiveness, and of the need to avoid overcriminalisation. Predictably, many difficulties have been anticipated in relation to their operation (Walklate et al. 2018; Tolmie 2018). Some commentators support coercive control models of domestic abuse yet are sceptical of the value of a specific criminal offence (Tyson, Chap. 4; Wangmann, Chap. 11). Yet it is arguable that failure to criminalise means that these harms and human rights abuses are privatised and remain a public health, not a legal issue. It may also leave victims in current domestic relationships in the curious position of having fewer legal protections from non-physical harms than they have in relationships with strangers and ex-partners. At the beginning of the twenty-first century, it is curious that criminal laws can punish physical contact as slight as a mere touch (*Collins v Wilcock* [1984]) but, in the absence of legislative initiatives, offer little protection to those in intimate relationships who are abused, often for prolonged periods of time, in non-physical ways by their partners. Consequently, exploring the ambit, aim and potential impact of the new offences is a significant undertaking. These matters are addressed in subsequent chapters.

References

Ambos, K. (2015). The overall function of the international criminal law: Striking the right balance between the *rechtsgut* and the harm principles. *Criminal Law and Philosophy, 9*(2), 301–329.

Arias, I., & Pape, K. T. (1999). Psychological abuse: Implications for adjustment and commitment to leave violent partners. *Violence and Victims, 14*(1), 55–67.

Australian Institute of Health and Welfare. (2014). *Specialist Homelessness Services: 2013–2014.* Canberra: Australian Institute of Health and Welfare. Retrieved from www.aihw.gov.au/WorkArea/DownloadAsset.aspx?id=60129549998.

Bagshaw, D., Thea, B., Wendt, S., Campbell, A., McInnes, E., Tinning, B., & Arias, P. F. (2010). *Family violence and family law in Australia: The experiences and views of children and adults from families who separated post-1995 and post-2006.* Canberra: Commonwealth Attorney General's Department. Retrieved from https://www.ag.gov.au/FamiliesAndMarriage/Families/FamilyViolence/Documents/Family%20violence%20and%20family%20law%20in%20Australia%20volume%201.pdf.

Baldry, A. (2003). 'Stick and stones hurt my bones but his glance and words hurt more': The impact of psychological abuse and physical violence by current and former partners on battered women in Italy. *International Journal of Forensic Mental Health, 2*(1), 47–57.

Barlow, C., Johnson, K., & Walklate, S. (2018). The coercive control offence and implications for the policing of domestic abuse. Paper presented at the *30th Annual Conference of the Australian & New Zealand Society of Criminology*, Melbourne, 7 December 2018.

Bernstein, E. (2007). The sexual politics of 'new abolitionism'. *Differences: A Journal of Feminist Cultural Studies, 18*(3), 128–151.

Bernstein, E. (2012). Carceral politics as gender justice? The 'traffic in women' and neoliberal circuits of crime, sex, and rights. *Theory and Society, 41*(3), 233–259.

Bettinson, V., & Bishop, C. (2015). Is the creation of a discrete offence of coercive control necessary to combat domestic violence? *Northern Ireland Law Quarterly, 66*(2), 179–197.

Bishop, C., & Bettinson, V. (2017). Evidencing domestic violence, including behaviour that falls under the new offence of 'controlling or coercive behaviour'. *International Journal of Evidence and Proof, 22*(2), 1–27.

Bolger, R. (2015, March 8). Domestic violence perpetrators using non-physical abuse 'to avoid being caught'. *ABC News.* Retrieved from http://www.abc.net.au/news/2015-03-08/domestic-violence-perpetrators-using-non-physical-abuse-to-avoi/6289278.

Brooks, L. (2018, February 1). Scotland set to pass 'gold standard' domestic abuse law. *The Guardian*. Retrieved from https://www.theguardian.com/society//feb/01scotland-set-to-pass-gold-standard-domestic-abuse-law.

Burke, A. (2007). Domestic violence as a crime of pattern and intent: An alternative reconceptualization. *George Washington Law Review, 75*(3), 552–612.

Burman, M., & Brooks-Hay, O. (2018). Aligning policy and law? The creation of a domestic abuse offence incorporating coercive control. *Criminology & Criminal Justice, 18*(1), 67–83.

Chalmers, J. (2014). Frenzied law making: Overcriminalization by numbers. *Current Legal Problems, 67*(1), 483–502.

Chalmers, J., & Leverick, F. (2008). Fair labelling in criminal law. *Modern Law Review, 71*(2), 217–246.

Chesney-Lind, M. (1991). Patriarchy, prisons, and jails: A critical look at trends in women's incarceration. *The Prison Journal, 71*(1), 51–67.

Cobbe, F. (1878). *Wife-Torture in England*. London: Contemporary Review.

Coker, A. L., Smith, P. H., Bethea, L., King, M. R., & McKeown, R. E. (2000). Physical health consequences of physical and psychological intimate partner violence. *Archives of Family Medicine, 9*(5), 451–457.

Council of Europe. (2011). *Convention on Preventing and Combating Violence Against Women and Domestic Violence*. Retrieved from https://rm.coe.int/16800848e.

Crowell, N. A., & Burgess, A. W. (Eds.). (1996). *Understanding violence against women*. Washington DC: National Academy.

Crown Prosecution Service. (n.d.). Offences against the Person, Incorporating the charging standard: Assault occasioning actual bodily harm. Retrieved from https://www.cps.gov.uk/legal-guidance/offences-against-person-incorporating-charging-standard.

Crown Prosecution Service. (2015). DPP: Controlling and coercive behaviour can 'limit victims' basic human rights' as new domestic abuse law introduced. Previously available at http://www.cps.gov.uk/news/latest_news/new_domestic_abuse_law_introduced/.

Crown Prosecution Service. (2017). Controlling or coercive behaviour in an intimate or family relationship. Retrieved from https://www.cps.gov.uk/legal-guidance/controlling-or-coercive-behaviour-intimate-or-family-relationship.

Cunneen, C. (2010). *Alternative and improved responses to domestic and family violence in queensland indigenous communities*. Brisbane, QLD: Department of Communities Queensland.

Department of Justice and Industrial Relations (Tas). (2003). *Safe at Home: A Criminal Justice Framework for Responding to Family Violence in Tasmania. Options Paper*. Tasmania: Tasmanian Government. Retrieved from https://www.safeathome.tas.gov.au/__data/assets/pdf_file/0006/28374/Options_Paper.pdf.

Devries, K., Watt, C., Yoshihama, M., Kiss, L., Schraiber, K. L., Deyessa, N., Heise, L., Durand, J., Jansen, M., Berhane, Y., Ellsberg, M., & Garcia-Moreno, C. (2011). Violence against women is strongly associated with suicide attempts: Evidence from the WHO multi-country study on women's health and domestic violence against women. *Social Science & Medicine, 73*(1), 79–86.

Dobash, R., & Dobash, R. (1979). *Violence against wives*. New York, NY: Free Press.

Dobash, R., & Dobash, R. (1998). *Rethinking violence against women*. London: Sage Publishing.

Douglas, H. (2007). Not a crime like any other: Sentencing breaches of domestic violence protection orders. *Criminal Law Journal, 31*(4), 200–219.

Douglas, H. (2015). Do we need a specific domestic violence offence? *Melbourne University Law Review, 39*(4), 434–471.

Douglas, H., & Stark, T. (2010). *Stories from survivors: Domestic violence and criminal justice interventions*. Brisbane: T.C. Bierne School of Law, University of Queensland. Retrieved from https://law.uq.edu.au/files/12453/Stories-From-Survivors-Douglas-Stark.pdf.

Dowling, C., Morgan, A., Hulme, S., Manning, M., & Wong, G. (2018). Protection orders for domestic violence: A systematic review, *Trends & Issues in Criminal Justice no. 551*, Canberra, ACT: Australian Institute of Criminology.

Dutton, M., & Goodman, L. (2005). Coercion in intimate partner violence: Toward a new conceptualization. *Sex Roles, 52*(11–12), 743–756.

Fitz-Gibbon, K., & Walklate, S. (2018). Coercive control: A clinical or legal concept? Problems and possibilities. Paper presented at the *30th Annual Conference of the Australian & New Zealand Society of Criminology*, Melbourne, 7 December 2018.

Follingstad, D. R. (2009). The impact of psychological aggression on women's mental health and behavior. *Trauma, Violence and Abuse, 10*(3), 271–289.

Follingstad, D., Rutledge, L., Berg, B., Hause, E., & Polek, D. (1990). The role of emotional abuse in physically abusive relationships. *Journal of Family Violence, 5*(2), 107–120.

Garcia-Moreno, C., Jansen, H. A., Ellsberg, M., Heise, I., & Watts, C. H. (2006). Prevalence of intimate partner violence: Findings from the WHO multi-country study on women's health and domestic violence. *The Lancet, 368*, 1260–1269.

Garfield, L. (2009). The case for a criminal law theory of intentional infliction of emotional distress. *Criminal Law Brief, 5*(1), 33–50.

Gottschalk, M. (2015). *Caught: The prison state and the lockdown of American politics*. Princeton, NJ: Princeton University Press.

Griffin, J. (2008). *On human rights*. Oxford: Oxford University Press.

Hessbruegge, J. (2004). The historical development of the doctrines of attribution and due diligence in international law. *New York University Journal of International Law and Politics, 36*(4), 265–306.

Hill, A. (2016, September 1). Police failing to use new law against coercive domestic abuse. *The Guardian*. Retrieved from https://www.theguardian.com/society//aug/31/police-failing-to-use-new-law-against-coercive-domestic-abuse.

Hirschel, D., & Hutchison, I. W. (2003). The voices of domestic violence victims: Predictors of victim preference for arrest and the relationship between preference for arrest and revictimization. *Crime & Delinquency, 49*(2), 313–336.

Hoffman, P. (1984). Psychological abuse of women by spouses and live-in lovers. *Women in Therapy, 3*(1), 37–47.

Hogg, R. (2017). Criminology, globalization and human rights. In L. Weber, E. Fishwick, & M. Marmo (Eds.), *Routledge international handbook of criminology and human rights*. London: Routledge.

Home Office. (2010). *Call to End Violence Against Women and Girls: Action Plan 2011*. Retrieved from https://assets.publishing.service.gov.uk/government/uploads/system/uploads/attachment_data/file/118153/vawg-action-plan.pdf.

Home Office. (2014). *Strengthening the Law on Domestic Abuse Consultation Summary of Responses*. Retrieved from https://www.gov.uk/government/uploads/system/uploads/attachment_data/file/389002/StrengtheningLawDomesticAbuseResponses.pdf.

Home Office. (2015). *Controlling or Coercive Behaviour in an Intimate or Family Relationship: Statutory Guidance Framework*. Retrieved from https://www.gov.uk/government/uploads/system/uploads/attachment_data/file/482528/Controlling_or_coercive_behaviour_-_statutory_guidance.pdf.

Hudson, B. (1998). Restorative justice: The challenge of sexual and racial violence. *Journal of Law and Society, 25*(2), 237–256.

Johnson, M. P. (1995). Patriarchal terrorism and common couple violence: Two forms of violence against women. *Journal of Marriage and the Family, 57*(2), 283–294.

Johnson, M. P. (2006). Conflict and control: Gender symmetry and asymmetry in domestic violence. *Violence Against Women, 12*(11), 1003–1018.

Johnson, M., & Ferraro, K. (2000). Research on domestic violence in the 1990s: Making distinctions. *Journal of Marriage and Family, 62*(4), 948–963.

Lacey, N., & Zedner, L. (2012). Legal constructions of crime. In Maguire, M., Morgan, R., & Reiner, R. (Eds.), *Oxford Handbook of Criminology* (5th ed.). Oxford: Oxford University Press.

Libal, K., & Parekh, S. (2009). Reframing violence against women as a human rights violation: Evan Stark's coercive control. *Violence Against Women, 15*(12), 1477–1499.

Marshall, J. (2008). Positive obligations and gender-based violence: Judicial developments. *International Community Law Review, 10*(2), 143–169.

Martin, D. (1998). Retribution revisited: A reconsideration of feminist criminal law reform strategies. *Osgoode Hall Law Journal, 36*(1), 151–188.

Mechanic, M., Weaver, T., & Resick, P. (2008). Mental health consequences of intimate partner abuse: A multidimensional assessment of four different forms of abuse. *Violence Against Women, 14*(6), 634–654.

Merry, S. (2003). Rights talk and the experience of law: Implementing women's human rights to protection from violence. *Human Rights Quarterly, 25*(2), 343–381.

McGorrery, P., & McMahon, M. (2018). Prosecutions of controlling or coercive behaviour in England and Wales. Paper presented at the *30th Annual Conference of the Australian & New Zealand Society of Criminology*, Melbourne, 8 December 2018.

McMahon, M., & McGorrery, P. (2016). Criminalising economic and emotional abuse and intimidation: The Tasmanian experience. *University of Tasmania Law Review, 36*(2), 1–22.

McQuigg, R. (2011). *International human rights law and domestic violence: The effectiveness of international human rights law.* Oxford: Routledge.

Monckton-Smith, J., Szymanska, K., & Haile, S. (2017). *Exploring the Relationship between Stalking and Homicide.* Gloucester: Suzy Lamplugh Trust. Retrieved from http://eprints.glos.ac.uk/4553/.

Neate, P. (2015, December 29). Women's Aid welcomes coercive control law. *Press Release.* Retrieved from https://www.womensaid.org.uk/womens-aid-welcomes-coercive-control-law/.

North, C. (2015). The classification of hysteria and related disorders: Historical and phenomenological considerations. *Behavioral sciences, 5*(4), 496–517.

O'Leary, D. (1999). Psychological abuse: A variable deserving critical attention in domestic violence research. *Victims and Violence, 14*(1), 3–23.

Padfield, N. (2016). Editorial: Controlling or coercive behaviour in an intimate or family relationship. *Criminal Law Review, 3,* 149–151.

Pleck, E. (1987). *Domestic tyranny: The making of American social policy against family violence from colonial times to the present.* New York, NY: Oxford University Press.

Pogge, T. (2001). How should human rights be conceived? In P. Hayden (Ed.), *The philosophy of human rights.* Paragon Hose: St Paul, MN.

Polavarapu, A. (2018). Global carceral feminism and domestic violence: What the west can learn from reconciliation in Uganda. *Harvard Journal of Law & Gender,* (forthcoming). Retrieved from https://papers.ssrn.com/sol3/papers.cfm?abstract_id=3188271.

Robertson, N., Busch, R., D'Souza, R., Lam Sheung, F., Anand, R., Balzer, R., & Paina, D. (2007). *Living at the cutting edge: Women's experiences of protection orders. Volume 2: What's to be done? A critical analysis of statutory and practice approaches to domestic violence.* Wellington: University of Waikato.

Römkens, R. (2001). Law as a trojan horse: Unintended consequences of rights-based interventions to support battered women. *Yale Journal of Law and Feminism, 13*(2), 265–290.

Royal Commission into Family Violence. (2016). *Report and Recommendations, Vol III.* Retrieved from http://www.rcfv.com.au/Report-Recommendations.

Sackett, L. A., & Saunders, D. G. (1999). The impact of different forms of psychological abuse on battered women. *Violence and Victims, 14*(1), 105–116.

Schelong, K. M. (1994). Domestic violence and the state: Response to and rationales for spousal battering, marital rape and stalking. *Marquette Law Review, 78*(1), 79–120.

Scottish Government. (2014). *Equally Safe: Scotland's Strategy for Preventing and Eradicating Violence Against Women and Girls.* Retrieved from http://www.gov.scot/Publications/2014/06/7483.

Scottish Government. (2015). *Equally Safe: Reforming the Criminal Law to Address Domestic Abuse and Sexual Offences. A Scottish Government Consultation Paper.* Retrieved from http://www.gov.scot/Publications/2015/03/4845/0.

Scottish Government. (2018a). *Protective Orders for People at Risk of Domestic Abuse: Consultation*. Retrieved from https://www.gov.scot/publications/consultation-protective-orders-people-risk-domestic-abuse/pages/2/.

Scottish Government, (2018b). *Equally Safe: Scotland's Strategy to Eradicate Violence Against Women*. Retrieved from https://www.gov.scot/publications/equally-safe-scotlands-strategy-prevent-eradicate-violence-against-women-girls/.

Sentencing Advisory Council (Vic). (2009). *Sentencing Practices for Breach of Family Violence Intervention Orders: Final Report*. Retrieved from https://www.sentencingcouncil.vic.gov.au/publications/sentencing-practices-breach-of-family-violence-intervention-orders-final-report.

Sheridan, J. B., & Bakewell, J. W. (1879). *The magistrates' guide*. Adelaide, SA: Government Printer.

Siegal, R. B. (1995). 'The rule of love': Wife beating as prerogative and privacy. *Yale Law Journal, 105*(8), 2117–2207.

Simester, A. P., Spencer, J. R., Sullivan, G. R., & Virgo, G. J. (2010). *Simester and sullivan's criminal law: Theory and doctrine*. London: Hart Publishing.

Snider, L. (1998). Toward safer societies: Punishment, masculinities and violence against women. *British Journal of Criminology, 38*(1), 1–39.

Special Taskforce on Domestic and Family Violence in Queensland. (2015). *Not now, not ever: Putting an end to domestic and family violence in Queensland*. Brisbane: Queensland Government. Retrieved from http://www.qld.gov.au/community/documents/getting-support-health-social-issue/dfv-report-vol-one.pdf.

Stannard, J. (2010). Sticks, stones and words: Emotional harm and the English criminal law. *Criminal Law Review, 74*(6), 533–566.

Stark, E. (2016). Coercive control. Paper presented at the *Chance for Change Conference*, Nottinghamshire, 9 March 2016.

Stark, E. (2012). Coercive control. In N. Lombard & L. McMillan (Eds.), *Violence against women: Current theory and practice in domestic abuse*. London: Jessica Kingsley.

Stark, E. (1995). Re-presenting woman battering: From battered woman syndrome to coercive control. *Albany Law Review, 58*(4), 973–1026.

Stark, E. (2009). Rethinking coercive control. *Violence Against Women, 15*(12), 1509–1525.

Stark, E. (2007). *Coercive control: How men entrap women in personal life*. Oxford: Oxford University Press.

Street, A. E., & Arias, I. (2001). Psychological abuse and posttraumatic stress disorder in battered women: Examining the roles of shame and guilt. *Violence and Victims, 16*(1), 65–78.

Straight, E., Harper, F., & Arias, I. (2003). The impact of partner psychological abuse on health behaviors and health status in college women. *Journal of Interpersonal Violence, 18*(9), 1035–1054.

Stubbs, J. (2002). Domestic violence and women's safety: Feminist challenges to restorative justice. In H. Strang & J. Braithwaite (Eds.), *Restorative justice and family violence*. Cambridge: Cambridge University Press.

Tadros, V. (2005). The distinctiveness of domestic abuse: A freedom based account. *Louisiana Law Review, 65*(3), 989–1014.

Taylor, C. (2018). Anti-carceral feminism and sexual assault—A defence. *Social Philosophy Today, 34*, 29–49.

Tolman, R. M. (1992). Psychological abuse of women. In R. T. Ammerman & M. Hersen (Eds.), *Assessment of family violence: A clinical and legal sourcebook*. Oxford: John Wiley & Sons.

Tolmie, J. (2018). Coercive control: To criminalize or not to criminalize? *Criminology & Criminal Justice, 18*(1), 50–66.

Travis, A. (2014, December 19). Domestic abuse charity criticises May's law criminalising coercive behaviour. *The Guardian*. Retrieved from http://www.theguardian.com/society/2014/dec/18/theresa-may-domestic-abuse-offence-coercive-behaviour.

Tuerkheimer, D. (2004). Recognizing and remedying the crime of battering: A call to criminalize domestic violence. *Journal of Criminal Law & Criminology, 94*(4), 959–1031.
van Hempen, P. (2014). Introduction—Criminal law and human rights. In Criminal Law & Human Rights (Eds.), *van Hempen, P*. Farnham: Ashgate.
VicHealth. (2004). *The Health Costs of Violence: Measuring the Burden Of Disease Caused by Intimate Partner Violence*. Retrieved from https://www.vichealth.vic.gov.au/media-and-resources/publications/the-health-costs-of-violence.
Walby, S., & Towers, J. S. (2018). Untangling the concept of coercive control: Theorizing domestic violent crime. *Criminology & Criminal Justice, 18*(1), 7–28.
Walker, L. E. (1979). *The battered woman*. New York, NY: Harper Perennial.
Walklate, S., Fitz-Gibbon, K., & McCulloch, J. (2018). Is more law the answer? Seeking justice for victims of intimate partner violence through the reform of legal categories. *Criminology & Criminal Justice, 18*(1), 115–131.
Whiting, N. (2014, May 30). Domestic violence: Victims call for tougher laws to combat abuse. *ABC News*. Retrieved from http://www.abc.net.au/news/2014-05-30/victims-call-for-introduction-of-tougher-laws-to-combat-abuse/5474070.
Williamson, E. (2010). Living in the world of the domestic violence perpetrator: Negotiating the unreality of coercive control. *Violence Against Women, 16*(12), 1412–1423.
Women's Legal Service Victoria. (2018). 'Officer she's psychotic and I need protection': Police misidentification of the 'primary aggressor' in family violence incidents in Victoria. Retrieved from https://www.womenslegal.org.au/files/file/WLSV%20Policy%20Brief%201%20MisID%20July%202018.pdf.

Legislation

Charter of Human Rights and Responsibilities Act 2006 (Vic)
Crimes Act 1958 (Vic)
Crimes Amendment (Gross Violence Offences) Act 2013 (Vic)
Crimes (Domestic and Personal Violence) Act 2007 (NSW)
Criminal Code Act Consolidation Act 1913 (WA)
Criminal Justice Act 1988 (UK)
Criminal Justice and Licensing (Scotland) Act 2010 (Scot)
Criminal Law Consolidation Act 1935 (SA)
Domestic Abuse (Scotland) Act 2018 (Scot)
Domestic and Family Violence Act 2007 (NT)
Domestic and Family Violence Protection Act 2012 (Qld)
Domestic Violence Act 2018 (IR)
Domestic Violence and Protection Orders Act 2008 (ACT)
Family Violence Act 2016 (ACT)
Family Violence Act 2004 (Tas)
Family Violence Protection Act 2008 (Vic)
Human Rights Act 2004 (ACT)
Intervention Orders (Prevention of Abuse) Act 2009 (SA)
Offences Against the Person Act 1861 (UK)
Protection From Harassment Act 1997 (UK)
Restraining Orders Act 1997 (WA)
Serious Crime Act 2015 (E&W)
Summary Offences Act 1986 (Vic)

Cases

Attorney-General (Tas) v CL [2018] TASFC 6
Collins v Wilcock [1984] 3 All ER 374
John Fairfax Publications Pty Ltd v Ryde Local Court [2005] NSWCA 101
Knight v R (1988) 35 A Crim R 34
R v Beaton; ex parte Smee [1997] QSC 176
R v Bourne [1939] 1 KB 687
R v Chan-Fook [1994] 1 WLR 689
R v Curtis [2010] All ER 849
RR v The Queen [2013] VSCA 147
R v Widdows [2011] EWCA Crim 1500
Shu Qiang Li v R [2005] NSWCCA 442

Other materials

Convention on the Elimination of all Forms of Discrimination against Women (1979)
Convention on the Rights of the Child (1989)
Declaration of Human Rights (1948)
International Covenant on Civil and Political Rights (1966)
International Covenant on Economic, Social and Cultural Rights (1966)

Chapter 2
The 'Coercive Control Framework': Making Law Work for Women

Evan Stark

Abstract The potential efficacy of a new offence of coercive control will be determined by the constellation of factors that surround its implementation. Drawing on experiences with s 76 of the *Serious Crime Act 2015* (E&W) in England and Wales and the *Domestic Abuse (Scotland) Act 2018* (Scot), these factors are identified as: a coherent national strategic framework; an articulation of the current dilemma posed to the justice system by policing domestic violence; centralised coordination by justice professionals; activist pressure from advocacy organisations such as Women's Aid; and exhibitions of political will. I endorse the comprehensive, bespoke offence crafted in Scotland; however, the cases of Northern Ireland and the Irish Republic also illustrate how meaningful reform can be achieved despite narrow or ambiguous statutory language. I conclude by responding to critics of the new offence as 'more law', and by clarifying the definition of coercive control and the underlying value commitments.

Keywords Domestic abuse offence · Coercive control · Human rights abuse · Law enforcement · Social change

2.1 Introduction: The Coercive Control Framework

This chapter does *not* defend the new offence of 'coercive and controlling behaviour' in s 76 of the *Serious Crime Act 2015* (E&W) that operates in England and Wales against its critics (Walby and Towers 2017; Burman and Brooks-Hay 2018; Padfield 2016; Douglas 2015; Tolmie 2018). However, I *do* reiterate my endorsement of 'coercive control', but conceived here as a comprehensive framework for approaching partner abuse, not as a specific offence. The 'coercive control framework' may include legislation such as the *Domestic Abuse (Scotland) Act 2018* (Scot) passed unanimously by the Scottish Parliament in 2018 and considered

E. Stark (✉)
School of Public Affairs and Administration, Rutgers University, NJ, USA
e-mail: starkevan342@gmail.com

© Springer Nature Singapore Pte Ltd. 2020
M. McMahon and P. McGorrery (eds.), *Criminalising Coercive Control*,
https://doi.org/10.1007/978-981-15-0653-6_2

a 'gold standard'. But more important than the specific law is that the consensus that led to its passage depended on a confluence of related factors that make it likely to be implemented in ways that are consistent with the meaning of the concept. Among the most important of these factors were: a coherent national strategic framework; an articulation of the dilemma facing the justice system; centralised coordination by justice professionals; activist pressure from *Women's Aid*; and exhibitions of political will. I call this loose constellation 'the coercive control framework' to denote the larger context in which a new offence of coercive control is likely to be most effective.

The overall coercive control framework is adaptable elsewhere, but particular constituent elements like a specific law are rarely replicable from one national context to the next. Even the best drawn laws function as a 'disguised betrayal' of women's justice claims without concurrent commitments of resources to infrastructure, nationally coordinated assistance to local surveillance and interdiction, and the comparable political will to pursue the equality agenda. By contrast, in a politically dynamic context such as Northern Ireland, for instance, even a narrowly drawn statute can be a vehicle for addressing coercive control. The closing sections of this chapter clarify my definition of coercive control and explain my value commitment to creating a bespoke offence to classify this class of behaviours as 'unjust', to make the suffering it causes 'grievable', and to hold those responsible to account.

2.2 The Scottish Framework: One Size May Not Fit All

By specifying multiple elements of coercion and control, subsuming violence and sexual assault along with controlling behaviours not currently crimes, extending coverage to former partners, stiffening the top sanction and shifting the weight of evidence to the perceived intent of the offender, the Scottish bespoke offence created by the *Domestic Abuse (Scotland) Act 2018* (Scot) responds to the more serious shortcomings critics identified in s 76 of the *Serious Crime Act 2015* (E&W) (Burman and Brooks-Hay 2018; Wiener, Chap. 8 in this volume). In England, the broad strategic framework for an appropriate 'cross-governmental response' was spelled out by the Home Office in a new 'working definition' of coercive control to include 'any incident or *pattern of incidents* of controlling, coercive or threatening behaviour, violence or abuse between those aged 16 or over who are or have been intimate partners or family members regardless of gender or sexuality' (Home Office 2015). *Coercion* encompasses psychological, physical, sexual, financial and emotional abuse, and *controlling* behaviour was defined as 'making a person subordinate and/or dependent by isolating them from sources of support, exploiting their resources and capacities for personal gain, depriving them of the means needed for independence, resistance and escape and regulating their everyday lives'. From 2012 to 2014, the new working definition replaced more than 20 other, conflicting definitions that guided the funding and delivery of services to abuse victims throughout Britain. But the new definition had no legal standing. As Wiener argues in this volume (Chap. 8), the Conservative Party Solicitor General crafted the offence of coercive and controlling behaviour in England and Wales far too narrowly to carry the weight or breadth of this definition.

To my mind, the weakness of s 76 lies less in its minimalist language than in the Solicitor General's decision to set aside the larger coercive control framework which makes the particular acts identified by the offence intelligible as part of a malign pattern of domination. The explicit enumeration of bad acts in the Scottish offence makes sense only against the background of this larger context. If other countries simply adapt a Scottish-type offence, they risk prematurely fixing a statutory gaze on a crime about which relatively little is known and where the government has little direct experience in ways that foreclose the institutional learning that is essential here. The working definition developed in England by the Home Office was the culmination of activism by women's organisations as well as two decades of local experimentation with broader definitions of abuse in London and more than 80 other local Councils (Stark 2018). Had the intent of s 76 been to introduce coercive control *de nuevo*, a broad, ambiguously worded statute might actually have evoked more local innovation in evidence gathering, charging, sentencing and related issues than a statute with exacting provisions of law (like Scotland's *Domestic Abuse Act*). Instead, s 76 left those whose experience and learning had produced the working definition out to dry.

Taking this point a bit further, the actual reception of coercive control by the justice system is likely to be as much a by-product of administration, enforcement, implementation and interpretation as of guidance received from statutory language. What happens in courts will depend on what is 'seen' and 'heard' there and how court officers are instructed to listen. The working definition and the Scottish Act expose many facets of the abuse experience that have eluded public scrutiny and accountability until now. Such areas include emotional abuse, historical abuse, isolation, sexual coercion, financial abuse, cyberstalking and other distal forms of intimidation. Perhaps most confounding are cases where high levels of fear appear to have been evoked in victims by offender behaviours other than violence. Tolmie (2018) and Walklate et al. (2017) have warned that, regardless of what definitions police are given, the narrow purview of a justice system attuned to physically violent incidents will constrain its response in these cases to extreme violence and thereby perpetuate the false impression that coercive control is rare. This is not, however, what has happened in England thus far. For one thing, there have been almost 1000 prosecutions brought to date (Crown Prosecution Service 2018). For another thing, the very ambiguity of s 76 with respect to violence (which Wiener (Chap. 8) and others justly criticise) has allowed cases to be brought, at least early on, that involve sustained periods of coercive and controlling behaviour other than violence (Stark 2018) and where no violence has occurred. For example, Paul Payle was convicted in January 2018 and sentenced to 3 years and 6 months imprisonment after he 'stalked' his wife online by hacking her accounts and sending messages to her family and friends while pretending the culprit was a previous boyfriend (BBC News 2018).

Despite a steep learning curve and the ambiguity in the statute, the cases I reviewed suggest English police are enforcing s 76 as well as can be expected. But their efforts have revealed that the targeted patterns of behaviour are often too widespread, too spatially diffuse and involve too many disparate elements for local jurisdictions to effectively pursue on their own, even after considering the effects of devolution on available support services. To make law that is 'effective' as well as well made in the abstract means to anticipate a system of law enforcement and justice administration that matches the scope of the offence being tackled. Here, this means having the versatility to confront a range of coercive and controlling tactics deployed over a considerable time period to monopolise a partner's access to the scarce resources without which she cannot thrive. Personal life is the primary siting of coercive control. But, in addition to threats relating to material resources such as money, food, transport, computers or cell phones, threats to survival also often target social activities, at school, work, market or leisure spaces, which an offender may 'enter' at multiple points, for sustained periods, over widely dispersed areas. Interdiction must be similarly designed to be sustained, versatile, geographically dispersed and equally capable of penetrating social and institutional space. Anticipating and/or allowing for this sort of versatility is an important element of the coercive control framework.

Law enforcement has been severely challenged by cases of historic child sexual abuse, though these involve far fewer victims overall than do cases of coercive control. Like cases of historic child sexual abuse, coercive control often lasts for years (more than 5 years on average: Stark 2007, p. 109) and its perpetrators relocate frequently to elude prosecution as well as to isolate their targets. For instance, a case reported to me recently in Cambridge, England resulted in successful prosecution only after 2 years of police work and jurisdictional negotiations between three area departments. Anticipating similar challenges to local resources in Scotland, the Crown Office and Procurator of Fiscal Services (COPFS) provides national direction for an overall prosecution strategy via a newly appointed National Domestic Abuse Prosecutor, and Police Scotland supplies intelligence on high risk offenders to local forces through its National Domestic Abuse Task Force. These initiatives, which were developed independently by COPFS, send a strong message of accountability to Police Scotland and set the stage on which Scottish Women's Aid was able to mobilise a 'consultation' into the new law (Police Scotland and COPFS 2013). This combination of centralised command, decentralised technical assistance and flexibility in law enforcement is as much a part of the coercive control framework as the identification of criminal elements.

Another facet of the Scottish experience that was important was the degree to which the judiciary made public its frustration with the existing response, thereby publicising a problem to which the *Domestic Abuse (Scotland) Act 2018* (Scot) s 1 was a solution. The result was fortuitous, but not accidental.

On 13 August 2013, national media in the United Kingdom featured the following story. Based on complaints by his three former wives and a stepdaughter, Bill Walker, a long-standing Labour Member of the Scottish Parliament (MSP), was convicted of breach of the peace and 23 assaults. The assaults stretched over

28 years (1967 to 1995) and included punching his wives in the face, leaving one with a black eye, brandishing an air rifle, repeatedly using a saucepan to hit another ex-partner, and putting all his partners through 'systematic physical and emotional abuse.' Walker's convictions included an assault using a frying pan on his 16-year-old stepdaughter (BBC 2013). In a public statement read from the bench, Edinburgh's Domestic Violence Sheriff (Katherine Mackie) outlined the chronic and heinous nature of Walker's 'controlling, domineering, demeaning … behaviors' (*PF v Bill Walker*, 23 August 2013). Sheriff Mackie voiced frustration with the 1-year sentencing limit in the Sheriff's Court without trial because she believed that this would make Walker's behaviour seem not to amount to a 'criminal' (i.e. serious) offence. Even if she sentenced the 71-year-old Walker to prison for the maximum period, he could remain in Parliament, where removal under Westminster rules was automatic only for members sentenced to more than a year in prison (Chilton 2013). He could voluntarily resign (and ultimately did), but was not legally compelled to do so.

Sheriff Mackie's sentencing statement got at the heart of how abstracting individual assaultive episodes (any of which may be trivial in themselves) from their historical context can lead to the mistaken conclusion that the abuse of women and children need not be taken seriously. She weighed the 'cumulative effect' of Walker's 'pattern of abusive behaviour' towards his wives and children against the single act of assault that would have been dismissed as 'just a domestic' in the past. In his defense, Walker claimed 'various conspiracies among former wives, political opponents and the media.' Sheriff Mackie rejected Walker's claims out of hand. Instead, she identified his incredulity at being convicted and his repeated claims of victimisation as 'further indications of your abdication of responsibility for your behaviour' (*PF v Bill Walker*, 20 September 2013). Though the crimes for which Walker was charged had occurred 18 years earlier, she noted his open expressions of 'contempt for your former wives and your stepdaughter and the derogatory manner in which you refer to them'. She highlighted the fact that his teenage stepdaughter 'thought it necessary to protect her mother from you and that you professed to be unaware of any injuries sustained' even though these were both visible and documented by medical records (*PF v Bill Walker*, 20 September 2013). Again and again, Sheriff Mackie identified and condemned the narcissistic behaviours for which abusive fathers are often rewarded in family cases in the United States. She observed that the only 'remorse' Walker seemed to feel was for himself and further noted that his extreme denial and minimisation, even in the face of extensive media coverage, made it unlikely domestic violence counselling would help. In the few instances where Walker acknowledged using physical force, she added, he had tried to justify his actions: (The Guardian 2013).

With respect to sentencing, Sheriff Mackie insisted that the overall or *cumulative* effect of Walker's course of criminal conduct merited a lengthy custodial sentence, even if some of the individual acts did not. Sheriff Mackie recognised what the law in Scotland would not fully comprehend until legal reform in 2018, that the seemingly diverse pieces of Walker's course of conduct were joined by a decipherable and singular behavioural logic, the *strategy of coercive control*, and it was to the various expressions of this ongoing strategy to which Walker's wives and children had responded. Thus, Sheriff Mackie found that it was Walker's behaviour that led his children to want no further contact with him, not the fact that his wives had turned them against him, as he alleged. To put it crudely, Walker's children hated him because he'd behaved hatefully towards them and towards his wives. The sentences Mackie imposed on Walker added up to 15 years' imprisonment, which is almost precisely the maximum penalty that the Scottish Parliament subsequently set for conviction at trial under the 2018 abuse law. Most of Walker's sentences were, however, concurrent. He would serve less than the year in prison required for him to resign his seat, a pyrrhic victory since public pressure forced his ouster (BBC News 2013).

In England, public awareness of coercive control became more widespread after *The Archers*, a hugely popular radio soap opera, made 'gas-lighting' and other elements of the coercive control of fictional character Helen Titchener by her husband Rob a long-running theme. Unable to withstand his relentless tormenting, Helen 'snapped' and stabbed her husband. She was arrested and charged (Kerley and Bates 2016). The story made the front pages of the tabloids and inspired a fundraising initiative that has raised £173,000 for British charity *Refuge* (Trueman 2018). When Helen was acquitted the Prime Minister's Office issued a statement supportive of victims of domestic abuse. Section 76 was used to illustrate the sort of legal protection that might have prevented the stabbing.

I was a Visiting Professor at the University of Edinburgh and lecturing on behalf of Scottish Women's Aid when Bill Walker went on trial. My book on Coercive Control (Stark 2007) had been directed at closing a gap similar to the one Sheriff Mackie identified between the patterns of 'cruel, terroristic and immoral behaviour' exhibited by men like Walker and Rob Titchener towards their wives and children and laws to stem abuse. The Walker and Titchener cases dramatised an objective reality that constrains the cost-effectiveness of all public investments in managing partner abuse as a type of assault. At most, these investments have produced incremental gains in safety and accountability. More often, as had been true with Walker, even when offending men were arrested, applying the calculus of physical harms to individual assaults had the effect of trivialising and normalising the common pattern of frequent, ongoing but generally low-level violence while masking the accompanying strategy of coercive control in which this ongoing violence was embedded. Among millions of men arrested dozens of times for similar offences against the same women and children, almost no one goes to jail (Hester 2006; Hamby et al. 2015). Abuse reporting and arrest rates are higher in the United States than in Britain because US States have specific domestic violence offences. However, there is still less than one chance in 20 that a reported offender will be convicted of a serious crime and jailed (Hamby et al. 2015). Nor does this likelihood increase in the United States or Britain after a man's 50th arrest for a domestic offence (Hester and Westmarland 2006). Listeners to *The Archers* were horrified at how she was mistreated. Equally shocking was that it was she who was targeted as the criminal by police when she responded, but not him (Kerley and Bates 2016).

The law's focus on physical injury led to declines in these types of severe assaults. But this positive outcome was overshadowed by increases in the proportions of women and children reporting historical abuse and coercive control. Proof of a large subpopulation of women who were experiencing long-standing abuse could be gleaned from government surveys, but only by looking behind official statistics. To critically assess the government's claim that violent crimes had declined in Britain, Walby et al. (2014) recorded all violence reported to the Crime Survey for England and Wales by female victims, disregarding the official cap of six on the number of reported crimes that was counted. Their review showed that the actual total of violent crimes women reported had been increasing so dramatically since 2009 that it offset the decline in almost all other forms of reported violent crime during this period, including most violent crime against men. This increase in reported violence against women was accounted for not by an increase in the number of women reporting stranger assaults or partner abuse, but by the growing proportion of 'high-frequency repeat female victims' among the reporting sample (Walby et al. 2014). The expanded definitions adapted throughout the United Kingdom responded to tragic statistics such as these by describing partner abuse as it is being experienced by its most prominent class of victims. Although the US has yet to take this step, the wisdom of adapting the broadened definition would seem unassailable given the saliency of coercive control for so many lives.

This discussion should not pre-empt discussion of the Scottish experience elsewhere in this volume. Suffice it to say here that while our countries share the apparent contradiction between the realities of coercive control and a systemic response that only targets acts of violence, the sociopolitical circumstances that gave Scottish lawmakers the courage to give coercive control its first explicit statutory definition are somewhat unique. Apart from any influence my book or *Scottish Women's Aid* had, Sheriff Mackie was already operating within a Scottish national strategy that had, since 2003, identified domestic violence as a pattern of 'gender-based abuse' perpetrated by partners or ex-partners that 'can include physical abuse (assault and physical attack involving a range of behaviour), sexual abuse (acts which degrade and humiliate women and are perpetrated against their will, including rape) and mental and emotional abuse (such as threats, verbal abuse, racial abuse, withholding money and other types of controlling behaviour such as isolation from family or friends) (Scottish Executive 2003). In sentencing Walker, Sheriff Mackie gave voice to the dilemma created for her by the failure of the Scottish Executive to translate its own strategic ideal into practical law, a tension she challenged the Scottish National Parliament to resolve.

2.3 Getting It Right: Does It Matter?

In my work, *psychological abuse* is a subset of the tactics used to control a partner who is simultaneously afraid to resist, respond, refuse or escape demands because of some combination of threats and physical and/or sexual coercion. In this approach, the *wrong* consists of denuding a target of the resources (material/subjective) needed for resilience, not the insults themselves, however inappropriate or vicious. At first look, the substantive focuses only on psychological abuse in recent coercive control legislation in England, the Irish Republic and Tasmania belie this broad political impulse. For example, in England, a mistaken belief that existing offences covered all but the psychological elements of coercive control led the Solicitor General in England to parse the coherent Home Office definition (Home Office 2015). But is this really so?

Work on coercive control is about changing the big picture, not adding new offensive behaviours to a series of (already unenforced) distinct offences. This means joining as many elements as possible under a single offence, as Scotland does, including those, like violent and sexual assault which are now crimes but not considered together as part of coercive control; those like stalking or harassment, which are rarely considered criminal in the context of a relationship (see the chapters by Wiener (Chap. 8) and McMahon, McGorrery and Burton (Chap. 5) in this volume); and then, yes, psychological abuse, degradation, regulation, deprivation, exploitation and other forms of 'control,' whose significance as part of a criminal pattern of domination, arises from their context. The aim is to identify a singular malevolent intent to dominate, whatever the interplay of the means deployed to instil fear of resistance/refusal and/or dependence/incapacitation. Properly drawn, coercive control sets physical and sexual violence against women in the context of myriad complementary nonviolent coercive and controlling tactics that make the serious criminal intent to dominate coherent over time and across social space.

Coercive control is most prevalent and has its most devastating consequences in heterosexual relationships where it is 'gendered' in its aim (male privilege) and its object (female subordination) and is linked to structural inequalities in the larger economy. But the process of coercive control is not per se gender specific and need not be legally specified as such; it may play off a host of vulnerabilities, including those associated with race, sexual orientation, sexual identity, age or immigration status that has been socially marginalised.

Exacting statutory language is not a sufficient condition for enacting an effective coercive control law. Nor may it even be necessary if other elements of the coercive control framework are prominent. Despite the absence of favourable statutory language, activist pressure in the Irish Republic matching activism in Scotland could elicit a comparably robust response from the justice system in that country, including the judiciary, regardless of whether the law is narrowly drawn. The recent success of the referendum in Ireland to remove the Constitutional ban on abortion appears to have reawakened consciousness there of the global woman's agenda, on which a comprehensive condemnation of 'violence against women' is a part. By contrast, despite a high level of activist pressure for reform in Belfast, problems in governance there may force a response directly from courts and police without the benefit of new law or coordinated leadership from government.

Even if the Scottish Act was copied verbatim elsewhere, it is unlikely that the quality of community life for women would appreciably improve without a similarly resourced and popularly supported national crime fighting strategy that makes a priority of combatting coercive control. Although the larger role of law enforcement is much debated in Scotland, the view of coercive control as a bespoke offence against women's rights is shared across a broad spectrum of actors. This view is not universally shared in England, Australia or America, however, not even among feminists (for example, see Walklate et al. 2017; Tolmie 2018).

2.4 'More Law' Versus Reframing How Law Works for Women

Some of our critics reject attempts to enhance the state police response to male tyranny in personal life as naïve or ill-conceived because 'more law' (sic!) simply adds weight to the already top-heavy patriarchal Golgotha (Walklate et al. 2017). A Marxist variant on this theme in the US highlights the extent to which, by highlighting individual 'causes,' the 'criminalisation' of social issues (like domestic violence) complements 'neo-liberal' (i.e. market-based) solutions to these problems (like the delivery of services) (Mehrotra, Kimball, Wahab 2016). The criminalisation of domestic violence in the United States occurred during a time of massive policy shifts towards criminalisation as a means of dealing with social problems in general. For instance, we were pressured by then-Senator Joe Biden and other allies in the U.S Congress to accept the *Violence against Woman Act*, the largest single source of federal funding for our shelter programmes, as shared funding with prosecutors and police and as part of a larger *Violent Crime Control and Law Enforcement Act of 1994* that is often cited as heralding the pro-incarceral policies of subsequent years. Some US feminists have argued against the criminalisation of social problems altogether (Bumiller 1987; Maguigan 2003; Rivera 1994; Coker 2001). But others make a credible case that framing domestic violence as a criminal issue rather than a human rights, civil rights or public health issue limits the frameworks for understanding its depth, breadth, causes and consequences (Coker and Macquaid 2015; Das Gupta 2003). Others have argued that criminalisation has not benefited all women (Mills 2003; Presser and Gaarder 2000). Still more have noted that increased criminalisation of domestic violence has had a range of unintended consequences for a number of marginalised populations, including women of colour, undocumented immigrants, poor, transgender people, lesbians, women with disabilities, older women and sex workers (Chesney-Lind 2006; Kohn 2012; Danis 2003; Richie 2015). Because of its alleged effects on the incarceration of men of colour, New York City and other areas with nonwhite majorities have given serious consideration to 'decriminalising' domestic violence (i.e. treating it as a violation akin to overtime parking rather than as an offence, except in the most serious cases).

How are we to negotiate between these two seemingly contradictory forces, one pushing to decriminalise domestic violence, the other to upgrade it to coercive control? Elements in both camps appear to be beyond reach of the other. Self-proclaimed 'conservative feminists' like Linda Mills (1999, 2003) or Christina Hoff Somers (1994) argue that women and men are equally responsible for violent dynamics; that criminal sanctions are inappropriate for intimate abuse; and that mainstream feminists are responsible for exploiting women and punishing men. Along with some more mainstream proponents of 'restorative justice' approaches, they would triage all but the worst cases into varied therapeutic modalities designed to win 'reconciliation' as 'all parties' 'come to terms' with their violence. I find the level of harm to women and children which these critics minimise, ignore or tolerate morally and politically unacceptable. At the other end of the spectrum are those who oppose reform because the little progress made in policing the most common partner assaults will be lost if the emphasis shifts from incidents to patterns, or from physical injury to such intangibles as control and subordination (Walby and Towers 2017; Walklate et al. 2017). Here the liberal state is seen as fixed in its capacity to respond to women at the status quo. Reform is only possible within existing terms of discourse. For me, s 76 and particularly the adaptation of the 'coercive control framework' in conjunction with Scotland's *Domestic Abuse (Scotland) Act 2018* (Scot) represent 'real reform'. This train has left the station.

Setting these extremes aside, it is indisputable that, since its inception, the opposition to woman abuse (represented most publicly by *Women's Aid* in the United Kingdom and the battered women's movement in the United States) has struggled with how to reconcile the state's indispensable role in securing safety, support and liberty for victims with its equally undeniable role in perpetuating the patterns of discrimination and privilege from which it continues to derive legitimacy. This dilemma is most vivid in low-income and minority communities where pre-existing vulnerabilities magnify the effects on personal, family and community life of woman battering and of government support for services and equal protection. Since the introduction of shelters/refuges and mandatory arrest policies in the US, severe and fatal violence has dropped far more sharply among black couples than any other group (Rennison and Welchans 2000), in large part because ready utilisation of shelters by women of colour in emergency confrontations with abusive men has provided a 'safety valve' for black women, which in turn led to a sharp drop in Black female-to-male homicide. At the same time, *all* state intervention in these communities is infused with a bias that disadvantages men as well as women and raises the spectre that in any particular instance, 'protection' can be more harmful than abuse (Stark 1993). Similar questions have arisen in Britain about the effects of more aggressive policing on immigrants, as well as racial and sexual minorities.

I have chosen to lean the weight of whatever expertise I have on the side of more criminal law with respect to abuse, not less. For me, the present response of the criminal justice system, by limiting itself to physical violence, serves to legitimate the exercise of male hegemony in personal life by whatever other means are available to men and thought necessary. By embodying the male definition of abuse as discrete incidents of criminal assault, current policies obscure the basic condition of relationships that enhances women's vulnerability in personal life, that afford males privileged access to means of ongoing intimidation and control and that makes the 'stranger assault' or 'mugging' a last resort rather than pre-emptive strike of choice. To this extent, the current response is not merely 'liberal' or even 'neo-liberal;' it is patriarchal. Just as 'waiting for 'real' violence distracts attention from the operative source of power in these relationships, it also masks the nature of the violence already occurring. Most of the frequent assaults typical of these cases are individually trivial, but the cumulative effect of 'a thousand cuts' can be devastating. Nevertheless, I count among the harshest critics of my position many whom I hold in the highest standing and who embody what Elizabeth Schneider (2000) calls 'feminist law making.' Needless to say, their arguments deserve far more weighty reply than I intend here.

2.5 The Rationale for Coercive Control

Having acknowledged that engaging the justice system is fraught, it would be as irresponsible to deny abuse victims the scarce justice resources without which they can merely endure coercive control as it would be to entrust a law to its makers to be delivered as writ. Making new law is never an end in itself. To belabour my point about Scotland: central to adapting the 'coercive control framework' is law with the wind of the women's movement at its back. When the wind breaks, so then does the cradle fall. No sooner does 'new law' cease to be a conveyance for new lawmakers, new levels of accountability and a new understanding of who is being held to account for what types of harm to whom, then it ceases to balance the scales of justice; it degrades into the burden of just 'more law' that critics warn us to avoid.

In my original formulation, I used 'coercive control' to describe the social phenomenon of male partner abuse. Coercive control answered key questions in my work with abused women, offenders and their children. When we asked a woman we hid in our Connecticut home almost 50 years ago to talk about the violence, she memorably replied 'violence wasn't the worst part'. She and her 9-year-old daughter had been hiding in their car for almost a week from a man stalking them with a gun. Years later, her story unfolded in response to questions about coercive control.

Much of my forensic practice is with women who have killed partners, often proactively, almost always after years of abuse; much of it physical, but not usually in response to an impending attack. Several of my clients never suffered severe physical abuse. As I shifted my focus to elements of their oppression other than violence, so too did their narrative make a corresponding turn towards liberties that had been affirmed and denied. As important as the shift in discourse was a shift in mood from the *pathos* that often accompanied accounts of victimisation to a sense of righteous indignation that often drove the fatal blow. Ironically, this sense of freedom defended against 'the liberty crime of coercive control' resonated more clearly with the predominantly male, non-abused court personnel and lay jurors who heard our cases.

Another question which coercive control answers concerns the durability of abusive relationships: *how* these relationships are held together is as important as *why*. A working assumption in assessments of coercive control is that the choice to end the abuse is not the victim's to make and that any ambivalence about leaving the relationship is subject to the abuser's global dictum 'It's over when I say its over'. The ostensible paradox, that relationships in constant turmoil appear 'unbreakable,' is explained by identifiable structural constraints (on resources, time, movement, etc.) that are 'rule' based and grounded in fear (the 'or else' proviso). In the past, even when an offender's controlling behaviour was correctly seen as a priority target, there was a common tendency for law enforcement to confound the objective fact of the relationship 'lasting' (due to the coercive control) with the survivor's subjective 'decision' to 'stay' and to then point to deficits in her personality or character to explain why she was unwilling to act in her best interest (for instance, because of misplaced affection for the offender) or was unable to do so. As a practical matter, so long as there was no means available to end the coercive control, case management via 'advocates,' support workers, Multi-Agency Risk Assessment Committees, Independent Domestic Violence Advisors and the like focused on 'hardening the 'targeted' victim so she would not return (Stark 2016).

Coercive control reframes the dimensions of abusive relationships, their scope and intensity as well as their durability, as the by-product of the offending partner's strategy. The *entrapment* that results from the imposition of this strategy has a prominent *structural* dimension comprised of the physical, material and spatial constraints on a woman's options. It also has a subjective/psychological dimension which can be experienced as a constant interior struggle between memories, thoughts, feelings and language of a 'true' self and the 'false' self superimposed by the malevolent other. In extreme cases of constraint, the true self is eviscerated and targeted women lose the ability to bring basic facets of their predicament to cognition, to 'know what they know,' (a condition termed 'perspecticide': Schneider 2018). In the rest, women's decision-making continues to be influenced by the same confluence of personality, gender ideology and culture as when individuation is not directly constrained. The critical point is that the space through which individuation operates is constantly changing shape, expanding or contracting, drawing on pride here or self-loathing there, according to how the offender is exercising his power over the ground of inequality. The psychological does not disappear, the bipolar or the dependent personality disorder, for instance, but goes underground and takes expression only as it can do so in the space afforded by the *political*.

In short, coercive control is the result of the gradual superimposition, over time, of a structure of domination/subordination over the processes of individuation. Self appears as the ghostly projection of 'the other.' The elements of this structure can be documented, photographed, recorded and observed directly or in their effects or otherwise evidenced and reoccur with reasonable frequency in close proximity to other, similar elements or other elements of the structure, so as to be attributable to a single, malevolent intent. It is this fungibility of coercive control that makes it possible to package it as a criminal offence. The diminished self that results is also demonstrable historically, both in relation to its prior achievements and potentialities and existentially, in its current endurance of adversity and prospectively, as it emerges from hiding onto centre stage.

Paralleling and complementing the paradoxical durability of abusive relationships is their seeming capacity to 'cross social space'; these relationships endure and abuse seemingly continues unchecked during numerous periods when couples are physically separated, living apart or even when they have never lived together. Again, accounts abound that fix blame on victim 'ambivalence' for this behaviour or, alternately, view 'staying and leaving' as a 'process' of gradual extrication rather than the single decision-point many civil protection orders suggest it is. Coercive control offers an account in which *men stay* by using stalking, surveillance, 'harassment through the network' and other convert means to continue to constrain their partners. This process is reflected in research which demonstrated that women's 'space for action' expanded post-separation when they entered *Refuge* but contracted when they left Refuge with the offending partners still at large. As Sharp-Jeffs, Kelly and Klein (2017, p. 182) noted, removing themselves from the immediate control of an abusive man was only the first step; over 90 per cent of the women in their study experienced post-separation abuse, which interfered with both being and feeling safe. The limited effectiveness of criminal and civil law enforcement requires women to undertake a huge amount of 'safety work'.

The 'privileges' derived from dominating women provide the material rationale for the behavioural strategy of coercive control. But its subjective underpinning is the psychological investment in staying. Unless the ultimate capacity to constrain a victim's access to time, space and other resources is challenged, whatever she does or decides, it is *he* who 'says its over'.

2.6 Ultimate Values

I am flattered to have my name associated with a class of 'law' so well intended as the offence of coercive control. My concern is to advance an approach that defines the wrong of partner abuse as the systemic, historical abrogation of individual (i.e. civil) rights and liberties in personal life, whatever the means deployed. Since these rights include dignity and autonomy, accountability for the sort of 'gas-light' games that were popularised on the British soap radio programme *The Archers* is obviously important. But so too is accountability for violating the rights to sexual choice, physical security and economic self-determination.

I take two facts as now incontrovertible. The first is that the vast majority of women everywhere who reach out for help for 'abuse' recognise that their rights have been abrogated in one or more of these ways, usually by males with whom they have had a relationship. The second is that none (very few, even now) of the systems we have put in place to stem abuse adequately protect these rights in personal life or fix accountability for their abrogation.

As our critics rightly suspect (Walby and Towers 2017; Walklate et al. 2017; Tolmie 2018), expanding the definition from domestic violence to coercive control shifts the level of behaviour on which the law focuses, not merely its empirical content. From the incident to historical abuse or the pattern or course of conduct; from violence to other 'bad' acts, some of which are already criminal, some of which are only crimes now when committed by strangers and some of which become elements of a criminal pattern only in combination with other 'bad' acts; from injury and the intent to harm to a range of less tangible outcomes, including a 'reasonable probability' of causing fear.

Illustrative is the case of Nigel Wolitter, a 30-year-old Nottinghamshire man sentenced in October 2015 to four-and-a-half years' imprisonment for his coercive and controlling behaviour, as well as for two acts of common assault and property damage. Wolitter was arrested after he poured paint on machinery belonging to his partner's family to punish her for refusing to give him money for marijuana (Henderson 2016). In the past, there would have been no case of partner abuse or harassment and Wolitter would probably have been fined for the damage and given a low-level community order. Instead, following statutory and police guidance for controlling or coercive behaviour, the Nottingham Police Domestic Abuse and Investigation Team used the episode as a window to investigate the possibility that his revenge vandalism was part of a much more serious pattern of dominance. Trawling through the couples' 13-year relationship, they collected information on Wolitter's past offences that would not previously have been admissible as evidence in court in relation to the current offence, including photos on his partner's cell phone of injuries he had inflicted during the last 2 years. Two of these assaults were charged separately. But the team also linked Wolitter's *ongoing* violence to the larger course of his oppressive conduct and highlighted his partner's assertion that he had 'controlled every aspect of my life from where I went to what I wore, to what possessions he allowed me to own. I wasn't a person, but an object to him' (Henderson 2016). It is the status of claims such as this—that I am not 'a person' unless I am free to go and come as I please, wear what I wish and own my possessions—that calls our attention to the value commitments embedded in coercive control. As a form of oppression/domination, coercive control is never reducible to physical violence or violations of security. It is by now well known that the most common coercive control tactics also constrain autonomy, offend dignity, abrogate rights to sociability, free speech and movement, and quash self-determination, including economic and sexual self-determination. It is to the defence of these rights that we spring into the fray.

But even where only physical violence is involved, attacks on women are considered 'violence against the State' only where women are considered full persons and free-state actors like other full persons. This does not appear to be the case before the law when their unencumbered status is subsumed as relational (by the term 'intimacy', e.g.) or 'dependent' ('wife') or is naturalised ('victim.'). I worry that 'psychological well-being' of the sort that is encoded in legislation such as the Tasmanian statute may also suggest less than full political standing. We are at the early stages of being able to portray what abuse entails. Only slowly are we learning to voice the capacities lost to coercive control that make it worthy of grieving with the most serious crimes.

References

BBC News. (2013, September 20). Bill Walker jailed for 12 months for domestic abuse. Retrieved from https://www.bbc.com/news/uk-scotland-edinburgh-east-fife-24173669.
BBC News. (2018, January 24). Paul Playle Jailed for Stalking Wife for Two Years. Retrieved from http://www.bbc.co.uk/news/uk-england-sussex-42805203.
Bumiller, K. (1987). Victims in the shadow of the law: A critique of the model of legal protection. *Signs, 12*(3), 421–439.
Burman, M., & Brooks-Hay, O. (2018). Aligning policy and law? The creation of a domestic abuse offence incorporating coercive control. *Criminology and Criminal Justice, 18*(1), 67–84.
Chesney-Lynd, M. (2006). Patriarchy, crime, and justice: Feminist criminology in an era of backlash. *Feminist Criminology, 1*(1), 6–26.
Chilton, J. (2013, September 7). Bill Walker: Law change could make him quit. *Sky News*. Retrieved from https://news.sky.com/story/bill-walker-law-change-could-make-him-quit-10435082.
Coker, D. (2001). Crime control and feminist law reform in domestic violence law: A critical review. *Buffalo Criminal Law Review, 4*(2), 801–860.
Coker, D., & Macquaid, A. (2015). Why opposing hyper-incarceration should be central to the work of the anti-domestic violence movement. *Race and Social Justice Law Review, 5*(2), 585–618.
Crown Prosecution Service. (2018). *Violence Against Women and Girls Report: 2017–18*. Retrieved from https://www.cps.gov.uk/sites/default/files/documents/publications/cps-vawg-report-2018.pdf.
Danis, F. (2003). The criminalization of domestic violence: What social workers need to know. *Social Work, 48*(2), 237–246.
DasGupta, S. (2003). *Safety and Justice for All: Examining the Relationship Between the Women's Anti-Violence Movement and the Criminal Legal System*. Retrieved from http://www.ncdsv.org/images/Ms_SafetyJusticeForAll_2003.pdf.
Douglas, H. (2015). Do we need a specific domestic violence offence? *Melbourne University Law Review, 39*(2), 434–471.
Hamby, S., Finkelhor, D., & Turner, H. (2015). Intervention following family violence: Best practices and helpseeking obstacles in a nationally representative sample of families with children. *Psychology of Violence, 5*(3), 325–336.
Henderson, E. (2016, October 18). Basford man who threatened his partner jailed under new 'controlling behaviour' law. *Notts TV*. Retrieved from https://nottstv.com/basford-man-threatened-partner-jailed-new-controlling-behaviour-law/.
Hester, M. (2006). Making it through the criminal justice system: Attrition and domestic violence. *Social Policy and Society, 5*(1), 1–12.
Hester, M., & Westmarland, N. (2006). Domestic violence perpetrators. *Criminal Justice Matters, 66*(1), 34–35.
Home Office. (2015). *Controlling or Coercive Behaviour in an Intimate or Family Relationship: Statutory Guidance Framework*. Retrieved from https://www.gov.uk/government/publications/statutory-guidance-framework-controlling-or-coercive-behaviour-in-an-intimate-or-family-relationship.
Kerley, P., & Bates, C. (2016, April 5). The Archers: What effect has the Rob and Helen story had? *BBC News Magazine*. Retrieved from https://www.bbc.com/news/magazine-35961057.

Kohn, N. (2012). Elder (in)justice: A critique of the criminalization of elder abuse. *American Criminal Law Review, 49*(1), 1–29.

Maguigan, H. (2003). Wading into professor Schneider's 'murky middle ground' between acceptance and rejection of criminal justice responses to domestic violence. *American University Journal of Gender, Policy and the Law, 11*(2), 427–446.

Mehrotra, G. R., Kimball, E., & Wahab, S. (2016). The braid that binds us: The impact of neoliberalism, criminalization, and professionalization on domestic violence work. *Affilia: Journal of Women and Social Work, 31*(2), 153–163.

Mills, L. G. (1999). Killing her softly: Intimate abuse and the violence of state intervention. *Harvard Law Review, 113*(2), 551–613.

Mills, L. G. (2003). *Insult to injury: Rethinking our responses to intimate abuse*. Princeton, NJ: Princeton University Press.

Padfield, N. (2016). Editorial: Controlling or coercive behaviour in an intimate or family relationship. *Criminal Law Review, 3*, 149–151.

PF v Bill Walker. (2013, August 23). Retrieved from http://www.scotland-judiciary.org.uk/8/1109/PF-v-BILL-WALKER.

PF v Bill Walker. (2013, September 20). Retrieved from http://www.scotland-judiciary.org.uk/8/1131/PF-v-BILL-WALKER.

Police Scotland and Crown Office and Procurator Fiscal Service. (2013). *Joint Protocol between Police Scotland and the Crown Office and Procurator Fiscal Service: In Partnership Challenging Domestic Abuse*. Retrieved from http://www.copfs.gov.uk/images/Documents/Prosecution_Policy_Guidance/Protocols_and_Memorandum_of_Understanding/Joint%20Domestic%20Abuse%20Protocol%20-%20Oct%2013.pdf.

Presser, L., & Gaarder, E. (2000). Can restorative justice reduce battering? Some preliminary considerations. *Social Justice, 27.1*(79), 175–195.

Rennison, C. M., & Welchans S. (2000). *Intimate Partner Violence*, Bureau of Justice Statistics: Special Report NCJ-178247. Retrieved from https://www.bjs.gov/index.cfm?ty=pbdetail&iid=1002.

Richie, B. E. (2015). Reimagining the movement to end gender violence: Anti-racism, prison abolition, women of color feminisms, and other radical visions of justice. *Miami Race and Social Justice Law Review, 5*(2), 257–274.

Rivera, J. (1994). Domestic violence against latinas by latino males: An analysis of race, national origin and gender differentials. *Third World Law Journal, 14*(2), 231–257.

Schneider, E. (2000). *Battered women and feminist law making*. New Haven, CT: Yale University Press.

Schneider, N. (2018). The mask of happiness: Unmasking coercive control in intimate relationships. *Journal of Psychiatric Practice, 24*(1), 48–50.

Scottish Executive. (2003). *Preventing Domestic Abuse—A National Strategy*. Retrieved from https://www2.gov.scot/Publications/2003/09/18185/26437.

Sharp-Jeffs, N., Kelly, L., & Klein, R. (2017). Long journeys toward freedom: The relationship between coercive control and space for action—Measurement and emerging evidence. *Violence Against Women, 24*(2), 163–185.

Somers, C. H. (1994). *Who stole feminism?*. New York, NT: Simon and Schuster.

Stark, E. (2007). *Coercive control: How men entrap women in personal life*. New York, NY: Oxford University Press.

Stark, E. (2018). Coercive control as a framework for responding to male partner abuse in the UK: Opportunities and challenges. In N. Lombard (Ed.), *The Routledge handbook of gender and violence*. London: Taylor and Francis.

Stark, E. (2016). Policing partner abuse and the new crime of coercive control in the United Kingdom. *Family & Intimate Partner Violence Quarterly, 8*(4), 345–353.

Stark, E. (1993). The myth of black violence. *Social Work, 38*(4), 485–491.

The Guardian. (2013, September 20). Former MSP Bill Walker jailed over violent domestic abuse. Retrieved from https://www.theguardian.com/politics/2013/sep/20/msp-bill-walker-jailed-domestic-abuse.

Tolmie, J. (2018). Coercive control: To criminalise or not to criminalise? *Criminology & Criminal Justice, 18*(1), 50–66.

Trueman, P. (2018). *The Helen Titchener (nee Archer) Rescue Fund.* Retrieved from https://www.justgiving.com/fundraising/helentitchener.

Walby, S., Towers, J., & Francis, B. (2014). Mainstreaming domestic and gender-based violence into sociology and the criminology of violence. *Sociological Review, 62*(S2), 187–214.

Walby, S., & Towers, J. (2017). Measuring violence to end violence: Mainstreaming gender. *Journal of Gender-Based Violence, 1*(1), 11–32.

Walklate, S., Fitz-Gibbon, K., & McCulloch, J. (2017). Is more law the answer? Seeking justice for victims of intimate partner violence. *Criminology and Criminal Justice, 18*(1), 1–17.

Chapter 3
Economic Abuse and Family Violence Across Cultures: Gendering Money and Assets Through Coercive Control

Supriya Singh

Abstract Across cultures, men control and use economic and financial resources to instill fear, intimidate and degrade their wives/partners so that women lose their sense of self and human rights. This form of abuse takes different pathways as it strips away the moral norms associated with the gender of money. In middle-income, Anglo-Celtic marriage, the joint banking account symbolises partnership in marriage, but can also become a medium of coercive control. Among recent Indian migrants, the culturally accepted male control of money becomes abusive when money is not used for the wellbeing of all members of the family. Drawing on ongoing qualitative research into cross-cultural experiences of economic abuse in Australia, this chapter argues that economic abuse constitutes a breach of trust which must be investigated within the broad context of the gender and morality of money. It should be criminalised in order to recognise that its impact on women and their safety can in some instances be greater than physical assault.

Keywords Economic abuse · Financial abuse · Coercive control · Joint bank account · Cross-cultural research

3.1 Introduction

This chapter provides an overview of economic abuse as it relates to coercive control. It also places economic abuse within its social and cultural context, for money is a social phenomenon that shapes, and is shaped by, social relationships and cultural norms. A brief review of the literature on economic abuse, coercive control and the gender and morality of money is followed by an outline of findings from a qualitative research project that investigated economic abuse among Anglo-Celtic and Indian women in Australia.

S. Singh (✉)
Graduate School of Business and Law, RMIT University, VIC, Australia
e-mail: Supriya.singh@rmit.edu.au

3.1.1 What Is Economic Abuse?

Economic abuse 'involves behaviours that control a woman's ability to acquire, use, and maintain economic resources, thus threatening her economic security and potential for self-sufficiency' (Adams et al. 2008, p. 564). It is a broader concept than financial abuse, which focuses exclusively on control of money in relationships. Economic abuse also includes control of other economic resources, such as the use of a car, a place to live, communications devices and enabling oneself to engage in paid work through enhancing language and skills and obtaining appropriate registration of qualifications (Sharp-Jeffs and Learmonth 2017).

Economically abusive behaviours in an intimate relationship (both ongoing and after separation) involve economic control, economic exploitation, and employment sabotage. Postmus et al. (2018) have described these behaviours as follows:

> Economic control tactics included: restricting access to finances, refusing to contribute financially for necessities or other items, restricting access to financial information or involvement with financial decision-making, and controlling the household spending. Economic exploitation included tactics such as misusing family finances; damaging property; stealing property, money, or identities; going into debt through coercion or in secret; kicking the victim out of the living situation; using wealth as a weapon or as a threat; selling necessary household or personal items; restricting access to health care or insurance; and denying or restricting access to transportation. Employment sabotage tactics includes anything related to interfering with or preventing a partner from work. (Postmus et al. 2018, p. 5)

3.1.2 Economic Abuse, Family Violence and Coercive Control

The tactics involved in economic abuse, as with other dimensions of family violence, frequently operate through coercive control. Evan Stark (2012, p. 207) argues that coercive control is 'used to hurt and intimidate victims (coercion) and ... designed to isolate and regulate them (control)'. He defines the tactics of coercive control as including:

> ... forms of constraint and the monitoring and/or regulation of commonplace activities of daily living, particularly those associated with women's default roles as mothers, homemakers, and sexual partners, and run the gamut from their access to money, food, and transport to how they dress, clean, cook, or perform sexually. (Stark 2012, p. 201)

Empirical research has confirmed that women who experience economic abuse are likely to suffer other forms of family violence such as physical assault, psychological or emotional abuse, and sexual abuse (Sharp-Jeffs and Learmonth 2017). A study in the United States by Stylianou, Postmus and McMahon (2013) reported that 76% of the women who experienced physical and/or psychological abuse also suffered economic abuse. Similarly, research by Adams et al. (2008) with 103 women who were survivors of family violence found that all had experienced psychological abuse and almost all of them (98%) had experienced physical abuse and economic abuse (99%). More than half (57%) had been sexually assaulted. The authors concluded that 'economic abuse is a significant component of the broad system of tactics used by abusive men to gain power and maintain control over their partners' (Adams et al. 2008, p. 580).

Coercive control underpins these diverse forms of abuse; it is the strategy men use to preserve their entitlements so that while women have achieved formal equality, gender inequalities remain in the home, economy and community. Men coerce through the use of extreme violence, isolation, intimidation, surveillance, micromanaging daily life through 'rules', withholding food, communication and money, degradation, the use of shaming tactics and threats to the safety of children. This control increases with time as the woman learns to fear the consequences of not obeying her husband (Stark 2009, 2012).

Coercive control over money involves men's reinterpretation of the gendered meanings of money to isolate women, instill fear and deny freedom. It violates the human rights of women, depriving them of freedom to shape their lives. When coercive control is the overarching framework, it becomes clear that family violence is articulated through physical assault, emotional and sexual abuse, and economic abuse. All these aspects of family violence, alone and together, are demeaning and disempowering.

There are certain cultural differences in how economic abuse is perpetrated, particularly in situations where joint family living is the norm. Moreover, the framework of migration law shapes a woman's options in the face of abuse. There are also, however, continuities of economic abuse across all cultures. For example, women across cultures who become dependent on their partner are less likely to leave abusive relationships for fear of not being able to provide for themselves and their children (Adams et al. 2008; Postmus et al. 2016; Sharp-Jeffs and Learmonth 2017). In addition, coerced debt, that is, 'all nonconsensual, credit-related transactions that occur in a violent relationship' (Littwin 2012, p. 954) is a further obstacle to leaving an abusive relationship and establishing financial sustainability.

Preparing to leave often involves trying to gain more education—sometimes covertly—and women may seek to do this by setting limits to their husband's use of their assets, hiding money (at times, through the help of trusted family or employers), family support, and ensuring access to relevant financial documents (Sanders 2015; Llyod 1997). Nevertheless, when women do leave, they are often encumbered with debt and have few resources because of economic abuse. Studies have shown that poverty, belonging to a cultural minority, having a background of gendered violence, low socioeconomic status and belonging to a racial or ethnic minority are all factors that increase the difficulties experienced by survivors of domestic abuse who are trying to achieve economic independence (Peled and Krigel 2016). And of course economic abuse can also continue after separation with perpetrators using fragmented legal and child support systems to keep their ex-partners and children in poverty (Douglas 2018; Camilleri et al. 2015; Fehlberg and Millward 2014; Macdonald 2012; Smallwood 2015; State of Victoria 2016).

The health impact of distinct forms of family violence across cultures has not been adequately investigated. Poverty associated with economic abuse is a significant predictor of adverse health impacts. On this issue, a US study of mothers is noteworthy because it found that economic abuse is more predictive of depression than psychological or physical abuse (Postmus et al. 2012a). More generally, intimate partner violence is the single most important factor leading to women's physical and mental health problems in Australia. According to research published by Australia's National Research Organisation for Women's Safety (ANROWS), intimate partner violence contributed more to the disease burden than any other risk factor among women aged 18-44 years with the range of health problems including 'poor mental health, problems during pregnancy and birth, alcohol and illicit drug use, suicide, injuries and homicide' (Webster 2016, p. 7). The grievous impacts of family violence are clear in the decimation of self-confidence, mental and physical health problems and continued financial insecurity for women and their children (Alhabib et al. 2010; Australian Law Reform Commission 2010; Bevin 2016; Cameron 2014; McMahon and McGorrery 2016; Pollett 2011; Postmus et al. 2012b; Sharp-Jeffs 2015; Sharp 2008; Smallwood 2015; State of Victoria 2016; Vaughan et al. 2016; VicHealth 2014).

3.1.3 *The Prevalence of Economic Abuse*

While it is clear that economic abuse is linked to other forms of domestic abuse, it is difficult to authoritatively identify the prevalence of economic abuse. Instruments that purport to measure it may be limited. For instance, Adams et al. (2008) created a 28-item Scale of Economic Abuse (SEA) with two subscales for economic control and economic exploitation. This was later modified to a 12-item SEA with three subscales that also included employment sabotage by Postmus et al. (2016). These constructs were developed in the United States and primarily based on low-income, heterosexual, African-American and Caucasian women who were receiving services from family violence organisations. Whether they accurately identify economic abuse in different cultural contexts for women who are ethnically diverse, middle or high income, in same sex relationships, disabled or have not engaged with family violence services is not known (Adams et al. 2008; Postmus et al. 2016).

Data from Australia suggests that 16% of women have experienced economic abuse (compared to 7% for men), though these figures must be treated with caution as the results depend on the number of relevant questions asked, sampling techniques and re-analysis of data (Kutin et al. 2017). In that research, five questions relating to economic abuse were extracted from 15 questions relating to emotional abuse in the Australian Bureau of Statistics' *Personal Safety Survey* and were re-analysed. Significantly, we still do not know whether women in culturally and linguistically diverse (CALD) communities experience more family violence than women in English speaking communities in Australia. CALD women are not adequately represented in surveys because of difficulties of language, at times a cultural acceptance of family violence, and difficulties of sharing the experience with outsiders (Vaughan et al. 2015). Women's unequal rights of inheritance and control of money and resources in the household also make them vulnerable to economic abuse (Singh 2013). In migrant communities, women are subject to additional coercive control because of greater isolation, unfamiliarity with their options in a new country, and migration regimes that permit greater control by the husband (Abraham 2000; Ghafournia 2011; Raj and Silverman 2002; Segrave 2017; Vaughan et al. 2016). However, education, employment and employability shape the options for migrant women in similar ways as other women.

3.1.4 Economic Abuse, Family Violence and the Law

Economic abuse is identified as a form of family violence in many legislative jurisdictions on domestic abuse, either expressly or implicitly. In Tasmania (Australia), it has been a criminal offence since 2005 to economically abuse a spouse or partner. Section 8 of the *Family Violence Act 2004* (Tas) criminalises the economic abuse of a spouse or partner. Economic abuse of an intimate partner can also fall within the scope of the criminal offence of controlling or coercive behaviour in England and Wales (*Serious Crime Act 2015* (E&W) s 76) a similar offence in Ireland (*Domestic Violence Act 2018* (IR) s 39); and the offence of domestic abuse in Scotland (*Domestic Abuse (Scotland) Act 2018* (Scot) s 1). Yet even when economic abuse is expressly criminalised, it may remain largely invisible. In Tasmania, since the enactment of the offence until November 2017 there had been only one prosecution for economic abuse and that charge was ultimately dropped by the prosecution (Barwick et al. Chap. 7). Similarly, an analysis of 35 successful prosecutions for the offence of controlling or coercive behaviour in England reported that two-thirds of these cases involved economic abuse—yet in none of these cases was the abuse named (Sharp-Jeffs and Learmonth 2017).

There are multiple consequences of this failure to criminally prosecute (in addition to the obvious failure to punish the perpetrator). In some jurisdictions, women who have experienced economic abuse are not seen to have experienced an 'act of violence' and so are not eligible for compensation as a victim of crime (*Attorney-General (Tas) v CL* [2018] TASFC 6). Another consequence is that this contributes to the physical assault being the dominant image of family violence for those who suffer it, the community, police and service providers. Safety is seen mainly in terms of keeping women and children *physically* safe.

As an alternative to direct criminal prosecution, in many jurisdictions, economic abuse is included in legislative definitions of family violence in civil matters. For instance, in Victoria (another Australian State) the *Family Violence Protection Act 2008* (Vic) s 6 recognises economically abusive behaviour and defines it as:

behaviour by a person...that is coercive, deceptive or unreasonably controls another person...without the second person's consent—

(a) in a way that denies the second person the economic or financial autonomy
(b) the second person would have had but for that behaviour; or
(c) by withholding or threatening to withhold the financial support necessary for meeting the reasonable living expenses of the second person or the second person's child, if the second person is entirely or predominantly dependent on the first person for financial support to meet those living expenses.

Under this law and similar laws relating to intervention orders, a person can obtain a civil order to gain protection from family violence. Once such an order is obtained, a respondent who breaches it—and in several jurisdictions this may include breaching the order by being economically abusive—commits a criminal offence. However, while economic abuse is a distinct form of domestic abuse, it is 'rarely identified as a form of family violence' by the community, the police, the judiciary, regulatory bodies and service providers (State of Victoria 2016, p. 118; see also Sharp-Jeffs and Learmonth 2017).

In summary, economic abuse works through the gendered rails of coercive control. Gender inequality is the broad context of family violence and coercive control. Traditional gendered roles mean it is men who 'almost exclusively' abuse women economically (Sharp-Jeffs and Learmonth 2017) and are rarely prosecuted. In addition, as Postmus et al. (2018) have noted, it is important to study the cultural context of economic abuse. We do not know whether culturally mandated control translates to abuse. In cultures like India and China, men traditionally control the family and household finances. Does this necessarily translate into coercive and controlling behaviour? This is an important question for the study of economic abuse in cultures of the Global South (Asia, the Pacific, Africa, Latin America, the Caribbean and the Middle East).

3.2 The Gender and Morality of Money

Economic abuse has to be addressed in its social and cultural context because money is a social phenomenon. It shapes, and is shaped by, social relationships and cultural norms (Zelizer 1994). Money has gender. Men and women use, inherit, manage and control money in different ways. The 'gender of money' varies across cultures. It reflects the ideology of marriage and cohabitation, kinship norms, household and family formation, socioeconomic differences and the legal and religious status of women. The gender of money also changes within a culture over time, life stage and migration. Because the gender of money is accompanied by moral norms, it is important to focus on the gender and morality of money, as coercive control in family violence operates by targeting a re-invented version of 'gender identity' (Stark 2009, p. 1509), abusing the woman for not being a good housekeeper and homemaker, as well as a poor mother, wife and lover.

In the cases of economic abuse that are subsequently described, it is relevant to bear in mind the reference points for coercive control identified by Wiener:

'grooming', 'coercive behaviour' and the 'victim's response' (Wiener 2017, p. 6). Grooming results in the woman becoming vulnerable as the 'initial courtship' gives way to behaviour that terrifies, emotionally abuses, and isolates' her (Wiener 2017, p. 9). The fear, self-blame, personality change, vulnerability and constant surveillance results in coerced behaviour. The victim's response is one of fear, instability and diminished personal control. She begins to blame herself, seeing the world through her abusive partner's eyes (Wiener 2017).

Comparing the gender of money among middle-income Anglo-Celtic couples in Australia and patrilineal joint families in urban India reveals how the gender of money can differ across and within cultures. This is due to differences in the position of women in society, the ideology of marriage, household and family formation, kinship systems, and migration.

3.2.1 Money in Middle-Income Anglo-Celtic Marriage in Australia

The ancestry of the Anglo-Celtic group in Australia is predominantly English, Irish and Scottish (Australian Bureau of Statistics 1995).This group is the dominant community in Australia, accounting for at least 39 per cent of the population in 2016 (Australian Bureau of Statistics 2018). As they are the largest ethnic group, their cultural money practices are seen as 'mainstream' and desirable.

It was only in the late 19th century that married women in Australia were able to own property (Singh 1997). In the 1930s and 1940s, it was more usual for the husband to hold the cheque book with the wife having a savings book account or an account with the corner store. The joint bank account among middle-income Anglo-Celtic married couples is relatively recent and in the 1990s was spoken of as a major generational change. Nevertheless, jointness is now the central norm in their gender of money, with joint bank accounts a ritual symbol of the ideology of marriage as a joint partnership. Though not all joint accounts are jointly managed and controlled, having a joint account emphasises the moral importance of 'togetherness' in marriage, blocking questions about equality and power. This ideology of marriage as a partnership coexists with the role of the husband as provider, particularly when the children are young (Singh 1997). Another important characteristic of the gender of money in Anglo-Celtic marriage in Australia is that the couple is the domestic financial unit. Money, and information about money is private to the married couple. Money is not usually transferred from parents to adult children. When money does flow across generations, it goes one way—from parents to children or from grandparents to grandchildren. This is partly because money is not the preferred gift among Anglo-Celtics as it is with many of the cultures of the global South. It is also because parents and grandparents are proud and revel in their ability to 'manage' (Singh 1997). In recent years, the flow of money across generations has increased to facilitate adult children to enter the increasingly expensive housing market. It is estimated that one-third to just over one-half (55 percent) of middle-income parents have helped children with housing deposits and/or guarantees (Olsberg and Winters 2005; Price 2018). However, this intergenerational money, for the most part, continues to flow in one direction.

3.2.2 Money in the Urban Patrilineal Joint Family in India

The gender of money in the urban, patrilineal, middle-income, joint family in India differs from the Anglo-Celtic in that it is male, rather than joint. Men across generations control and often manage the money. The patrilineal joint family is commonly a three-generational unit marked by male descent, comprising parents, married sons and grandchildren. Though there is a diversity of family forms in India, the patrilineal Hindu joint family in India is *the* Indian family celebrated in popular culture (Uberoi 2004). Another major difference in the gender of money is that money belongs to the family rather than the couple. So, information about money is not private to the couple but is shared across generations, including a two-way exchange of information between parents and children (Singh and Bhandari 2012).

Male control of money is supported by an ideology of male dominance. But the morality of money is that the man who controls the money is also charged with responsibility for the welfare of the whole family. Parents prioritise giving to their children in a timely manner to increase the children's wellbeing. Children, particularly sons, have a filial duty to look after the parents (Singh 2017). This duty is confirmed in court judgments (Tripathi 2016) and lies behind India receiving the highest level of international remittances (money transferred through formal financial channels such as banks, money transfer organisations and via mobile money); in 2016, the value of these remittances was estimated at US$65.5 billion (Ratha et al. 2016a). Issues that arise when discussing the gender and morality of money in India have wider implications. The gender and morality of money in the Indian patrilineal joint family has many shared characteristics with many of the countries in the global South. The family is the unit of domestic money. There is sharing of money across generations. This has led to formal international remittances constituting one of the largest international flows of funds estimated at US $441 billion in 2015 to developing countries, nearly three times the amount of international foreign aid (Ratha et al. 2016b). The gender of money is changing in India, particularly in the metropolitan cities and as women become more educated and are earning higher salaries. Money management and control can change with migration, particularly if women become the major earners (George 2005; Singh 2016).Despite the fact that 'coercive control', which is at the centre of family violence, has much to do with gender identity and continuing inequality, there has been little in the sociology of money and the discussion of gender and morality that has intersected with the literature on family violence. Results from a project in Australia will now be outlined to try to remedy some of the gaps in this area.

3.3 Studying Economic Abuse Across Cultures: The Empirical Investigation

The qualitative study focused on the experience of female survivors of family violence among the Anglo-Celtic and Indian communities in Australia, through interviews with 30 women who had a history of family violence. A particular focus was on the management and control of money in the household and economic abuse.

3.3.1 The Participants

The participants in this study were accessed through the professional, community and personal networks of the researchers (myself, Dr Marg Liddell and Dr Jasvinder Sidhu). Unlike many studies of family violence, this study included women who had sought professional help *and* those who did not. Snowballing also occurred in recruitment: two of the Anglo-Celtic women referred a woman who they knew experienced abuse, and one of the Indian participants also referred another two women. Indian and Anglo-Celtic communities were selected because of my previous research and knowledge of some of the languages and networks in these two groups. It was particularly important to study money, gender and family violence in the Anglo-Celtic community, for that is the norm against which the gender of money and economic abuse is assessed in Australia.

The study is based on 47 interviews conducted between 2016 and 2017. Of these, 30 interviews were with women in Australia who had previously experienced family violence: 17 were from the Indian community, and 13 were from the Anglo-Celtic community. The information obtained from these women was supplemented by interviews with 17 community leaders, service providers and leaders of faith communities.

All the women in the Anglo-Celtic group were born in Australia or came with their families before they were 12 years old; three of these women were married or partnered with men from South Asia and the Middle East and another three were of European background but were married to Anglo-Celtic men. Unlike the Anglo-Celtic women, all but one of the Indians were migrants with a varied migration history: three were multiple migrants, having migrated from India to Europe, the United States or Africa before migrating to Australia. All the Indian women had a graduate or postgraduate education. All were fluent in English; none had to contend with language barriers. They represented different phases of Indian migration to Australia (see Table 3.1) Of the recent migrants : one came as a spouse on a tourist visa; two came on skilled visas; and the initial visa status of 9 of the 12 remaining recent migrants was as a spouse or student.

It is noteworthy that the participants in the Anglo-Celtic and Indian communities varied in terms of age, education and income (Table 3.1). The Anglo-Celtic women

Table 3.1 Characteristics of Anglo-Celtic and Indian participants, n = 30

Characteristics	Anglo-Celtic (n = 13)	Indian (n = 17)
Age		
25–34	0	8
35–44	2	2
45–54	3	4
55–64	4	2
65 and above	4	1
Period of migration		
Born in Australia or arrived before age 12	13	1
Early migrant 1970–1995	0	4
Recent migrant 1996—present	0	12
Children		
Yes	13	11
No	0	6
Education		
School/Diploma	3	0
Undergraduate degree	8	5
Postgraduate/professional	2	12
Current Occupation		
Professional (Health, Education and Law)	7	11
Community/Customer services	1	2
Housewife/retired/unemployed	3	3
Creative Arts	1	0
Business	1	0
Volunteer	0	1

were older and less educated than the Indians; fewer had a postgraduate education. They were also less likely to be employed as professionals. Migration was a major factor only for the Indian community. The names of the participants in this chapter are pseudonyms to preserve the participants' privacy. To comply with ethics requirements, some identifying details have been changed.

3.3.2 The Interviews

All interviews were open-ended. Twenty-eight interviews with victims were conducted face-to-face, audio-recorded with permission and were at a location chosen by the interviewee; two further interviews were conducted with Indian participants, one by email (with responses to the interview questions) and another by telephone (recorded with the permission of the interviewee). The face-to-face interviews were conducted wholly in English or in a mixture of English, Hindi and Punjabi.

Each interview lasted for about two hours with the associated visit component going further. The interview began with the woman telling the story of her family and marriage; her access to money, resources and paid work; patterns of decision-making; the role of the husband and his family; remittances if any; dimensions of family violence; the effect of visa conditions; support from family, friends, community and service providers; and how she survived economic abuse. For some, aspects of family violence continued after separation and divorce. Moreover, in the telling of their stories, the experience of family violence seemed very present.

The interviews were transcribed and coded using *NVivo*, a computer programme for the analysis of qualitative data. This involved sorting and broadly coding the data according to the themes mentioned above. The codes were descriptive. The fit between data and theory progressed with memoing and writing as analysis, building matrices to uncover patterns in the data, and checking for negative cases. This later stage of analysis revealed that the women had suffered coercive control as morality was stripped from the gender of money in their culture.

3.4 Narratives of Economic Abuse

There are continuities and differences in the narratives of economic abuse across cultures. They show that economic abuse in all cultures focuses on economic control, economic exploitation and employee sabotage. In all cultures, coercive control of economic sources focuses on gendered cultural practices of money but strips them of morality. Economic abuse leads to isolation, the denial of a woman's human rights and denial of self. The differences lie in the way economic abuse is shaped by the gender and morality of money.

3.4.1 No Money of Her Own

The qualitative research shows coercive control of money is at its most extreme when the woman is denied money, has none of her own, and must ask or beg her husband/partner for money. In this section, I outline the story of two women—one Indian and one of European background with an Anglo-Celtic husband. Both had young children, were not earning when the children were young and were financially dependent on their husbands. They had no bank accounts they could use.

In these stories, economic abuse is accompanied by emotional and physical abuse. The husband exercised coercive control by denying the woman money, isolating her, making her afraid, and causing her to doubt her own capacities. Instead of providing, the husband caused his wife to experience trauma and degradation. The women did not identify their treatment as abuse, and in some cases continued to think that they were the ones at fault.

1. 'I was terrified of the world'

Helen, 51, was of European ancestry but born in Australia. She left home at the age of 16, and was in paid work before she had a child with her first partner. She met her second partner, an Anglo-Celtic man, soon after the end of the first relationship. She left this second relationship after five and a half years. Talking about this relationship 23 years later, Helen said 'he controlled everything, absolutely everything.' He was developing a business so she was not eligible for Centrelink (welfare) payments. She had young children at home and so could not earn. She had no money of her own and no access to his. 'So I would ask him for money, for food, for clothes.' Her total economic dependence, combined with his physical violence to her and her children, led to her living in fear. She said:

> I was terrified of the world. And for me, there was an unspoken agreement that he will protect me from the world and for that I gave over total control.... He changed my name, the way I dressed, my makeup, my hair, who I could see.

Helen described her partner as a violent and vengeful man. He kept guns and bullets in the closet. She said 'he used to handcuff the children,' referring to her two children (including one from her first partner and one that he had fathered). He would punch Helen, drag or pull her against the wall so that there were only a few bruises or a bit of blood, nothing serious enough to go to the doctor. She felt that she couldn't call the police because some of his friends were policemen. She added, 'The physical violence was not the biggest thing. It was more everything else.' She lived in fear:

> I was safe in some ways and not in all. I remember I would sleep hours after he would go to sleep just to make sure that he was fast asleep. I would sleep in my clothes. And I would sleep at the very, very, very edge of the bed as far as possible. Then I used to wake up early in the morning before him.

She was wholly isolated. Her relationship with her family was fractured, increasing her isolation because of his coercive control. She had no friends. His friends would come to the house and would know what was happening but not say anything. She said:

> I was just in survival mode trying to take care of the children... I was never happy in the relationship but I had no money, I had no friends and I had no alternative as to what to do. So I kept staying. I didn't realise it was abusive. I knew it wasn't good but I didn't know it was abusive.

Around 1991 Helen saw something about domestic violence on a notice board at a doctor's clinic and recognised that she experienced similar abuse. She finally left because her partner was hospitalised, and she felt freer of him. When she brought him home from the hospital, she told him, 'I am taking my life back.' He stalled and suggested counselling but the counsellor told her to leave. She was terrified to leave because she thought her husband would kill her. But she contacted Centrelink—which she was only emboldened to do because her husband was ill at the time—and got help with money and accommodation and her father helped her move. After separation, the abuse continued with the children as the court granted her ex-partner access to his child and step-child, believing his word over hers. She and the children were in trauma therapy for years. Now she counsels others who experience domestic abuse.

3.5 He Gave Her Coins, not Notes

Geeta, in her late 30 s, with two children, was married for ten years. She was born in India, has an MBA and had worked in Human Resources in South India before marrying against her family's wishes. When Geeta moved with her husband to Australia, he did not want her to earn. She was pregnant within six months. She had to ask him for money. She did not have a debit card. She had a bank account but he had the ATM card and knew the password. He gave her coins, not notes. She knew he was stingy but said 'It was his wish whatever he wants to buy, he'll buy for us. It's like that. And whatever he likes me to wear, I have to wear.' But she said, 'I trusted him … I was held up with household duties. He got the groceries and paid the bills.' She had never travelled alone by train because she didn't have the money to pay the fare. She tried to please him by giving him a good breakfast. She would ask for AU$20-30 for housekeeping. From this, she saved money and walked to Target and bought a $40 mobile telephone, for he had earlier taken away her Indian mobile phone and had prohibited her from talking to her parents.

After giving birth to their first child she experienced postnatal depression. Geeta said 'I didn't know what was happening with me. I thought "It's Australia, new place, I have to listen to him." … I never questioned him.' He kept her passport and her Medicare card. After discovering her new mobile telephone he smashed it. Geeta's sister in India couriered her long nighties to wear. When he saw her wearing one of them, he stomped on it. He took a knife and cut the nighties. He dragged her wearing the remaining nightie and threatened her with the knife; this was observed by their children who were three and eight years old. She went to a neighbour's house and they called the police. She spent the night there and the police only came at 5 am the next day.

Later, when her husband refused to give her $40 to pay library fines, she went to the bank and found there was $200 in her account. She withdrew $100. Her husband discovered this because he had access to her account, and beat her. The police came again. Thinking she would take the remaining $100 from her account, she went to the bank and found he had withdrawn that. But the teller told her there was a fixed deposit account in her name with $25,000 in it. Geeta took it out and deposited it into a new account. After discovering this her husband slapped her and told her to go to the bank and withdraw the money. She refused. He beat her again, saying 'I can't trust you,' and that she had stolen his money. The assault continued. She woke up hearing her son screaming because his father was beating him. He then beat her again, saying 'You took my money.' The police came again and arrested him.

At the end of the interview, Geeta wondered whether she had done wrong by taking the money, by calling the police. She said her dreams of a happy marriage had been shattered. She wanted her husband to understand her. But he had left the home and initiated divorce proceedings. Geeta was meeting with lawyers trying to secure some money from the sale of the marital home. She is retraining to be able to work while looking after her young children. But the overwhelming feeling for her was 'I'm alone.'

Helen and Geeta's stories show some of the ways in which men perpetrate economic abuse. As Postmus et al. (2018) have noted, it includes a gamut of tactics such as denying their wife/partner access to economic resources, information about money, controlling expenditure, appropriating money and sabotaging their partners' ability to generate money and assets through paid work. This is true across cultures. Men do it through coercive control. These stories illustrate the way coercive control works (Stark 2009, 2012). The man isolated the woman, instilled fear, degraded and intimidated her, denied her a voice and made her feel she was responsible for the abuse. The woman knew the relationship was not good but did not recognise non-physical abuse as family violence.

However, coercive control does not always operate through absolute denial of money. Most often, the man uses traditional cultural practices related to the gender of money. Most Anglo-Celtic women willingly have a joint banking account, assuming there will be a partnership in marriage. Similarly, an Indian woman like Chitra (below) may agree to put money into her husband's account because she thinks he will take care of her welfare. But when the man acts immorally all that is left is the shell of the cultural practices around money.

3.5.1 The Joint Account Minus the Jointness

The joint bank account, a symbol of togetherness and partnership in middle-income Anglo-Celtic marriage in Australia, becomes a medium of abuse when the husband does not provide in any consistent fashion. He may not have paid work or may keep his money in a separate account, spending it on 'men's toys' rather than the household. In some cases, he also controls a joint account that only has his wife's money. The husband can then use or remove her money from the joint account as he wishes and monitor her expenditure. At the same time, his wife does not have information about his money. Instead of being the symbol of the partnership of marriage, the joint account becomes a medium of economic abuse.

Eight of the 13 women in the Anglo-Celtic group had joint accounts for much of the period of their relationship with their husbands but their cultural expectations of jointness were overturned. All eight husbands failed to provide for much of the time. In Carol's story below, the joint account was an expected part of marriage. When she put her savings, and then her earnings, into the joint account with her second husband, his coercive control was nearly unstoppable. Her husband did not provide but controlled her money through the joint account. She lived in fear, lost her voice and was shunted into a nightmare.

3.6 The Joint Account—'My Model of a Marriage'

Carol, 67, was a teacher when her 20-year first marriage ended. When she married her second husband, Carl, it was against the advice of her family and friends. Carol expected they would have a joint account because, in her words, 'that was my model of marriage.' She put her savings of $60,000 into their joint account. She said, 'He didn't *actually* ask for it, but I think it was in the whole culture of the relationship.'

Carl did not have a regular wage. Carol had a credit card but said she 'wouldn't *dare* spend it on anything without speaking to him. So I bought groceries [knowing] he would check, he would go over the statements.' Without telling her, Carl sold Carol's sewing machine that she had owned for years and which had allowed her to do some complicated sewing. He put her adored roll-top desk in a garage sale. When Carol began teaching again a year after they married, she said of her earnings 'He took it all. He took it all and that paid off the house we were in.' Carol said she felt there was the looming threat of physical violence. She worked out that if she curled up at the bottom of the big walk-in cupboard, Carl would not be able to see her. One day, she hid there for three hours knowing 'he was going to turn on me'. She said, 'I'd nearly gone crazy.'

What she minded most was not being able to give generous gifts to her family and friends. When her sons from her first marriage sent her $15,000, she opened a separate account, a 'sneaky account'. She says she felt 'a bit unfaithful.' When she decided to leave Carl two and a half years later, she directed her pay to this separate account. This gave her access to money, though she did not feel free to take any money out of the joint account. Despite this experience, Carol continues to feel that joint money is central to marriage. When she married for the third time, she pooled her money again. But this time her husband also shares, and respects the partnership of marriage. They have two joint accounts and each of them also has a separate account. Now that Carol has retired, her husband transfers a set amount to her account every month, to ensure she has money for personal use.

3.6.1 *Male Control Without Morality*

Most Indian participants in the study did not initially worry about the male control of money, as money in India is traditionally controlled by a man. Eleven of the 17 Indian participants began their marriage with the husband controlling the money. The control was exercised through the women's money being deposited in the husband's account (3 of 11) or a joint account that he controlled (5 of the 11). Alternatively, the woman may have had no account at all, because she was not earning or because she was working in her husband's business (3 of 11). As with the Anglo-Celtic community, the expectation was that the husband would look after his wife and children. It was only when these moral norms were flouted that the wife moved to separate her money.

This norm of male control is so strong that when Asha, 32, set up a joint account for joint expenses and a separate account for her personal expenses and to send money home, her husband opposed it vehemently. Yet Asha had already discussed this with him before marriage, for they had met in Australia and then got married. Asha stated:

> [R]ight from the beginning ... I was clear ... I will not be giving him my salary. And that's when he started to give me more problems. He saw this as a trust issue. He wanted me to give him my salary to him and then he manages all the finances.

Two months after their marriage her husband also began questioning why she was sending money to her parents. Now, she belonged to him and his family. They divorced in less than two years. Asha's sending money home to her parents reflected a change in the gender and morality of money. It was no longer just a 'good son' who sent money home; a 'good daughter' could also do this. This is part of a larger questioning that is taking place among urban educated women in India, as well as Australia, that their money does not necessarily belong to their husbands' families (Singh 2018a).

The joint account among the Indian participants, however, was not a sign that the Indian migrants were changing the gender of money by adopting the Anglo-Celtic jointness of money. Joint accounts in India are used to protect wives and children, rather than enable joint transactions and information (Singh 2009). Among the Indian participants, two women said their husbands believed that having a joint account would be evidence of a continuing marriage and would help the wife's case for permanent residence. In fact, this does reflect current practice in that evidence of having a joint account for a 'reasonable period' is one of the points showing a continuing marriage (Department of Home Affairs, n.d.). So, the male-controlled joint account among the Indian participants was also a medium of control. In all the cases, the husband had a separate account, with the wife's earnings going into an additional joint account that he controlled.

1. *'You want to spend money now?'*

Chitra's husband went further than others previously described, for he not only controlled what she spent from the joint account that contained only her earnings but he and his family also appropriated her assets and involved her in joint debt. Her husband and his family beat her, making her feel like a 'slave'. Chitra, 29, had been a health professional in India and had agreed to an arranged marriage because the family was affinally connected and Chitra and her family thought this would keep her safe and happy. But within three years her marriage was over. The honeymoon grooming period was short. Soon after Chitra arrived in Australia in 2015, her husband told her she talked too much. His family laughed at her, saying she was a liar, that she was from a poor family unlike the older daughter-in-law, and she was pretending to have asthma attacks.

In the first year and a half, they prevented Chitra from earning and her mother-in-law took away Chitra's jewellery. They prevented her from driving though she had an Indian driving licence. This was accompanied by emotional abuse with the mother-in-law saying Chitra was not good enough for her son, although it was an arranged marriage. Her husband was suspicious of her talking to anyone, including her family. He monitored her use of her mobile phone, isolating her from her family in India. And her doctor's receptionist told Chitra her husband had come to check whether she really had an appointment with the doctor. Chitra's husband and his brother, encouraged by their mother, beat Chitra. Her husband blamed Chitra saying, he wouldn't hit her if she behaved 'like a good wife.' Chitra said:

> I tried my best all the time to be a good wife and do whatever he wanted me to do. I was so scared all the time that I was so careful about what I was saying, because anything I said or did, they would start scolding me. I was so scared to tell this to anyone because they always made me believe that I was the wrong one. I had lost trust in myself.

Her husband and his family threatened they would have Chitra deported from Australia because she was only on a spousal visa. This malevolent instilling of fear, deprivation, isolation, and accusations of not being a good wife followed the usual pattern of coercive control. When Chitra began working—not as a health professional—her earnings went into a joint account controlled by her husband. When she saw the balance was getting lower in the account she asked him to leave some for her personal needs. He replied, 'Oh you want to spend money now.' She later found she was also entangled in 'coercive debt' through a directorship in the joint family business and a loan. Chitra passed the first step of her professional registration examination, despite her husband and family saying she was too stupid to pass. The day after, her husband beat her 'mercilessly'. Chitra tried to escape but her husband's brother and his wife pulled her back. She then ran out again, straight to the police station, fearing for her life. As she was on a spousal visa, she was eligible for refuge facilities and associated services. It also helped she was employed. After she left the refuge, she moved interstate to stay with extended family for a few months before moving to a rented place. At the time of the interview, Chitra's mother and brother were staying with her.

3.7 Conclusion: Criminalising Coercive Control

Economic abuse in all cultures leads to a woman losing her sense of freedom and agency, with harmful mental effects. Yet unlike physical assault, economic abuse is not presently recognised in some common law countries as a criminal offence, despite it being established that economic abuse and other non-physical aspects of family violence are serious and not acceptable. The arguments against criminalising economic abuse revolve around two issues. The first involves the difficulty of policing and prosecuting economic abuse and coercive control. The second focuses on the gendered nature of coercive conduct and the difficulty of distinguishing between normal gendered behaviour and coercive behaviour that amounts to economic (or other non-physical) abuse.

First, as Wiener (Chap. 8) has outlined, difficulties in policing and prosecuting coercive control impact on prosecuting economic abuse through this offence. Similarly, the experience of Tasmania (which criminalised economic and emotional abuse in 2005) reveals that only a small number of prosecutions of economic abuse have occurred in that State, partly because there is little understanding of the nature of economic abuse—among victims as well as the police. As Barwick et al. (Chap. 7) note in relation to prosecutions, 'the lack of community awareness is undoubtedly a major impediment'. Consequently, the Tasmanian experience, in conjunction with more recent reports of the operation of the offence of controlling or coercive behaviour in England and Wales, demonstrates that a public education campaign, as well as specific training for police, will have to be introduced if successful prosecutions for economic abuse are to occur. The emphasis will need to move from an incident-based approach to a broader narrative, where it is the history of intimidation and deprivation that established the significance of even small acts of economic control, exploitation and sabotage within a more encompassing pattern of abuse (Barwick 2017; Wiener 2017).

In contrast, this chapter largely addresses the second issue in criminalising economic abuse: that coercive control can be invisible. Tolmie (2018, p. 56) has argued:

> … male dominance is to some degree *naturalized* because heterosexual norms permit men a certain degree of dominance in the minutia of everyday living even in non-abusive relationships … If abusive behaviour exploits existing gender norms when does 'normal' end and 'abuse' begin?

This chapter has shown that economic abuse in any culture results when the gender of money is stripped of its morality. It is this that differentiates what is 'normal' from what is 'abusive', whether we are speaking of joint accounts in the Anglo-Celtic group or dowry in the Indian community in Australia. The gender of money, whether it is characterised by joint or male control, is accompanied by moral norms. These norms are readily recognisable in one's own culture and have to be sought in cultures other than one's own. The treatment of Helen and Carol in the Anglo-Celtic culture is recognised as coercive because it does not represent the jointness of marriage and the husband's duty to provide. For Geeta and Chitra among Indians in Australia, the husband has acted against his moral duty to ensure the wellbeing of his wife and children. The common aspect of economic abuse across the two cultures is that the men have transgressed moral norms around the gender of money.

As this chapter has shown, there are cultural dimensions of financial abuse in all communities. I have sought to challenge the ease with which we see money practices of other cultures as abusive, while not seeing economic abuse as a cultural phenomenon in mainstream Australian culture. For instance, dowry related abuse is now one of the examples of family violence in Victoria's amended *Family Violence Protection Act 2008* (Vic) and a Senate Inquiry focused on the 'Incidence of Dowry and Dowry Abuse in Australia'. This focus on dowry abuse directs the spotlight on its immorality in some 'other' culture, without realising that coercive control by definition strips away morality from money practices. It sends the message that the mainstream way of managing and controlling money is culture-free, ignoring the fact that money in all cultures is a social and cultural phenomenon (Singh 2018b). Additionally, focusing on criminalising specific practices in one culture ignores the complexity of family violence in that culture as well as in other cultures. Economic abuse can also take place through the coercive control of a bank account and/or denying a woman access to money, appropriating her money, preventing her from undertaking paid work, abusing cultural practices like joint bank accounts in Anglo-Celtic communities or remittances, dowry and bride-price in communities of the global South.

Economic abuse results from coercion on a wide front. It is by definition immoral according to the dictates of its own culture. It exploits the trust and vulnerability of intimate relationships. Economic abuse and other forms of non-physical aspects of family violence lead women across cultures to live in fear, lose their sense of self, making their world unsafe and unpredictable. The trauma lasts long, not only for the woman but also for her children. Consequently, it is particularly important to ensure that economic abuse—a key aspect of non-physical family violence—is criminalised in all its forms across cultures, including one's own. Criminalising economic abuse in the context of family violence is the beginning of protection and redress. Not criminalising this form of abuse sends the message that economically abusive behaviour is acceptable and will not have negative consequences for the perpetrator.

References

Abraham, M. (2000). Isolation as a form of marital violence: The South Asian migrant experience. *Journal of Social Distress and the Homeless, 9*(3), 221–236.

Adams, A. E., Sullivan, C. M., Bybee, D., & Greeson, M. R. (2008). Development of the scale of economic abuse. *Violence Against Women, 14*(5), 563–588.

Alhabib, S., Nur, U., & Jones, R. (2010). Domestic violence against women: Systematic review of prevalence studies. *Journal of Family Violence, 25*(4), 369–382.

Australian Bureau of Statistics. (1995). *1301.0—Year Book Australia, 1995: Ethnic and Cultural Diversity in Australia.* Retrieved from http://www.abs.gov.au/Ausstats/abs@.nsf/94713ad445ff1425ca25682000192af2/49f609c83cf34d69ca2569de0025c182!OpenDocument.

Australian Bureau of Statistics. (2018). *2016 Census QuickStats.* Retrieved from http://quickstats.censusdata.abs.gov.au/census_services/getproduct/census/2016/quickstat/036?opendocument.

Australian Law Reform Commission. (2010). *Family Violence–A National Legal Response.* Retrieved from http://www.alrc.gov.au/sites/default/files/pdfs/publications/ALRC114_Whole Report.pdf.

Bevin, E. (2016, August 1). Tasmanian man accused of preventing wife from making decisions, accessing joint accounts. *news.com.au.* Retrieved from http://www.abc.net.au/news/2016-08-01/tasmanian-man-prosecuted-for-alleged-economic-abuse/7679922.

Cameron, P. (2014). *Relationship Problems and Money: Women Talk about Financial Abuse.* WIRE. Retrieved from https://www.aph.gov.au/DocumentStore.ashx?id=3938c7bf-ab6b-4b0e-b2d3-56177777334b&subId=411337.

Camilleri, O., Corrie, T., & Moore, S. (2015). *Restoring Financial Safety: Legal Responses to Economic Abuse*. Good Shepherd Australia New Zealand and Wyndham Legal Service. Retrieved from https://www.goodshep.org.au/media/1220/restoring-financial-safety_legal-responses-to-economic-abuse_web.pdf.

Douglas, H. (2018). Legal systems abuse and coercive control. *Criminology & Criminal Justice, 18*(1), 84–99.

Fehlberg, B., & Millward, C. (2014). Family violence and financial outcomes after parental separation. In A. Hayes & D. Higgins (Eds.), *Families, policy and the law: Selected essays on contemporary issues for Australia*. Australian Institute of Family Studies: Melbourne, VIC.

George, S. M. (2005). *When women come first: Gender and class in transnational migration*. Berkley, CA: University of California Press.

Ghafournia, N. (2011). Battered at home, played down in policy: Migrant women and domestic violence in Australia. *Aggression and Violent Behavior, 16*(3), 207–213.

Kutin, J., Russell, R., & Reid, M. (2017). Economic abuse between intimate partners in Australia: Prevalence, health status, disability and financial stress. *Australian and New Zealand Journal of Public Health, 14*(3), 269–274.

Littwin, A. (2012). Coerced debt: The role of consumer credit in domestic violence. *California Law Review, 100*(4), 951–1025.

Lloyd, S. (1997). The effects of domestic violence on women's employment. *Law & Policy, 19*(2), 139–167.

Macdonald, F. (2012). *Spotlight on economic abuse: A literature and policy review*. Melbourne, VIC: Good Shepherd Youth and Family Service.

McMahon, M., & McGorrery, P. (2016). Criminalising controlling and coercive behaviour: The next step in the prosecution of family violence? *Alternative Law Journal, 41*(2), 98–101.

Olsberg, D., & Winters, M. (2005). *Ageing in place: Intergenerational and interfamilial housing transfers and shifts in later life*. AHURI Research & Policy Bulletin No. 67. Melbourne, VIC: Australian Housing and Urban Research Institute.

Peled, E., & Krigel, K. (2016). The path to economic independence among survivors of intimate partner violence: A critical review of the literature and courses for action. *Aggression and Violent Behavior, 31*(November–December), 127–135.

Pollett, S. L. (2011, February). Economic abuse: The unseen side of domestic violence. *New York State Bar Association Journal*, 40–44.

Postmus, J. L., Hoge, G. L., Breckenridge, J., Sharp-Jeffs, N., & Chung, D. (2018). Economic abuse as an invisible form of domestic violence: A multicountry review. *Trauma, Violence & Abuse*, 1–23.

Postmus, J. L., Huang, C. C., & Mathisen-Stylianou, A. (2012a). The impact of physical and economic abuse on maternal mental health and parenting. *Children and Youth Services Review, 34*(9), 1922–1928.

Postmus, J. L., Plummer, S. B., McMahon, S., Murshid, N. S., & Kim, M. S. (2012b). Understanding economic abuse in the lives of survivors. *Journal of Interpersonal Violence, 27*(3), 411–430.

Postmus, J. L., Plummer, S. B., & Stylianou, A. M. (2016). Measuring economic abuse in the lives of survivors: Revising the Scale of Economic Abuse. *Violence Against Women, 22*(6), 692–703.

Price, J. (2018). Leave nothing but huge amounts of money. Expect only grandchildren. *The Age*. Retrieved April 23, 2018, fromhttps://www.smh.com.au/business/the-economy/leave-nothing-but-huge-amounts-of-money-expect-only-grandchildren-20180423-p4zb7h.html

Raj, A., & Silverman, J. (2002). Violence against immigrant women: The roles of culture, context, and legal immigrant status on intimate partner violence. *Violence Against Women, 8*(3), 367–398.

Ratha, D., Plaza, S., Wyss, H., De, S., Schuettler, K., & Yi, S. (2016a). Trends in Remittances, 2016: A New Normal of Slow Growth. *People Move: A blog about migration, remittances and development*. Retrieved October 6, 2016, from http://blogs.worldbank.org/peoplemove/trends-remittances-2016-new-normal-slow-growth.

Ratha, D., Eigen-Zucchi, C., & Plaza, S. (2016b). *Migrant Remittances Factbook 2016* (3rd ed.). Washington DC: World Bank Group's Global Knowledge Partnership on Migration and Development(KNOMAD).

Sanders, C. K. (2015). Economic abuse in the lives of women abused by an intimate partner: A qualitative study. *Violence Against Women, 21*(1), 3–29.

Segrave, M. (2017). *Temporary Migration and Family Violence: An Analysis of Victimisation, Vulnerability and Suport*. Melbourne: Monash University. Retrieved from https://www.ntv.org.au/wp-content/uploads/2016/12/Temporary-migration-and-family-violence_Full-Report-2017.pdf.

Sharp-Jeffs, N. (2015). *Money Matters: Research into the Extent and Nature of Financial Abuse within Intimate Relationships in the UK*. London: Co-operative Bank and Refuge. Retrieved from http://www.refuge.org.uk/files/Money-Matters.pdf.

Sharp-Jeffs, N., & Learmonth, S. (2017). *Into Plain Sight: How Economic Abuse is Reflected in Successful Prosecutions of Controlling or Coercive Behaviour*. London: Surviving Economic Abuse. Retrieved from http://survivingeconomicabuse.org/wp-content/uploads/2017/12/PlainSight.pdf.

Sharp, N. (2008). *'What's Yours is Mine': The Different Forms of Economic Abuse and its Impact on Women and Children Experiencing Domestic Violence*. London: Refuge. Retrieved from http://www.refuge.org.uk/files/Whats-yours-is-mine-Full-Report.pdf.

Singh, S. (1997). *Marriage money: The social shaping of money in marriage and banking*. St Leonards, NSW: Allen & Unwin.

Singh, S. (2009). Balancing separateness and jointness of money in relationships: The design of bank accounts in Australia and India. (13th Annual Conference on Human Computer Interaction, San Diego, 19–24 July 2009).

Singh, S. (2013). *Globalization and money: A global South perspective*. Lanham, MD: Rowman & Littlefield.

Singh, S. (2016). *Money, migration and family: India to Australia*. New York, NY: Palgrave Macmillan.

Singh, S. (2017). The future of money is shaped by the family practices of the global South. In K. Hart (Ed.), *Money in a human economy*. New York, NY: Berghahn.

Singh, S. (2018a). The daughter-in-law questions remittances: Changes in the gender of remittances among Indian migrants to Australia. *Global Networks. Advance online publication:*. https://doi.org/10.1111/glob.12215.

Singh, S. (2018b). *Submission to the Senate Inquiry on the Practice of Dowry and the Incidence of Dowry Abuse in Australia*. Retrieved from https://www.aph.gov.au/DocumentStore.ashx?id=752fd61e-ca4e-4c2d-b9eb-be4cdb61087c&subId=658070.

Singh, S., & Bhandari, M. (2012). Money management and control in the Indian joint family across generations. *The Sociological Review, 60*(1), 46–67.

Smallwood, E. (2015). *Stepping Stones: Legal Barriers to Economic Equality after Family Violence*. Melbourne: Women's Legal Service Victoria. Retrieved from https://womenslegal.org.au/files/file/Stepping%20Stones%20Report(1).pdf.

Stark, E. (2012). Looking beyond domestic violence: Policing coercive control. *Journal of Police Crisis Negotiations, 12*(2), 199–217.

Stark, E. (2009). Rethinking coercive control. *Violence Against Women, 15*(12), 1509–1525.

State of Victoria, Royal Commission into Family Violence. (2016). *Report and Recommendations*. Melbourne: Royal Commission into Family Violence. Retrieved from http://www.rcfv.com.au/Report-Recommendations.

Stylianou, A. M., Postmus, J. L., & McMahon, S. (2013). Measuring abusive behaviors: Is economic abuse a unique form of abuse? *Journal of Interpersonal Violence, 28*(16), 3186–3204.

Tolmie, J. R. (2018). Coercive control: To criminalize or not to criminalize? *Criminology & Criminal Justice, 18*(1), 50–66.

Tripathi, S. (2016). Restricting son to fulfil duties to aged parents a valid ground for divorce: SC. *Firstpost*. Retrieved October 7, 2016, from https://www.firstpost.com/india/restricting-son-to-fulfil-duties-to-aged-parents-a-valid-ground-for-divorce-sc-3040124.html.

Uberoi, P. (2004). The family in India. In V. Das (Ed.), *Handbook of Indian Sociology* (pp. 275–307). New Delhi: Oxford University Press.

Vaughan, C., Davis, E., Murdolo, A., Chen, J., Murray, L., Block, K., Quiazon, R., & Warr, D. (2015). *Promoting Community-Led Responses to Violence Against Immigrant and Refugee Women in Metropolitan and Regional Australia: The ASPIRE Project: State of Knowledge Paper*. Alexandria, NSW: Australia's National Organisation for Women's Safety. Retrieved from https://d2c0ikyv46o3b1.cloudfront.net/anrows.org.au/s3fs-public/12_1.2%20Landscapes%20ASPIRE%20web.pdf.

Vaughan, C., Davis, E., Murdolo, A., Chen, J., Murray, L., Quiazon, R., Block, K., & Warr, D. (2016). *Promoting Community-Led Responses to Violence Against Immigrant and Refugee Women in Metropolitan and Regional Australia: The ASPIRE Project: Research Report*. Alexandria, NSW: Australia's National Organisation for Women's Safety. Retrieved from http://media.aomx.com/anrows.org.au/Aspire_Horizons_FINAL.pdf.

VicHealth. (2014). *Australians' Attitudes to Violence Against Women: Findings from the 2013 National Community Attitudes Towards Violence Against Women Survey (NCAS)*. Melbourne: VicHealth. Retrieved from https://www.vichealth.vic.gov.au/media-and-resources/publications/2013-national-community-attitudes-towards-violence-against-women-survey.

Webster, K. (2016). *A Preventable Burden: Measuring and Addressing the Prevalence and Health Impacts of Intimate Partner Violence in Australian Women: Key Findings and Future Directions*. Sydney: Australia's National Organisation for Women's Safety. Retrieved from http://media.aomx.com/anrows.org.au/s3fs-public/28%2010%2016%20BOD%20Compass.pdf.

Wiener, C. (2017). Seeing what is 'invisible in plain sight': Policing coercive control. *The Howard Journal of Crime and Justice, 56*(4), 500–515.

Zelizer, V. A. (1994). *The social meaning of money*. New York, NY: Basic Books.

Chapter 4
Coercive Control and Intimate Partner Homicide

Danielle Tyson

Abstract Over the past decade, there has been a paradigm shift away from understanding intimate partner violence (IPV) as comprising single discrete instances of physical abuse towards a more comprehensive and accurate paradigm based on coercive control: a model of abuse that encompasses a range of strategies or tactics used by men to dominate individual women in their personal life. Despite this shift, domestic violence laws continue to coalesce around an incident-specific focus and weigh the severity of abuse by the level of force used or injury inflicted. This chapter considers how coercive control as a criminological concept has become central to contemporary understandings of domestic abuse and intimate partner homicide. It discusses how the concept of coercive control challenges the focus on physical injury in the development of risk assessments for domestic abuse and intimate partner homicide. The chapter also considers how coercive control has the potential to inform the criminal defences of women who are victims of domestic violence and who kill their abusers. While there is controversy about the desirability of introducing a specific family violence offence modelled on coercive control, this approach to domestic abuse is not restricted to the introduction of new offences. Recent efforts to tender evidence of coercive control in the trials of women who have killed an abusive partner have confronted significant difficulties, but feminist commentators suggest it is a strategy that should be pursued. While the concept of coercive control has increasingly become part of the language and thinking of feminist research and legal and policy responses to domestic abuse and intimate partner homicide, the chapter concludes that more work needs to be done if we are to truly reorient our understandings of IPV as a liberty crime.

Keywords Intimate partner homicide · Coercive control · Risk assessment · Criminal defences

D. Tyson (✉)
School of Humanities and Social Sciences, Deakin University,
VIC, Australia
e-mail: danielle.tyson@deakin.edu.au

4.1 Introduction

Over the past decade there has been a paradigm shift in criminal justice policy and research away from an understanding of intimate partner violence (IPV) as consisting of a one-off or series of isolated physical incidents towards a more comprehensive and accurate paradigm that accounts for coercive control. Evan Stark's (2007) work has been particularly influential in reorienting understandings of IPV as coercive control, a model of abuse that encompasses a range of strategies or tactics used by men to dominate individual women in their personal life. Stark emphasises that it is a misrepresentation of the harm of IPV to understand it as an incident-specific or assault crime; rather, it should be understood as a liberty crime that involves:

> a course of conduct that subordinates women to an alien will by violating their physical integrity (domestic violence), denying them respect and autonomy (intimidation), depriving them of social connectedness (isolation) and appropriating or denying them access to the basic rights resources required for personhood and citizenship (control). (Stark 2007, p. 15; also see Buzawa et al. 2017, p. 105)

Despite this shift, physical assault and injury continue to be the dominant and most commonly identified form of abuse in police, legal and policy responses to domestic violence. Indeed, the failure to recognise that IPV frequently manifests as an ongoing and systematic process of controlling behaviours aimed at disempowering the victim has not yet fully permeated legal understandings (Bishop 2016, p. 60). This has created a legal system that perpetuates a 'hierarchy of harm' where other forms of abuse (verbal, emotional, financial, manipulation using children, and harassment) are considered less serious and less in need of legal intervention, and fails to protect, prevent and intervene in domestic violence cases (Bishop 2016, p. 60).

In order to enhance protections for victims of IPV, some jurisdictions have taken the bold step of enacting offences that criminalise a broader range of coercive and controlling behaviours than just physical violence (McMahon and McGorrery 2016). This shift was manifest to some degree in stalking and harassment offences that were introduced over the last 30 years in England and Wales (*Protection from Harassment Act 1997* (E&W)), Scotland (*Criminal Justice & Licensing (Scotland) Act 2010* (Scot)), New Zealand (*Harassment Act 1997* (NZ)) and all Australian jurisdictions (McMahon et al. 2018). The shift is also discernible in the introduction in many jurisdictions of intervention orders (variously labelled civil protection orders, domestic violence protection orders, apprehended violence orders, etc.) that can be taken out by police or an affected person to protect them against abuse (including non-physical abuse) by a family member (for a discussion of the efficacy of such approaches in Australia, see: Douglas 2018). However, the boldest step that has been taken is the enactment of criminal offences that directly criminalise coercive control in domestic relationships. In 2004, Tasmania, Australia introduced the summary offences of emotional and economic abuse through the *Family Violence Act 2004* (Tas) ss 8–9. In 2015 England and Wales enacted an offence that criminalises coercive and controlling behaviour (*Serious Crime Act 2015* (E&W) s 76). A similar offence was introduced in Ireland in 2018 (*Domestic Violence Act 2018* (IR) s 39) and that same year Scotland enacted a specific offence of domestic abuse (*Domestic Abuse (Scotland) Act 2018* (Scot) s 1). The merits of enacting specific offences that criminalise non-physical abuse, grounded primarily on a recognition of the centrality of controlling and coercive behaviour in domestic violence, has been examined by a range of scholars (e.g. Bettinson 2016, 2018; Bettinson and Bishop 2015; Burman and Brooks-Hay 2018; Douglas 2015; McMahon and McGorrery 2016; Ortiz 2018; Stark 2012a; Tolmie 2018; Walklate et al. 2018).

In addition to these legislative developments, an understanding of the role of coercive control in IPV has been used to inform claims of self-defence in cases where women have killed their abusive male partners and then sought to rely on this defence. This understanding is particularly important where the fatal act in self-defence occurred in non-confrontational circumstances (e.g. Arnold 2009; Bettinson 2018; Hanna 2009; Midson 2016; Sheehy 2018; Sheehy et al. 2014; Tarrant 2018; Wake 2015). Understanding the broader dynamics of coercive control in IPV relationships reveals how domestic violence:

> spans a period of time (often lengthy), has a cumulative impact on those who survive it that affects how they see and respond to the world, is a pattern of behaviour ... is hidden ... and is more complex than an account of the physical incidents of violence that have taken place would suggest. (Sheehy et al. 2012, p. 707)

According to Stark, understanding this broader context is critical to understanding how men entrap women, and if lawyers and judges could better understand this context, it would render more just results for women who kill their abusers (Stark 2007, p. 12, 2012a, p. 12).

Underpinning these developments has been an increasing body of research that identifies and analyses coercive control in intimate partner relationships. This research emphasises the micromanagement of victims' lives by their abusive partners (Stark 2007, p. 5; Kelly and Westmarland 2016, pp. 114–115), constructs abuse through patterns of behaviour rather than discrete events, and recognises the importance of non-physical harms (Hanna 2009). These insights have not only contributed to the development of new offences but have also significantly contributed to the development of risk assessment tools structured around coercive control (rather than based on 'incident-by-incident' responses to physical violence) (Myhill and Hohl 2016, p. 2; Bettinson 2016). It is this research and its contribution to an understanding of domestic abuse that is the focus of this chapter.

In particular, this chapter contributes to an understanding of the role of coercive control in domestic abuse and intimate partner homicide. It identifies coercive control as a risk factor for both abuse and homicide. Although the emphasis is on jurisdictions in Australia, recent developments and reforms to the law of homicide in other jurisdictions, including Canada and New Zealand, are considered. The chapter has three aims:

- First, it outlines the findings of prior research on domestic abuse and intimate partner homicide, emphasising the importance of coercive controlling behaviour.
- Second, having established the centrality of coercive control in domestic homicide, it then considers how this can inform claims of self-defence by women charged with killing their abusers.
- Third, the contribution of coercive control to understanding domestic abuse and intimate partner homicide is evaluated, with the conclusion that it has contributed to more nuanced understandings of family violence. However, ongoing challenges include the continuing greater recognition of physical violence rather than other forms of abuse (such as psychological abuse or fear of physical violence following a sustained period of coercive and controlling behaviour) and a likely difficulty in expert evidence of coercive and controlling behaviour satisfying evidentiary admissibility standards in the trials of women who have killed their abusive partners, thereby preventing juries from obtaining a comprehensive understanding of the abuse experienced by these defendants.

4.2 Domestic Abuse and Coercive Control: The Golden Thread

Concepts of coercion and control, frequently associated with models of abuse developed by Michael Johnson (1995, 2008) and especially Evan Stark (2007), have become increasingly influential in understanding domestic abuse and intimate partner homicide and have guided the formulation and introduction of new domestic abuse offences in England and Wales, Scotland and Ireland.

Coercion and control emphasise the psychological abuse involved in domestic abuse. Strategies used by abusers frequently involve humiliation, manipulation, degradation, gaslighting (using 'mind games' to make the other person doubt their sanity), economic abuse and the micromanagement of a woman's life so that even minor aspects of her day-to-day activities are generally monitored and controlled. This often leads to the abused woman becoming isolated and dependent on the abuser. Evan Stark (2007, 2009, 2010) emphasises that abusive intimate relationships characterised by coercive control are gendered (men control women) and are not simply characterised by physical violence, but are best understood as men's attempts to destroy women's autonomy and reinstate patriarchy in intimate relationships. Similarly, the American sociologist Michael Johnson (1995) emphasises that IPV is gendered, and that emotionally abusive intimidation, coercion and control coupled with physical violence—what he labels 'intimate terrorism' (originally 'patriarchal terrorism')–characterises severely abusive relationships (Kelly and Johnson 2008, p. 322).

Whether termed coercive control or intimate terrorism, these approaches to domestic abuse build on and expand what has long been understood as central to victim's experiences of abuse in intimate relationships: the coercion and control is ongoing (rather than merely repeated), is *cumulative* and *routine* (Stark 2007), and generates a condition of entrapment that comes through the suppression of a victim's autonomy, rights and liberties (Stark 2012b, p. 4). These insights into the underlying dynamics of coercive control have increasingly permeated criminological discourse on domestic abuse and intimate partner homicide, with notions of 'power and control' (Pence and Paymar 1993; Straka and Montminy 2008), and 'jealousy' and 'possessiveness' being routinely used in the literature (e.g. Polk 1994; Dobash and Dobash 2004, 2007). The recognition of the influence of coercive controlling behaviours on women's experiences in abusive relationships has assisted researchers to move beyond the stereotypical image of women victims as 'helpless' and 'passive' victims. This insight has had implications for reframing the question, 'why didn't she leave' into 'why did he do it?' (Hanna 2009, p. 1464, 1460). In the coercive control approach, abused women are aggressive help-seekers who are as likely to be assaulted and entrapped when they are legally and/or physically separated from their abuser as when they are married or living together. This conceptualisation of separation as a continuum, as opposed to a single moment in time, has led researchers to account for the ways in which women victims adopt a range of resistance strategies to counter their partner's control, as opposed to solely resisting physical violence or isolated incidents (Hayes 2013, p. 3; Meyer 2012, 2016). Despite these inroads, coercive control remains marginal in the mainstream thinking of some professionals, and the wider public, including the perceptions of perpetrators and victims (Kelly and Westmarland 2016).

As previously noted, explanations of domestic abuse that utilise concepts of coercion and control highlight that the abuse is gendered and 'ongoing, rather than episodic, cumulative rather than incident-specific, and the harms it causes are more readily explained by these factors than its severity' (Stark 2007, p. 35). Coercive control deprives victims of respect and autonomy (intimidation), deprives them of social connectedness (isolation), and appropriates or denies their access to the resources required for personhood and citizenship (control) (Stark 2007, p. 15). The cumulative impact of these tactics is to make abused women constantly fearful and ashamed, undermining their self-respect, reminding them that they are dependent on their abusive partners for their well-being, cutting them off from other sources of support, diminishing their sense of identity, and infringing on their rights to make their own decisions (Arnold 2009, p. 1435). It results in the experience of *entrapment*, which Stark describes as 'hostage-like in the harms it inflicts on dignity, liberty, autonomy and personhood as well as to physical and psychological integrity' (2012b, p. 7). Entrapment is characterised by escalating isolation, risk and fear; the fear prevents victims from keeping themselves and their children safe and inhibits their resistance to, or escape from, the abuse and, in some instances, from leaving the relationship (Stark 2007). But entrapment involves more than an emotional and psychological response to the abuse; it is compounded by the indifference of powerful institutions to the victim's suffering and exacerbated by class and racism (Stark 2007, p. 13).

Models of IPV that emphasise the centrality of coercion and control help to explain why separation is such a dangerous time for women and a clearly established risk factor for intimate partner homicide (e.g. Walby and Myhill 2001; Campbell et al. 2003; Sheehan et al. 2015) as separation is often perceived as an extreme threat by controlling partners. This insight has important implications for understanding a woman's decision to remain within an abusive relationship. Research with victims of abuse has found that while women display a diverse range of proactive help-seeking decisions, most stay with their abusive partner for a prolonged period of time after the onset of abuse (Meyer 2012). Many women report attempting to terminate the relationship but returning to their abusive partner on one or more occasion. They are aware of the risks associated with leaving their abusive partner, including risks to their children's safety, financial hardship, a lack of accommodation and the risk of fatal retaliatory violence (Meyer 2012, p. 182). A distinctive feature of the coercion and control approach to domestic abuse is that it understands women as 'active' agents who make rationally informed choices about the future safety of themselves and their children, rather than passive victims in the process of enduring and overcoming victimisation (Meyer 2012, p. 182, 2016, p. 208; Bruton and Tyson 2018). Many women in coercive relationships adopt a range of resistance strategies in response to their abusive partner's ongoing control, which are based on their experience of the abuser's behaviour and the history of the relationship. Women's resistance strategies may be an overt challenge to the abusive partner's behaviour, or they may be more covert about their resistance if they believe the direct challenge will further fuel the abuser's behaviour (Hayes 2013, p. 3). Women's experience of coercive control and their resistance strategies vary when domestic violence intersects with other characteristics such as race, class, ethnicity, language, familial structures, social exclusion and immigration status (Hayes 2013, p. 3).

Crucially, coercive control is a pattern of behaviour that may or may not involve physically injurious violence (Stark 2007, p. 18). This is not to say that severe acts of physical violence are unimportant but that some victims may experience relatively little physical violence, while others may experience low-level violence and others still may not experience physical violence at all (Myhill and Hohl 2016, p. 25). This understanding contrasts with the 'violence model' (or 'violent incident model') of abuse, which is built on discrete acts of (injurious) physical violence (Stark 2007). Stark attributes the limited effectiveness of criminal justice responses to domestic abuse less to failures in policing, for example, 'than from the fact that current laws, training, and procedures are based on a 'violence model' that bears little resemblance to the forms of oppression that drive most abused women to require outside assistance' (Stark 2012b, p. 201). Accordingly, Stark argues that 'this gap between what the law defines as the crime of domestic violence and the actual tactics abusers use to subjugate their partners severely limits the efficacy of even the most dedicated and well-trained police' (2012b, p. 201).

There is a now small but growing body of evidence to suggest that risk assessment tools structured around coercive control may assist police officers to move beyond an incident-by-incident response towards identifying dangerous patterns of behaviour that are potentially lethal but where there is no overt physical violence (Myhill and Hohl 2016, p. 2; Bettinson 2016). These assessment instruments have been slow to be adopted, which may partly be related to the fact that there are different forms of domestic abuse that have different underlying dynamics and represent different levels of harm. Myhill and Hohl have noted that the challenge of using risk assessment for those working with abused women is to accurately identify the type of harm that the victim is experiencing and its associated degree of harm (Myhill and Hohl 2016, p. 8). Nevertheless, the presence of control and coercion can be a highly significant matter. For instance, analysis of 488 completed risk assessment interviews conducted by members of a medium size police force in England and Wales with victims of domestic violence using the national 'Domestic abuse, stalking and harassment risk identification, assessment and management model' (DASH) found that several risk factors demonstrating coercion or control were consistently present (Myhill and Hohl 2016). The study found that perpetrators engaged in 'jealous, controlling, threatening and sexually coercive behaviours', and that victims' sense of isolation, fear and escalation, formed a consistent cluster of factors at the heart of domestic abuse and that these factors were linked with separation, choking and the use of weapons. Notably, physical injury was not central to most incidents of domestic abuse (Myhill and Hohl 2016, p. 20), a finding that accords with the theorising of Stark and Johnson. The researchers concluded that focusing on physical violence would lead police to fail to identify many instances of domestic abuse, and that coercive control was the 'golden thread' running through risk identification and assessment in cases of domestic violence' (Myhill and Hohl 2016, p. 25).

4.3 Coercive Control as a Risk Factor for Intimate Partner Homicide

Early formulations of risk assessments were based on a 'violence model', which equated domestic abuse with discrete assaults or threats (Stark 2012b, p. 3). This approach tended to either ignore or minimise the range of tactics used by abusive partners to intimate, dominate, coerce, isolate and control and ultimately subjugate their victims (Stark 2012b, p. 6). Yet interventions that are not informed by an appreciation of coercive controlling behaviours fail to respond to the harms that the majority of victims who seek outside assistance are experiencing (e.g. multiple tactics to frighten, isolate, degrade and subordinate them, as well assaults, threats, sexual exploitation, material deprivation, imprisonment, micromanagement of victims' lives, and the imposition of rules for how victims carry out their daily affairs). As most of these activities were (until the introduction of the new offences) not crimes, they were not investigated, prosecuted or even identified as risk factors (Stark 2012b, pp. 6–7). Although risk assessment tools and policies aimed at predicting and preventing domestic abuse and intimate partner homicide still tend to prioritise factors associated with physical violence (which may lead to the mistaken minimisation of risk: Myhill and Hohl 2016; Johnson et al. 2019), there has been increasing recognition. The following two parts of this chapter outline this increasing understanding of the role of coercion and control in domestic abuse and intimate partner homicide.

Well-established findings in the literature and research (including data obtained from domestic and family violence death reviews) on intimate partner homicide are that:

- it is a gendered crime, with men the primary perpetrators, and women the primary victims (Johnson 2008; Stark 2007, 2010; Bryant and Bricknell 2017, p. 4; Walsh et al. 2012; New South Wales Domestic Violence Death Review Team (NSWDVDRT) 2017; Queensland Domestic and Family Violence Death Review and Advisory Board (QDFVDRAB) 2017; Australian Domestic and Family Violence Death Review Network (ADFVDRN) 2018; Family Violence Death Review Committee (FVDRC) 2016);
- an identifiable history—either reported or anecdotal—of domestic violence exists in these homicides (Campbell et al. 2007; McKenzie et al. (2016); Domestic Violence Death Review Committee (DVDRC) 2017; NSWDVDRT 2017; Walsh et al. 2012, p. 4), with some offenders also having been violent towards a previous intimate partner other than the deceased (McKenzie et al. 2016, p. 42); and
- relationship separation, or a declared intention by the woman to separate, is a strong risk factor (Johnson and Hotton 2003; Dobash and Dobash 2007, 2009; Dawson et al. 2009), with the most dangerous time being the point at which the male partner realises that he has lost control of the relationship and/or over his female partner or ex-partner (Johnson et al. 2019; Juodis et al. 2014; Sheehan et al. 2015). In some cases, this risk of lethal violence may extend to the children (Jaffe et al. 2014).

In addition to these well-established risk factors, death reviews—reviews of the deaths of victims killed by their abusers, usually conducted in conjunction with coronial investigators—have facilitated a clearer focus on abusive behaviours (in addition to physical violence) that precede the killings, and have sometimes expressly used Stark's concept of coercive control (e.g. New Zealand Law Commission (2016), FVDRC (2016)), especially his concepts of resistance and entrapment.

Significantly, coercive controlling behaviours have been identified as an important risk factor for fatal violence (NSWDVDRT 2017, p. 149). A review of domestic violence-related deaths from March 2008 to June 2014 in New South Wales, Australia reported that in 77 of the 78 identified intimate partner homicides (99%), there was a clear primary domestic violence victim and a primary domestic violence abuser (NSWDVDRT 2017, p. 122) and that in these 77 cases the relationship was characterised by the abuser's use of coercive and controlling behaviours towards the victim. The abusive partners (all of whom were male) engaged in diverse behaviours, including psychological and emotional abuse (NSWDVDRT 2017, p. 123). In most cases, the perpetrator's controlling behaviour continued following separation (NSWDVDRT 2017, p. 14). Following on from this research the NSWDVDRT made two key recommendations

- that the operational training of police should 'include specific training concerning where non-physical domestic violence behaviours manifest as coercive and controlling conduct by the perpetrator' (NSWDVDRT 2017, p. 146); and
- that a public education campaign be conducted with the aim of improving the reporting of domestic violence, including physical violence and controlling and coercive behaviour (NSWDVDRT 2017, p. 174).

Another report from Queensland, Australia, also identified controlling and coercive behaviours in the history of men who killed their intimate partners. The authors noted that although many forms of domestic violence are criminalised (physical violence, sexual assault, stalking, property damage, threats and homicide), other non-physical forms of abuse—including coercive control—that did not constitute criminal offences could be just as harmful to victims and their families, causing them to experience fear, emotional and psychological torment, financial hardship and social isolation (QDFVDRAB 2017, p. 71). Disturbingly, when non-physical abuse (social isolation, belittling, humiliation, threatening behaviour, restricting financial resources and abuse of children, pets, and relatives), sexual (morbid) jealousy and even non-fatal strangulation were reported by victims prior to their deaths, the authors noted that this information was often 'not considered within the context of previous reports or other concerning behaviours, thereby further limiting the provision of effective supports or assistance' (QDFVDRAB 2017, p. 51). The authors further observed that from an evidentiary perspective, non-physical abuse such as stalking, threats to harm or kill and other controlling behaviour were often the hardest to establish as abuse, with victims having a difficult task establishing that apparently 'minor' or innocuous' acts could cumulatively cause trauma and a sense of victimisation (QDFVDRAB 2017, p. 57). This, in turn, could adversely affect the quality of police investigations and whether the evidence that is gathered was likely to be perceived as sufficient to sustain a prosecution (QDFVDRAB 2017, p. 71).

Further information about the role of coercive control in intimate partner homicide comes from a study by McKenzie et al. (2016). The researchers analysed 64 intimate partner homicides that took place in Victoria, Australia, between November 2005 and December 2014; 51 were committed by men. The researchers identified 43 men who had killed a female intimate partner, ex-partner or an actual or perceived male sexual 'rival'. Predictably, these perpetrators demonstrated many of the key risk factors for lethality identified in previous research and domestic/family violence death reviews. In over half the cases (27, 53%), there was evidence that the accused had been threatening, physically violent and/or controlling (for example, being jealous and/or possessive of his partner or being domineering and/or verbally abusive or preventing her from working in paid employment or engaging in social activities). While most cases involved a history of actual or threatened physical violence, in two cases there were evidence of controlling behaviour but no apparent history of physical violence. For example, in one case the deceased's mother described the accused as 'controlling' and as having engaged in 'mental bullying', saying that he 'wouldn't allow [the deceased] to go to work until it suited him' and that he 'resented' her going to social functions *(R v Baxter* (2009), cited in McKenzie et al. 2016, p. 53).

Despite mounting evidence of the significance of coercion and control in abusive relationships as a risk factor for domestic homicide, there is some evidence that judges do not adequately appreciate the significance of this abuse. For instance, in *The Queen v McPhee* [2013] VSC 581 (*'McPhee'*), there was evidence that the accused had been possessive and controlling towards his wife prior to killing her. At social functions, he would follow her to the toilet and wait outside (cited in McKenzie et al. 2016, p. 53). During a counselling session his wife had told the counsellor that when she told him that she wanted to separate, he became 'agitated and aggressive' and threatened to kill himself (*McPhee* at [3]). Commenting on the accused's previous possessive, jealous and controlling behaviour, the judge rejected McPhee's claim that he had lost control, but also went on to tell him that although the 'marriage had its strains and you had reacted aggressively in the presence of the psychologist, the marriage was not marked by violence' (*McPhee* at [25]). The judge further remarked on McPhee's lack of prior convictions and testimonials from his family, friends and colleagues which described him as 'hard working and reliable' and found that 'this conduct was totally out of character for you' and was, therefore, 'otherwise inexplicable' (*McPhee* at [25]–[27]). However, in this case, several 'red flag' indicators of a risk of lethal violence were present, including the accused's obsessive jealousy, controlling behaviour, alcohol misuse and threats to suicide using a weapon, plus the victim's desire to separate. The finding that the homicide was an 'inexplicable' out of character event sits at odds with the presence of multiple risk indicators.

4.4 Coercive Control and Self-defence

The concept of coercive control has not only informed understandings of domestic abuse and risks associated with intimate partner homicide, but has also contributed to understandings of claims of self-defence by women who have killed their abusive partners by giving considerable attention to the impact of non-physical abuse (emotional, psychological, economic) and the reasonableness of the reaction of an abused woman in such circumstances.

Self-defence is available for most crimes, most commonly homicide and assault charges, involving the use of, or the threat of, force to a person. A successful defence of self-defence results in a complete acquittal (Bronnitt and McSherry 2017, p. 349). The defence of self-defence now has a statutory footing in many jurisdictions, and while the definition varies across jurisdictions, the statutory versions of the defence are largely derived from the common law version (Crofts et al. 2016, p. 941). Until 2004 in Australia, the traditional (or common law) formulation of self-defence required consideration of several matters when determining whether a defendant's conduct was necessary and reasonable in the circumstances: the honesty of the belief, the imminence of the threat, the proportionality of the response and the possibility of escape (Crofts and Tyson 2013, p. 878). These formulations of self-defence developed in the context of a conflict or a physical confrontation between two people (usually men) of relatively equal strength, the traditional scenario being a barroom brawl or one-off duel (Victorian Law Reform Commission 2004, p. 61). As a consequence, women who kill their abusers have faced, and continue to face, numerous obstacles when trying to establish that their actions were taken in lawful self-defence, particularly in those cases where the killing occurs in non-confrontational circumstances (Hanna 2009, p. 1469). As Tarrant observes

> [a]t the heart of the criticisms of … [self-]defence is its inability to provide justice to an accused where they were responding to violence embedded in their everyday life, as opposed to violence in a once-off physical attack. (Tarrant 2018, p. 5)

It is perhaps unsurprising that most women charged with the murder or manslaughter of their abusive partners do not successfully assert self-defence at trial (Sheehy et al. 2012, 2014, 2015, 2018; Tarrant 2018; Tyson et al. 2015). There are many well documented reasons for this, including

> [j]urors may not hear all the testimony about the deceased's violence offered by the defence … [t]he woman's claim to self-defence may be hobbled by the fact she failed to disclose the abuse, seek help or leave the relationship … [a]nd, woman's credibility will be challenged by prosecutors who point to evidence of independence or prior violence by the woman to contest whether she was a "real" battered woman who faced lethal danger …' (Sheehy et al. 2015, p. 110)

While expert evidence of battered woman syndrome was previously tendered in the trials of women who killed their abusive partners, over the past decade researchers and advocates have moved away from the stereotypical view of the woman victim as 'helpless' and pathological, and now emphasise the impact of coercive controlling behaviours on abused women (Hayes 2013, p. 3; Dobash and Dobash 2004; Loveless 2014). Using coercive control models of domestic abuse has been identified as a strategy to support claims of self-defence and thereby obtain more just outcomes for women who kill their abusive partners (Sheehy et al. 2015, p. 110; Sheehy 2018). The particular value of expert evidence of coercive control as a framework for establishing a claim of self-defence is that it can provide social framework evidence that helps judges and juries to understand the dynamics of coercive control and the defendant's mental state (including the reasonableness of her conduct) within the broader context and realities of abused women's lives (Arnold 2009, pp. 1437–1438; Hanna 2009, pp. 1473–1474; Kirkwood et al. 2013; Naylor and Tyson 2017; Sheehy 2014, p. 696; Tyson et al. 2015).

The coercive control approach essentially shifts consideration away from an individualised, psychological focus on the defendant woman's behaviour and mental state to a broader consideration of the dynamics of the relationship and the context of her acts (Stark 2009, pp. 389–390). Stark describes his approach—as an expert witness for the defence, utilising the concept of coercive control—as one that 'stories' coercive control in a way that conveys 'the degree of subjugation battered women experience while still presenting them as autonomous subjects' (Stark 2009, pp. 1521–1522; see also Hanna 2009, p. 1469).

Tendering evidence of coercive control in the trials of women who have killed an abusive partner will likely confront significant difficulties. This is illustrated in the recent Canadian case involving Teresa Craig, who was charged with murdering her husband, Jack Craig, in 2008. Her claim of self-defence relied on evidence of battered woman syndrome and post-traumatic stress disorder. Additionally, expert evidence that Teresa Craig was a victim of coercive control was to be given by Evan Stark (Sheehy 2018, p. 102). The case was apposite for this evidence as, unlike the more frequent cases involving women who kill their abusers after experiencing physical abuse, Teresa acknowledged that she had never been physically assaulted by her husband during their 10-year relationship (Sheehy 2018, p. 100). However, she stated that she was fearful of him because he had been verbally and physically abusive towards their son, and verbally abusive toward, and very controlling of, her (Sheehy 2018, p. 101). The defence strategy provoked resistance from Crown prosecutors who successfully applied to have crucial sections of Stark's report redacted, which ultimately resulted in her claims of self-defence and defence of another being removed from the jury's consideration (Sheehy 2018, pp. 109–110). Teresa was convicted of manslaughter; her appeal against the trial judge's removal of self-defence was dismissed, but her sentence was reduced to time served (three years: Sheehy 2018, p. 111). Given the withdrawal of self-defence at trial, the benefits of using a defence based on coercive control can be questioned.

Despite this lack of success, feminist commentators suggest that it is a strategy that should be pursued because labelling victims of violence or coercion like Teresa Craig as 'murderers' or 'killers' when they acted to end their abuse is inconsistent with their degree of moral blameworthiness (e.g. Midson 2016, p. 418), and maybe the basis of a new defence for abused women (Sheehy 2018, p. 112). Recent developments in England provide some support for the latter possibility, at least in jurisdictions that enact an offence based on coercive control. In March 2018, Sally Challen's (second) appeal against her conviction for the murder of her husband was successful. Challen's original defence had been based on a claim of diminished responsibility. At the appeal hearing, her lawyers submitted new psychiatric evidence and an expert report showing how a framework of coercive control provided a mechanism for understanding Sally's conduct as occurring in the context of legally recognised provocation (psychological and economic abuse) by her husband (Justice for Women, n.d.). Although the re-trial will be based on a defence of provocation rather than self-defence, the outcome of this case will be broadly instructive in developing strategies for criminal defences based on the concept of coercive control. However, it is possible that future legislative reform may be required to ensure that notions of coercive control can inform criminal defences (Bettinson 2018, pp. 85–86).

Recent developments in Australian case law suggest the increasing effectiveness of using family violence evidence provisions as a social framework for understanding how coercive controlling behaviour can inform the context of homicide. The Victorian case of Bonnie Sawyer-Thompson involved a woman who killed an innocent male victim in the belief that it was necessary to do so to prevent her family from being killed by her abusive male partner. Bonnie Sawyer-Thompson's original defence to the charge of murder was duress, but on day two of the trial, after the jury had been empanelled, she entered a plea of guilty to defensive homicide (a lesser form of homicide than murder); the plea was accepted by the prosecution and she was sentenced to 10 years' imprisonment with non-parole period of 7 years (*R v Sawyer Thompson* [2016] VSC 767). In June 2018 her appeal against sentence was successful and her term of imprisonment was reduced to six-and-a-half years with a non-parole period of 5 years (*Sawyer-Thompson v The Queen* [2018] VSCA 161 ('*Sawyer-Thompson*')). In a joint judgement, Maxwell ACJ and Tate JJA observed that expert evidence of the *general* effects of family violence was helpful in establishing a context for a relevant accused's conduct and endorsed the statutory reforms that had facilitated the admissibility of this evidence (*Sawyer-Thompson* at [30]–[31]). The appellate judges referred to the submission by the applicant (Bonnie) both on her plea and in this Court, which was that 'this should be seen as a case' in which her belief may be said to have been reasonable:

> because of the threat by [her abusive male partner] that he would kill [her] family unless she killed [the victim], and because of the cumulative effect on her of [her abusive partner's] sadistic and controlling behaviour. (*Sawyer-Thompson* at [14])

In agreement with that submission, they further observed that Sawyer-Thompson's case 'fell "just shy"' of self-defence (*Sawyer-Thompson* at [14–15]). In this case, evidence of the general effects of family violence, including the impact of coercive and controlling behaviour, assisted the appellate judges to reframe the narrative of the homicide so that the family violence could be seen in its 'proper context' (*Sawyer-Thompson* at [43]). However, despite the reduction in Bonnie's sentence, it is significant that the murder charge was exchanged with a plea of guilty to defensive homicide. Many still argue that the preponderance of manslaughter convictions (or similar outcomes) in cases involving women who kill their abusive partners over time and across jurisdictions, suggests a court's willingness to show sympathy for the circumstances of victims of domestic violence who kill, but there is still a reluctance on the part of legal professionals to assess these circumstances in the framework of self-defence (Tarrant 2018, p. 212–213; Sheehy 2014; Sheehy et al. 2012).

4.5 Conclusion

The concept of coercive control has increasingly become part of the language and thinking of feminist researchers. It has informed research on domestic abuse and homicide and been identified as a significant risk factor for both non-fatal abuse and intimate partner homicide. It also has the potential to inform the criminal defences of women who kill their abusive partners (e.g. Bettinson 2018).

The push to criminalise coercive control in England and Wales, Scotland and Ireland has been underpinned by this research. While there is some controversy about the desirability of introducing a specific family violence offence modelled on coercive control (e.g. Walklate et al. 2018), this approach to domestic abuse is not restricted to facilitating the development of new offences. Models of domestic abuse and intimate partner homicide that centralise coercion and control and construct abuse as 'social entrapment' (FVDRC, 2016, p. 39) offer a potentially more complex and comprehensive conceptual model to use when investigating, presenting and interpreting facts in IPV, assessing risk, developing policies and responses, and developing criminal defences for women who kill their abusive partners (Tolmie et al. 2018; Tarrant 2018). Clearly, there is much more work to be done if we are to fully relinquish the 'violence model' or 'fight' paradigm of IPV in favour of one that takes account of coercive control. Until then, the law will continue to fail to protect those women who are killed by their partners, as well as those who kill their abusers and have limited access to a claim of self-defence.

References

Australian Domestic and Family Violence Death Review Network. (2018). *Data Report*. Domestic Violence Death Review Team: Sydney. Retrieved from https://www.whiteribbon.org.au/wp-content/uploads/2018/06/ADFVDM-Report_2018.pdf.

Arnold, G. (2009). A battered women's movement perspective of coercive control. *Violence Against Women, 15*(12), 1432–1443.

Bettinson, V. (2016). Criminalising coercive control in domestic violence cases: Should Scotland follow the path of England and Wales? *Criminal Law Review, 3*, 165–180.

Bettinson, V. (2018). Aligning partial defences to murder with the offence of coercive or controlling behaviour. *Journal of Criminal Law, 83*(1), 71–86.

Bettinson, V., & Bishop, C. P. (2015). Is the creation of a discrete offence of coercive control necessary to combat domestic violence? *Northern Ireland Legal Quarterly, 66*(2), 179–197.

Bishop, C. P. (2016). Domestic violence: The limitations of a legal response. In S. Hilder & V. Bettinson (Eds.), *Domestic violence: Interdisciplinary perspectives on protection, prevention and intervention*. London: Palgrave.

Bronnitt, S., & McSherry, B. (2017). *Principles of criminal law* (4th ed.). Sydney, NSW: Thomas Reuters.

Bruton, C., & Tyson, D. (2018). Leaving violent men: A study of women's experiences of separation in Victoria, Australia. *Australian & New Zealand Journal of Criminology, 51*(3), 339–354.

Bryant, W., & Bricknell, S. (2017). *Homicide in Australia 2012–13 to 2013–14: National Homicide Monitoring Program Report*, Statistical Report 02. Australian Institute of Criminology: Canberra. Retrieved from https://aic.gov.au/publications/sr/sr002.

Burman, M., & Brooks-Hay, O. (2018). Aligning policy and law? The creation of a domestic abuse offence incorporating coercive control. *Criminology & Criminal Justice, 18*(1), 67–83.

Buzawa, E. S., Buzawa, C. G., & Stark, E. D. (2017). *Responding to domestic violence: The integration of criminal justice and human services* (5th ed.). Thousand Oaks, CA: Sage.

Campbell, J. C., Webster, D., Koziol-McLain, J., Block, C., Campbell, D., Curry, M. A., et al. (2003). Risk factors for femicide in abusive relationships: Results from a multisite case control study. *American Journal of Public Health, 93*(7), 1089–1097.

Campbell, J., Glass, N., Sharps, P., Laughon, J., & Bloom, T. (2007). Intimate partner homicide: Review and implications of research and policy. *Trauma, Violence & Abuse, 8*(3), 246–269.

Crofts, T., & Tyson, D. (2013). Homicide law reform in Australia: Improving access of women who kill their abusers to defences. *Monash University Law Review, 39*(3), 864–893.

Crofts, T., Crofts, P., Gray, S., Naylor, B. G., Kirchengast, T., & Tudor, S. (2016). *Waller & Williams criminal law: Text and cases* (13th ed.). Chatswood, NSW: LexisNexis.

Dawson, M., Bunge, V. P., & Balde, T. (2009). National trends in intimate partner homicides: Explaining the decline, Canada 1976–2001. *Violence Against Women, 15*(3), 276–306.

Dobash, R. E., Dobash, R. P., Cavanagh, K., & Lewis, R. (2004). Not an ordinary killer—Just an ordinary guy: When men murder an intimate woman partner. *Violence Against Women, 10*(6), 577–605.

Dobash, R. P., & Dobash, R. E. (2007). Lethal and nonlethal violence against an intimate female partner. *Violence Against Women, 13*(4), 329–353.

Dobash, R. E., & Dobash, R. P. (2009). The murder in Britain study: Broadening the analysis of men who murder an intimate woman partner. In *Domestic-related Homicide: Keynote Papers from the 2009 International Conference on Homicide*, Research and Public Policy Series 104. Australian Institute of Criminology, Canberra. Retrieved from https://aic.gov.au/file/5742/download?token=A7fUDWye.

Domestic Violence Death Review Committee. (2017). *Domestic Violence Death Review Committee 2016 Annual Report*. Office of the Chief Coroner: Ontario. Retrieved from https://www.mcscs.jus.gov.on.ca/english/Deathinvestigations/OfficeChiefCoroner/Publicationsandreports/2016DomesticViolenceDeathReviewCommitteeAnnualReport.html.

Douglas, H. (2015). Do we need a specific domestic violence offence? *Melbourne University Law Review, 39*(2), 434–471.

Douglas, H. (2018). Legal systems abuse and coercive control. *Criminology & Criminal Justice, 18*(1), 84–99.

Family Violence Death Review Committee. (2016). *Fifth Report: January 2014 to December 2015*. Wellington: Health Quality and Safety Commission of New Zealand. Retrieved from https://www.hqsc.govt.nz/assets/FVDRC/Publications/FVDRC-5th-report-Feb-2016.pdf.

Hanna, C. (2009). The paradox of progress: Translating Evan Stark's coercive control into legal doctrine for abused women. *Violence Against Women, 15*(12), 1458–1476.

Hayes, B. E. (2013). *Women's resistance strategies in abusive relationships: An alternative framework* (pp. 1–10). July–September: Sage Open.

Jaffe, P., Campbell, M., Olszowy, L., & Hamilton, L. (2014). Paternal filicide in the context of domestic violence: Challenges in risk assessment and risk management for community and justice professionals. *Child Abuse Review, 23*(2), 142–153.

Johnson, M. P. (1995). Patriarchal terrorism and common couple violence: Two forms of violence against women. *Journal of Marriage and the Family, 57*(2), 283–294.

Johnson, M. P. (2008). *A typology of domestic violence: Intimate terrorism, violent resistance, and situational couple violence*. Boston, MA: Northeastern University Press.

Johnson, H., & Hotton, T. (2003). Losing control: Homicide risk in estranged and intact intimate relationships. *Homicide Studies, 7*(1), 58–84.

Johnson, H., Eriksson, L., Mazerolle, P., & Wortley, R. (2019). Intimate femicide: The role of coercive control. *Feminist Criminology, 14*(1), 3–23.

Juodis, M., Starzomski, A., Porter, S., & Woodworth, M. (2014). A comparison of domestic and non-domestic homicides: Further evidence for distinct dynamics and heterogeneity of domestic homicide perpetrators. *Journal of Family Violence, 29*(3), 299–313.

Justice for Women. (n.d.). *Sally Challen*. Retrieved from https://www.justiceforwomen.org.uk/sally-challen-appeal/.

Kelly, J. B., & Johnson, M. P. (2008). Differentiation among types of intimate partner violence: Research update and implications for interventions. *Family Court Review, 46*(3), 476–499.

Kelly, L., & Westmarland, N. (2016). Naming and defining 'domestic violence': Lessons from research with violent men. *Feminist Review, 112*(1), 113–127.

Kirkwood, D., McKenzie, M., & Tyson, D. (2013). *Justice or judgement: The impact of victorian homicide law reforms on responses to women who kill intimate partners, discussion paper 9*. Melbourne, VIC: Domestic Violence Resource Centre Victoria & Monash University.

Loveless, J. (2014). R v GAC: Battered woman 'syndromization'. *Criminal Law Review, 9*, 655–677.

McKenzie, M., Kirkwood, K., Tyson, D., & Naylor, B. (2016). *Out of Character? Legal Responses in Intimate Partner Homicides by Men in Victoria 2005-2014*, Discussion Paper 10. Melbourne, VIC: Domestic Violence Resource Centre Victoria. Retrieved from https://www.dvrcv.org.au/sites/default/files/out_of_character_dvrcv.pdf.

McMahon, M., & McGorrery, P. (2016). Criminalising controlling and coercive behaviour: The next step in the prosecution of family violence? *Alternative Law Journal, 41*(2), 98–101.

McMahon, M., McGorrery, P., & Burton, K. (2018). Prosecuting non-physical abuse between current intimate partners: Are stalking laws an under-utilised resource? *Melbourne University Law Review, 42*(2), (forthcoming).

Meyer, S. (2012). Why women stay: A theoretical examination of rational choice and moral reasoning in the context of intimate partner violence. *Australian & New Zealand Journal of Criminology, 45*(2), 179–193.

Meyer, S. (2016). Examining women's agency in managing intimate partner violence and the related risk of homelessness: The role of harm minimisation. *Global Public Health, 11*(1–2), 198–210.

Midson, B. (2016). Coercive control and criminal responsibility: Victims who kill their abusers. *Criminal Law Forum, 27*, 417–442.

Myhill, A., & Hohl, K. (2016). The 'golden thread': Coercive control and risk assessment for domestic violence. *Journal of Interpersonal Violence*. https://doi.org/10.1177/088626-516675464.

Naylor, B. G., & Tyson, D. (2017). Reforming defences to homicide in Victoria: Another attempt to address the gender question. *International Journal of Crime, Justice and Social Democracy, 6*(3), 72–87.

New South Wales Domestic Violence Death Review Team. (2017). *Domestic Violence Death Review Team Report 2015–2017*. Domestic Violence Death Review Team: Sydney. Retrieved from https://www.parliament.nsw.gov.au/lc/papers/DBAssets/tabledpaper/WebAttachments/72106/2015-2017_DVDRT%20REPORT%20PDF.pdf.

New Zealand Law Commission. (2016). *Strangulation: The Case for a New Offence*, NZLC report 138. New Zealand law Commission: Wellington. Retrieved from https://www.lawcom.govt.nz/sites/default/files/projectAvailableFormats/NZLC-R138.pdf.

Ortiz, A. M. (2018). Invisible bars: Adapting the crime of false imprisonment to better address coercive control and domestic violence in Tennessee. *Vanderbilt Law Review, 71*(2), 681–714.

Pence, E., & Paymar, M. (1993). *Education groups for men who batter: The duluth model/*. New York, NY: Springer.

Polk, K. (1994). *When men kill: Scenarios of masculine violence*. Cambridge: Cambridge University Press.

Queensland Domestic and Family Violence Death Review and Advisory Board. (2017). *2016–2017 Annual Report*. Queensland Government: Brisbane. Retrieved from https://www.courts.qld.gov.au/__data/assets/pdf_file/0003/541947/domestic-and-family-violence-death-review-and-advisory-board-annual-report-2016-17.pdf.

Sheehan, B. E., Murphy, S. B., Moynihan, M. M., Dudley-Fennessey, E., & Stapleton, J. G. (2015). Intimate partner homicide: New insights for understanding lethality and risks. *Violence Against Women, 21*(2), 269–288.

Sheehy, E. (2014). *Defending battered women on trial: Lessons from the transcripts.* Vancouver: University of British Columbia Press.

Sheehy, E., Stubbs, J., & Tolmie, J. (2012). Defences to homicide for battered women: A comparative analysis of laws in Australia, Canada and New Zealand. *Sydney Law Review, 34*(3), 467–492.

Sheehy, E., Stubbs, J., & Tolmie, J. (2014). Securing fair outcomes for battered women charged with homicide: Analysing defence lawyering in *R v Falls*. *Melbourne University Law Review, 38*(2), 666–708.

Sheehy, E., Stubbs, J., & Tolmie, J. (2015). When self-defence fails. In K. Fitz-Gibbon & A. Freiberg (Eds.), *Homicide law reform in victoria: Retrospect and prospects.* Leichardt: Federation Press.

Sheehy, E. (2018). Expert evidence on coercive control in support of self-defence: The trial of Teresa Craig. *Criminology & Criminal Justice, 18*(1), 100–114.

Stark, E. (2007). *Coercive control: How men entrap women in personal life.* Oxford: Oxford University Press.

Stark, E. (2009). Rethinking coercive control. *Violence Against Women, 15*(12), 1509–1525.

Stark, E. (2010). Do violence acts equal abuse? Resolving the gender parity/asymmetry dilemma. *Sex Roles, 62*(3–4), 201–211.

Stark, E. (2012a). Looking beyond domestic violence: Policing coercive control. *Journal of Police Crisis Negotiations, 12*(2), 199–217.

Stark, E. (2012b). Representing battered women: Coercive control and the defence of liberty. Paper presented at the *Violence Against Women: Complex Realities and New Issues in a Changing World* Conference, Québec, 29 May 2011.

Straka, S. M., & Montminy, L. (2008). Family violence: Through the lens of power and control. *Journal of Emotional Abuse, 8*(3), 255–279.

Tarrant, S. (2018). Self defence against intimate partner violence: Let's do the work to see it. *University of Western Australia Law Review, 43*(1), 196–220.

Tolmie, J. R. (2018). Coercive control: To criminalize or not to criminalize? *Criminology & Criminal Justice, 18*(1), 50–66.

Tolmie, J., Smith, R., Short, J., Wilson, D., & Sach, J. (2018). Social entrapment: A realistic understanding of the criminal offending of primary victims of intimate partner violence. *New Zealand Law Review, 2*, 181–217.

Tyson, D., Kirkwood, D., McKenzie, M., & Naylor, B. (2015). The effects of the 2005 reforms on legal responses to women who kill intimate partners. In K. Fitz-Gibbon & A. Freiberg (Eds.), *Homicide law reform in victoria: Retrospect and prospects.* Leichardt: Federation Press.

Victorian Law Reform Commission. (2004). *Defences to Homicide: Final Report.* Melbourne, VIC: Victorian Law Reform Commission. Retrieved from www.lawreform.vic.gov.au/sites/default/files/FinalReport.pdf.

Walby, S., & Myhill, A. (2001). New survey methodologies in researching violence against women. *British Journal of Criminology, 41*(3), 502–522.

Walsh, C., McIntyre, S. J., Brodie, L., Bugeja, L., & Hauge, S. (2012). *Victorian Systemic Review of Family Violence Deaths—First Report.* Melbourne, VIC: Coroners Court of Victoria. Retrieved from https://www.coronerscourt.vic.gov.au/sites/default/files/2018-11/vsrfvd%2Bfirst%2Breport%2B-%2Bfinal%2Bversion.pdf.

Walklate, S., Fitz-Gibbon, K., & McCulloch, J. (2018). Is more law the answer? Seeking justice for victims of intimate partner violence through the reform of legal categories. *Criminology & Criminal Justice, 18*(1), 115–131.

Wake, N. (2015). 'His home is his castle. And mine is a cage': A new partial defence for primary victims who kill. *Northern Ireland Legal Quarterly, 66*(2), 149–175.

Cases

Sawyer-Thompson v The Queen [2018] VSCA 161
The Queen v Sawyer-Thompson [2016] VSC 767
The Queen v McPhee [2013] VSC 581

Part II
Fixing a 'Gap' in the Law?

Chapter 5
An Alternative Means of Prosecuting Non-Physical Domestic Abuse: Are Stalking Laws an Under-Utilised Resource?

Marilyn McMahon, Paul McGorrery and Kelley Burton

Abstract The criminal law traditionally has focused exclusively on physical violence and some forms of financial wrongdoing. The recent interest in non-physical abuse has led to consideration of how this harm also might be addressed. Currently, much domestic abuse—including economic and psychological abuse—is indirectly criminalised via breaches of civil orders. This chapter investigates whether that abuse can, is and should also be directly criminalised through stalking laws, particularly in the context of an ongoing intimate relationship where the partners are cohabiting. In doing so, we discuss the broader issue of whether these laws constitute an adequate mechanism for dealing with non-physical abuse. We conclude that although stalking provisions can be used to prosecute non-physical domestic violence, restricted community and expert understandings of stalking suggest that the enactment of a domestic abuse-specific offence is a more appropriate solution to comprehensively deal with this form of abuse.

Keywords Stalking · Harassment · Family violence · Fair labelling

5.1 Introduction

Stopping domestic abuse has become one of the top priorities of governments in common law countries. Governments in England, Scotland, Ireland, Australia and New Zealand have adopted plans and introduced initiatives to reduce family vio-

---

An earlier version of Chap. 5 was published in the Melbourne University Law Review. We are grateful to the editors for permission to publish.

M. McMahon (✉) · P. McGorrery
School of Law, Deakin University, VIC, Australia
e-mail: marilyn.mcmahon@deakin.edu.au

K. Burton
School of Law and Criminology, University of the Sunshine Coast, QLD, Australia

lence. Underpinning these diverse government strategies are consistent themes: family violence involves more than physical violence, combatting it requires a coordinated and collaborative response between agencies and organisations, and the problem must be addressed in a cohesive, multifaceted and holistic manner (HM Government 2010; Scottish Government 2015, paras [1.1]–[1.9]); Department of Justice and Equality, n.d; Department of Social Services, n.d.; New Zealand Ministry of Justice 2016).

Contemporary strategies for dealing with domestic abuse now incorporate broad definitions that encompass more than physical violence; they include non-physical abuse as an integral component. While the dynamics of 'physical abuse' and 'non-physical abuse' are interactive, 'non-physical abuse' broadly refers to conduct that may result in myriad diverse harms, variously described in terms such as 'psychological', 'mental', 'emotional', 'social' and 'economic'. There is considerable overlap between these various terms, but collectively they operate to distinguish these harms from physical harms. What the non-physical harms generally share is intangibility; they are subjectively experienced by the victim without any necessary and invariant physical manifestation.

Definitions of domestic abuse, family violence and harassment in civil legislation (such as laws governing protection, molestation, harassment or intervention orders) often incorporate these broader definitions and include psychological or mental harm, alarm or distress, economic abuse and threatening or coercive behaviour. Indeed, many legislative definitions expressly acknowledge that 'domestic violence extends beyond physical violence and may involve the exploitation of power imbalances and patterns of abuse over many years' (*Family Violence Protection Act 2008* (Vic) s 5). In many jurisdictions, those who are at risk can obtain a civil order to obtain protection against a broad range of abusive behaviours. A respondent who breaches an order thereby commits a criminal offence (England and Wales: *Family Law Act 1996* (UK) s 42A; Scotland: *Domestic Abuse (Scotland) Act 2011s* 2(2); Australia: *Intervention Orders (Prevention of Abuse) Act 2009* (SA) s 31(2); *Crimes (Domestic and Personal Violence) Act 2007* (NSW) s 14; *Restraining Orders Act 1997* (WA) s 61), *Domestic and Family Violence Protection Act 2012* (Qld) s 177(2)(a); *Family Violence Protection Act 2008* (Vic) ss 123A(2), 125A(1); *Family Violence Act 2004* (Tas) s 35(1)(d)). Consequently, this two-step prohibition process is a mechanism by which economic, social, emotional and psychological abuse is *indirectly* criminalised.

There are a number of concerns in relation to this two-step process (Simester and von Hirsch 2011), particularly in the context of domestic abuse. Subjecting those who engage in non-physical abuse to criminal sanctions only when they are in breach of a court order can misidentify the real harm of the behaviour, may result in inappropriately low penalties, and can give the impression that the abuse *per se* is decriminalised in the absence of a protection/intervention order (Douglas 2007, 2015, p. 438). An overreliance on civil preventive orders may also constitute *under*criminalisation (a failure to adequately employ the criminal law) given that the true targets are significant wrongs and harms (Ashworth and Zedner 2011). Further, this civil/criminal hybrid form of criminalisation may negatively affect the legitimacy of the law as a whole, because it bypasses the procedural rights that should accompany the criminal process (Hendry and King 2017). The intermingling of civil orders and criminal sanctions for their breach raises the issue of how far the criminal law's reach should extend in *directly* regulating domestic abuse. In particular, to what extent should governments intervene and use the coercive power of the criminal law to directly protect family members from harms that have not been traditionally recognised by the criminal law, such as non-physical abuse?

The parliaments of England and Wales, Scotland, Ireland and Tasmania have answered this question by extending direct (rather than two-step) criminal liability to those who engage in non-physical abuse of their intimate partners. The offences of controlling or coercive behaviour (*Serious Crime Act 2015* (E&W) s 76; *Domestic Violence Act 2018* (IR) s 39), domestic abuse (*Domestic Abuse (Scotland) Act 2018* (Scot) s 1) and economic abuse or emotional abuse or intimidation (*Family Violence Act 2004* (Tas) ss 8–9) significantly extend the legal regulation of domestic abuse. When evaluating these offences and considering whether they appropriately broaden the reach of the criminal law, there is a need for a principled approach, one which balances the gendered and substantive harms associated with non-physical abuse with the appropriate limits of the criminal law. On the one hand, there are significant negative outcomes associated with long-term psychological abuse by an intimate partner, including human rights abuse (Stark 2007), substance abuse, psychiatric and physical disorders, homelessness and involvement in the criminal justice system (see McMahon and McGorrery, Chapter 1). On the other hand, the criminal law is 'a powerful, expensive, and invasive tool' (Simester and von Hirsch 2011, p. 211) which should only be used as a last resort (Husak 2004), and when used, should extend only as far as absolutely necessary (Moore 2013).

An even more fundamental consideration is whether, despite many common law jurisdictions not having *specifically* criminalised non-physical intimate partner abuse, such behaviours might already be *generally* criminalised through existing criminal laws. After all, a new law should generally only be introduced if there is a 'gap' that needs filling. The most immediately relevant laws that might be used to prosecute offenders for some forms of non-physical abuse of an intimate partner are those that prohibit stalking. The new family violence offences and stalking laws both prohibit conduct that is likely to result in non-physical harms to victims (Bjerregaard 2000; Davis et al. 2002), and are both premised on the proscription of *repeated* behaviours (i.e. 'courses of conduct') that are likely to result in those harms. A key feature of incidents of both intimate partner abuse and stalking is that the effect of recurrent incidents is cumulative; that is, the impact of the totality of the behaviour is almost invariably greater than the simple additive effect of each individual incident. Indeed, not only are there significant conceptual overlaps between stalking and domestic abuse, but many jurisdictions expressly link the two concepts. In Scotland, domestic abuse is linked to harassment (*Protection from Harassment Act 1997* (E&W) s 8A). In Australia, legislative definitions of domestic or family violence in several States and Territories include stalking (*Domestic and Family Violence Protection Act 2012* (Qld) s 8(2)(h); *Domestic and Family Violence Act* (NT) s 5(d); *Family Violence Act 2004* (Tas) s 7(a)(iv); *Family*

Violence Act 2016 (ACT) s 8(2)(d)). Additionally, in New South Wales, stalking provisions expressly specify that, in determining whether a person's conduct amounts to stalking, courts may have regard to any previous domestic violence by the offender (*Crimes (Domestic and Personal Violence) Act 2007* (NSW) s 8(2)). This seems to acknowledge that there is at least a link, and perhaps even overlap, between stalking and domestic violence. Indeed, when stalking legislation was originally introduced in New South Wales it was *limited* to domestic relationships (*Crimes Act 1900* (NSW) ss 562A, 562AB).

However, when stalking occurs within domestic relationships, traditional attitudes and practices associated with domestic violence may impede legal responses. For instance, research with police suggests that they are less likely to perceive behaviour as stalking when perpetrated by a domestic partner, as opposed to a stranger (Weller et al. 2013), are less likely to charge an offender with stalking when the victim is an ex-intimate partner, and are more likely to recommend that the victim obtain a family violence intervention order rather than commence a criminal prosecution for stalking (Pearce and Easteal 1999). Additionally, there has been some reluctance by the judiciary and prosecuting authorities to accept behaviour as stalking when the abuse was directed at a *current* intimate partner. In *R v GSH* [2000] the English Court of Appeal concluded that an ongoing relationship between the parties precluded the application of England's stalking laws, making 'estrangement' a precondition of criminal liability for stalking (*R v GSH* at [31]). This is, however, no longer the position at common law. There have now been several cases where men have been convicted of stalking their then-current female partners (see *R v Curtis* [2010]; *R v Widdows* [2011]). Nevertheless, guidance published by the Crown Prosecution Service of England and Wales still advises that stalking and harassment charges 'may be appropriate if the victim and perpetrator were previously in a relationship *but no longer live together*' (Crown Prosecution Service, n.d., emphasis added), thereby suggesting that if the parties were cohabiting at the time of the offence, stalking would not be an appropriate charge. These 'mixed messages' concerning the applicability of stalking laws to persons who were cohabitating at the time of the alleged offending indicates that the issue warrants further exploration and clarification.

This chapter explores the relationship between stalking laws and domestic abuse. In particular, using stalking laws from jurisdictions in Australia that do not have a stand-alone offence that criminalises non-physical domestic abuse, it investigates three key issues:

- whether stalking laws *can* be used to prosecute non-physical abuse between intimate (and especially cohabitating) partners;
- whether stalking laws *are* being used to prosecute non-physical abuse between intimate partners; and
- whether stalking laws *should* be used to regulate non-physical abuse between intimate partners.

5.2 Can Stalking Laws Be Used to Prosecute Non-Physical Abuse?

Stalking legislation was first enacted in California in 1990 and within a decade related legislation was introduced in most common law jurisdictions (Finch 2001). Although originally triggered by the stalking of celebrities, debates about stalking soon encompassed discussions of family violence (Burgess et al. 1997). A crisis was identified, particularly in relation to women who were being harassed by their ex-partners. The new stalking offences allowed courts to hear about courses of conduct in which the impact of the totality of incidents greatly exceeded that of individual events (Finch 2001). These offences also addressed a matter central to stalking, but traditionally regarded as largely outside the ambit of the criminal law: protection from mental harm (Finch 2001).

Stalking laws were often introduced as part of a system of dual regulation that incorporated both civil and criminal responses. That is, not only were criminal offences of stalking introduced but so too were civil orders prohibiting stalking (variously referred to as protection, molestation, harassment and personal safety intervention orders). In many jurisdictions the definitions of stalking in both the civil and criminal legislation are identical, although the maximum penalty for breaching the civil order is often much lower than the maximum penalty for the criminal offence of stalking (despite there being an aggravating feature where the behaviour occurs in breach of a court order: e.g. in Victoria, Australia a breach of an intervention order can incur a maximum penalty of 2 years' imprisonment whereas a conviction for stalking can incur a maximum penalty of 10 years' imprisonment: *Personal Safety Intervention Orders Act 2010* (Vic) s 100; *Crimes Act 1958* (Vic) s 21A). In practice, stalking has often been dealt with via the civil process (Willis and McMahon 2000).

In the context of domestic abuse, there would appear to be considerable scope for stalking laws to operate in this space. Stalking provisions are generally drafted very broadly. They do not require a particular prior relationship between offender and victim, and they extend to conduct well beyond the stereotypic stalker who is jealous, obsessively attached or delusional about another person. Criminal prosecutions for stalking have been initiated in diverse situations such as disputes between neighbours (*R v Dunn* [2001]) and bullying by fellow school students (*R v Barking Youth Court ex p B* [1999]). Further, as described in more detail below, stalking laws require a relatively low threshold of harm (if at all), and the mental element of the offence can usually be imputed to an alleged offender when it cannot be proven. Moreover, the offences often do not contain, as many other offences do, the qualifying phrase 'without lawful excuse' (e.g. see *Crimes Act 1958* (Vic) s 21A (4)). In the following section, we engage in a more detailed exploration of Australia's and New Zealand's various stalking provisions in order to unpack how they could be used in the context of non-physical domestic abuse, particularly where the abuse is perpetrated by a current intimate partner. In doing so, we apply three fundamental rules of statutory interpretation: the literal rule, which requires courts to interrogate the ordinary and natural meaning of a provision (*Amalgamated Society of Engineers v Adelaide Steamship Co Ltd* (1920); the golden rule, which permits courts to ignore the ordinary and natural meaning of the provision if it would lead to some absurdity or inconsistency (*Grey v Pearson* (1857)); and the mischief rule, which permits courts to have regard to the purposes of objects of the legislation if a provision is ambiguous (*Mills v Meeking* (1990). In the present context, we applied the literal rule to the various stalking laws in Australia and New Zealand in order to identify the mental elements (*mens rea*), behavioural elements (*actus reus*) and harm elements (*malum reus*) of each offence. We then assessed whether the meanings of these provisions, if used in the context of a charge of non-physical intimate partner abuse between cohabitating intimate partners, were clear and not absurd.

5.2.1 The Proscribed Behaviours

Stalking laws frequently include a unique list of specified behaviours that can constitute stalking. In some jurisdictions, the list is relatively brief and narrow in application; in others, the list of behaviours is not only lengthy and broad in application, but also includes a catch-all provision that prohibits *any* behaviour that could reasonably be expected to cause mental harm or arouse apprehension or fear. The relevance of a catch-all definition of stalking behaviour to non-physical domestic abuse is clear: there are countless behaviours by one partner against another—such as persistent humiliation, degradation, gaslighting and verbal abuse —that courts would likely have no trouble classifying as being reasonably expected to cause psychological harm, apprehension or fear. Indeed, in the context of an intimate relationship history characterised by years of physical and/or emotional abuse, the potential to cause such harm is magnified. Even certain 'gestures and eye contact' that the rest of the world would view as innocuous can be 'devastating to the person who is the target' (Scottish Parliament 2017, p. 92).

Of course, it could be argued that the *ejusdem generis* principle (which holds that 'words derive meaning from the context in which they appear') limits the ambit of the catch-all stalking provisions, because their reach should be contextualised and restricted by the preceding list of specific, prohibited behaviours (Pearce and Goodes 2014, p. 171). That rule, is, however, only applicable if there is a common or dominant thread, feature or genus that ties together the preceding list (*R v Regos* (1947) at 624). If no such thread or genus exists, the catch-all must be read broadly, as appears to be the case here. Indeed, Emily Finch has pointed out that the very purpose of the catch-all provisions in stalking laws is to capture behaviours that could not have been predicted, and to thereby future-proof the legislation (Finch 2001, p. 16).The catch-all provision should, therefore, not be considered limited by the context of the preceding enumerated behaviours; it is nearly impossible to discover a common thread between the behaviours in these lists (such as using offensive words at a person and following them surreptitiously). Examples of these catch-all provisions can be found in the stalking laws of Victoria (*Crimes Act 1958* (Vic) s 21A(2)(g)), South Australia (*Criminal Law Consolidation Act 1935* (SA) s 19AA(1)(a)(vi)), Tasmania (*Criminal Code Act 1924* (Tas) sch 1 s 192 (1)(j) and the Northern Territory (*Criminal Code Act* (NT) sch 1 s 189(1)(g)).

In the remaining jurisdictions, which do not have catch-all definitions of stalking, the enumerated specific behaviours could still often apply in the context of non-physical partner abuse, such as: intimidating, harassing or molesting another person (*Crimes Act 1900* (ACT) s 35(2)(j)); performing an intimidating, harassing or threatening act towards another person (*Criminal Code 1899* (Qld) s 359B(c)(vi)); and repeated communications, both direct and indirect, constituted by words or some other medium (*Criminal Law Consolidation Act 1913* (WA) App B, s 338D). Indeed, the New South Wales offence of stalking *coexists* in the same provision as an offence titled 'intimidation' (*Crimes (Domestic and Personal Violence) Act 2007* (NSW) s 13(1)), and these offences were expressly intended to capture family violence behaviours. 'Stalking' is exhaustively and relatively narrowly defined in New South Wales in a way that accords with traditional public conceptions of stalking behaviours: following a person; watching a person; or frequenting the vicinity of their residence, business, work or other place they frequent (*Crimes (Domestic and Personal Violence) Act 2007* (NSW) s 8). 'Intimidation', on the other hand, has slightly more *prima facie* overlap with family violence behaviours: harassment or molestation; approaching the other person—including via telephone or the Internet—in a way that causes them to fear for their safety; and any conduct that causes a reasonable apprehension of violence, injury or damage to a person or their property (*Crimes (Domestic and Personal Violence) Act 2007* (NSW) s 7).

5.2.2 The Harm Requirement

In contemporary criminal law, one of the most difficult elements of any criminal offence that prosecutors are required to prove is the experience of non-physical harm by a victim. There are a number of reasons for this difficulty. Establishing psychological, mental or emotional harm beyond reasonable doubt is an onerous task, given the 'invisibility' of such harms (Cassin 2013, p. 931); they are not as tangible as broken bones and bruises. Additionally, not only is it difficult to establish the presence of these harms, it is also just as difficult (if not more so) to establish beyond reasonable doubt that the offender *caused* that harm (e.g. see *Wodrow v Commonwealth of Australia* (1993)). Finally, courts occasionally retain a certain level of scepticism about the reliability of psychological diagnoses, particularly where reasonable experts disagree about the appropriate diagnosis (see, e.g., *R v Dhaliwal* [2006]).

Perhaps in light of these difficulties, stalking provisions often provide for circumstances in which the prosecution is under no obligation to prove that the victim actually suffered any harm. In South Australia, New Zealand and the Australian

Capital Territory, this is always the case; when prosecuting a stalking charge, it is not necessary for the prosecution to establish that the victim actually suffered any harm. In three other jurisdictions, the context will dictate whether the prosecution is required to prove actual harm. In particular, in Western Australia and Tasmania, the prosecution is only required to prove that the offender actually caused mental harm or apprehension or fear if the case is prosecuted (or resolved) on the basis that the offender was *reckless* about causing such harm (*Criminal Code Act 1924* (Tas) sch 1 s 192(3); *Criminal Law Consolidation Act 1913* (WA) app B, ss 338E(2), 338D, defining 'intimidate'). There is no such obligation to prove actual mental harm if the case is conducted on the basis that the offender *intended* to cause such harm. Somewhat similarly in Victoria, the question of whether the prosecution is required to establish actual harm is predicated on whether the offender was subjectively reckless (*actually* knew harm was likely), in which case there is no harm element required, or objectively reckless (*ought* to have known harm was likely), in which case the prosecution must prove actual harm (*Crimes Act 1958* (Vic) s 21A(3)(a)-(b)).

In the remaining Australian jurisdictions, the prosecution is (almost) always under an obligation to establish actual harm in order to prove the stalking offence. The Northern Territory requires the prosecution to establish either that the victim suffered mental harm, or that they experienced apprehension or fear (*Criminal Code* (NT) s 189(1)). In Queensland the specified harms (referred to as 'detriment') are relatively broad, and include: serious mental, psychological or emotional harm; preventing the person from doing something they are lawfully entitled to do; compelling the other person to do something that are lawfully entitled to not do; or arousing apprehension or fear (*Criminal Code 1899* (Qld) s 359A). In New South Wales, 'intimidation' requires that the prosecution prove actual harm (*Crimes (Domestic and Personal Violence) Act 2007* (NSW) s 7(1)(c)).

5.3 Are Stalking Laws Being Used to Prosecute Non-Physical Abuse?

Analysis of crime statistics published by various police and government agencies provides a snapshot of the types of relationships between victims and offenders in stalking prosecutions. There is significant variation in the rates of stalking recorded by police between jurisdictions, and this is likely due to differences both in the legislation and in police practices.

A number of jurisdictions expressly link family violence and stalking in relevant statutory provisions, and this may encourage police to more readily identify stalking as family violence, and vice versa (e.g. New South Wales: *Crimes (Domestic and Personal Violence) Act 2007* (NSW) ss 8(2), 13(2)). This could explain why in 2015–16, 21% of reported stalking/intimidation offences in New South Wales involved intimate partners: 8% involved current partners and 13% involved ex-partners (Bureau of Crime Statistics and Research, personal communication).

A similar link between family violence and stalking exists in legislative definitions of domestic and family violence in Queensland, the Northern Territory, Tasmania and South Australia (*Domestic and Family Violence Protection Act 2012* (Qld) s 8(2)(h); *Domestic and Family Violence Act* (NT) s 5(d); *Family Violence Act 2004* (Tas) s 7(a)(iv)). In Queensland, about 8% of all stalking cases recorded by police in 2015–16 (n = 720) involved a current partner, while 10% involved an ex-partner (Queensland Police Service 2016). This accords with a survey of Queensland magistrates in 2000, which reported that magistrates believed that family violence and stalking legislation worked well together and that they were comfortable making orders when harassment was non-physical (Currie 2000). Older data from South Australia presents a different picture. Analysis of criminal stalking incidents reported to police in South Australia from January 1995 to December 1999 reveals that stalking was most commonly perpetrated by ex-partners (44% of reports by female victims and 28% of reports by male victims), while only a small proportion involved current partners (4% of reports by female victims and 2% of reports by male victims: Marshall 2001). Data from Victoria, where there is no legislative linking of stalking and family violence, present a somewhat similar outcome; from 1 July 2016 to June 2017, 11% of reports of criminal stalking to police-involved current partners, and one-third of reports involved previous partners (Crime Statistics Agency, personal communication).

These data reveal considerable variation in the use of stalking laws to protect intimate partners from abuse, particularly those who were still in a relationship when the stalking occurred. With the exception of South Australia, it appears that jurisdictions that statutorily link family violence and stalking report relatively similar rates of criminal stalking by current and ex-intimate partners. What is particularly concerning are the low rates of criminal prosecutions of stalking of current partners in Victoria (where no such link exists) and South Australia, despite research indicating that most men who stalk their ex-partners begin the stalking while the relationship is ongoing (Brewster 2003; Mullen et al. 2009; Senkans et al. 2017). There could, though, be a number of explanations for this. It may be that victims are less likely to identify the behaviour as stalking while the relationship is ongoing. Additionally, victims may be more reluctant to report the behaviour if they hope to continue the relationship. Or police might be more willing to charge the behaviour as a criminal offence if the intimate relationship between the parties has ended (perhaps because it signifies a higher likelihood of a cooperative victim during the proceedings). It may also be that police do not identify non-physical abuse between intimate partners as stalking unless it occurs through the use of stereotypical stalking behaviours such as GPS tracking or other surveillance. In any event, these statistics indicate that stalking offences are sometimes being used to prosecute behaviours by current intimate partners. The next section of this chapter considers the final, and most important, question. Having established that stalking laws *can* apply in the context of domestic abuse, and that they sometimes *are* applied in that context, the normative question arises: *should* stalking offences apply to non-physical abuse between current intimate partners?

5.4 *Should* Stalking Laws Be Used to Prosecute Non-Physical Abuse?

The potential for stalking laws to be used to prosecute non-physical abuse between current, and especially cohabitating, intimate partners, raises important and competing rule of law considerations. On the one hand, the criminal law is deemed to be a knowable institution; to retain its legitimacy, it applies as equally to those aware of its contents as it does to those who are intentionally or inadvertently ignorant of them. From this perspective, all offenders are deemed to have constructive knowledge of the criminal law and can, therefore, be held accountable, even if they are caught unawares. This proposition is supported by what some have termed the authoritarian and 'thin ice' principles, which are described in more detail below.

In contrast, just because the criminal law is deemed a knowable institution does not automatically make it so. Penal legislation may be drafted ambiguously, judicial activism can operate to functionally criminalise that which was not previously criminal, or there may be so much discord between the content of criminal law and the public's understanding of it that its application would be incongruous. Ignorance of the law may not be an excuse, but perhaps justifiable confusion could be (see, e.g., Keedy 1908, p. 90; Cass 1975, p. 682). The criminal process is not simply a black-letter compilation of rules, regulations and judgments; it is also a 'social practice' (Lacey, 2007, p. 26), and as such must, in appropriate circumstances, bend to accommodate a level of normativity by reference to contemporary standards. From this perspective, offenders should only be deemed to have constructive knowledge of the criminal law if an ordinary person, fully aware of the substance of the law, could have (note the low bar of 'could' versus 'would') foreseen that they would be held accountable. This proposition is primarily supported by the principle of fair labelling, also discussed in more detail below.

5.4.1 *Principles Supporting Criminal Liability*

The authoritarian principle 'holds that a wide-reaching and flexible criminal law is justified, if it ensures that wrongdoing worthy of criminalization can more easily be brought within the scope of offences' (Horder 2016, p. 89). This principle effectively demands that, where appropriate, offenders should expect the unexpected and not casually assume that the criminal law is so rigid that it could not possibly adapt to their behaviour, particularly where the behaviour is clearly socially undesirable.

The related 'thin ice' principle then holds that 'citizens who know their conduct is on the borderline of illegality take the risk that their behaviour will be held to be criminal' (Horder 2016, p. 89). That is, even a particularly astute offender who studies the law for technical loopholes in order to flout their continuing wrongdoing should recognise that a court may shift the boundaries of which behaviours are criminal and which are not. Although reservations have sometimes been expressed about this principle (e.g. *R v Lavender* (2005) at 96), there is perhaps broader scope for its application in the present instance. Courts would not be engaging in the controversial task of 'creating' criminal liability where once it did not exist (see *Director of Public Prosecutions v Withers* [1975]; *R v Rogerson* (1992) at 304). Instead, the issue that courts would need to grapple with would be whether to actively stand in the way of this unanticipated (yet apparently already enforced) form of criminal liability, despite its patent application.

5.4.2 A Principle Opposing Criminal Liability

In contrast, a key principle that militates *against* using stalking laws to prosecute non-physical abuse of an intimate partner when the parties are cohabitating is *fair labelling*. This principle posits that 'the definition of an offence [should] *itself* give us an accurate moral grasp of what the defendant has done' (Horder 1994, p. 339, emphasis in original). The principle acknowledges that the criminal law has an important communicative function (Chalmers and Leverick 2008, p. 238). Labelling an offence with appropriate language informs would-be offenders that their behaviour will be wrong, and denounces it in the same language afterward (Simester and von Hirsch 2011, p. 205), allowing people to 'plan their lives with confidence' and 'live autonomous lives' (Simester and von Hirsch, pp. 225–226). A fair label also lets would-be victims know in advance that they have a right not to be subjected to that particular behaviour (and validates their understanding of what has been done to them afterward). It permits the community to engage in a unifying discourse about the behaviour, letting them gauge its seriousness at a glance. A proper label is particularly important in the context of describing an offence, because offence labels are often truncated descriptions of complex behaviours that exist on a spectrum. Conversely, labelling an offence with inappropriate language, or using vague or incomplete descriptions, can create false assumptions and speculations (Chalmers and Leverick 2008, p. 227). Moreover, attributing the wrong label to an offence can potentially undermine public confidence in the criminal law's ability to identify and punish that behaviour.

5.4.3 Balancing Competing Principles

The question then, taking into account these competing considerations, is whether courts should prefer strict construction principles and hold perpetrators of non-physical abuse criminally liable pursuant to what appears to be a relatively clear interpretation of stalking legislation, or whether they should prefer the principle of fair labelling and acknowledge that ordinary persons would not appreciate that non-physical abuse against current and cohabitating intimate partners could be classified as the criminal offence of stalking. Balancing competing rule of law principles, particularly when they are in direct opposition to one another, is no simple task (Horder 2016, pp. 65–70; Lacey 2012, pp. 24–25), but it is our reluctant conclusion that the latter consideration is more significant and that stalking laws should not be used in this manner.

The primary reason that we consider the use of stalking provisions to be under-utilised in the context of non-physical abuse by a current intimate partner is because—despite the distinctive manner in which the word 'stalking' has occasionally evolved in the last three decades (see Douglas 2015, p. 452; Parkinson et al. 2011, p. 1)—labelling family violence between cohabitating intimate partners as stalking does not accord with community or expert understandings of stalking. There is considerable resistance, in both socio-legal and psychological discourses, and in popular understandings, to the notion that current intimate partners might 'stalk' one another, particularly with behaviours that do not conform with stereotypical conceptions of stalking.

1. Fair labelling and understandings of stalking

It is now recognised that a great deal of stalking involves attempting to coercively control a victim, and that it is a crime predominantly perpetrated by men against women (Stark 2007). However, a review of community attitudes and professional discourses by criminologists, psychiatrists and psychologists reveals a major limitation in this understanding. While stalking is linked to domestic violence, a sharp bifurcation is manifest: 'family violence' occurs in ongoing intimate relationships, while 'stalking' occurs in relationships that have ended. Commentators routinely expressly refer to, or implicitly accept that, stalking occurring only after the ending of an intimate relationship (e.g. Goldsworthy and Raj 2014, p. 185). The pervasive, unconscious and taken for granted nature of this belief, shared by those who may be called upon to become jurors and those who may be called to appear as expert witnesses, makes it extremely powerful. Insofar as police, experts and members of the community (including victims and jurors) accept this bifurcation, it is likely to significantly underpin a reluctance to apply stalking laws to non-physical abuse that occurs between intimate partners who are living together at the time of the alleged offending.

2. Expert discourses on stalking

The dominant ways in which experts understand stalking are most clearly manifest in taxonomies of stalkers and/or stalking behaviours. These classification schemes originate from two principal sources: forensic psychiatric studies (e.g. Mullen and Pathé 2002; Mullen et al. 1999; Pathé and Mulllen 1997) and criminal justice reports (Mohandie et al. 2006; Spitzberg 2002; Wright et al. 1996). Despite the wide variety of definitions of 'stalking' employed, these taxonomies invariably use a previous relationship between stalker and victim as a key discriminating variable. Both forensic psychiatric studies and criminal justice research emphasise the significance of this relationship and identify stalking by a *previous* intimate partner as the most dangerous form of stalking (Mohandie et al. 2006, pp. 150–151; Pathé and Mullen 1997; Wright et al. 1996), with the risk of violence increasing if there is physical proximity between victim and perpetrator (Mohandie et al. 2006, p. 154; Meloy 2003) and rates of re-offending being highest in this group (Mohandie et al. 2006, p. 151). The possibility of stalking occurring between *current* intimate partners is almost entirely absent from this research.

This inherent (but not expressly identified) distinction in most professional discourses on stalking is even shared by researchers who have specifically researched both stalking and domestic violence. That research confirms a link between non-physical abuse by current partners and stalking (Mechanic et al. 2000; Mohandie et al. 2006, p. 152; Tjaden and Thoennes 1998) and identifies that many women who are stalked by an ex-partner were subjected to non-physical abuse while the relationship was ongoing (Brewster 2003; Mohandie et al. 2006, p. 149; Mullen et al. 2009; Walker and Meloy 1998). Thus, a history of abuse while the parties were in a relationship and cohabitating is frequently noted as part of the 'background' to stalking (Wright et al. 1996, p. 499; Mechanic et al. 2000; Brewster 2000). Links between the two phenomena are also established through common behaviours and shared characteristics of perpetrators. Sev'er (1997), for example, notes multiple characteristics shared by perpetrators of family violence and stalking, and suggests that violence by an ex-partner takes much the same form, and has many of the same dynamics, as violence by a current partner. Walker and Meloy (1998, p. 140) also note the close relationship; after describing the types of monitoring and control that exist in abusive relationships where the parties are cohabitating they observe that stalking is an extreme endpoint of these behaviours: 'when it reaches the point of monitoring, surveillance, and overposessiveness, and induces fear, it approaches stalking'.

Overall, these specialised studies simultaneously confirm a clear link between non-physical abuse between cohabitating couples and subsequent post-separation stalking, yet persist in labelling many of the shared behaviours separately and distinctively as family violence (pre-separation) and stalking (post-separation). The distinction is so entrenched that it seems to be natural and unquestioned; it also permeates popular understandings of stalking.

3. Community perceptions of stalking

Community perceptions of stalking and stalkers have been extensively investigated (e.g. Dennison and Thomson 2000; Weller et al. 2013; Scott et al. 2015). Again, a notable feature of this research is that it almost uniformly excludes the possibility of stalking occurring in an *ongoing* relationship; stalking is depicted as occurring only *after* the termination of an intimate relationship. It also reveals some interesting findings regarding perceptions of non-physical abuse. Research from Australia and the United Kingdom consistently indicates that there is a 'hierarchy of harms' with stalking that involves physical injury to the victim being regarded as more serious (Scott et al. 2010; Sheridan and Scott 2010). It also confirms the pervasive and continuing impact of the 'stranger danger' myth, demonstrated in the finding that stalking is most readily identified when there was no prior relationship between the parties (Scott et al. 2013; Sheridan et al. 2003; Hills and Taplin 1998). Curiously, and contrary to actual risk, members of the community are likely to view a stalker as less dangerous, are less likely to involve police, and will attribute more responsibility to the victim, when stalking is by a former intimate partner rather than a stranger.

In summary, constructions of stalking by criminological and forensic mental health experts, as well as by members of the community, most readily identify a perpetrator as a stalker when the relevant behaviour occurs *after* an intimate relationship has ended. The implications of this distinction are significant: non-physical abuse (such as putting a victim under surveillance or following her) that occurs after a relationship has ended is recognised as stalking (and may thereby constitute a criminal offence), whereas when those same behaviours occur in an ongoing intimate relationship when the parties are cohabiting they are more likely to be labelled as family violence and, therefore, not directly criminalised.

In our view, these findings undermine the potential use of stalking laws to protect victims from non-physical abuse by their current intimate partners. It might be argued that stalking statistics from some jurisdictions (particularly those that link stalking and family violence) appear to demonstrate that this limitation can be overcome by direct legislative linking of stalking and family violence and perhaps a strong public education campaign around the adapted meaning of stalking in a criminal sense. But even these strategies are likely to be insufficient to address the problem. For the reasons previously identified, we believe that the stalking of a current intimate partner is under-recognised and consequently is very likely to be under-prosecuted. Additionally, stalking laws do not capture the full ambit of non-physical abuse; for instance, they do not include economic abuse. Consequently, a new offence criminalising the unique forms of non-physical abuse that occur between current intimate partners appears warranted.

5.5 Conclusion

Various types of non-physical abuse are defined as family violence, but this abuse has usually not been directly criminalised. We have identified that under existing stalking laws, some perpetrators engaging in non-physical forms of abuse of intimate partners can be, and are being, prosecuted for stalking. However, given (1) that stalking of current intimate partners appears to be under-reported (and perhaps under-policed), (2) the broad legislative ambit of stalking provisions is incompatible with expert and community understandings of stalking, and (3) stalking laws do not prohibit significant types of non-physical abuse (such as economic or social abuse), we argue that stalking laws are not only very likely to be under-utilised in this context, but are inappropriate as the sole mechanism by which non-physical abuse is directly criminalised. The criminal justice system should no longer tolerate stalking laws being used as mental harm's catch-all provision in the criminal law (McMahon and McGorrery 2016).

So, how should we move forward? Although there appears to be concern that a specific family violence offence is inappropriate (e.g. Walklate et al. 2018), we fail to see how the ongoing humiliation, isolation and control of a current intimate partner could never warrant a criminal justice response. At the moment, in jurisdictions that do not have such an offence, victims' legal protection from this form of abuse is largely relegated to the questionable civil/criminal hybrid of intervention orders. There are, of course, legitimate concerns: the criminal law is not a panacea, and it would be a travesty indeed if a new offence were misused against victims rather than perpetrators. We therefore, suggest that the most appropriate response to this legal lacuna is to review the legislative models adopted in Tasmania, England and Wales, Scotland and Ireland, to conduct empirical research on their impact, and to then adapt and adopt the appropriate features of those models to directly and specifically criminalise non-physical domestic abuse.

References

Ashworth, A., & Zedner, L. (2011). Preventive orders: A problem of undercriminalization? In R. A. Duff, L. Farmer, S. E. Marshall, M. Renzo, & V. Tadros (Eds.), *The boundaries of the criminal law*. Oxford: Oxford University Press.

Bjerregaard, B. (2000). An empirical study of stalking victimization. *Violence and Victims, 15*(4), 389–406.

Brewster, M. P. (2003). Power and control dynamics in pre-stalking and stalking situations. *Journal of Family Violence, 18*(4), 2017–2217.

Brewster, M. P. (2000). Stalking by former intimates: Verbal threats and other predictors of physical violence. *Violence and Victims, 15*(1), 41–54.

Burgess, A. W., Baker, T., Greening, D., Hartman, C. R., Burgess, A. G., Douglas, J. E., et al. (1997). Stalking behaviors within domestic violence. *Journal of Family Violence, 12*(4), 389–403.

Cass, R. A. (1975). Ignorance of the law: A maxim revisited. *William and Mary Law Review, 17*(4), 671–699.

Cassin, S. (2013). Eggshell minds and invisible injuries: Can neuroscience challenge longstanding treatment of tort injuries? *Houston Law Review, 50*(3), 929–962.

Chalmers, J., & Leverick, F. (2008). Fair labelling in criminal law. *Modern Law Review, 71*(2), 217–246.

Crown Prosecution Service. (n.d.) Controlling or coercive behaviour in an intimate or family relationship. Retrieved from https://www.cps.gov.uk/legal-guidance/controlling-or-coercive-behaviour-intimate-or-family-relationship#a09.

Currie, S. (2000). Stalking and domestic violence: Views of Queensland magistrates. Paper presented at the *Stalking: Criminal Justice Response Conference*, Sydney, 7 December 2000.

Davis, K. E., Coker, A. L., & Sanderson, M. (2002). Physical and mental health effects of being stalked for men and women. *Violence and Victims, 17*(4), 429–443.

Department of Justice and Equality. (n.d.). *Second National Strategy on Domestic, Sexual and Gender-Based Violence, 2016–2021*. Retrieved from http://www.cosc.ie/en/COSC/Second%20National%20Strategy.pdf/Files/Second%20National%20Strategy.pdf.

Department of Social Services. (n.d.). *The National Plan to Reduce Violence Against Women and Their Children 2010–2022*. Retrieved from https://www.dss.gov.au/sites/default/files/documents/08_2014/national_plan1.pdf.

Dennison, S., & Thomson, D. (2000). Community perceptions of stalking: What are the fundamental concerns? *Psychiatry, Psychology and Law, 7*(2), 159–169.

Douglas, H. (2015). Do we need a specific domestic violence offence? *Melbourne University Law Review, 39*(4), 434–471.

Douglas, H. (2007). Not a crime like any other: Sentencing breaches of domestic violence protection orders. *Criminal Law Journal, 31*(4), 200–233.

Finch, E. (2001). *The criminalisation of stalking: Constructing the problem and evaluating the solution*. London: Cavendish.

Goldsworthy, T., & Raj, M. (2014). Stopping the stalker: Victim responses to stalking. *Griffith Journal of Law and Human Dignity, 2*(1), 174–198.

Hendry, J., & King, C. (2017). Expediency, legitimacy, and the rule of law: A systems perspective on civil/criminal procedural hybrids. *Criminal Law and Philosophy, 11*(4), 733–757.

Hills, A. M., & Taplin, J. L. (1998). Anticipated responses to stalking: Effect of threat and target-stalker relationship. *Psychiatry, Psychology and Law, 5*(1), 139–146.

HM Government. (2010). *Call to End Violence Against Women and Girls*. Retrieved from https://assets.publishing.service.gov.uk/government/uploads/system/uploads/attachment_data/file/118150/vawg-paper.pdf.

Horder, J. (2016). *Ashworth's principles of criminal law* (8th ed.). Oxford: Oxford University Press.

Horder, J. (1994). Rethinking non-fatal offences against the person. *Oxford Journal of Legal Studies, 14*(3), 335–351.

Husak, D. (2004). The criminal law as last resort. *Oxford Journal of Legal Studies, 24*(2), 207–235.

Keedy, E. R. (1908). Ignorance and mistake in the criminal law. *Harvard Law Review, 22*(2), 75–96.

Lacey, L. (2012). Principles, policies, and politics of criminal law. In L. Zedner & J. V. Roberts (Eds.), *Principles and values in criminal law and criminal justice: Essays in honour of Andrew Ashworth*. Oxford: Oxford University Press.

Marshall, J. (2001). *Stalking in South Australia: The Criminal Justice Response*, Information Bulletin No 25. Office of Crime Statistics. Retrieved from http://www.ocsar.sa.gov.au/docs/information_bulletins/IB25.pdf.

McMahon, M., & McGorrery, P. (2016). Criminalising controlling and coercive behaviour: The next step in the prosecution of family violence? *Alternative Law Journal, 41*(2), 98–101.

Mechanic, M., Weaver, T., & Resick, P. (2000). Intimate partner violence and stalking behavior: Exploration of patterns and correlates in a sample of acutely battered women. *Violence Victims, 15*(1), 55–72.

Meloy, J. R. (2003). When stalkers become violent: The threat to public figures and private lives. *Psychiatric Annals, 33*(10), 658–665.

Mohandie, K., Meloy, J. R., McGowan, M., & Williams, J. (2006). The RECON typology of stalking: Reliability and validity based upon a large sample of North American stalkers. *Journal of Forensic Sciences, 51*(1), 147–155.

Moore, M. S. (2013). Liberty's constraints on what should be made criminal. In R. A. Duff, L. Farmer, S. E. Marshall, M. Renzo, & V. Tadros (Eds.), *Criminalization: The political morality of the criminal law*. Oxford: Oxford University Press.

Mullen, P., & Pathé, M. (2002). Stalking. *Crime and Justice, 29*, 273–318.

Mullen, P., Pathé, M., Purcell, R., & Stuart, G. (1999). Study of stalkers. *American Journal of Psychiatry, 158*(8), 1244–1249.

Mullen, P., Pathé, M., & Purcell, R. (2009). *Stalkers and their victims* (2nd ed.). Cambridge: Cambridge University Press.

New Zealand Ministry of Justice. (2016). *Safer Sooner: Strengthening Family Violence Laws*. Retrieved from https://www.justice.govt.nz/assets/Documents/Publications/safer-sooner-report.pdf.

Parkinson, P., Cashmore, J., & Single, J. (2011). Post separation conflict and the use of family violence orders. *Sydney Law Review, 33*(1), 1–38.

Pathé, M., & Mullen, P. (1997). The impact of stalkers on their victims. *British Journal of Psychiatry, 170*(1), 12–17.

Pearce, A., & Easteal, P. (1999). The 'domestic' in stalking. *Alternative Law Journal, 24*(4), 165–169.

Pearce, D. C., & Goodes, R. S. (2014). *Statutory interpretation in Australia* (8th ed.). Canberra, ACT: LexisNexis Butterworths Australia.

Queensland Police Service. (2016). *Annual Statistical Review 2015–2016*. Retrieved from https://www.police.qld.gov.au/corporatedocs/reportsPublications/statisticalReview/2015-2016.htm.

Scott, A., Rajakaruna, N., Sheridan, L., & Gavin, J. (2015). International perceptions of relational stalking: The influence of prior relationship, perpetrator sex, target sex, and participant sex. *Journal of Interpersonal Violence, 30*(18), 3308–3323.

Scott, A., Lloyd, R., & Gavin, J. (2010). The influence of prior relationship on perceptions of stalking in the United Kingdom and Australia. *Criminal Justice and Behavior, 37*(11), 1185–1194.

Scott, A., Rajakaruna, N., Sheridan, L., & Sleath, E. (2013). International perceptions of stalking and responsibility: The influence of prior relationship and severity of behavior. *Criminal Justice and Behavior, 41*(2), 220–236.

Scottish Government. (2015). *Equally Safe: Reforming the Criminal Law to Address Domestic Abuse and Sexual Offences*. Retrieved from https://www2.gov.scot/Publications/2015/03/4845/4.

Scottish Parliament. (2017). *Official Report*, 28 September 2017.

Sev'er, A. (1997). Recent or imminent separation and intimate violence against women: A conceptual overview and some Canadian examples. *Violence Against Women, 3*(6), 566–589.

Sheridan, L., Gillett, R., Davies, G. M., Blaauw, E., & Patel, D. (2003). 'There's no smoke without fire': Are male ex-partners perceived as more 'entitled' to stalk than stranger or acquaintance stalkers? *British Journal of Psychology, 94*(1), 87–98.

Sheridan, L., & Scott, A. (2010). Perceptions of harm: Verbal versus physical abuse in stalking scenarios. *Criminal Justice and Behavior, 37*(4), 400–416.

Simester, A. P., & von Hirsch, A. (2011). *Crimes, harms, and wrongs: On the principles of criminalisation*. Oxford: Hart Publishing.

Senkans, S., McEwan, T., & Ogloff, J. (2017). Assessing the link between intimate partner violence and postrelationship stalking: A gender-inclusive study. *Journal of Interpersonal Violence, advance online publication,*. https://doi.org/10.1177/0886260517734859.

Spitzberg, B. (2002). The tactical topography of stalking victimization and management. *Trauma Violence and Abuse, 3*(4), 261–288.

Stark, E. (2007). *Coercive control: How men entrap women in person life*. Oxford: Oxford University Press.

Tjaden, P., & Thoennes, N. (1998). *Stalking in America: Findings From the National Violence Against Women Survey*. National Institute of Justice Centers for Disease Control and Prevention: Research Brief. Retrieved from https://www.ncjrs.gov/pdffiles/169592.pdf.

Walker, L., & Meloy, J. R. (1998). Stalking and domestic violence. In J. R. Meloy (Ed.), *The psychology of stalking: Clinical and forensic perspectives*. San Diego, CA: Academic Press.

Walklate, S., Fitz-Gibbon, K., & McCulloch, J. (2018). Is more law the answer? Seeking justice for victims of intimate partner violence through the reform of legal categories. *Criminology & Criminal Justice, 18*(1), 115–131.

Weller, M., Hope, L., & Sheridan, L. (2013). Police and public perceptions of stalking: The role of prior victim-offender relationship. *Journal of Interpersonal Violence, 28*(2), 320–339.

Willis, J., & McMahon, M. (2000). Stalking: Intervention orders. Paper presented at the *Stalking: Criminal Justice Response Conference*, Sydney, 7 December 2000.

Wright, J., Burgess, A., Burgess, A., Laszlo, A., McCrary, G., & Douglas, J. (1996). A typology of interpersonal stalking. *Journal of Interpersonal Violence, 11*(4), 487–502.

Legislation

Crimes Act 1900 (NSW)
Crimes Act 1958 (Vic)
Crimes Act 1900 (ACT)

Crimes (Domestic and Personal Violence) Act 2007 (NSW)
Criminal Code 1899 (Qld)
Criminal Code RSC 1985
Criminal Code Act 1997 (NT)
Criminal Code Act 1924 (Tas)
Criminal Code Amendment Act 1994 (WA)
Criminal Law Consolidation Act 1935 (SA)
Criminal Law Consolidation Act 1913 (WA)
Domestic Abuse (Scotland) Act 2018 (Scot)
Domestic Violence Act 2018 (IR)
Domestic and Family Violence Protection Act 2012 (Qld)
Domestic and Family Violence Act (NT)
Domestic Violence Act 1995 (NZ)
Family Law Act 1996 (UK)
Family Violence Act 2016 (ACT)
Family Violence Act 2004 (Tas)
Family Violence Protection Act 2008 (Vic)
Harassment Act 1997 (NZ)
Intervention Orders (Prevention of Abuse) Act 2009 (SA)
Personal Safety Intervention Orders Act 2010 (Vic)
Protection from Harassment Act 1997 (UK).
Restraining Orders Act 1997 (WA)
Serious Crime Act 2015 (E&W)

Cases

Amalgamated Society of Engineers v Adelaide Steamship Co Ltd (1920) 28 CLR 129
Barton v Armstrong (1969) 2 NSWR 451
Director of Public Prosecutions v Withers [1975] AC 842
Grey v Pearson (1857) 6 HL Cas 61
Knuller v Director of Public Prosecutions [1973] AC 435
Mills v Meeking (1990) 169 CLR 214
Ostrowski v Palmer (2004) 218 CLR 493
Phillips v Police [2016] SASC 135
R v GSH [2000] EWCA Crim 93
R v Barking Youth Court ex p B (Unreported, England and Wales High Court, Rose LJ and Forbes J, 27 July 1999)
R v Curtis [2010] EWCA Crim 123
R v Dhaliwal [2006] EWCA Crim 1139
R v Dunn [2001] Crim LR 130
R v Hills [2001] 1 FLR 580
R v Lavender (2005) 222 CLR 67, 96
R v Miller [1954] 2 All ER 529
R v Regos (1947) 74 CLR 613 at 624
R v Rogerson (1992) 174 CLR 268
R v Widdows [2011] EWCA Crim 1500
Wodrow v Commonwealth of Australia (1993) 45 FCR 52

Chapter 6
Evaluating Criminalisation as a Strategy in Relation to Non-Physical Family Violence

Julia Quilter

Abstract This chapter reflects broadly on the use of criminalisation as a strategy for addressing the harms and risks related to non-physical family violence. It aims to contribute to constructive dialogue over whether we should adopt new forms of criminalisation to combat non-physical family violence and, if so, how we should criminalise. This chapter is organised around three lines of inquiry. First, a consideration of whether a different 'logic' of criminalisation operates in relation to domestic violence when compared to other subject matter or 'sites' of criminal lawmaking. Secondly, a discussion about the care that needs to be taken when 'borrowing' criminalisation innovations to address coercive non-physical forms of domestic violence from other policy settings and jurisdictions. Finally, an examination of how we should approach the detection of a 'gap' in existing legal arrangements and the considerations that should inform what statutory architecture is appropriate for filling any gap so identified.

Keywords Criminalisation · Family violence · Law reform

6.1 Introduction

This chapter reflects broadly on the use of criminalisation as a strategy for addressing the harms and risks related to non-physical family violence. It aims to contribute to constructive dialogue over whether we *should* adopt new forms of criminalisation to combat non-physical family violence and, if so, *how* we should criminalise? The chapter is organised around three lines of inquiry, which are designed to assist in the production of answers to these larger questions. First, I consider whether, when compared to other subject matter or 'sites' of criminal lawmaking, a different 'logic' of criminalisation operates in relation to domestic violence. Second, I discuss the care that needs to be taken when 'borrowing'

J. Quilter (✉)
School of Law, University of Wollongong, NSW, Australia
e-mail: jquilter@uow.edu.au

© Springer Nature Singapore Pte Ltd. 2020
M. McMahon and P. McGorrery (eds.), *Criminalising Coercive Control*,
https://doi.org/10.1007/978-981-15-0653-6_6

criminalisation innovations to address coercive non-physical forms of domestic violence from other policy settings and jurisdictions. Third, I examine how we should approach the detection of a 'gap' in existing legal arrangements and the considerations that should inform what statutory architecture is appropriate for filling any gap so identified.

6.2 A Particular 'Logic' of Criminalisation?

In collaboration with other researchers (Luke McNamara, Russell Hogg, Heather Douglas, Arlie Loughnan and David Brown), I am involved in a project which examines the different 'logics' of criminalisation, including why and how it happens, and what forms it takes (McNamara et al. 2018, 2019). Criminalisation' includes 'the creation and enforcement of criminal offences, and the punishment of detected transgressions, as well as investing police and other state agencies with coercive powers in the name of crime prevention (McNamara et al. 2018). In this, I include punishment as part of criminalisation (cf McGorrery 2018). To bracket off punishment, it seems to me, assumes that it only commences at the moment of declaring a person's guilt which neglects the myriad ways in which police powers and pre-conviction orders operate as forms of punishment on the individual. As Malcolm Feely (1979) wrote many years ago, often the 'process is the punishment'.

In the first part of this chapter, I want to reflect on the logics that appear to be associated with criminal lawmaking in relation to family violence.

Our larger project's two key organising concepts are *processes* and *modalities* of criminalisation, for which we have developed novel typologies. I will briefly introduce these in turn, and then draw on a recent pilot study to offer a flavour of how these concepts might be deployed to support a more nuanced understanding of criminal lawmaking in relation to family violence.

6.2.1 Processes of Criminalisation

Our typology for illuminating the processes by which criminal laws are commonly made contains six categories:

1. *judge-made*: typically in relation to common law offences (and principles)—noting that lawmaking of this sort is a product of the adversarial system and is influenced by a range of actors and factors apart from judges, including prosecutorial decisions to initiate charges, defence strategies, submissions and arguments on both sides as well as jury verdicts.
2. *single-stage, executive controlled*: tends to be fast and driven by Cabinet with limited or no opportunity for consultation or independent input.

3. *internal government agency initiative*: legislative changes that have their origins in the discussions and workings of government departments, and which typically proceed on the basis of internal deliberation, with little or no external consultation, and are generally reflective of dominant intra-departmental imperatives and policy priorities, influenced by a range of factors, including ideological factors and considerations of budgetary efficiency.
4. *mandated statutory review*: legislative reforms that arise from a formal review of an existing statute, conducted by a government department (typically Department of Justice/Attorney General), but with some external consultation and opportunity for submissions, etc.
5. *government appointed inquiry/review*: describes situations in which governments establish a publicly announced inquiry, typically by a former politician or judge, which gives a degree of independence or appearance thereof from executive government.
6. *independent review by standing commission/committee*: a process sometimes characterised as 'textbook' or 'best practice', which has as a 'centrepiece' research undertaken by an expert organisation that is (relatively) independent of government.

Criminalisation scholars, particularly those concerned about overcriminalisation, have tended to focus on, and critique, the second of the six processes of our typology: single-stage executive driven lawmaking. It has been criticised as knee-jerk 'law and order' criminal lawmaking (Hogg and Brown 1998) and 'hyper-criminalisation' (McNamara and Quilter 2016). Examples of this process of criminal lawmaking often involve the creation of a new offence or other legislative mechanism through which the coercive and punitive parameters of the criminal law are expanded (such as restrictions on bail and parole, and serious sex offender schemes; see McNamara et al. 2018).

The single-stage, executive driven process of criminalisation often follows a tragic fatality involving an ideal victim (what may be called 'signal crimes': Innes 2014), which leads to a 'quick fix' legislative change usually in the form of the creation of a new offence. Such offences are created in haste, without regard to any expert input such as a Law Reform Commission or other expert groups, or any public or stakeholder consultation process, and often demonstrate the pitfalls of poor drafting, lack of coherence and operational difficulty. Often such laws have exceptional features (e.g. objective fault standards or strict liability, reverse onus of proof, mandatory minimum sentences), derogating from fundamental principles of the criminal law (e.g. the presumption of innocence, proportionality, individualisation and sentence finality).

Common targets of such processes are 'demonised' groups (McNamara and Quilter 2016) such as terrorists, bikie gang members and coward-punchers. A recent classic example of this process is the introduction of a new 'one punch law' in New South Wales (NSW) in 2014 following the deaths of Thomas Kelly and Daniel Christie (Quilter 2014). The new homicide offence, the first since 1952, was passed by Parliament in a single day without any known consultation, expert input or evidence base, and with exceptional features including a mandatory minimum sentence.

In addition to underpinning instances of hurried offence creation, the single-stage executive driven process is also often the motivating force behind changes to pre- and post-conviction orders, such as bail (Brown and Quilter 2014), parole (Bartels 2013; Fitzgerald et al. 2016) and regimes for the preventive detention or post-sentence monitoring of serious sex offender laws (McNamara et al. 2018, 2019). In these contexts, 'speed' is somehow constructed as symbolising a government that is taking community concerns seriously, means business and is 'in control' of the problem—rather than what it often does signify: a lack of understanding of the complexity of the legal and social issues and a willingness to make law 'on the run' for perceived electoral advantage.

Ashworth has reflected on this 'unprincipled and chaotic construction of the criminal law', which is deeply dependent on 'the fortunes of successive governments, on campaigns in the media' and the 'activities of various pressure groups' and has posed the question: is the criminal law a lost cause? (Ashworth 2000, pp. 225–226). The answer to that question is a very important one for the issues addressed in this collection.

There is a tendency amongst critical criminalisation scholars to tar all or most contemporary criminal lawmaking with the same knee-jerk and overcriminalisation brushes. One of the objectives of the larger long-term criminalisation project in which I am involved is to adopt a more nuanced approach to understanding processes of criminalisation, with a stronger empirical foundation. Our early work suggests that processes of criminalisation are more diverse than is often assumed, and that this point is exemplified by criminalisation directed at family violence.

In a recent pilot study (McNamara et al. 2018), we collected all criminal law statutes related to 10 selected criminalisation sites enacted by the legislatures of NSW, Queensland and Victoria during the 5 year period from 2012–2016. One of our sites was domestic violence.

For the purpose of this study, 'criminal law statute' was defined broadly as a statute that:

- creates or deletes/removes a new offence or contracts/expands an existing offence;
- increases/decreases a penalty, establishes a mandatory penalty or changes sentencing laws;
- increases/decreases the powers of police or other state agencies; and/or
- changes the procedures by which criminal offences and allied powers are administered.

Our primary aim with this initial deployment of our novel conceptual framework was to shed light on the range of different processes and modalities in contemporary Australian criminal lawmaking. We also sought to identify any noteworthy jurisdictional similarities and differences, in a context where there is evidence that the turn to criminalisation can be triggered by 'local' events and drivers, and be a

Table 6.1 Process of criminalisation—domestic violence statutes, 2012–2016

	NSW	QLD	VIC	Total[a]
1. Judge-made	–	–	–	–
2. Single-stage executive controlled	–	–	–	–
3. Internal government agency initiative	4	–	3	7
4. Departmental statutory review	2	–	–	2
5. Government appointed inquiry/review	0	5	–	5
6. Independent review commission/committee	2	2	1	5

[a]The total sums to 20 as four statutes attracted two processes codes and different parts of the statute were the product of different processes

product of cross-jurisdictional 'borrowing' (Quilter 2015; McNamara and Quilter 2016; McNamara 2017).

Our search identified 107 criminal law statutes that were enacted between 2012 and 2016: 45 in NSW; 42 in Victoria; and 20 in Queensland. Sixteen of these statutes (7 in NSW; 4 in Victoria; 5 in Queensland) addressed domestic violence, constituting a significant 15% of the total number of statutes passed during the review period.

Even more notable than the volume of criminal lawmaking concerned with domestic violence is that, in stark contrast to its influence in other criminalisation sites, there was not a single instance in the review period of domestic violence legislation that was the product of process 2: single-stage executive-driven process (see Table 6.1). All instances of domestic violence-related criminal lawmaking resulted from one or more of processes 3, 4, 5 and 6. Sound stakeholder consultation and backing, and bipartisan political support, were routinely associated with domestic violence-related criminal lawmaking during the period under review.

While it fell outside of the study period, I note one exception to this 'rule' that I am aware of, involving the tragic murder of Teresa Bradford in Queensland on 31 January 2017 by her estranged husband David Bradford. He was on bail in relation to serious domestic violence offences against her. Her death was subject to significant media attention. Although the Queensland Attorney General announced a review of the bail system on 2 February 2017, the Opposition Leader proposed a private members Bill with numerous punitive changes. The Bill was referred to the Legal Affairs and Community Safety Committee which found, unsurprisingly, that the Bill required more consultation and significant amendment in light of potential unintended consequences. Despite this, three business days later, the government moved a number of amendments and passed the Bill into law (*Bail (Domestic Violence) and Another Act Amendment Act 2017* (Qld)). Presumptions against bail were created for a number of domestic violence offences, a consideration regarding domestic violence risk was added to the unacceptable risk determination, and a bail condition requiring bailees to wear GPS tracking devices was created. (It is worth noting that these quick-fire changes were directed at bail laws, which have long been a focus of fast executive driven 'law and order'-style criminal lawmaking; Brown and Quilter 2014.)

This exception aside, it is striking that while one-punchers, outlaw motorcycle gangs, terrorists, sex offenders and other demonised groups are often subject to quick fix high visibility legislative changes, usually involving draconian offences and other pre- and post-conviction regulation, the hallmarks of legislative change in relation to domestic violence are quite different. Processes tend to be unhurried and evidenced-based, involving thorough consultation with experts and stakeholders. In 2012–2016 alone—that is, the 5 year period we examined in our pilot criminalisation study (McNamara et al. 2018)—legislative change was informed by numerous reports and inquiries: ALRC and NSWLRC 2010; NSW Legislative Council Standing Committee on Social Issues 2012; NSW Domestic Violence Death Review Team 2012, 2013, 2015, 2017; NSW Attorney General & Justice 2012; Council of Australian Governments 2015; NSW Justice 2015; NSW Legislative Council Select Committee on Partial Defence of Provocation 2013; Commonwealth Department of Social Services 2011; Queensland Government 2015; Queensland Special Taskforce on Domestic and Family Violence 2015; Parliament of Australia, Senate Finance and Public Administration References Committee 2015; Royal Commission into Family Violence (Victoria) 2016; Victorian Department of Justice 2013; and Victorian Government 2012.

We are still unpacking the complex pictures that are being revealed by exploratory analysis of data on processes of criminalisation, but here I offer some initial reflections. There seems to be asymmetry or disjunction between the need and speed in offence creation: the speed of enacting one punch laws despite the infrequency of one-punch deaths, versus the daily urgency of domestic violence in women's lives and the relatively glacial pace of change. This observation presents a conundrum: the slow, evidence-based pace of change is ironically what criminalisation scholars would advocate as 'good practice' against the 'bad practice' of 'knee-jerk' and single-stage executive processes. Yet I am uncertain whether to condemn or exalt this difference, given it so overwhelmingly operates in the family violence context. At a minimum, this seems to have symbolic implications. Arguably, the 'hasten' slowly approach reflects a troubling lack of urgency and an undervaluing and de-prioritisation of the needs of family violence victims. What should we make of the fact that the tragedies of the victims of 'one punch' drunken violence or 'drive-by shootings' animate urgent law reform action, whereas years of tallying the annual number of 'dead women', killed by their (current or former) domestic partners, does not?

6.2.2 Modalities of Criminalisation

The second organising concept in our criminalisation project is what we call 'modalities' of criminalisation (McNamara et al. 2018)—that is, the particular 'method or procedure' (Stevenson 2015) by which the coercive and punitive parameters of the criminal law are set and changed. While the focus of many critiques of overcriminalisation is on the creation of new offences, our conception of modalities argues that criminalisation is much more diverse than that, and takes a multiplicity of forms. Offence creation is simply one of the ways in which the reach of the criminal justice system is extended (for better or worse). Our project adopts four high-level characterisations to account for legislation that:

1. *expands* or extends the parameters of criminalisation;
2. *contracts* or narrows the parameters of criminalisation;
3. represents a relatively 'neutral' attempt to *rationalise* the statute books; or
4. attempts to better support the interests of *victims* of criminal harm.

We have identified nine sub-modalities of *expanding* criminalisation (1a–1i), and six sub-modalities of *contracting* criminalisation (2a–2f):

1a   offence creation
1b   offence expansion
1c   penal intensification (including increasing penalties, mandatory penalties, sentencing aggravating factors and other related procedural changes)
1d   restricting defences (including reverse onus provisions)
1e   expanding enforcement powers (including police powers as well as the powers of other state agencies including prosecution and corrections)
1f   expanding pre/post-correctional powers (including pre-conviction remand and bail conditions, post-sentence detention and post-release conditions)
1g   reducing procedural safeguards
1h   civil–criminal hybridity (that is, 'two-step' criminalisation, where conditions are imposed under a civil order and breach is a criminal offence)
1i   compliance regimes (that is, where criminal sanctions form part of a regulatory compliance regime)
2a   enhancing procedural safeguards
2b   expanding defences
2c   depenalisation
2d   diversionary programs
2e   narrowing offences
2f   decriminalisation

Further, the fourth modality (the 'victims' modality) is defined by—

> …legislative changes that have as their object, improvement in the victim's experience of the criminal justice system. This may involve a more active role for the victim in the process (like victim impact statements), protective measures to ensure minimisation of criminal trial trauma (such as permitting victims to give evidence via special arrangement such as video link), or formally articulating the rights of victims. We recognise that many modalities of criminalisation (e.g. higher penalties) are motivated by (or are said to be motivated by) a desire to better respond to crime victimisation or, more amorphously, enhance the 'safety' of members of the public. Such measures are more likely to fit within our 'expanding criminalisation' modality. However, we believe there is value in attempting to identify a separate and discrete 'victims' modality encompassing laws that attempt to respond to the needs of victims by enhancing their experience of the criminal justice system. (McNamara et al. 2018, p. 97)

Table 6.2 Modalities of criminalisation—domestic violence statutes, 2012–2016

	NSW	QLD	VIC	Total
Expanding	5	14	5	24
Contracting	–	1	2	3
Rationalisation	–	–	2	2
Victims	5	2	4	11

Table 6.3 Most common sub-modalities of expanding criminalisation—domestic violence statutes, 2012–2016

	NSW	QLD	VIC	Total
Offence creation (1a)	2	3	1	6
Increasing penalties (1c)	–	3	1	4
Expanding enforcement powers (1e)	1	3	1	5
Civil–criminal hybridity (1h)	1	2	1	4

As noted earlier, 16 of the 107 statutes in our study directly related to domestic violence. The majority of these were amendments to specialist domestic violence statutes (such as the *Crimes (Domestic and Personal Violence) Act 2007* (NSW)), but there were some instances related to general defences (e.g. extreme provocation in NSW) and new offences (e.g. strangulation) in primary general criminal law statutes (e.g. *Crimes Act 1900* (NSW)).

Table 6.2 summarises the findings from applying the modalities categories to the 16 statutes enacted during the period under review (2012–2016) that directly impact on domestic violence.[1] Expanding the parameters of criminalisation was the most frequent modality in operation (as it was for all sites in our study). Table 6.3 summarises findings on the most common sub-modalities of expanding criminalisation.

Offence creation was the most common form of expansion with new family violence-related offences created in the review period including: strangulation in NSW and Queensland; copying/publishing to any other person a recording of a domestic violence complainants' evidence in chief in NSW; contravening a police protection notice and contravening a release condition in Queensland; failing to comply with a direction given by police to remain at a particular place in order to serve a protection order in Queensland; and breaching a family violence safety notice in Victoria. Note, however, that 13 of the 24 instances (Table 6.3) of

---

[1]We did not set out to offer a precise quantitative analysis of the nature of criminalisation legislation. Nor were we attempting to produce a comprehensive calculation of the volume of criminal law making in the selected jurisdictions. As noted above, we limited the scope of our study to laws affecting 10 important 'sites' of criminalisation. Note that, consistent with our project objectives, we identified whether a statute reflected a particular modality, not how many times that modality was reflected. For example, a statute may have created three new offences. (See further McNamara et al., 2018).

domestic violence-related expanded criminalisation did not involve the creation of new offences. Rather, they involved increasing penalties, expansions in state (typically police) powers and/or the adoption of 'hybrid' civil–criminal models.

The three instances of contracting criminalisation related to an enhanced procedural safeguard in Queensland, requiring a court to ensure parties understand the DVO, and the abolition of defensive homicide in Victoria (which was coded as both expanding defences and decriminalisation).

Eleven domestic violence-related statutes were categorised as involving the victims modality (including five in NSW, two in Queensland and four in Victoria). This figure accounts for more than half of all instances in our study of 107 Acts in which the victims modality was in play (21 instances in total: McNamara et al. 2018). Apart from domestic violence, the other 'site' in our study where the victims modality was common was sexual assault. Many of these instances (both domestic violence and sexual assault) reflect amendments which are part of a wider strategy of easing the burden imposed on victims giving evidence in criminal trials. For example, the *Criminal Procedure Amendment (Domestic Violence Complainants) Act 2014* (NSW) amended the *Criminal Procedure Act 1999 (NSW)* to allow a domestic violence complainant's evidence in chief to be recorded by video/audio statement in criminal proceedings for a domestic violence offence.

What broader implications can we draw from this analysis? It seems to me that in addition to the evidence-based, slow-paced legislative reform revealed by our processes analysis, another feature of domestic violence-focused criminal lawmaking is an emphasis on attempting to ease the burden of criminal justice system involvement on domestic violence complainants. This may reflect a number of possible issues relevant to the criminalisation of non-physical family violence.

First, criminalisation in the form of creating new offences may not be the priority of domestic violence victims. Many studies have underscored the significant problem of what has been called 'legal systems abuse' for domestic violence complainants in their treatment by the criminal justice system (e.g. Douglas 2018). It appears that ameliorating these issues are, appropriately, at the forefront of the minds of legislative reformers. Criminalisation may also be a high-stakes strategy, with 'victims' themselves being subjected to criminalisation (Tolmie 2018), 'mandatory arrest' (as that policy operates in some jurisdictions in the USA) and/or the subject of cross-orders in AVOs (e.g. Chesney-Lind 2006, pp. 14–20; Douglas 2008).

Second, one of the strengths of the modalities approach is the way it helps to illuminate the interrelationship between forms of criminalisation. The creation of a new offence—such as for non-physical family violence—will have impacts on other aspects of criminal justice administration and associated legislation, including: investigation and policing powers; bail laws; how and what evidence is collected and later led in any proceedings; how evidence is to be given and how cross-examination is to occur; what defences are available; sentencing options and the availability of forms of therapeutic justice. Any consideration of a new offence of psychological or non-physical harm, must be approached in conjunction with consideration of allied reforms of this sort.

6.3 Models of Criminalisation: Pitfalls of Policy Transfer and Cross-Jurisdictional Borrowing in a Federation

The focus of this collection is on the criminalisation of psychological abuse or non-physical family violence. And there is clearly significant evidence that much family violence involves a 'course of conduct' or 'pattern' of harmful behaviour (e.g. Stark 2007; NSW Domestic Violence Death Review Team 2017). The harm involved in such behaviour is often non-violent or psychological in nature.

The concept of 'coercive control' is one attempt to capture both this pattern and type of harm. A notable example of statutory take-up of this formula is the offence in s 76 of the *Serious Crime Act 2015* (E&W) entitled 'Controlling or coercive behaviour in an intimate or family relationship'. Australian legislators have also adopted definitions of family violence that feature coercive control. For example, the *Family Law Act 1975* (Cth) s 4AB(1) provides that 'family violence':

(1) … means violent, threatening or other behaviour by a person that *coerces or controls* a member of the person's family (the family member), or causes the family member to be fearful.
(2) Examples of behaviour that may constitute family violence include (but are not limited to) as follows:

  …

  (g) unreasonably denying the family member the financial autonomy that he or she would otherwise have had; or
  (h) unreasonably withholding financial support needed to meet the reasonable living expenses of the family member, or his or her child, at a time when the family member is entirely or predominantly dependent on the person for financial support; or
  (i) preventing the family member from making or keeping connections with his or her family, friends or culture; or
  (j) unlawfully depriving the family member, or any member of the family member's family, of his or her liberty.

Against this trend, Scotland recently created the offence of 'domestic abuse'—involving a course of behaviour which is abusive of the partner or ex-partner (*Domestic Abuse (Scotland) Act 2018* (Scot)). And well over a decade ago, in 2004, Tasmania opted for new offences of economic and emotional abuse (*Family Violence Act 2004* (Tas) ss 8 and 9), which focus on a course of conduct with the specific intent of 'unreasonably controlling or intimidating, or causing mental harm, apprehension or fear' (s 9)—noting that that specific intent may be proved by knowledge or what a person 'ought to know, is likely to' have that effect.

Rather than assessing the legal and operational merits of these different legal formulations (noting that such work has been done by others, see for example, Douglas 2015; Bettinson 2015; McMahon and McGorrery 2016a), I want to highlight two broader and related issues in relation to cross-jurisdictional 'borrowing' when considering the criminalisation of these forms of harm. The first relates to the issue of crime policy transfer, and the second relates to the Australian federal context in which criminal laws operate.

On the first issue, we should be cautious of any simple criminalisation policy transfer strategy (Newburn 2002; Jones and Newburn 2002a, b) whether from the UK, Scotland (or Tasmania) that does not engage in a course of proper 'translation' to the local context. As has been discussed by others, the offences in the UK and Scotland have different origins and motivating factors. None, or perhaps only some, may be relevant to the Australian domestic context. For example, Bettinson (2016) has highlighted that the impetus for the UK offence was recognition of the inadequacy of police responses and particularly the inability of police officers to accurately identify dangerous patterns of abusive behaviour in perpetrators. By contrast, Scotland's commitment to the implementation of *Preventing Domestic Abuse: A National Strategy* (Scottish Government, 2003) provides a different context for criminalisation. Bettinson (2016) argues that Scottish laws 'capture a wider range of conduct and harm compared to England and Wales' (p. 175). Further, Bettinson (2016) emphasises that the Scottish National Strategy led to significant changes to address domestic abuse including 'a specialist pro-active police force that works constructively with the prosecution authorities in matters of domestic abuse', the use of specialist domestic abuse courts, and a context in which family violence cases are already treated as an aggravated offence (pp. 175–176).

Other issues—although perhaps of lesser significance—include the fact that there appear to be significant differences between UK understandings of existing offences, such as stalking, compared to Australia. The Home Office *Controlling or Coercive Behaviour in an Intimate or Family Relationship: Statutory Guidance Framework* (p. 6, decisions cited at [15]) indicates that judicial treatment of the laws of stalking and harassment means that they do not apply to controlling or coercive behaviour that takes place in an *ongoing* intimate relationship. While it would not be decisive of the decision to criminalise, Australian laws on stalking and intimidation do not appear to be limited in this way (see, e.g. *Crimes (Domestic and Personal Violence) Act 2007* (NSW) ss 5, 7, 13; c.f. McMahon et al., Chap. 4).

Finally, it has been noted that the language of 'controlling or coercive' behaviour may have particular significance in the Australian context. Douglas (2015, p. 466) has pointed out that in the Australian context the work of Kelly and Johnson in developing a typology of violence (e.g. Kelly and Johnson 2008; Johnson 2008) has been influential. In this typology, 'controlling or coercive violence is merely one of a variety of forms of violence that may occur between intimates…' and 'Rathus has argued that if the language of "controlling or coercive" behaviours was to be interpreted in line with the typologies of violence literature, one of the effects may be to exclude some very valid experiences of domestic violence from criminalisation' (Douglas 2015, p. 466, citing Rathus (2013), pp. 388–389).

Jane Wangmann's (2016) study of how Johnson's five-part typology has been utilised in parenting decisions may also reflect the difficulties of translating concepts in the Australian criminal context. Her study demonstrates among other things that cases characterised as 'coercive controlling violence' in family proceedings reflect a continuum and involve multiple forms of violence and abuse—from the physical to emotional to property damage (Wangmann 2016, p. 6). These cases show that ultimately the focus on *physical violence* had a 'disqualifying function'— typically leading to the granting of sole parenting responsibility to the mother. However, Wangmann concludes that while the cases reflect how violence is being taken into account in proceedings, the typologies themselves do not appear to be adding 'depth or complexity to understandings of violence' (p. 12).

We thus need to be cognisant of the 'baggage' any language may bring with it when drafting an offence—the assumptions, interpretations and expectations—but also of the fact that there is no guarantee that simply adding an offence with words such as 'coercive' and 'controlling' (or any other formulation for that matter) will mean that the offence is interpreted in accordance with the 'intentions' of legislators (Quilter 2011).

On the second question of how such an offence might be enacted in Australia we should be mindful of the context in which Australian criminal laws operate. Australia's federal compact means that most criminal law is left to the eight State and Territory-based legislatures. The Commonwealth Parliament's criminal law-making jurisdiction is relatively limited. There are significant differences across the nine criminal jurisdictions and only broad commonality between the 'common law' states (NSW, Victoria and SA) and the Code based jurisdictions (Qld, Tasmania, WA, NT, ACT and the Cth). Attempts at national harmonisation have largely failed. Loughnan (2017) has argued that the Commonwealth *Model Criminal Code* (MCC) (Parliamentary Counsel's Committee 2009) signalled a 'high point of faith in the value and possibility of systematising, rationalising and modernising criminal law' (Loughnan 2017, p. 9), but ultimately that project failed to produce the hoped-for unification of Australian criminal laws. This means that if only some jurisdictions enact an offence of controlling or coercive behaviour, the level of protection afforded to victims will be uneven.

Furthermore, the recent 'history' of criminal law cross-jurisdictional 'borrowings' (Quilter 2015; McNamara and Quilter 2016; McNamara 2017) should also make us think carefully about how best to criminalise forms of non-physical harm. The statute books in Australia testify to the problematic reality that governments may 'borrow' a regime from other jurisdictions because it has been found to be a *valid* exercise of lawmaking power (typically measured against constitutional validity criteria), rather than because it has been shown to be a well-adapted, effective and proportionate response to the crime problem at which it is directed (Appleby 2015). Worse still, governments may be emboldened to enact draconian or over-criminalising legislation (McNamara and Quilter 2016) because of the 'success' of governments in other States and Territories in enacting such laws (McNamara and Quilter 2018). Examples of such problematic borrowings include control order regimes, serious sex offender and high-risk offender schemes, one-punch laws and protest laws, but also borrowings in relation to bail (show cause offences) and parole risk factors.

It may be that this more negative view of inter-jurisdictional borrowing may have less currency in relation to criminalisation measures introduced to combat domestic violence. If I am right that a different logic operates in the family violence space, it may be that the risks associated with cross-jurisdictional borrowing are reduced. For example, the 2014 changes to the offence of 'strangulation' in NSW in 2014 (by amending s 37 of the *Crimes Act 1900* (NSW)) were later 'borrowed' by the Queensland legislature in 2016 (although, in a different form, with specific reference to domestic violence inserted into s 315A of the *Criminal Code 1899* (Qld)). There also appears to be evidence of goodwill and genuine embrace of opportunities for reciprocal learning about 'best practice' models in the family violence contexts—that may or may not be present in other criminalisation sites. For example, the most recent *NSW Domestic Violence Death Review Team Report 2015–2017* (2017) recommended reviewing the operation of the NSW offence of strangulation (rec 5) and noted: '… the Team was of the perspective that, in form, this legislation [the Queensland offence] was promising and may overcome some of the challenges that persist in prosecuting the NSW offence' (p. 80).

While I am drawing attention to a somewhat dubious history when it comes to cross-jurisdictional borrowings in criminal law reform in Australia, and suggest that borrowing should be approached with caution, I would nonetheless advocate that enhanced national harmonisation of Australian criminal laws should be one of our goals in any efforts to more appropriately criminalise non-physical domestic violence.

How then can this be best achieved? At one extreme there is the possibility of State referral of powers to the Commonwealth (under s 51(xxxvii) of the *Constitution*) as occurred for example, in relation to terrorism in 2003 (see *Criminal Code Amendment (Terrorism) Act 2003* (Cth)). This is probably an unlikely and difficult goal to achieve. It might be possible to pursue enhanced uniformity through both standing institutional arrangements (such as the Council of Australian Governments' (COAG) Standing Council on Police and Emergency Management (SCPEM)), and ad hoc processes leading to enhanced uniformity. There is already a history of such reform in relation to family violence. For example, in 2015, COAG agreed on a national scheme for domestic violence orders and states have begun to enact legislation for cross-jurisdictional recognition and enforcement of such orders (see Parliamentary Counsel's Committee 2015; *Crimes (Domestic and Personal Violence) Amendment (National Domestic Violence Orders Recognition) Act 2016* (NSW); *National Domestic Violence Order Scheme Act 2016* (Vic); *Domestic and Family Violence Protection and Other Legislation Amendment Act 2016* (Qld); *Family Violence Act 2016* (ACT); *Domestic Violence Orders (National Recognition) Act 2016* (Tas); *Intervention Orders (Prevention of Abuse) (Recognition of National Domestic Violence Orders) Amendment Act 2017* (SA)). Given the significant and multiple jurisdictional inquiries in relation to family violence, there does appear to be an appetite for, and goodwill towards, harmonised national reform (e.g. Queensland Special Taskforce on Domestic and Family Violence, 2015; Parliament of Australia, Senate Finance and Public Administration References Committee 2015; Royal Commission into Family Violence (Victoria) 2016).

6.4 The Implications of 'Gap'-Filling as a Criminalisation Paradigm

One of the most powerful tropes in criminalisation debates is the identification of an alleged 'gap' that needs to be 'filled' by *more* law. In Australia, the 'gap' trope is often used dubiously by Police Associations to justify calls for more police powers because of a perceived deficiency in existing legislative arrangements (e.g. the 2013 amendments to arrest powers in s 99 of the *Law Enforcement (Powers and Responsibilities) Act 2002* (NSW); see also Sentas and McMahon 2014).

Conversely, in some contexts, criminalisation scholars have appropriated and subverted the 'gap' paradigm to argue *against* the new criminalisation of certain harms or risks. For example, in relation to 'one punch' fatal violence I argued strongly that there was no need for the NSW Parliament to introduce the new offence of Assault Causing Death (ACD) in 2014 because the behaviour at which it was directed was already 'covered' by the existing offence of manslaughter, by virtue of the low bar that already applied to the test for 'dangerousness' in manslaughter by unlawful and dangerous act, and the fact that the accident defence does not apply in the common law states. Furthermore, a review of decided cases revealed a long history of 'one punch' manslaughter convictions—meaning that there was neither a legal nor operational gap to be filled by the ACD offence (Quilter 2014, 2015).

So, how does the discourse of the 'gap' operate in the context of non-physical family violence? The parliamentary debates on the *Domestic Abuse (Scotland) Bill 2017* (Scot) are a good example. Indeed, almost every speaker justified the introduction of the new offence on the basis of an alleged 'gap' in the criminal laws. For example, Margaret Mitchell, speaking on behalf of the Justice Committee, stated:

> The new domestic abuse offence in the bill is intended to address a gap in the law: the lack of a criminal remedy when domestic abuse is primarily psychological in nature, in a relationship in which one party seeks to control and dominate the other. The committee heard that the current law is not well equipped to handle situations in which abuse consists of a course of behaviour, as opposed to an isolated incident. That means that the current law does not effectively reflect the lived experience of many victims. (Scottish Parliament 2017, p. 66)

Similarly, Liam Kerr (North East Scotland) (Conservative) stated:

> In its current form, the criminal law focuses on discrete incidents of physical violence or threatening behaviour that causes fear or alarm, and it can fail to recognise the lived experience of domestic abuse as a course of conduct over a period of time. The bill seeks to bridge that gap, making it possible *inter alia* to convict an individual on the basis of a course of conduct that includes psychological abuse. (Scottish Parliament 2017, p. 69).

In these debates, the trope of the 'gap' functions largely at the level of formal criminalisation. (For further insight into the debates see Claire Baker (Scottish Parliament 2017, pp. 71–72); Sandra White (p. 77); Rona MacKay (p. 81); John Finnie (p. 82); Ben Macpherson (p. 84); Liam McArthur (p. 86); Fulton MacGregor (p. 88); Christina McKelvie (p. 92); Rhoda Grant (p. 95); Michelle Ballantyne

(p. 96); Ministry of Justice (UK) (2018, p. 54).) This trope is employed to mark a claim that, on the face of the statute books, there is no other offence which could be considered to cover the harm in question. Such assertions then lead to exercises of categorising and cataloguing current criminal laws to determine whether or not such a gap indeed exists (e.g. Douglas 2015; McMahon and McGorrery 2016a, b). Exercises of this sort identify a range of existing criminal law tools, including:

- statutory provisions that provide for intervention orders (and associated breach offences);
- stalking and intimidation offences;
- offences that address the recording and distributing of intimate images (e.g. *Crimes Act 1900* (NSW) Pt 3 Div 15C, added in 2017);
- strangulation offences;
- common assault and 'aggravated' assault offences;
- offences covering emotional and economic abuse (e.g. *Family Violence Act 2004* (Tas) ss 8–9); and
- statutory provisions that provide for tailored bail conditions (e.g. *Bail (Domestic Violence) and Another Amendment Act 2017* (Qld)).

On the positive side, such cataloguing exercises highlight the growth in volume and diversity of attempts to recalibrate the criminal law to better redress the specific harms and risks involved in family violence. This approach fosters further 'gap analysis' as to whether existing offences are adequate for addressing psychological harms (e.g. McMahon and McGorrery 2016a, b; Douglas 2015). Such examinations are important, but I want to draw attention to one of the negatives of the gap-filling paradigm. It can encourage a dynamic of 'arguing the toss', in a lawyerly fashion, about, for example, whether the NSW offence of 'intimidation' may actually be a 'model' with broader application to the kind of conduct under discussion in this book, or whether the relative 'elasticity' of an offence like stalking can cover such behaviours (cf McMahon and McGorrery 2016b). There is a danger that the gap paradigm can tend to focus so closely on statutory drafting that existing or proposed offences are abstracted or decontextualized, and operate with the implicit assumption that the solution lies in 'perfecting' statutory formulations to ensure 100% coverage of those harmful behaviours deemed sufficiently serious to warrant criminalisation.

The point I want to emphasise here is that 'gap' analyses are too narrow if they only draw attention to the 'absence' of an appropriately drafted offence on the statute books. They must also investigate and highlight absences or deficits in the *structural and operational settings* for any proposed new offence. This involves developing a more holistic picture of criminalisation.

A gap paradigm which assumes a simple 'lacuna' into which a new offence can be inserted to 'fill' that space has at least two interconnected problems. First, it has the capacity to obfuscate the well documented problematic operation of current criminal laws in respect of physical violence in intimate partner relationships (see e.g. Douglas 2008). In other words, by focusing on creating an offence of non-physical violence we may impliedly endorse the idea (fiction) that *physical* family violence is currently well policed and adequately addressed by the criminal law. Secondly, and relatedly, it misunderstands the difference between what Lacey and Zedner (2012) have called formal and substantive criminalisation. Formal criminalisation is effected when a crime is added to the statute books. Substantive criminalisation remains unchanged until police, prosecutors and courts act on that new law (Lacey and Zedner 2012, p. 162). How they do or don't act is crucial. Effective substantive criminalisation, therefore, depends on many factors beyond offence creation and other forms of lawmaking, including reporting decisions, official policing and prosecutorial practices, and exercises of various other forms of discretion. As Lacey and Zedner (2012) have argued, party political interests, administrative pressures and constraints upon the implementation of laws, including training of criminal justice officials and the influence of professional cultures, all play a significant factor in criminalisation: 'These extra-legal factors play an important part in determining how crime is actually policed and prosected through the criminal justice process.' (p. 178)

Any consideration of the necessity or desirability of drafting a new offence to fill a 'gap' in relation to non-physical violence must address the interrelationship with substantive criminalisation. Going further, we should also think through other relevant interconnections; that is, not just between criminal law 'on the books' and criminal law in operation, but the interconnections with other areas of law such as family and property law. We should resist the tendency to bracket off and compartmentalise the criminal law from other areas of law. It is clear that many family violence victims have multiple sets of proceedings on foot at any one time and are unlikely to see or understand their situation or needs in 'siloed' terms (Wangmann 2016). This may also include thinking through how definitions of family violence (e.g. and the role of coercive conduct) may be harmonised—or even whether harmonisation is desirable—in different legal domains.

These claims, particularly regarding the problems related to substantive criminalisation, are not new. It is widely recognised that the criminal law is largely based on a single incident/act/event paradigm rather than a pattern of behaviour that occurs within a relationship, and some have argued that the operational failures in relation to policing perpetrators of family violence makes it state-sanctioned violence (Douglas 2008). There are also the all too common strategies of harm down-playing and victim blaming that occur at all levels of the criminal justice system (see Douglas 2008) that may serve to undermine prosecutions. Indeed, these problems have led Walklate et al. (2018) to argue that more law is not the answer.

This leads me to my final point, which is a more optimistic take on how a better and more sophisticated gap analysis might be conducted. Gap analyses tend to be utilitarian, technical and doctrinal. I argue that in approaching criminalisation as a preventative strategy in relation to family violence, we should take more seriously the *symbolic* power of the criminal law (Tadros 2005, p. 1011). Criminalisation is the state's most coercive and powerful tool that may be used against an individual. It has a strong symbolic power—to declare which behaviours are not simply undesirable, but so unacceptable that they should attract criminal punishment. The criminal law has the capacity to send a powerful message of public disapproval and reprobation. It speaks of the unacceptability and moral culpability of family violence perpetration—not only to the wider community, but to key decision-makers in the justice system, including police, prosecutors, and the judiciary.

To create an offence that is framed around non-physical harms, and which treats such harms as discrete from physical harms, seems to me to undermine the symbolic and communicative function of the criminal law. Such an offence, however it is drafted, will inevitably attract debate and disagreement about which behaviours fall within in it, and which remain outside it. The more energy that is devoted to drafting precision, the greater the risk that the exercise will give rise to the pitfalls of 'particularism' (Horder 1994, p. 340). Such an approach to criminalisation reform is unlikely to reflect the continuum of harms experienced by many victims of family violence; and, more worryingly, may lead to judgments being made (by complainants themselves, police, prosecutors, judges and juries) about the 'morality' of a particular relationship rather than the wrongfulness of the harm perpetrated and experienced.

I argue that we need a *general* offence related to family violence or abuse that fairly labels (Chalmers and Leverick 2008), and captures, what Tadros (2005, p. 1004) has argued is the moral gravity of the wrong. For example, the wrongness of rape, stalking, sexual servitude, torture, child cruelty, strangulation, voyeurism, bigamy is embedded in the 'labels' attached to these crimes. I advocate avoiding clinical and formulaic approaches and language of the sort that have been adopted in Scotland. The terminology of 'person A' and 'person B' is suggestive of a simple formula for proving the offence $(X + Y = Z)$ that belies the complexity of the violence that is experienced by many victims of domestic violence and how it must be proven. Such offences exhibit the 'moral vacuity' of which Horder (1994) warns; they are stripped of context and fail to symbolise the gravity of the wrong.

Although I have been critical of the role of 'emotionalism' and (penal) 'populist' drivers of criminal lawmaking in other contexts (such as alcohol-related 'one punch' violence: Quilter 2014, 2015), I argue that they have an important role to play in the effective criminalisation of family violence. Offences should be drafted in such a way as to ensure that the symbolic power of the law resonates with the community. I believe that family violence is a terrain in relation to which we should embrace, rather than dismiss, the common claim of governments that new criminal laws are required to make the 'community safer' (Australian Bureau of Statistics 2017). As Horder has said:

> The important point here is that the moral warrant for creating a separate offence is that the offence protects an important value whose worth is not merely separable from other values, but is partly constituted by its separateness. (Horder 1994, p. 343)

Harm is contingent: there is nothing necessary or natural about it. As Lacey and Zedner (2012, p. 169) have argued, 'the concept of "harm" is neither fixed nor analytically robust'. At any given time, a society can authorise its lawmakers to employ the criminal law as the vehicle for symbolically denouncing harms previously unsanctioned by the criminal law, and as the warrant for using the state's most coercive power to prosecute it. That time should be now.

Appendix 1

Crimes (Domestic and Personal Violence) Amendment Act 2013 (NSW)
Crimes and Courts Legislation Amendment Act 2013 (NSW)
Crimes Amendment (Provocation) Act 2014 (NSW)
Crimes Amendment (Strangulation) Act 2014 (NSW)
Criminal Procedure Amendment (Domestic Violence Complainants) Act 2014 (NSW)
Crimes (Domestic and Personal Violence) Amendment (National Domestic Violence Orders Recognition) Act 2016 (NSW)
Crimes (Domestic and Personal Violence Amendment (Review) Act 2016 (NSW)
Domestic and Family Violence Protection Act 2012 (Qld)
Criminal Law (Domestic Violence) Amendment Act 2015 (Qld)
Domestic and Family Violence Protections and Another Act Amendment Act 2015 (Qld)
Criminal Law (Domestic Violence) Amendment Act 2016 (Qld)
Domestic and Family Violence Protection and Other Legislation Amendment Act 2016 (Qld)
Justice Legislation Amendment (Family Violence and Other Matters) Act 2012 (Vic)
Corrections Amendment (Abolition of Defensive Homicide) Act 2014 (Vic)
Family Violence Protection Amendment Act 2014 (Vic)
National Domestic Violence Order Scheme Act 2016 (Vic)

References

Appleby, G. (2015). The high court and *Kable*: A study in federalism and human rights protection. *Monash University Law Review, 40*(3), 673–697.
Ashworth, A. (2000). Is the criminal law a lost cause? *Law Quarterly Review, 116*(Apr), 225–256.
Australian Bureau of Statistics. (2017). *4906.0—Personal Safety, Australia, 2016*. Retrieved from http://www.abs.gov.au/ausstats/abs@.nsf/mf/4906.0.
Australian Law Reform Commission and NSW Law Reform Commission. (2010). *Family Violence—A National Legal Response*, ALRC Report No. 114, NSWLRC Report No. 128.
Bartels, L. (2013). Parole and parole authorities in Australia: A system in crisis? *Criminal Law Journal, 37*(6), 357–376.
Bettinson, V. (2016). Criminalising coercive control in domestic violence cases: Should Scotland follow the path of England and Wales? *Criminal Law Review, 3,* 165–180.
Bettinson, V., & Bishop, V. (2015). Is the creation of a discrete offence of coercive control necessary to combat domestic violence? *Northern Ireland Legal Quarterly, 66*(2), 179–197.

Brown, D., & Quilter, J. (2014). Speaking too soon: The sabotage of bail reform in New South Wales. *International Journal for Crime, Justice and Social Democracy, 3*(3), 73–97.

Chalmers, J., & Leverick, F. (2008). Fair labelling in criminal law. *Modern Law Review, 71*(2), 217–246.

Chesney-Lind, M. (2006). Patriarchy, crime, and justice: Feminist criminology in an era of backlash. *Feminist Criminology, 1*(1), 6–26.

Commonwealth Department of Social Services. (2011). *The National Plan to Reduce Violence Against Women and their Children 2010–2022*. Retrieved from https://www.dss.gov.au/women/programs-services/reducing-violence/the-national-plan-to-reduce-violence-against-women-and-their-children-2010-2022.

Douglas, H. (2018). Legal systems abuse and coercive control. *Criminology & Criminal Justice, 18*(1), 84–99.

Douglas, H. (2015). Do we need a specific domestic violence offence? *Melbourne University Law Review, 39*(2), 434–471.

Douglas, H. (2008). The criminal law's response to domestic violence: What's going on? *Sydney Law Review, 30*(3), 439–469.

Feeley, M. (1979). *The process is the punishment: Handling cases in a lower criminal court*. New York, NY: Russell Sage Foundation.

Fitzgerald, R., Bartels, L., Freiberg, A., Cherney, A., & Buglar, S. (2016). How does the Australian public view parole? Results from a national survey on public attitudes towards parole and re-entry. *Criminal Law Journal, 40*(6), 307–324.

Ministry of Justice (UK). (2018). *Transforming the Response to Domestic Abuse: Government Consultation*. Retrieved from https://consult.justice.gov.uk/homeoffice-moj/domestic-abuse-consultation/.

Hogg, R., & Brown, D. (1998). *Rethinking Law and Order*. Sydney, NSW: Pluto Press.

Home Office. (2015). *Controlling or coercive behaviour in an intimate or family relationship: Statutory guidance framework*. London: Home Office.

Horder, J. (1994). Rethinking non-fatal offences against the person. *Oxford Journal of Legal Studies, 14*(3), 335–351.

Innes, M. (2014). *Signal crimes: Social reactions to crime, disorder and control*. Oxford: Oxford University Press.

Johnson, M. (2008). *A typology of domestic violence: Intimate terrorism, violent resistance and situational couple violence*. Lebanon, NH: Northeastern University Press.

Jones, T., & Newburn, T. (2002a). Policy convergence and crime control in the USA and the UK: Streams of influence and levels of impact. *Criminology and Criminal Justice, 2*(2), 173–203.

Jones, T., & Newburn, T. (2002b). Learning from Uncle Sam? Exploring US influences on British crime control policy. *Governance, 15*(1), 97–119.

Kelly, J., & Johnson, M. (2008). Differentiation among types of intimate partner violence: Research update and implications for interventions. *Family Court Review, 46*(3), 476–499.

Loughnan, A. (2017). 'The very foundations of any system of criminal justice': Criminal responsibility in the Australian model criminal code. *International Journal for Crime, Justice and Social Democracy, 6*(3), 8–24.

Lacey, N., & Zedner, L. (2012). Legal constructions of crime. In M. Maguire, R. Morgan, & R. Reiner (Eds.), *The Oxford handbook of criminology* (5th ed.). Oxford: Oxford University Press.

McGorrery, P. (2018). The philosophy of criminalisation: A review of Duff et al.'s criminalisation series. *Criminal Law and Philosophy, 12*(1), 185–207.

McMahon, M., & McGorrery, P. (2016a). Criminalising emotional abuse, intimidation and economic abuse in the context of family violence: The Tasmanian experience. *University of Tasmania Law Review, 35*(2), 1–22.

McMahon, M., & McGorrery, P. (2016b). Criminalising controlling and coercive behaviour: The next step in the prosecution of family violence? *Alternative Law Journal, 41*(2), 98–101.

McNamara, L. (2017). Editorial: In search of principles and processes for sound criminal law-making. *Criminal Law Journal, 41*(1), 3–6.

McNamara, L., & Quilter, J. (2018). High Court constitutional challenges to criminal law and procedure legislation in Australia. *University of New South Wales Law Journal, 41*(4), forthcoming.

McNamara, L., & Quilter, J. (2016). The 'bikie effect' and other forms of demonisation: The origins and effects of hyper-criminalisation. *Law in Context, 34*(2), 5–35.

McNamara, L., Quilter, J., Hogg, R., Douglas, H., Loughnan, A., & Brown, D. (2018). Theorising criminalisation: The value of a modalities approach. *International Journal for Crime, Justice and Social Democracy, 7*(3), 91–121.

McNamara, L., Quilter, J., Hogg, R., Douglas, H., Loughnan, A., Brown, D., & Farmer, L. (2019). Understanding *processes* of criminalisation: Insights from an Australian study of criminal law-making. *Criminology & Criminal Justice*. (online) https://doi.org/10.1177/1748895819868519.

NSW Attorney General & Justice. (2012). *The NSW Domestic Violence Justice Strategy: Improving the NSW Criminal Justice System's Response to Domestic Violence 2013–2017*. Retrieved from https://www.women.nsw.gov.au/news/2012/domestic_violence_justice_strategy_for_nsw.

NSW Domestic Violence Death Review Team. (2012, 2013, 2015, 2017). *Annual Reports*. Retrieved from http://www.coroners.justice.nsw.gov.au/Pages/Publications/dv_annual_reports.aspx.

NSW Justice. (2015). *Statutory Review of the Crimes (Domestic and Personal Violence) Act 2007 (NSW)*. Retrieved from https://www.justice.nsw.gov.au/justicepolicy/Pages/lpclrd/lpclrd_publications/lpclrd_complete_reviews.aspx.

NSW Legislative Council Select Committee on Partial Defence of Provocation. (2013). *The Partial Defence of Provocation*. Retrieved from https://www.parliament.nsw.gov.au/committees/listofcommittees/Pages/committee-details.aspx?pk=235#tab-reportsandgovernmentresponses.

NSW Legislative Council Standing Committee on Social Issues. (2012). *Domestic Violence Trends and Issues in NSW*, Final Report. Retrieved from https://www.parliament.nsw.gov.au/lcdocs/inquiries/1687/120827%20Final%20report.pdf.

Newburn, T. (2002). Atlantic crossings: 'Policy transfer' and crime control in the USA and Britain. *Punishment and Society, 4*(2), 165–194.

Parliament of Australia, Senate Finance and Public Administration References Committee. (2015). *Domestic Violence in Australia*. Retrieved from https://www.aph.gov.au/Parliamentary_Business/Committees/Senate/Finance_and_Public_Administration/Domestic_Violence/Report.

Parliamentary Counsel's Committee. (2015). *Domestic Violence Orders (National Recognition) Model Provisions*. Retrieved from https://www.pcc.gov.au/uniform/Domestic-Violence-Orders-Model-Provisions-11December2015.pdf.

Queensland Government. (2015). *Queensland Says: Not Now, Not Ever. Domestic and Family Violence Prevention Strategy 2016–2026*. Retrieved from https://www.communities.qld.gov.au/resources/gateway/campaigns/end-violence/dfv-prevention-strategy.pdf.

Queensland Special Taskforce on Domestic and Family Violence. (2015). *Not Now, Not Ever: Putting an End to Domestic and Family Violence in Victoria*. Retrieved from https://www.communities.qld.gov.au/resources/gateway/campaigns/end-violence/about/special-taskforce/dfv-report-vol-one.pdf.

Quilter, J. (2015). Criminalisation of alcohol fuelled violence: One-punch laws. In T. Crofts & A. Loughnan (Eds.), *Criminalisation and criminal responsibility in Australia*. Oxford: Oxford University Press.

Quilter, J. (2014). One-punch laws, mandatory minimums and 'alcohol-fuelled' as an aggravating factor: Implications for NSW criminal law. *International Journal for Crime, Justice and Social Democracy, 3*(1), 81–106.

Quilter, J. (2011). Re-framing the rape trial: Insights from critical theory about the limitations of legislative reform. *Australian Feminist Law Journal, 35*(1), 23–56.

Rathus, Z. (2013). Shifting language and meanings between social science and the law: Defining family violence. *University of New South Wales Law Journal, 36*(2), 359–389.

Royal Commission into Family Violence (Victoria). (2016). *Report and Recommendations: Vol III*.

Scottish Government. (2003). *Preventing Domestic Abuse: A National Strategy*. Retrieved from https://www.gov.scot/Publications/2003/09/18185/26437.

Scottish Parliament. (2017). *Official Report: Meeting of the Parliament*, 28 September. Retrieved from http://www.parliament.scot/parliamentarybusiness/report.aspx?r=11111&mode=pdf.

Sentas, V., & McMahon, R. (2014). Changes to the police power of arrest. *Current Issues in Criminal Justice, 25*(3), 785–801.

Stark, E. (2007). *Coercive control: How men entrap women in personal life*. Oxford: Oxford University Press.

Stevenson, A. (2015). *Oxford Dictionary of English*, 3rd ed. Oxford University Press: Online.

Tadros, V. (2005). The distinctiveness of domestic abuse: A freedom based account. *Louisiana Law Review, 65*(3), 989–1014.

Tolmie, J. (2018). Coercive control: To criminalise or not to criminalise? *Criminology & Criminal Justice, 18*(1), 50–66.

Victorian Department of Justice. (2013). *Defensive Homicide—Proposals for Legislation*. Retrieved from https://assets.justice.vic.gov.au/justice/resources/f9d7181e-5bef-47b6-814b-183eeb8d8be5/defensivehomicideconsultationpaper2013.pdf.

Victorian Government. (2012). *Action Plan to Address Violence against Women and Children 2012–2015: Everyone Has a Responsibility to Act*. Retrieved from https://awava.org.au/wp-content/uploads/2012/10/VIC-Action-Plan-To-Address-Violence-against-Women-Children.pdf.

Walklate, S., Fitz-Gibbon, K., & McCulloch, J. (2018). Is more law the answer? Seeking justice for victims of intimate partner violence through the reform of legal categories. *Criminology and Criminal Justice, 18*(1), 115–131.

Wangmann, J. (2016). Different types of intimate partner violence—what do family law decisions reveal? *Australian Journal of Family Law, 30*(2), 77–111.

Part III
New Initiatives

Chapter 7
Ahead of Their Time? The Offences of Economic and Emotional Abuse in Tasmania, Australia

Kerryne Barwick, Paul McGorrery and Marilyn McMahon

Abstract More than a decade before the offences of controlling or coercive behaviour and domestic abuse were introduced in England and Wales, Ireland and Scotland, the parliament of Tasmania in Australia enacted the offences of economic abuse and emotional abuse of a person's spouse or partner. The introduction of these novel provisions constituted a significant move away from criminal law conceptions of family violence that relied solely upon physical acts and, instead, recognised that the infliction of psychological and economic harm were core features of that violence. This chapter analyses the Tasmanian offences, identifying difficulties in their construction and exploring the reasons for their slow uptake. Analysis of prosecutions that have occurred reveals interesting patterns of offending starting to emerge that have implications for how the offences are prosecuted and how family violence is understood.

Keywords Economic abuse · Emotional abuse · Family violence · Tasmanian offences · Police training

7.1 Introduction

When the offence of 'controlling or coercive behaviour' was introduced in England and Wales by s 76 of the *Serious Crime Act 2015* (E&W) it generated considerable controversy. Commentators were concerned about the apparent unprecedented extension of the criminal law to penalise conduct that *psychologically or eco-*

A significant portion of Chap. 7 is derived from an article in the University of Tasmania Law Review. We are grateful to the editors for permission to publish.

P. McGorrery · M. McMahon (✉)
School of Law, Deakin University, VIC, Australia
e-mail: marilyn.mcmahon@deakin.edu.au

K. Barwick
Prosecution Services, Tasmania Police, TAS, Australia

© Springer Nature Singapore Pte Ltd. 2020
M. McMahon and P. McGorrery (eds.), *Criminalising Coercive Control*,
https://doi.org/10.1007/978-981-15-0653-6_7

nomically abused another person, rather than conduct that had an adverse physical effect. That new offence was not, however, the first time the criminal law had been used to combat non-physical aspects of family violence. In 2004, Tasmania enacted the *Family Violence Act 2004* (Tas) ('the Act'), which introduced two novel criminal offences in the context of family violence: economic abuse (s 8) and emotional abuse or intimidation (s 9). Whilst other jurisdictions had definitions of family or domestic violence which included coercive control and intimidation for the purpose of protective orders, Tasmania was the first state in Australia (and, it appears, in common law countries) to criminalise this conduct directly.

In this chapter, we begin by providing some background to the introduction of the two Tasmanian offences, as well as some context to emphasise just how novel these offences were, given their focus on non-physical harms (Parts II and III). We then deconstruct the two offences in order to better understand their elemental components (Part IV), before providing a summary of criminal prosecutions that occurred until the end of 2017 (Part V). Finally, we consider reasons for the relative scarcity of prosecutions but also note the increasing rate at which these prosecutions have occurred in recent years (Part VI).

7.2 Background to the Reforms

The enactment in Tasmania of two specific offences criminalising emotional abuse and economic abuse was intended to cover patterns of psychological and emotional abuse, such as intimidation and bullying behaviour, committed against the person's spouse or partner. That behaviour, if taken as individual incidents, would in most cases not have reached a sufficient level of seriousness to constitute a crime under pre-existing laws, even though it can create or maintain a climate of fear which affects the family (Department of Justice (Tas) 2003, p. 24). As noted in Chap. 1, research on the effects of domestic violence provided the impetus for the introduction of these offences. In particular, battered woman syndrome—which describes the psychological and behavioural effects of domestic violence, and the cyclic nature of violence that occurs in abusive relationships (Walker 1980)—was relied upon to establish the profound and adverse effects of non-physical abuse.

The new offences were not, however, created in isolation, but were instead part of a reform package that significantly changed how family violence is addressed in Tasmania. The State government's *Safe at Home* program was designed to be an integrated criminal justice response to family violence. It combines both policy and legislative change, with a focus squarely on criminalising family violence and protecting the safety, well-being and interests of persons affected by family violence (Department of Justice (Tas) 2003). The reforms took time to implement and the new offences were neither the most controversial part of the new legislation, nor were they well-publicised. Indeed, in a subsequent review of the legislation, little was reported about the prosecution of the offences (Grealy et al. 2008). There are no readily available statistics and no reported case authorities about their operation.

This perhaps gives the impression that the offences have not been used at all. While this is not true, their uptake has been slow. Within the first 3 years, no charges had been laid, with a 2008 review of the impact of the new legislation indicating that stakeholders were still awaiting the first case involving the new offences (Grealy et al. 2008). As will be explored later in this chapter, several factors contributed to the slow uptake of the provisions, including a lack of community awareness of the offences, and the difficulty posed to first responding police in identifying course of conduct offending. In addition, until 2015 prosecutions were handicapped by a statutory time limitation of 6 months for laying complaints.

To better understand the Tasmanian offences, the current chapter explores their background, construction and impact. The *Safe at Home* Coordination Unit, under the Department of Justice, kindly provided the authors with statistical data on the offences. This data forms the basis of the empirical analysis in Part V of this chapter. By the end of 2017, 73 charges of emotional and economic abuse had been finalised, and some patterns in offending behaviour had emerged. Dispute in these cases has been on the facts (including simple denials of the conduct alleged). There has been no legal challenge to the mental element of the offences; that is, no accused has denied an intent to unreasonably control or intimidate, cause mental harm, apprehension or fear (economic abuse) or the less onerous recklessness —'knew or ought to have known'—about their conduct being likely to have that effect (emotional abuse).

7.3 Family Violence Reform in Tasmania

In 2004 the Tasmanian Parliament enacted the *Family Violence Act 2004* (Tas), introducing significant changes to the manner in which police and the courts dealt with domestic violence. The Act was passed in reaction to a number of previous criticisms of the criminal justice response to family violence, such as not treating domestic violence seriously, low charge and conviction rates, a lack of systemic coordination, victim safety not being addressed and ineffective sentencing options (Department of Justice (Tas) 2003, p. 24). It would be fair to say that prior to implementation of the Act, there was an entrenched attitude that much domestic violence was a private matter. This was reflected in the low rate of reporting, the minimal effort invested by police in investigating charges that were likely to be withdrawn at the victim's request, and in the nominal sentences imposed by the courts. There was previously no provision for specific protective orders to be made by the court, with victims generally left to seek their own restraining order (only about 5% of all restraint orders—related to family violence or otherwise—were initiated by police) (Department of Justice (Tas) 2003, p. 26).

As well as creating the new offences of economic and emotional abuse (ss 8–9), other changes introduced by the Act included;

- introducing an expansive definition of family violence (s 7) to include: assaults, threats, coercion, intimidation or verbal abuse, abduction, stalking, economic abuse, emotional abuse or intimidation, contravening a family violence order (including an interim order or an order made by police) and property damage;
- giving police new powers in relation to entry, search and arrest in family violence cases, including arrest for the purpose of making a protective order, and arrest on suspicion of family violence (ss 10–11);
- giving police the power to issue a protective order (known as a Police Family Violence Order, or PFVO) (s 14);
- establishing a procedure for review of PFVOs by magistrates and giving magistrates the power to make a Family Violence Order, or FVO (pt 4); and
- creating a presumption against bail for offenders charged with family violence offences (s 12).

The reversal of the presumption of bail in s 12 in particular sent a clear message that family violence would be taken seriously. As well as placing the onus on the applicant to establish why bail should be granted, s 12 requires the court to assess the risk to the victim, and any affected children, that may be posed by the defendant's release from custody. Bail is to be granted only if it 'would not be likely to adversely affect the safety, wellbeing and interests' of an affected person or child. Additionally, police bail is not to be granted if the defendant has been charged with breaching an intervention order (s 12(3)): the defendant must be brought before a court. This has meant that there is now greater judicial oversight and management of repeat offenders, and considerably more offenders are remanded in custody. In the first few months after enactment, a defendant who was facing a family violence charge was almost always remanded in custody as the judiciary grappled with parliament's intent, and what would be necessary to satisfy a court that the defendant's release would not be 'likely to adversely affect' a victim or their children. It is notable that in the first few years of the Act being in operation, case law relating to the reform legislation exclusively considered the operation of s 12 (see, for example, *Re S* [2005] TASSC 89; *Director of Public Prosecutions (Acting) v JCN* [2015] TASFC 13).

In addition to these changes introduced by the *Family Violence Act 2004* (Tas), other legislative amendments also directly targeted family violence. Those reforms affected the giving of evidence in family violence matters, further amended the provisions relating to bail, and affected the sentencing of family violence offenders. For example, child witnesses in family violence matters (automatically) and adult victims (on application) may now give their evidence via remote video link (*Evidence (Children and Special Witnesses) Act 2001* (Tas) ss 6 and 8). Further protections were introduced to prevent family violence offenders from cross-examining the complainant themselves (*Evidence (Children and Special Witnesses) Act 2001* (Tas) s 8A). These reforms sought to recalibrate the right of an accused to face their accuser against concerns about victimising complainants, and in effect amended the common law position in *Kerrison v Buxton* [2000] TASSC 135. In that case, which defence lawyers regularly cited in arguments opposing prosecution applications for witnesses and victims to give evidence via videolink, the court had concluded that 'there remains a need that a person ... be enabled to confront the accuser. Technology or convenience ought not to supplant the human dimension, unless Parliament determines otherwise.'

These various reforms were all part of a package of reforms called *Safe at Home*:

> *Safe at Home* is an integrated whole-of-government criminal justice response and intervention system to family violence that aims to: improve the safety and security for adult and child victims of family violence in the short and long term; ensure that offenders are held accountable for family violence as a public crime and change their offending behaviour; reduce the incidence and severity of family violence in the longer term; and minimise the negative impacts of contact with the criminal justice system on adult and child victims. (Tasmanian Government 2005a; Tasmania Police 2018)

A number of government departments are part of *Safe at Home*, with funding specifically provided to address victims' needs, including accommodation, security upgrades, counselling and access to legal services (see, for instance, the breakdown of how more than $7 million was allocated to various initiatives in 2012–2013; Tasmanian Government 2013, p. 28). There is also provision under the Act for information sharing and voluntary reporting of family violence incidents between government agencies, though at the time of writing this has not yet commenced (*Family Violence Act 2004* (Tas) ss 37–39). There is also a structure in place for weekly meetings of agencies to discuss ongoing cases, known as 'integrated case coordination' (ICC) meetings. They occur weekly in each region of Tasmania (South, North and North-West). Agencies include police, prosecutors, the Child Safety Service, the Court Support and Liaison Service, Community Corrections, and more. Software programs—known as the *Family Violence Management System* (FVMS) and the *Safe at Home Information Management System* (SIMS)—were developed to enable this information sharing to occur efficiently and consistently. This both informs the police and prosecution response and keeps the service providers who are working with the families apprised of how matters are progressing.

A significant change in police culture was made by the imposition of a pro-arrest and pro-prosecution policy (now referred to as a pro-intervention policy). Essentially, where police discover evidence of family violence, an arrest and prosecution will result; the victim does not determine the response of the justice system (Grealy et al. 2008, p. 4). In practice this means where there is evidence of family violence, even if a victim is unwilling to make a formal complaint, police will charge the alleged offender; they will not accept a 'withdrawal' of the charge or allegations by the victim (cf. Porter 2018). Indeed, family violence matters are being more thoroughly investigated so that the prosecution can proceed with charges even where a victim is unfavourable or even unavailable (as defined in ss 38, 65 and 66 of the *Evidence Act 2001* (Tas)). In addition, a specialised section of Tasmania Police, known as the Family Violence Unit (FVU), was established to investigate and have oversight of complicated or 'high risk' family violence cases; until 2017, these units were known as the Victim Safety Response Teams (VSRTs). Tasmania Police Prosecution Services was also provided with additional funding to employ legal practitioners to provide specialist legal representation in the prosecution of family violence matters. That department is predominantly staffed by police, who usually receive internal training in prosecuting, rather than being appointed because of legal qualifications.

In effect, the process for Tasmanian police dealing with family violence is now radically different to the situation before the 2004 Act. Operationalising the new offences was not simply a matter of absorbing new offences into the existing lexicon. The policy behind the Act meant very different processes would be employed for all points at which family violence and the criminal justice system intersect. The workload, complexity, and of course the paperwork, have considerably increased, and continue to evolve. For instance, the *Tasmanian Police Family Violence Manual* was revised in March 2017 to allow for additional supervision of 'high risk' matters. This was a direct response to criticisms of Tasmania Police in the findings of the Coroners Inquiry into the murder of Jessica Kupsch (*Record of Investigation into Death (With Inquest)* [2016] TASCD 217).

We raise each of the above reforms in order to emphasise that any analysis of the Tasmanian family violence offences as a reform measure must not be viewed in isolation. Their effect must be understood in the context of a whole-of-government reform of criminal justice responses to family violence. Introducing legislation to criminalise behaviour that was previously not captured is a valuable measure in reducing both the seriousness and prevalence of family violence, but must be located within processes and practices that better inform community attitudes and understandings and which shift the cultures and norms of how agencies (including police and courts) respond to family violence. In short, the offences are a part of a larger suite of reforms, and evaluation is necessary to determine whether they are fulfilling their particular intended role.

7.4 The New Offences

The offences of economic abuse and emotional abuse or intimidation came into force on 30 March 2005. The offences do not have retrospective effect. They are both summary offences. Although specifically developed with female victims of domestic abuse in mind, both provisions are gender neutral. The offences apply where they are committed against a person's 'spouse' or 'partner', defined as a person to whom they either are or have been married to, or with whom they are in a 'significant relationship', essentially a de facto or 'marriage-like' relationship, including same sex relationships (*Family Violence Act 2004* (Tas) s 4). For both offences, the penalty is a fine not exceeding 40 penalty units (currently $6,720) or imprisonment for a term not exceeding 2 years.

7.4.1 Emotional Abuse or Intimidation

Section 9 prohibits a person from pursuing a course of conduct that is likely to unreasonably control or intimidate, or cause mental harm, apprehension or fear in, their spouse or partner. The types of scenario to which it is anticipated that section 9 could apply might include where a victim's social interaction (such as contact with family or friends) is limited by their spouse or partner, or where a victim is verbally abused, humiliated or 'put down' by their spouse or partner.

s 9. Emotional abuse or intimidation

(1) A person must not pursue a course of conduct that he or she knows, or ought to know, is likely to have the effect of unreasonably controlling or intimidating, or causing mental harm, apprehension or fear in, his or her spouse or partner…
(2) In this section—a course of conduct includes limiting the freedom of movement of a person's spouse or partner by means of threats or intimidation.

The offence has some inbuilt limitations. First, it is restricted to 'spouses' and 'partners'. A 'spouse' or 'partner' is defined by the Act to mean a person with whom the person is or has been in a 'family relationship'. A 'family relationship' means a marriage or a significant relationship within the meaning of the *Relationships Act 2003* (Tas). A 'significant relationship' under that Act is defined as a relationship between two adult persons who (a) have a relationship as a couple and (b) are not married to one another or related by family. In determining whether two people are in a significant relationship the court may have regard to all the circumstances of the relationship; including duration, cohabitation, financial dependence, children and reputation (*Relationships Act 2003* (Tas) s 4. For a discussion on how the definition is applied see *Bromwell v Robinson* [2017] TASFC 11). Consequently, the offence does not capture elder abuse or abusive conduct by adolescents or adult children directed towards their parents or siblings. Second, the qualifier that the perpetrator knew or ought to have known that the conduct was *unreasonably* controlling or intimidating allows the possibility that some conduct by one member of a domestic partnership towards the other may be *reasonably* controlling or intimidating (McMahon and McGorrery 2016). Further, the offence seems to require more than a single instance of the requisite conduct ('a course of conduct'). It is interesting to note that the legislation non-exhaustively defines a 'course of conduct' not by referring to temporal matters (as might be expected) but by referring to 'limiting [a partner's] freedom of movement … by means of threats or intimidation' (see *Howe v S* [2013] TASMC 33). Finally, there is a statutory period of limitation for the offence, originally 6 months but now (from 6 October 2015) 12 months from the day on which the most recent act constituting part of the 'course of conduct' occurred (*Family Violence Act 2004* (Tas) s 9A).

The offence is expansively defined in several ways. The *mens rea* of the offence exceeds the subjective intent and recklessness standards usually employed for assault offences by importing an additional (and alternative) objective recklessness standard ('ought to have known'). Additionally, the *mens rea* is distinctive because it relates to knowledge of the *likely effect* of conduct on a victim. An accused will be liable under section 9 if, all other elements being satisfied, they knew, actually or constructively, that their conduct was likely to (1) unreasonably control, (2) unreasonably intimidate, (3) cause mental harm to, (4) cause apprehension in or

(5) cause fear in, the victim. It is not necessary that their behaviour actually has that effect.

Although the construction of the section raises some uncertainty about whether it actually prohibits *emotional* abuse (see McMahon and McGorrery 2016, pp. 15–18), the scope of the psychological harm from which the offence protects the victim is relatively broad: it prohibits conduct by the accused that they know is likely to have the effect of being unreasonably controlling or intimidating, or causing mental harm, apprehension or fear, is proscribed. There is no requirement that the accused knows that the likely effect of their conduct will be serious, or that it will impair the victim's ability to go about their daily activities. Moreover, there does not seem to be any requirement that the conduct of the accused *actually* controlled, intimidated, or caused mental harm, apprehension or fear in the victim; the requirement is simply that the accused knew, or should have known, that the conduct was likely to have that effect. Of course, as a practical and evidentiary matter, a prosecution would be unlikely to succeed in the absence of such an effect. In this respect the Tasmanian offences significantly differ from the 'controlling or coercive behaviour' offences that have subsequently been introduced in England and Wales and Ireland; the latter offences require that the prohibited conduct actually have a serious effect on the victim.

Finally, there does not appear to be any requirement of a direct relationship between the accused's conduct and the object of that conduct. That is, the unlawful course of conduct does not necessarily have to be directed towards the victim; the wording of the provision would seemingly allow for the accused's conduct to be directed towards a third party, or even a pet animal, where this could have the effect of unreasonably controlling or intimidating the victim.

7.4.2 Economic Abuse

The offence created by section 8 prohibits a person from intentionally and unreasonably controlling or intimidating their spouse or partner or causing them mental harm, apprehension or fear by pursuing a course of conduct involving a range of specified behaviours relating to financial matters. The categories of behaviour prohibited under ss 8(a)–(e) include: coercing a partner to relinquish control over property; disposing of property without consent; preventing a partner from participating in decisions about spending; preventing a partner from accessing property for normal household expenses; and withholding (or threatening to withhold) financial support. There may be considerable overlap of these behaviours. For example, if a person prevented their spouse from taking money out of a jointly owned bank account to meet normal household expenses (s 8(d)), it is likely that they will have thereby prevented their spouse from participating in decisions over household expenditure (s 8(c)) and coerced their spouse into giving up control over assets (s 8(a)).

s 8. Economic abuse

A person must not, with intent to unreasonably control or intimidate his or her spouse or partner or cause his or her spouse or partner mental harm, apprehension or fear, pursue a course of conduct made up of one or more of the following actions:

(a) coercing his or her spouse or partner to relinquish control over assets or income;
(b) disposing of property owned—(i) jointly by the person and his or her spouse or partner; or (ii) by his or her spouse or partner; or (iii) by an affected child—without the consent of the spouse or partner or affected child;
(c) preventing his or her spouse or partner from participating in decisions over household expenditure or the disposition of joint property;
(d) preventing his or her spouse or partner from accessing joint financial assets for the purposes of meeting normal household expenses;
(e) withholding, or threatening to withhold, the financial support reasonably necessary for the maintenance of his or her spouse or partner or an affected child.

As with the section 9 offence of emotional abuse or intimidation, there are some common built-in limitations to section 8; the offence of economic abuse is restricted to intimate domestic relationships; it requires that a 'course of conduct' be established; it has a short statutory period of limitation (as previously noted this was originally 6 months but since October 2015 is 12 months); and implicit in the wording of the section is the possibility of 'reasonable' control or intimidation of a spouse or partner (the offence only proscribes *unreasonable* conduct).

A further, notable feature of the *mens rea* required by section 8 is the requirement that the offender engaged in the proscribed economically abusive behaviours *while intending to* unreasonably control or intimidate his or her spouse or partner or cause his or her spouse or partner mental harm, apprehension or fear. This formulation of economic abuse, requiring a specific intent to unreasonably control or intimidate, etc., while engaging in the proscribed behaviours, may constitute an additional difficulty in prosecuting this offence (Wilcox 2007).

The offences both require a 'course of conduct', however, economic abuse requires that conduct to be made up from a list of specified actions relating to control of income, assets and property. Emotional abuse does not prescribe what that conduct might be, except to specifically include limiting freedom of movement by means of threats or intimidation. The ambit of behaviour that may be covered by the emotional abuse is therefore very broad. Further, the *mens rea* for these charges contain similar concepts but is phrased differently. Economic abuse requires 'intent to' unreasonably control or intimidate or cause mental harm, apprehension or fear by pursuing the course of conduct alleged. That is, the prosecution must prove that the offender in fact intended the conduct to have one of the alleged effects. The mental element for emotional abuse is, in contrast, more broadly phrased as pursuing a course of conduct that the offender 'knew or ought to have known' was likely to produce the effect of unreasonably controlling or intimidating, or causing mental harm, apprehension or fear. That is, it doesn't require the offender to have any specific intent in his actions, provided he knew or ought to have known their effect. The broad ambit of conduct and less restrictive *mens rea* is likely why the offence of emotional abuse has seen consistently more use.

7.5 The Prosecutions

Thus far, there have been no decisions of superior courts in relation to either sections 8 or 9 of the Act. There appears to be only two reported lower court cases that have considered the offence of emotional abuse or intimidation, and none in relation to economic abuse. The first was an application to revoke a family violence order (FVO) and involved only cursory mention of section 9: *K v K* [2012] TASMC 3. The second, *Howe v S* [2013] TASMC 33, was a change of plea application and had slightly more (but still limited) consideration of section 9. There have also been some unreported decisions. By the end of 2017, 73 complaints had been finalised for the new offences (with some additional cases still being processed); only eight cases had proceeded to a contested hearing (six were proven, and two were dismissed). Thus, the key source of information about the operation of the offences comes from an analysis of prosecutions.

7.5.1 *Prosecutions for Economic Abuse (s 8)*

There have been only five cases of economic abuse prosecuted to date. One of the authors (KB) appeared for the prosecution at the hearing of one of these cases in 2014. The offender had coerced his partner to relinquish control of her income, sold property belonging to her and her children without their consent, and withheld financial support for her and her children. The prosecution alleged that the offender was keeping the complainant socially isolated and dependent on him. This had continued for years, but the complaint could only allege 6 months of conduct due to the (as it was then) statute of limitations. There was evidence from the complainant and her 16-year-old daughter that the offender would make the complainant (by threats and intimidation) withdraw all her Centrelink benefits and give them to him. He would spend most of the money on himself and dole out small sums to the complainant or children to buy things, at his discretion. When he ran out of money he would pawn or sell their property. One of the primary difficulties in prosecuting these charges was the absence of corroborating evidence to support the allegations. It is difficult to prove someone is controlling a victim's money, where seemingly they had their own bank account and income. The abuse can also be sporadic or cyclical, making a course of conduct hard to prove on documentary evidence alone, and witness accounts of the relationship tend to vary. In this case, there was a cumulation of evidence that corroborated the alleged economically abusive behaviours as follows:

- *the complainant's bank records*: these demonstrated a pattern of bank withdrawals that indicated that when her Centrelink income was deposited it was immediately withdrawn in its entirety. This pattern ceased after she got help from the police to separate from him, and subsequently showed a pattern of regular household purchases;
- *records from pawnshops*: this confirmed that the offender had pawned items that were likely to belong to women and children (such as bicycles, toys, handbags, and hair straighteners);
- *testimony from the victim's extended family*: this indicated that the complainant was not 'allowed' to see them, and on the rare occasions that they did have contact, she was desperate for money to buy food, and stated that she was too afraid of the offender to leave him; and
- *testimony from others*: the principal at the younger children's school gave evidence that the children were frequently sent to school without lunches and had no uniforms, and that the school had tried to support the family but the offender would not engage.

As the case was tried in the Magistrates' Court, there was no jury; the Magistrate made findings of fact and law. The arguments in this case very much centred on establishing the facts. It was not disputed that the conduct, if proved, would amount to an intent to unreasonably control the complainant, or to cause her apprehension or fear.

The economic abuse charge was found to have been proven. The offender was also convicted of emotional abuse, and assault with indecent intent (towards his daughter). Indeed, consultation with members of the Tasmanian Police Prosecution Service established that in each of the five cases in which there has been a successful prosecution for economic abuse, the offender was, in the same case, also charged with emotional abuse. This is perhaps predictable, as it seems unlikely that an offender would be controlling and abusive in regards to financial matters in the relationship, without also being controlling and abusive in other respects (especially where his aim is to prevent the victim from being able to leave the relationship).

7.5.2 *Prosecutions for Emotional Abuse (s 9)*

In comparison to the dearth of economic abuse charges, there have been far more emotional abuse charges, covering a wide range of scenarios. By the end of 2017, there had been 68 cases of emotional abuse prosecuted.

Perhaps surprisingly, in some of these cases, the charge has been applied to discrete incidents, where the course of conduct only covers minutes or hours (as opposed to the years of abuse envisaged by parliament). For example, in the early, unreported decision in *McLean v Rundle* [2011] TASMC (unreported, 4 November 2011) the offender had caused a lockdown at a service for people with disabilities. He made threats to stab anyone that got in his way (including his wife), and stated that he would go home and burn his house down with himself inside it. Staff at the service spoke to him, telling him that they took the matter seriously, but he did not retract his comments. He showed staff a knife that was in his possession. There was evidence that the offender and the complainant were married and that the offender's conduct in fact caused her to become upset. The court was satisfied that the threats (which took place over a number of minutes), as well as the showing of the knife, amounted to a 'course of conduct'. As to whether the offender 'knew or ought to have known' that his behaviour would have the prohibited effect of emotionally abusing his wife, the magistrate concluded as follows:

> So I am therefore of the view that I must, in considering whether Mr Rundle knew or ought to have known, take into account what he, with his actual knowledge and capacity, ought to have known in the circumstances in which he was placed, that he ought to have thought about the likely consequences of his actions and if he had stopped to think to the extent that he ought to have, whether he would have known or appreciated that his actions were likely to have the effect of causing apprehension or fear in Mrs Rundle (*McLean v Rundle* [2011] TASMC (unreported, 4 November 2011), citing *Hawkins v R (No 3)* (1994) 76 A Crim R 47, *Wilkinson v R* [1985] TASSC 43 and *Tame v New South Wales* (2002) 211 CLR 317).

The court concluded that the phrase 'likely to have the effect of' is intended to mean a substantial or real chance, as distinct from a mere possibility (*McLean v Rundle* [2011] TASMC (unreported, 4 November 2011), citing *Simpson v R* [1996] TASSC 137; see also *Boughey v R* (1986) 161 CLR 10, 22), and that the words 'mental harm, apprehension or fear' should be given their ordinary meaning given that they are not elsewhere defined in the Act (s 8B(3) of the *Acts Interpretation Act 1931* (Tas) defines 'ordinary meaning' as the ordinary meaning conveyed in a provision, having regard to its context in the Act and to the purpose or objective of the Act). In finding the charge proven the court took into account that the accused and the victim were a married couple, that the defendant had pleaded guilty to assaulting his wife the night before these events took place, that the nature of the threats was serious, and that the complainant in fact became upset on hearing them. The court concluded that the nature of the threats and the circumstances in which they were delivered were likely to cause apprehension and fear in the complainant, and that if the offender had stopped to consider his actions that he ought to have known this.

In *Thomas v Stewart* [2017] TASMC (unreported, 4 September 2017). The offender was alleged to have:

- caused damage to the residence in which he lived with his spouse;
- caused damage to personal property jointly owned by himself and his spouse;
- stated to police, in the presence of his spouse, that 'I can smash my own fucking stuff, I can even burn the fucking house down';
- yelled and swore at his spouse; and
- yelled and swore at police in the presence of his spouse.

The court found that the offender and his wife had started arguing after lunch, and that the damage was done by the offender during the course of the argument. There were photographs showing considerable damage to the residence and property across a number of rooms of the house, and the offender was agitated and aggressive towards police when they arrived. When considering whether this could constitute a 'course of conduct' the court concluded as follows:

> ...a course of conduct would normally be interpreted as 'conduct which is protracted or conduct which is engaged in on more than one separate occasion'. I note also that the definition of 'family violence' in section 7 of the *Family Violence Act* includes 'stalking' within the meaning of section 192 of the *Criminal Code*. That section defines stalking as a course of conduct. Section 192(2) provides that for the purposes of that definition:

(a) A person pursues a course of conduct if the conduct is sustained or the conduct occurs on more than one occasion.

> On the other hand, section 9 itself defines 'a course of conduct' to include 'limiting the freedom of movement of a person, spouse or partner by means of threats or intimidation'. It seems to me that if a threat or act of intimidation had the effect of limiting the freedom of movement of a person, spouse or partner, that a single act of threat or intimidation could, in those circumstances, amount to 'a course of conduct' and hence amount to an offence contrary to that section. (*Thomas v Stewart* [2017] TASMC (unreported, 4 September 2017), citing *Gunes v Pearson* (1996) 89 A Crim R 297, 306 and *Howe v S* [2013] TASMC 33).

From the amount of damage across the rooms of the house, the court found that it could not have happened simultaneously. There were, therefore, a number of separate acts spanning a period of a few hours. The court was satisfied that this amounted to a course of conduct.

There was no direct evidence about how the conduct affected the complainant (she was uncooperative with police and was cross-examined by the prosecution as an unfavourable witness). The court did, however, accept that the offender ought to have known that his conduct was likely to have the effect of intimidating or causing apprehension and fear in his spouse. There was no analysis of the law in this regard; this conclusion appears to have been reached from the facts as the court found them.

These cases are, it should be noted, unusual, in the sense that the 'course of conduct' occurred over a relatively brief period of time. Most complaints involved offending that took place over a period of time and involved separate incidents. It might be anticipated that these lengthy courses of conduct would involve a variety of behaviours. However, as discussed below, the offending behaviours tended to be more repetitive, with only slight variations (for example, in the wording of particular threats or insults).

7.5.3 Types of Behaviour Supporting Prosecutions

In addition to the types of conduct engaged in by individual offenders being somewhat persistent and repetitive, there are also patterns of behaviours engaged in by all offenders convicted of Tasmania's family violence offences. These behaviours accord with what Evan Stark (2007) has identified as the four key aspects of coercive control: violence, intimidation (which itself includes threats, surveillance, degradation, and withholding money), isolation, and control (the institution of rules and behavioural expectations). Broadly speaking, the behaviours exhibited by men charged with emotional abuse fall into three categories: socially isolating the victim, degrading the victim, and intimidating the victim (see Table 7.1 below). There is considerable overlap; for example, controlling behaviours tend to be effectuated through a degree of actual or threatened violence. The behaviours can also have different contexts. For instance, throwing out or damaging a victim's treasured possessions could be degrading or intimidating in some circumstances, and in others, such as destroying or throwing out the victim's mobile phone, can be socially isolating.

The literature on non-physical domestic abuse often discusses social isolation and causing the victim to live in fear (e.g. Walker 1980). However, many of these cases also involved extremely degrading conduct that was confronting for police to hear and difficult for the complainant to come forward and talk about. The difficulties in speaking about degrading conduct are further exacerbated in the court process, as giving evidence about it in public and in front of the defendant forces a complainant to relive it, which is humiliating in itself. One of the authors (KB) has personally observed hearings in which the accused, in the dock, scoffed at the complainant as she recounted the degrading experiences to which she had been subject. Whilst the behaviour served to demonstrate the defendant's attitude, the experience was a difficult one for the complainant. Secondary victimisation, this time through public exposure of degrading conduct and the offender being given yet another opportunity to perpetuate their abuse, has consistently been identified as a factor inhibiting victims from coming forward. (e.g. Laing 2016; see also Douglas (2018) on what she describes as 'legal systems abuse') (Table 7.1).

As noted previously, the issue in prosecuting emotional abuse cases has largely been establishing the facts to the satisfaction of the court, rather than legal argument about whether the *mens rea* is proven. This may well be because the cases that have been prosecuted have been extreme cases, where if the facts were established then it was obvious that the offender knew his conduct was likely to have the effect of unreasonably controlling or intimidating, or causing mental harm, apprehension or fear. Alternatively, it may be because elements of the charge ('a course of conduct', 'knew or ought to have known', and 'likely to have the effect of') are elements of other offences and the law is already familiar with them, leaving little room for argument. They are, for example, similar concepts that arise in the existing crime of stalking (*Criminal Code Act 1924* (Tas) s 192; *Allen v Tasmania Police* [2004] TASSC 30; Wilcox 2007, p. 214; more generally see Chap. 5 of this book).

7 Ahead of Their Time? The Offences of Economic ... 149

Table 7.1 Offender behaviours in emotional and economic abuse prosecutions

Effect on victim	Offender behaviours
Social isolation	• Controlling whether, and when, the victim can come and go from their home • Not letting the victim leave the home unless in the offender's company • Controlling the victim's access to, and usage of, their telephone and social media • Not permitting the victim to have contact with specified people • Supervising the victim's conversations
Degradation	• Insulting and degrading the victim (telling them they are useless/worthless, or not capable of making their own choices) • Sending the victim to their bedroom as a means of discipline • Using abusive language towards the victim • Stopping the victim from showering • Controlling what the victim is allowed to wear • Controlling what and when the victim is allowed to eat • Telling the victim they are 'crazy' and threatening to have them involuntarily admitted to a psychiatric facility • Throwing out the victim's property
Intimidation	• Actual or threatened violence against the victim, their children, their friends and their family • Damaging property • Threatening to take the victim's children away or have them put into departmental care • Stopping the victim from using contraception

7.6 Impediments to Prosecuting the New Offences

To the outside observer is it undoubtedly curious that there have been so few prosecutions (73) in more than a decade of the Tasmanian offences being in operation. By way of comparison, in 2015–2016 there were eight prosecutions for either of the two new offences, yet there were 3,174 incidents of family violence recorded by Tasmania Police that same year, and this only refers to incidents that resulted in charges being laid (Department of Justice (Tas) 2016).

There are a number of explanations for this lack of usage. There was some predictable antipathy from some key members of the legal profession to the introduction of the new offences (e.g. Ellis 2004). And the difficulties generally associated with the prosecution of family violence offences remain relevant: it typically involves acts committed without the presence of witnesses (other than the victim and the offender), delayed reporting is widespread, and initially-eager-but-later-reluctant victims and witnesses are common. But these factors cannot explain the dearth of prosecutions. Instead, a number of difficulties, specific to the offences, may be identified, involving a lack of community awareness about non-physical domestic abuse, deficiencies in police training and investigative practices, and the existence of an unduly restrictive statutory time limit on filing charges.

7.6.1 Community Awareness

Victims frequently do not *initially* report emotional or economic abuse to the police. What they report is that they have been assaulted, threatened, had their property damaged or some other 'emergency' situation that requires immediate police intervention. The author KB has personally prosecuted 20 cases involving the new offences since 2013; each case was precipitated by the reporting of an assault. In the course of making a statement about that physical assault, the victim alluded to controlling or coercive behaviours by the perpetrator, often in a description of the circumstances of the relationship, or by way of explanation for a delay in reporting the assault matter. There are a number of comments—such as 'I couldn't leave the house before now,' 'I have no phone because he broke it,' and 'I knew he would be suspicious if I left straight away so I waited and tried not to make him angry again'—that can be indicative of additional non-violent domestic abuse that a victim either has not recognised or that they are unaware may amount to an offence. The controlling behaviour by the offender may well have been going on for months or years, but it is the last act(s) of physical violence that typically brings the matter to the attention of the police.

Prior to the implementation of the *Family Violence Act 2004* (Tas), there was criticism of the community perception that family violence is primarily limited to physical assault (Department of Justice (Tas) 2003). Even after the passage of the Act and the introduction of the new offences, that perception remains. The most likely cause for the persistence of this view is that there has been no campaign to educate the public about the new offences. A perusal of the media releases relating to the *Safe at Home* program reveals that the new offences of emotional and economic abuse received only brief mention when they were introduced (Tasmanian Government 2005b). Moreover, the limited information that has been published is sometimes misleading. For instance, in 2016 the ABC reported that the first person to be prosecuted for economic abuse in Tasmania would face court in October (Bevin 2016). The reporter also stated that the offence of emotional abuse 'is rarely prosecuted in Tasmania because of the difficulty in proving the intent of the alleged behaviour' (Bevin 2016). Yet at the time the article was published, there had already been at least two prosecutions for economic abuse and, as previously noted, proving intent for emotional abuse has not been a problem. It is also noteworthy that limited detailed information about the offences is available on the internet (which would likely be victims' first source of information if they were seeking information about their partner's non-physical abuse). There is no readily available definition or explanation of what the offences require, even from sources such as the Legal Aid Commission of Tasmania, the Women's Legal Service Tasmania or Tasmania Police. In addition, although there are support services that offer counselling for intimidating and coercive behaviour, there is very little readily available information to explain that what victims are experiencing is actually family violence *and* that it constitutes a criminal offence. The omission and confusion are also perhaps at least partly explained by inconsistency in laws across

Australia, with Tasmania still the only jurisdiction to have directly criminalised non-physical abuse. In summary, it is trite but true that police cannot charge people with offences that are not reported to them. The lack of community awareness about these offences is undoubtedly a major impediment to such reporting.

7.6.2 Police Training

Another impediment to identifying and prosecuting the new offences is the lack of police training in identifying and investigating these offences. When the *Safe at Home* program was rolled out, police training addressed the immediate changes to processes and police powers that came with the new pro-arrest model that the government had promised. However, there was no training on what constituted an economic or emotional abuse offence. There was confusion over how these offences would apply and what sort of conduct would be covered. The police and the legal profession were waiting for a test case to explain the provisions, including via appellate proceedings—but, thus far, such a case has not occurred (Department of Justice (Tas) 2009). The lack of guidance has likely negatively impacted on the ability of Tasmania Police generally to recognise indicators that this kind of offence is occurring to prompt an investigation.

Part of the difficulty in recognising economic and emotional abuse is that police need to be able to see the bigger picture of what is happening in the relationship to identify those behaviours: patterns of abusive conduct and collective acts of unreasonable control. This conflicts with the priority of first responders to resolve the particular incident to which they were called (see, e.g., Wiener 2017; Segrave et al. 2018). First responders are looking to secure the immediate safety of the victim, which puts the focus squarely on risks of physical harm. This is not dissimilar to the experience in the United Kingdom, where research into the coercive control legislation has found that officers tend to prioritise physical violence and focus on the incident reported. Robinson, Myhill and Wire (2018, pp. 44–45), for example, recently identified aspects of police behaviour and acts of the offender that contribute to a focus on physical violence:

> First, frontline police responses to domestic abuse is organized primarily around calls for service which are regarded as 'incidents'. Prior to the introduction of the coercive control law, it was not possible to prosecute a 'course of conduct', so it perhaps is not surprising that patterns of abuse that do not fit into traditional crime strategies have been less likely to be recognized. Second, this 'incidentalism' is also reflected in how men speak about their abusive behaviour, and police practitioners are likely to be less adept at recognizing the narratives of primary perpetrators than are specialist advocates. Finally, although the [risk identification tool] contains numerous questions relating to coercive control, it requires officers to have sufficient understanding of the concept to probe around victims' responses in order to recognize and record it effectively.

7.6.3 Investigations

What has commonly occurred in Tasmania is that the potential for a charge of economic or emotional abuse has been identified by prosecutors when they have reviewed a file to lay the complaint, or by members of the Family Violence Unit (FVU) in their review of 'high risk' cases. Even then, this file review process is reliant on the quality of material provided by first responders, and the time between the incident and the file review could result in valuable evidence, and the opportunity for victim cooperation, to have been lost. Once the potential for these charges has been identified, the FVU then tend to actively direct the course of the investigation. That investigation can be very labour intensive. Inevitably, a further statement must be obtained from the victim to obtain more detail about what happened, and any potential supporting evidence (including statements from other witnesses) must be obtained. This ensures that evidence is available to support the various elements of the offence (for example, that the victim suffered mental harm, apprehension or fear as a result of the perpetrator's conduct). In long-standing abusive relationships, these statements can be lengthy; in one case, the statement was close to 50 pages long and had to be taken over several days.

Following the taking of that statement, corroborative evidence must be collected. This often includes obtaining statements from friends, family, and neighbours, and obtaining banking and financial records, phone records, downloads from social media and medical records. The witness list usually includes a much wider circle of persons than those involved in the initial incident to which police first responded. Police will try to obtain evidence from people who have had dealings with the parties over time. This evidence is quite often circumstantial, involving reports from family who were suddenly cut off from the complainant, or from an employer who had to terminate the employment of the complainant because of frequent unexplained absences and being uncontactable. That evidence can be difficult to track down given the passage of time between the early stages of the 'course of conduct' and the time that police become aware of it. For economic abuse cases in particular, the investigation can be akin to a fraud investigation, requiring investigators to determine where the money has gone. This would normally require specialist detective skills, but generally these matters are investigated by the same uniformed first responders who attended the initial reported assault incident. It is not usually their role to conduct complex investigations, and they generally do not have the necessary time to dedicate to it.

7.6.4 The Statutory Limitation Period

The delay in recognising and investigating these offences impacts on the ability to prosecute them in multiple ways. Not only is there a loss of important evidence and deterioration of witness' memory, but for a decade police and prosecutors were

7 Ahead of Their Time? The Offences of Economic …

running against the clock. The time limit for initiating proceedings for both economic and emotional abuse was, for a long time, 6 months. This was because no specific statute of limitations was legislated, therefore the default time limit for summary offences specified in s 26 of the *Justice Act 1959* (Tas) applied.

In effect, this meant that on the date the defendant was charged, the only conduct that he could be held accountable for was that carried out in the immediately preceding 6 months. This was inappropriate given the scope of offending that parliament seemingly intended the offences to cover. It was referred to in the second reading speech by the Deputy Leader of the Government in Council as including 'a pattern of behaviour which is calculated to keep a spouse or partner in a state of fear *for a period of years*' (Parkinson, 2004, p. 58). A 6-month limitation period simply did not sit well with an offence that is constituted by a (n often lengthy) 'course of conduct'.

This short limitation period raised two issues. First, the requirement for a course of conduct means that the prosecution must string together a number of examples of offending conduct. Any conduct outside that 6-month limitation could not be relied upon to prove the charge. Delays in reporting the offence, and the time needed to conduct proper investigations, meant that police and prosecutors were often out of time before the offending conduct was even 'discovered'. Often victims will not report anything (or, at least, not the full extent of the behaviour) until they have escaped the relationship and feel safe. Some cases are not reported until months or even years after the offending has ended. In those circumstances, Tasmania Police can still assist by issuing protective orders (*Family Violence Act 2004* (Tas) ss 14(1) and 16(1)), but they cannot pursue charges for emotional or economic abuse. The second issue raised by the short limitation period is that the conduct alleged can be behaviour that has persisted for years. What started as actual violence and threats of violence to control the victim can have conditioned the victim to placate the perpetrator. The earlier conduct may be the more serious, in terms of actual violence, but could only be relied upon at hearing as 'relationship evidence' in an attempt to contextualise the controlling behaviour (for a discussion of relationship evidence in Tasmania, see *Tasmania v Farmer* [2004] TASSC 104 and *Tasmania v Finnegan (No 2)* [2012] TASSC 1).

In 2015 these issues were addressed. Section 9A was inserted into the Act, commencing on 6 October 2015, and it provides:

> A complaint for an offence against section 8 or 9 must be made against a person within 12 months from the day on which the action, or the last action, that made up the course of conduct to which the matter of complaint relates, occurred.

This did not simply extend the time limit for the laying of charges (from 6 months to 12 months) but also rephrased the manner in which that time limit is to be interpreted. So long as the most recent act constituting the course of conduct occurred within the 12 months prior to the charge being laid, the offence can now extend to capture behaviours extending over many years of abuse. The rationale for the extension was provided by Lara Giddings (Shadow Attorney-General), who observed:

It takes time for a behaviour to be totally understood in its context. An important point that needs to be understood is that it can be a behaviour that repeated over and over again can amount to emotional or economic abuse. To have a time limit of six months is arguably not long enough. (Giddings, 2015)

This amendment has been almost solely responsible for the increase in charges being laid in 2016 and 2017. Twenty complaints were laid in the 2016–2017 financial year, whereas only seven or eight charges had been laid in the preceding 5 years in total.

7.7 Conclusion: Have the New Offences Been Worthwhile?

The novel contributions of Tasmania's family violence offences to the extant criminal law have been that victims should be protected against the non-physical harms of psychological abuse and economic abuse and the recognition that family violence may be constituted not by any single incident, but by a course of conduct. The offences constitute a groundbreaking extension of the criminal law. Pre-existing offences—such as assault, damage to property, and even family violence specific breaches of protective orders—could only address specific incidents. They could also only take into account conduct directed towards the victim, as opposed to other conduct intended to intimidate, isolate or humiliate them, such as the perpetrator damaging his own property, or making threats towards the victim's family members or pets.

The offences therefore fill a gap in the criminal law. The only other criminal offence that might have been relevant to the same conduct is the offence of stalking, which also requires a course of conduct. In Tasmania, s 192(1)(j) of the *Criminal Code* 1924 (Tas) defines stalking to include 'acting in another way that could reasonably be expected to cause the other person to be apprehensive or fearful'. However, there are some limitations with using this offence, such as the questionable label of 'stalking' to prohibit emotional abuse between intimate partners (Chalmers and Leverick 2008), and to date there has been no attempt to use it to cover conduct that socially isolates or degrades a current partner. Moreover, the offence of stalking does not include, as a mental element, an intent that the perpetrator's behaviour will have the effect of 'unreasonably controlling' the victim. Furthermore, the listed actions amounting to stalking include using covert means to cause harm or fear, following the person, keeping them under surveillance, loitering outside their residence or place of work, interfering with their property, or using postal services or electronic devices to send offensive material (*Criminal Code Act 1924* (Tas) s 192(1)(a)-(i)). Arguably the rules of statutory interpretation would require the more general subsection in the stalking provision ('acting in any other way...')—a provision that could theoretically extend to some emotionally or economically abusive behaviours—to be restricted to 'matters of the same kind' as those others listed (see *Campbell v Smith* [2005] TASDT 7 for a discussion of the principles of *ejusdem generis* and *noscitur a sociis*). In summary, 'stalking' is not a good descriptor for the economic and emotional abuse scenarios dealt with thus far, and may simply add a layer of confusion to an area where the community is already poorly informed (see Chap. 5 for a more expansive consideration of the limitations of prosecuting stalking in cases of family violence).

The Tasmanian experience of tackling non-physical domestic abuse through the creation of new statutory offences has certainly not been 'smooth sailing'. However, it is possible that previous evaluations (e.g. McMahon and McGorrery 2016) were unduly pessimistic. While it is true that the number of prosecutions has been very small, much has been learned and it is possible that the full potential of these offences is only just beginning to emerge, especially with the amended statute of limitations. Of those prosecutions that have occurred, convictions were obtained in more than half of the 73 cases identified; the offender either pleaded guilty (34) or the charge was found proven by the court (6). In only two cases was the charge dismissed after hearing. The remainder were withdrawn as part of plea negotiations or because police were unable to proceed with the charges. Notably, all prosecutions to date have involved male offenders. This is consistent not only with the manner in which the United Kingdom's new controlling or coercive behaviour offence has been utilised (Sharp-Jeffs and Learmonth 2017) but also accords with decades of research finding that coercive control is in fact a highly gendered form of behaviour, with women the victims and men almost exclusively the perpetrators (Robinson et al. 2018).

One of the authors (KB) is a police prosecutor and has experienced the benefit of being able to pursue an offence that covers the totality of morally abhorrent conduct in family violence situations. In her experience it is a common feature of emotional abuses cases that the victim's confidence and sense of self-worth, previously undermined by the abuse that they have experienced, is somewhat restored. It can only be seen as a positive development to have police take victims' accounts seriously, to pursue those charges, and for those charges to be found proven. These prosecutions are embedded within programs such as the *Safe at Home* initiative in Tasmania, and, more broadly, an increasing trend to criminalise family violence in its various forms. Building on the increasing body of research on the extent and long-term effects of domestic violence, including non-physical domestic abuse, on victims and their children (Laing 2000; Evans 2007), these offences allow courts to sentence offenders for the psychological harm that their behaviour causes, or was likely to cause, to victims (e.g. *Belbin v Bennett* (2011) 218 A Crim R 42).

Family violence has been described by the courts as a breach of trust, often because the victim is vulnerable:

> When a man assaults his wife or other female partner, his violence towards her can be accurately characterised as a breach of the position of trust which he occupies. It is an aggravating factor. Men who assault their wives are abusing the power and control which they so often have over the women with whom they live. The vulnerability of many such women is increased by the financial and emotional situation in which they find themselves,

which makes it difficult for them to escape: *Her Majesty's Attorney-General v O* [2004] TASSC 53, citing *R v Brown* (1992) 73 CCC (3d) 242, 249 (Alberta Court of Criminal Appeal).

The availability of charges of economic and emotional abuse have allowed police and prosecutors to pursue cases where the exploitation of that vulnerability is itself the larger offence, rather than the assault that drew police's attention. The value of the offences cannot be measured simply by the number of prosecutions to date, or what parliament intended them to achieve. The potential for the charges to deal with the many and varied social evils that arise in domestic abuse scenarios is only just starting to be seen and is certainly yet to be exhausted.

References

Bevin, E. (2016, August 1). Tasmanian man accused of preventing wife from making decisions, accessing joint accounts. *ABC News (online)*. Retrieved from http://www.abc.net.au/news/2016-08-01/tasmanian-man-prosecuted-for-alleged-economic-abuse/7679922.

Chalmers, J., & Leverick, F. (2008). Fair labelling in criminal law. *Modern Law Review, 71*(2), 217–246.

Department of Justice (Tas). (2003). *Safe at Home: A Criminal Justice Framework for Responding to Family Violence in Tasmania*, Options Paper. Retrieved from http://www.safeathome.tas.gov.au/__data/assets/pdf_file/0006/28374/Options_Paper.pdf.

Department of Justice (Tas). (2009). *Review of the Integrated Response to Family Violence: Discussion Paper*. Retrieved from http://www.safeathome.tas.gov.au/__data/assets/pdf_file/0004/124978/SAH_discussion_paper_FINAL-web.pdf.

Department of Justice (Tas). (2016). *Family Violence: Strengthening Our Legal Responses*, Consultation Paper. Retrieved from https://www.justice.tas.gov.au/__data/assets/pdf_file/0005/358682/Public_Consultation_Paper_Strengthening_Legal_Responses_to_Family_Violence_October_2016.pdf.

Douglas, H. (2018). Legal systems abuse and coercive control. *Criminology & Criminal Justice, 18*(1), 84–99.

Ellis, T. (2004, September 11). "Cure" as Flawed as the Ill. *The Hobart Mercury*.

Evans, I. (2007). *Battle-scars: Long-term effects of prior domestic violence*. Melbourne, VIC: Centre for Women's Studies and Gender Research, Monash University.

Giddings, L. (2015, November 25). Tasmania, *Parliamentary Debates*, Legislative Council.

Grealy, C., Wilczynski, A., Smith, K., & Henning, T. (2008). *Review of the Family Violence Act 2004 (Tas)*, report prepared for the Department of Justice (Tas). Hobart: Urbis. Retrieved from http://www.safeathome.tas.gov.au/__data/assets/pdf_file/0004/97636/Review_Report_March_2008.pdf.

Laing, L. (2000). *Children, Young People and Domestic Violence*, Issues Paper. Australian Domestic and Family Violence Clearinghouse. Retrieved from http://pandora.nla.gov.au/pan/34659/20030410-0000/issuespaper2.pdf.

Laing, L. (2016). Secondary victimisation: Domestic violence survivors navigating the family law system. *Violence Against Women, 23*(11), 1314–1335.

McMahon, M., & McGorrery, P. (2016). Criminalising emotional abuse, intimidation and economic abuse in the context of family violence: The Tasmanian experience. *University of Tasmania Law Review, 35*(2), 1–22.

Parkinson, D. (2004, August 25). Tasmania, *Parliamentary Debates*, House of Assembly.

Porter, A. (2018). Prosecuting domestic abuse in England and Wales: Crown Prosecution Service 'working practice' and new public managerialism. *Social & Legal Studies*, advance online publication. Retrieved from https://doi.org/10.1177/0964663918796699.

Robinson, A. L., Myhill, A., & Wire, J. (2018). Practitioner (mis)understandings of coercive control in England and Wales. *Criminology & Criminal Justice, 18*(1), 29–49.

Segrave, M., Wilson, D., & Fitz-Gibbon, K. (2018). Policing intimate partner violence in Victoria (Australia): Examining police attitudes and the potential of specialisation. *Australian & New Zealand Journal of Criminology, 18*(1), 99–116.

Sharp-Jeffs, N., & Learmonth, S. (2017). *Into Plain Sight: How Economic Abuse is Reflected in Successful Prosecutions of Controlling or Coercive Behaviour*. Retrieved from http://survivingeconomicabuse.org/wp-content/uploads/2017/12/PlainSight.pdf.

Stark, E. (2007). *Coercive control: How men entrap women in personal life*. Oxford: Oxford University Press.

Tasmanian Government. (2005a). About Safe at Home. Retrieved from http://www.safeathome.tas.gov.au/about_us.

Tasmanian Government. (2005b). Media Releases. Retrieved from http://www.safeathome.tas.gov.aunews/media_releases.

Tasmanian Government. (2013). *Safe at Home Annual Report 2012–2013*. Retrieved from http://www.safeathome.tas.gov.au/__data/assets/pdf_file/0007/305647/2012-13_Annual_Report.pdf.

Tasmania Police. (2018). Family Violence. Retrieved from http://www.police.tas.gov.au/what-we-do/family-violence/.

Walker, L. (1980). *The battered woman*. New York: Harper & Row.

Wiener, C. (2017). Seeing what is 'invisible in plain sight': Policing coercive control'. *Howard Journal of Crime and Justice, 56*(4), 500–515.

Wilcox, K. (2007). Island innovation, mainland inspiration: Comments on the Tasmanian. *Family Violence Act Alternative Law Journal, 32*(4), 213–218.

Legislation

Acts Interpretation Act 1931 (Tas)
Criminal Code Act 1924 (Tas)
Evidence Act 2001 (Tas)
Evidence (Audio and Audio Visual Links) Act 1999 (Tas)
Evidence (Children and Witnesses) Act 2001 (Tas)
Family Violence Act 2004 (Tas)
Family Violence Amendment Act 2015 (Tas)
Justice Act 1959 (Tas)
Relationships Act 2003 (Tas)
Serious Crime Act 2015 (E&W)

Cases

Allen v Tasmania Police [2004] TASSC 30
Belbin v Bennett (2011) 218 A Crim R 42
Boughey v R (1986) 161 CLR 10
Campbell v Smith [2005] TASDT 7
Director of Public Prosecutions (Acting) v JCN [2015] TASFC 13
Gunes v Pearson (1996) 89 A Crim R 297
Hawkins v R (No 3) (1994) 76 A Crim R 47
Her Majesty's Attorney-General v O [2004] TASSC 53

Howe v S [2013] TASMC 33
K v K [2012] TASMC 3
Kerrison v Buxton [2000] TASSC 15
McLean v Rundle [2011] TASMC (unreported, 4 November 2011)
R v Brown (1992) 73 CCC (3d) 242 (Alberta Court of Criminal Appeal)
R v Goldman [2004] VSC 165
Re S [2005] TASSC 89
Record of Investigation into Death (With Inquest) [2016] TASCD 217
Simpson v R [1996] TASSC 137
Tame v New South Wales (2002) 211 CLR 317
Tasmania v Farmer [2004] TASSC 104
Tasmania v Finnegan (No 2) [2012] TASSC 1
Thomas v Stewart [2017] TASMC (unreported, 4 September 2017)
Wilkinson v R [1985] TASSC 43

Chapter 8
From Social Construct to Legal Innovation: The Offence of Controlling or Coercive Behaviour in England and Wales

Cassandra Wiener

Abstract In December 2015, a new offence was introduced in England and Wales: controlling or coercive behaviour in an intimate or family relationship. This chapter reviews the societal, political, and legislative developments that paved the way for the introduction of that offence. In particular, this chapter discusses an apparent frustration with societal and governmental understandings of what constitutes domestic abuse, particularly in light of continued resistance to utilising the *Protection from Harassment Act 1997* (UK) to prosecute domestic abuse offenders. A change to those understandings was made possible by the groundbreaking work of Evan Stark, who highlighted that domestic abuse could be better understood as an ongoing strategy of domination, and that the harm inflicted on victims is as much structural (the deprivation of liberty) and psychological (emotional) as it is physical (injuries). This chapter describes and evaluates the attempt in England and Wales to translate Stark's construct of 'coercive control' into the criminal offence of 'controlling or coercive behaviour'.

Keywords Coercive control · Controlling or coercive behaviour · Serious Crime Act 2015 s 76

8.1 Introduction: Understanding the Problem

The criminal law in the context of domestic abuse has been the subject of significant scrutiny and criticism for the last half-century. The obstacles faced by criminal justice systems across the world are myriad and complex. This is not least because, in relatively recent history, there was little criminal justice recognition that domestic abuse is a crime at all. Feminists have been partly responsible for 'significant shifts

---

C. Wiener (✉)
School of Law, Politics & Sociology, University of Sussex, Brighton, UK
e-mail: C.Wiener@sussex.ac.uk

© Springer Nature Singapore Pte Ltd. 2020
M. McMahon and P. McGorrery (eds.), *Criminalising Coercive Control*,
https://doi.org/10.1007/978-981-15-0653-6_8

towards seeing domestic violence as a social and public problem in the United Kingdom, elsewhere in Europe and many other countries' (Hester 2013, p. 1; also see Bunch 1990). They have contributed to a rich body of research detailing 'powerful, vivid accounts of sexual violence and battering relationships and initial explanations of the phenomena'. (Johnson 1998, p. 23). Since at least 1990 there has also been heightened public awareness of the suffering caused as a practical consequence of a lack of criminal justice attention.

These developments have been responsible for the state, in England and Wales and elsewhere, having increasingly regarded domestic abuse as a serious criminal justice issue, such that 'the law no longer recognises a private realm in which a man is free to beat his wife' (Cretney and Davis 1996, p. 162). One aspect of this recognition of state responsibility has been a concerted effort in England and Wales by the Home Office, the Ministry of Justice, the Crown Prosecution Service (CPS) and the police to make tackling domestic abuse a criminal justice priority. This focus, and the shift toward seeing domestic abuse as a social and public problem, has had far-reaching ramifications. There has, since the 1990s, been a plethora of policy initiatives aimed at improving the criminal justice response to domestic abuse (Hester 2013, p. 79). In addition to amendments to the criminal law, these initiatives have been directed at police and CPS working culture and criminal justice procedure, but it is the improvements in the criminal law that are the focus of this chapter.

One of the difficulties for the intersection of domestic abuse and the criminal law, as has been observed in the United States, Australia and the United Kingdom, is the 'disconnect' between domestic abuse as it has historically been criminalised, and what social science research says about how it is perpetrated (Tuerkheimer 2004; Burke 2007; McMahon and McGorrery 2016). This disconnect is in part because the traditional focus of the criminal law has been 'transactional'; it frames crime in an incident-specific way. This transactional focus makes it ill-suited for the prosecution of behaviour that is ongoing and continuous. The offences against the person regime, that is the *Offences Against the Person Act 1861* (E&W) and associated common law offences, was, and still is, the framework most commonly used in England and Wales for the prosecution of domestic abuse. The regime conceives of crimes as a violation of a physical boundary that takes place at a particular instant in time. Emphasising transactional specificity and harm that is physical means that much of the harm experienced by survivors of domestic abuse and coercive control is excluded altogether. Deborah Tuerkheimer refers to this exclusion as 'cloaking' (Tuerkheimer 2004, p. 980).

The 'cloaking' occurs because of the very nature of domestic abuse: 'abusive behaviour does not occur as a series of discrete events' (Dutton 1992, p. 1208). Framing assaults in an incident-specific way causes difficulties for survivors who often cannot pinpoint ongoing abuse to specific dates on which particular assaults took place. While the date of a one-off incident, such as a mugging by a stranger, is memorable, dates of attacks that occur regularly are not. Instead, the nature of living with attacks that are continuous prompts a tendency on the part of victims to 'blend, generalise and summarise' (Tuerkheimer 2004, p. 979). This makes it difficult to prove domestic abuse offences in court (Burke 2004; Douglas 2015). Defence barristers can attack victims' credibility in a way that is reasonable in light of the evidential requirements of the relevant criminal law, but that is extremely distressing for the victim. Juries too find it difficult to understand the relationship and the abuse when presented with isolated acts divorced from the narrative necessary to give those acts meaning (Burke 2007; Mulligan 2009; Youngs 2015).

Finally, and perhaps most importantly, the rich body of research detailing abuse referred to above has had an impact on the way that abuse is framed and understood. Feminist scholars and activists have long described domestic abuse as a gendered phenomenon that is perpetrated almost entirely by men against a backdrop of an imbalance of power and control (Dobash and Dobash 1979). Typologies introduced by Michael Johnson in the 1990s supported the feminist framework via the development of distinct paradigms. Johnson's key insight, which has been extremely influential in the social science academic literature, was that 'in order to understand the nature of an individual's use of violence in an intimate relationship, you have to understand its role in the general control dynamics of that relationship' (Johnson 1995, p. 2). But the most significant contribution to the reframing of domestic abuse—from an academic, political and societal perspective—has been the work of Evan Stark. Drawing on his extensive caseload as a forensic social worker, Stark conceptualises domestic abuse as coercive control, a form of entrapment. He explains that the harm of domestic abuse is the 'subordin[ation] of women to an alien will' (Stark 2007 p. 15) via a combination of physical, psychological and intimidatory tactics. The wrong of the abuse is enacted on the terrain of the relationship, and it is the perpetrator's strategic intent that provides the thread that connects and organises the acts.

Subordination, domination and a perpetrator's strategic intent to control a victim are not captured by the existing offences against the person regime. Stark (2007, p. 63) begins his agenda for a criminal justice revolution by pointing out that legislation introduced to address stranger violence and public order offences does not provide the best framework for the prosecution of domestic abuse. In many ways, it should not be surprising that legal provisions introduced in the nineteenth century 'to address bar brawls and street fights' (Bishop 2016, p. 66) are ill-suited for the prosecution of domestic abuse well over a 100 years later.

This chapter reviews s 76 of the *Serious Crime Act 2015* (E&W) ('s 76'), an ambitious attempt by the UK government to translate Stark's construct of coercive control (hereafter referred to as 'coercive control') into the criminal law of England and Wales. In addition to this introduction, the chapter is divided into two parts. Part II provides the context and background to s 76 and reviews the *Protection from Harassment Act 1997* (UK), which was originally introduced to deal with stalking, but has proved invaluable to police and prosecutors in the context of domestic abuse. As societal and governmental understandings of what constitutes domestic abuse developed in the 2000s, resistance by the judiciary to the use of the *Protection from Harassment Act 1997* in the context of intimate relationships appeared anachronistic, and led to calls for further reform. Part III of this chapter then describes the consultation process initiated by Prime Minister Theresa May in

2014, asking for feedback on her proposals for a new offence based loosely on coercive control, with s 76 coming into force on 29 December 2015. Part IV concludes with a doctrinal review of s 76, with a particular focus on where the translation of Stark's construct into law has been relatively smooth, and where it has been rather more difficult.

8.2 The Protection from Harassment Act

The *Protection from Harassment Act* is important in part because it was the first attempt by the government of England and Wales to move away from the 'transactional' paradigm referred to above, and as such paved the way for the later s 76. It was not, however, originally intended by Parliament to be used in conjunction with domestic abuse at all. In the 1990s in England and Wales, pressure to legislate came about because of an increasingly strident media focus on stalking as a form of criminal behaviour in need of political attention. Emily Finch's research (Finch 2001) tracks the development of the concept of stalking in the UK via a content analysis of newspaper articles in the 1990s; she found that the media portrayal of stalking in the UK followed a distinct trajectory. Early reports focused on non-relational stalking, which takes place where the victim and perpetrator have never been intimately involved. In particular, the kinds of cases that received media attention were high-profile celebrity cases that had previously been reported in the US. The Home Office also conducted a review of stalking at around this time and its findings supported Finch's: 'public perceptions of stalking have been coloured by the media attention given to high-profile cases involving public figures or personalities' (Harris 2000). This media focus—on stalkers as 'dangerous and mentally ill with a tendency towards the commission of violent crime' (Finch 2001, p. 109) —fed a public preoccupation with celebrity victims in need of protection from delusional strangers (Campbell 1997). This placed 'stalking' *outside the domestic abuse paradigm*.

The social construction of stalking as non-relational and therefore as outside the domestic abuse paradigm had consequences. When the draft *Protection from Harassment Bill* was debated in the House of Commons on 17 December 1996, for example, there was no reference to domestic abuse. In particular there was no explicit recognition of 'relational' versus 'non-relational' stalking. Instead, there seems to have been an assumption throughout that references to stalking are to non-relational stalking. The discussion in Parliament centres around stranger stalking, neighbourhood disputes, and nuisance neighbours (House of Commons Debates, 1996), and it is likely, therefore, that the *Protection from Harassment Act* was not designed to capture harassment within an intimate relationship. Certainly, this was the conclusion later drawn by the Court of Appeal (*R v Curtis* [2010] EWCA Crim 123; *R v Widdows* [2011] EWCA Crim 1500).

The Home Office originally anticipated (in line with its construction of the celebrity stalking paradigm) that the *Protection from Harassment Act* would be used relatively infrequently, perhaps around 200 cases a year (Harris 2000). This turned out to be a dramatic underestimation: in 1998 there were a total of 5,800 charges laid (Povey and Prime 1999). By 2016 this number had more than doubled to 12,986 for harassment and stalking (Crown Prosecution Service 2016). What became apparent was that the new stalking laws were not, in fact, being used to prosecute 'stranger' non-relational stalking offences. Instead, they were proving to be invaluable to police for the prosecution of insidious behaviours in the context of domestic abuse (Harris 2000). As it became clear that the *Protection from Harassment Act* was being used most frequently in the context of domestic abuse, it began to fall to the courts to determine the boundaries of actionable harassment. While the courts were prepared to allow the extension of the *Protection from Harassment Act* to cover relational stalking where a couple had separated, they were resistant if the abuse in question took place while a couple were still together.

The first judicial 'push-back' was Otton LJ's judgement in *R v Hills* [2001] 1 FLR 580 (henceforth '*Hills*'). The offender, in that case, was convicted at first instance of harassment, which consisted of two assaults that took place six months apart while he was still living with the victim. Otton LJ found that those assaults did not amount to harassment for the purposes of the *Protection from Harassment Act*, and his conclusion was influenced by his understanding of Parliament's intention for the *Protection from Harassment Act* (at [31]):

> It is to be borne in mind that the state of affairs which was relied upon by the prosecution was miles away from the "stalking" type of offence for which the Act was intended. That is not to say that it is never appropriate so to charge a person who is making a nuisance of himself to his partner or wife when they have become estranged. However, in a situation such as this, when they were frequently coming back together and intercourse was taking place (apparently a video was taken of them having intercourse) it is unrealistic to think that this fell within the stalking category which either postulates a stranger or an estranged spouse.

Otton LJ was correct to conclude that there was a '"stalking" type of offence for which the Act was intended'. As stated above, the only kind of stalking referred to in Parliament as the Bill was debated was non-relational 'stranger' stalking. Otton LJ was prepared to countenance some movement away from this parliamentary position, and to extend the application of the legislation to include 'a person who is making a nuisance of himself to his partner or wife when they have become estranged' (at 31). He was not, however, prepared to extend the application of the *Protection from Harassment Act* to include relational stalking where the partners are still in a relationship. This judicial push-back that began with *Hills* also continued with Pill LJ's judgements in *Widdows* and *Curtis*, in 2010 and 2011.

There are two points of importance here. First, by 2010 it was becoming hard to avoid the conclusion that Parliament based its intentions for the *Protection from Harassment Act* on a construction of the nature of stalking that had been superseded. The use to which the *Protection from Harassment Act* had been put by police and the courts since 1997 was not that intended by Parliament, but was necessary in light of what was becoming increasingly apparent about the nature of harassment and stalking (Bishop and Bettinson 2015). Pill LJ's 'judicial reluctance' (Bishop and Bettinson 2015) to allow the application of the *Protection from Harassment Act* in cases where a couple were still together hampered the ability of the police to take action and became, to use the government's own wording in their later report, 'an unhelpful barrier' (Home Office 2014b).

Second, and relatedly, governmental and societal understandings of domestic abuse have shifted since the enactment of the *Protection from Harassment Act*. Stark's articulation of control—he published his key text in 2007—proved to be extremely influential. Reframing domestic abuse as coercive control and incorporating (as he does) as agenda for a criminal justice revolution has had an important impact. Stark's vision is to put the power imbalance, 'entrapment', at the centre of a new domestic abuse offence, rather than at the periphery. One reason for the 'judicial reluctance' was a lack of judicial consideration of the existence of power imbalances in the context of domestic abuse. This lack of focus can be detected in all three of the cases referred to above that limited the police use of the *Protection from Harassment Act* in the context of domestic abuse. Thus, at the same time that the courts were turning their attention away from power imbalances, there was a heightened governmental recognition, post-Stark, of their significance.

8.3 The Governmental Consultation

The attempt in England and Wales to translate Stark's coercive control into a criminal offence began with an effective political campaign run by a coalition of women's groups who were heavily influenced by Stark's work (e.g. Sara Charlton Foundation, Women's Aid and Palladin). This led to the consultation that was launched by then Home Secretary Theresa May in 2014 (Home Office 2014a). It was at this point that translation of coercive control met with its first obstacle. Theresa May was clear about the scope of her consultation: its remit was limited. The central question of the consultation was to establish whether or not a new criminal offence was needed (Home Office 2014a, p. 5):

> [T]his consultation is specifically focused on whether we should create a specific offence that captures patterns of coercive and controlling behaviour in intimate relationships, in line with the Government's non-statutory definition of domestic abuse.

One important factor was overlooked: no time was spent defining what the government meant by 'patterns of coercive and controlling behaviour'. In particular, an assumption was made that coercive control amounts to psychological rather than physical abuse. May explained that 'the consultation asks whether reinforcing the law to capture patterns of non-violent behaviour within intimate relationships will offer better protection' (Home Office 2014a, p. 5). This assumption, that coercive control is psychological abuse, is at odds with Stark's framework. Stark is clear: he conceptualises coercive control as a strategy of domination that incorporates non-physical *and* physical behaviours (Stark, 2007).

Later, during the parliamentary debate that took place in January 2015 on the question of coercive control and physical violence, then Attorney General Robert Buckland (2015, p.172) said:

> In the consultation we identified a gap in the law—behaviour that we would regard as abuse that did not amount to violence. Violent behaviour already captured by the criminal law is outside the scope of the offence. Within the range of existing criminal offences a number of tools are at the disposal of the police and prosecution, which are used day in and day out. We do not want duplication or confusion; we want an extra element that closes a loophole.

In these comments, Buckland has moved away from Stark's coercive control. The last sentence gives an insight into why: 'we want an extra element that closes a loophole'. It is possible that in his desire for an 'extra element' he was over-influenced by the 'loophole'. In other words, the Attorney General appears to construct his understanding of coercive control around a legal lacuna that he previously identified, and not the other way around. It would have made more sense to reverse that process, to begin with an understanding of coercive control, and then conduct a review of legislation. By approaching the project in terms of a legislative gap rather than as a newly identified form of behaviour in need of a fresh approach, the Attorney General unintentionally reinforced some of what was unhelpful about the old regime. In particular, while it is entirely appropriate to state that 'violent behaviour already captured by the criminal law is outside the scope of the offence', the Attorney General did not appear to consider the difficulties that exist with prosecuting violent coercive behaviour under the existing offences against the person regime.

The government published a summary of responses with a clear conclusion: 85% of respondents felt that the current law did not provide adequate protection for victims of coercive control (Home Office 2014b, p. 5). Work began on the draft clauses immediately, and the Government introduced new clauses on what it referred to as 'controlling or coercive behaviour' in the *Serious Crime Bill*, which was the government's major crime bill of 2014–15. The new clauses received considerable cross-party support and became law as s 76 of the *Serious Crime Act 2015* (E&W) on 29 December 2015.

8.4 The New Offence: *Serious Crime Act 2015* (E&W) s 76

The remainder of the chapter consists of a doctrinal review of s 76. The most important components of s 76 for the purposes of this chapter are subsections (1), (2) and (4), which are set out in full below:

76. Controlling or coercive behaviour in an intimate or family relationship

(1) A person (A) commits an offence if—

   (a) A repeatedly or continuously engages in behaviour towards another person (B) that is controlling or coercive;

(b) at the time of the behaviour, A and B are personally connected;
  (c) the behaviour has a serious effect on B;
  (d) A knows or ought to know that the behavior will have a serious effect on B.

(2) A and B are 'personally connected' if—

  (a) A is in an intimate personal relationship with B, or
  (b) A and B live together and—

   (i) they are members of the same family or
   (ii) they have previously been in an intimate personal relationship with each other

(4) A's behaviour has a "serious effect" on B if

  (a) it causes B to fear, on at least two occasions, that violence will be used against B, or
  (b) it causes B serious alarm or distress which has a substantial adverse effect on B's usual day-to-day activities.

Subsection (1) thus sets out the new crime. It is immediately apparent that there is a move away from an incident-specific focus with the use of the phrase 'repeatedly or continuously'. This allows for a properly contextual approach that is more in line with Stark's coercive control. Also, and most importantly, the power imbalance is placed, correctly and for the first time, at the centre of the offence. While it is still early days (at the time of writing there has only been one reported Court of Appeal decision: *R v Conlon* [2017] EWCA Crim 2450 (henceforth '*Conlon*')) this appears to have had a positive impact on the way in which the Court of Appeal understands the significance of perpetrator behaviour in the context of domestic abuse.

It is not surprising that there are areas where the translation from social construct to law has been imperfect; translating a complex sociocultural phenomenon into law is inevitably a difficult exercise. In its determination to 'close a loophole', the government positioned 'controlling or coercive behaviour' as primarily non-physical (the definition of *serious effect* in subsection (4) refers to fear, alarm and distress, but not to actual physical violence). Further, s 76(1)(b) requires that the perpetrator and victim are 'personally connected', using the status of the relationship to define the offence. Former intimate partners are thus excluded from the offence's operation unless they live together. Both of those aspects of the new offence, the targeting of 'non-physical' behaviour and the restriction of its application to those who are in a continuing relationship, are examples of the government's determination to avoid 'duplication' with existing legislation. This has, however, resulted in the creation of unhelpful artificial boundaries.

8.4.1 The Difficulty with Coercive Control as Psychological Abuse

Possibly the most significant deviation from Stark's coercive control is its construction as purely 'psychological' or 'non-violent' abuse. The Attorney General made it clear in the House of Commons debate that 'violent behaviour already captured by the criminal law is outside the scope of the offence'. But Stark is also clear: psychological abuse and coercive control are not the same thing. In a recent interview for *New York Magazine* Stark was asked directly about the difference between psychological abuse and coercive control (Romm 2018). He explained:

> [S]ometimes the terms are used interchangeably, but I think that's a misnomer. Psychological abuse is not defined to include the elements of coercive control, such as taking people's money, such as stalking, such as physical violence, such as sexual abuse. So all those other elements of coercive control are not really elements of psychological abuse.

One of the problems caused by excluding physical abuse from the crime of controlling or coercive behaviour is that the physical abuse that most often forms part of coercive control is often not investigated by police or charged by the CPS. In the same interview (Romm 2018), in answer to the question: 'is physical violence typically part of coercive control?', Stark explained:

> In about 70, 75 per cent of cases, it is. But it's not always the kind of bone-breaking violence that you see on TV or on posters. In a typical case, which goes on for an extended period of time, the typical path is low-level violence—slaps, pushes, shoves, grabbing. The significance lies in its cumulative effect.

The 'low-level violence' described by Stark above causes, cumulatively, significant harm to the victim. It is, of course, open to the CPS to charge all violence as individual assaults, yet for the reasons already mentioned this violence rarely gets charged separately under the offences against the person regime. Furthermore, even if it were to be charged separately, common law offences of assault and/or battery recognise physical harm to the person, but not the more profound harm caused by entrapment that survivors say is by far and away the most significant harm of coercive control.

At the time of writing, there has only been one reported Court of Appeal decision reviewing the application of s 76. In *Conlon*, the Court of Appeal (at [26]) defined coercive control as psychological abuse: 'The new offence targets psychological abuse in which one partner to a relationship coerces or controls the life of the other without necessarily or frequently using threats or violence.' Although Robert Conlon was charged separately with only one charge of assault occasioning actual bodily harm there were numerous references throughout the judgement to his frequently violent behaviour to the victim. For example:

> [O]n 28th October 2015 ... [Conlon] punched the complainant in the face and when she fell to the floor he continued to punch her. (at [4])

> While on police bail, on 8th November 2015 the appellant jumped on top of the complainant when she was in bed, she screamed and to stop her screaming the appellant put his fingers in the complainant's mouth. (at [5])
>
> [On 19th November 2015] In anger he repeatedly punched the complainant to the head and face, kicked her to the back and pulled her by the hair to prevent her from leaving. (at [18])
>
> [O]n occasions the complainant reported that the appellant had been violent to her, pinning her to the wall and shouting at her. (at [8])
>
> On 15th July ... the appellant refused to leave her house as she tried to push him out and [he] punched her in the right breast. (at [13])

Conlon was only charged with one of the incidents of violence described in the above paragraphs, namely the incident on 19 November. The violence exhibited by Conlon in this case supports Stark's conceptualisation of coercive control, and is typical of perpetrator behaviour. Constructing the new offence of 'controlling or coercive behaviour' as something separate to 'physical violence' in *Conlon* meant that a significant amount of violence went uncharged. In its summing up of the harm suffered by the victim the Court of Appeal referred to Conlon's behaviour as 'persistent and sustained over a period of some 14 months' and 'secondly that it included one incident of serious physical violence' (at [30]). The fact that she was punched, kicked and pinned to the wall on other occasions goes unmentioned—to use Tuerkheimer's terminology, it is still, despite s 76, 'cloaked'.

The violence that goes uncharged is the ongoing violence that Stark highlights is typical of coercive control. As already discussed, the incident-specific nature of the offences against the person regime is inconsistent with victims' experiences of physical abuse that are consistent and ongoing. Thus the separation of the physical and psychological aspects of coercive control causes problems for the prosecution of both types of offence. Survivors still have to pinpoint physical abuse to specific dates on which particular assaults took place, which is difficult when that abuse is ongoing. Furthermore, coercive control is harder to understand in the absence of the physical abuse that is a key component. In other words, 'the binary juxtaposition of physical and psychological/emotional abuse fails to capture the embodied physicality and brutality of coercive control' (Barnett 2017, p. 380).

8.4.2 Using the End of the Relationship as a Legal Boundary

Section 76(1)(b) states that, in order for a crime to be committed, at the time of the behaviour, the defendant and the victim must be 'personally connected'. Section 76(4) states that two people are personally connected if they are in an intimate personal relationship (but not necessarily living together); or, if they live together and are members of the same family; or, if they live together and have previously been in an intimate personal relationship. This is the second example where Stark's version of coercive control has not been accurately translated into law. The end of the relationship becomes a legal boundary. If the relationship is ongoing, then the perpetrator behaviour might be 'controlling or coercive' contrary to s 76. If, on the other hand, the perpetrator and victim are no longer in a relationship, then the police will typically investigate whether or not the perpetrator's actions amount to harassment contrary to the *Protection from Harassment Act 1997*. The decision to use the end of the relationship as a marker is also related to the Attorney General's comment that s 76 'close[d] a loophole'. It was felt that victims who had left their partners were adequately protected by the *Protection from Harassment Act* (House of Commons Debates, 2015).

Using the end of the relationship to determine which of two crimes has occurred is dangerous for a number of reasons. First, it assumes a transactional moment (of separation) that often does not exist, and this is logistically challenging for police and other organisations that are working to keep the victim safe. It is well established that leaving a relationship is the point at which a victim is most at need of protection, partly because, as Tuerkheimer (2013, p. 82) explains, it is a difficult and protracted process:

> The paradigm of the transactional breakup—one that occurs at a distinct moment in time, upon mutual agreement by two parties hopelessly fails to capture the complexities that attend ending abusive relationships. In these relationships, separation is a process. Breaking up is often difficult, but the realities confronting battered women make separating from a partner distinctly dangerous, complicated, and protracted. For these women, there is typically no moment of breakup; rather, domestic violence victims "leave" relationships multiple times, in different ways, to varying degrees of success.

The danger to the victim that is implicit in the breakup of an abusive relationship together with its protracted (rather than transactional) nature means that using it as a pivotal legal moment is especially ill-advised.

Second, it is confusing from a 'fair labelling' perspective, especially for the victim. The control does not necessarily end with the relationship, and to prosecute it as a different crime (or not at all) is unhelpful. This also means that separation, even if it could be said to exist as a meaningful moment in time, should not be imbued with unwarranted significance in the context of control. As Tuerkheimer (2013) explains: 'control is ratcheted up when women attempt to separate' (p. 85). The behaviour patterns manifested by the perpetrator might take a different form (such as 'legal systems abuse': Douglas 2018), but the malevolent strategic intent (that gives meaning to the patterns) continues in much the same way as it did before. What distinguishes the abuser from all the other people in the victim's life is his desire to continue controlling her. In other words, the boundary between the period of her life when she is in an intimate relationship and the period when she could be finally said to have left it is not always a particularly conceptually significant one—*to the victim*—in the context of the coercive control exerted by him over her. This is backed up by social science research that shows that 'the behaviour itself is a much more important indicator (of harm) than the relationship state' (Monckton-Smith 2017, p. 5; Tuerkheimer 2013; Barnett 2017). Using that boundary to determine whether the victim is experiencing 'harassment' under the

Protection from Harassment Act or 'controlling or coercive behaviour' contrary to s 76 makes little sense.

One last point in relation to the definition of 'personally connected' is the subsection 76(6) definition of 'members of the same family' for the purposes of s 76 (4). This part of the definition is unnecessarily wide. The defendant and victim are members of the same family, and therefore personally connected, if they are 'relatives' (s 76(6)(c)). Stark argues that coercive control is perpetrated almost always by men who are, or who have been, in an intimate relationship with their victims. From the 'clear labelling' perspective it is detrimental to draft the offence so widely that it could include, for example, an overbearing parent or a controlling sibling (Youngs 2015). Reece argues that extending definitions of domestic abuse to include family members as well as intimate partners devalues 'the specificity of the category of domestic violence' (Reece 2006, p. 791). She emphasises that 'if domestic violence occurs everywhere then domestic violence occurs nowhere' (Reece 2006 p. 791).

8.4.3 Moving Away from the Incident-Specific Focus: 'Repeatedly or Continuously'

Section 76(1)(a) states that a person commits an offence if they 'repeatedly or continuously' engage in behaviour that is controlling or coercive. The use of 'repeatedly or continuously' is a novel way of moving beyond the incident-specific focus. The difficulty of the transactional specificity requirements of the criminal law in the context of domestic abuse has already been discussed. The *Protection from Harassment Act* attempted to deal with this problem by referring to a 'course of conduct', which must involve 'in the case of conduct in relation to a single person, conduct on at least two occasions in relation to that person' (s 7(3)(a)). The idea of a 'course of conduct' crime was thus an attempt to accommodate the ongoing nature of the behaviour patterns that constitute stalking. In fact, defining a crime by reference to two separate incidents instead of just one incident did not 'move' the transactional nature of the legal structure very far. In some ways, it had the unintended effect of increasing the incident-specific focus. If the intention of the 'course of conduct' element' of the *Protection from Harassment Act* was to better accommodate the patterns of behaviour experienced by victims, what actually happened was that judges 'confounded such an analysis by lapsing back into an examination of individual incidents of assault and battery' (Bishop 2016, p. 68; see also Ormerod and Rees 2001, p. 319; Infield and Platford 2000, p. 10; Addison and Lawson-Cruttenden, pp. 30–32; *R v Hills* [2001] 1 FLR 580; *Lau v DPP* [2000] Crim LR 580; *R v Qosja* [2016] EWCA Crim 1543).

The case of *Hills* is an example of just such a 'lapse'. Gavin Hills was convicted at first instance of harassment consisting of two assaults that took place six months apart while he was still living with his victim. Otton LJ found that the assaults did not amount to harassment for the purposes of the *Protection from Harassment Act*. There was plenty of evidence before Otton LJ of the abusive nature of the relationship in that case, with multiple incidents of abuse that the victim found it difficult (in court) to pin to specific times and dates: 'over a period of time and on a fairly regular basis, [the victim] had been ill-treated by the appellant' (at [10]). The particulars on the indictment included that 'the appellant assaulted the complainant on a number of occasions by throwing a stool at her, hitting her, restricting her breathing by putting his hands over her mouth or around her throat and attempting to smother her with a pillow' (at [11]). Otton LJ nevertheless found that the two incidents of assault that formed the basis of the harassment charge could not constitute a course of conduct, because the two incidents were isolated and separated by six months, and 'the prosecution might have been wiser to have abandoned the harassment count and to have concentrated on the two substantive counts of violence, and with more prospects of success' (at [32]).

Bishop (2015) described this as 'judicial disbelief of the alleged behaviour between the two incidents' (p. 188). Otton LJ did not need to consider the relationship as a whole or think about whether or not there may have been a power imbalance between the defendant and his victim that might explain the longevity of the relationship. Instead, Otton LJ (correctly) focused on an examination of the two individual incidents of assault, both abstracted from the abusive backdrop that the prosecution unsuccessfully tried to argue demonstrated the necessary course of conduct for the harassment offence.

Thus, s 76(1)(a)'s use of 'repeatedly or continuously' marks significant progress. It allows the victim to move away from dates/times of 'incidents' of control, and instead take a more contextual approach, which is much more in line with Stark's coercive control because it reflects the way in which victims 'story' their experiences. If the *Protection from Harassment Act* had required 'repeated or continuous' conduct, rather than 'conduct on at least two occasions', then the ongoing nature of the abuse in *Hills* might have carried more weight. Media reporting of early s 76 cases appears to reflect an appropriately contextual approach to the abuse. For example, the *Express* described how defendant Robert Simmons—

> Hosed his wife with cold water, forced her to keep a "mistake book", 'created an "almost cult-like" atmosphere and regularly tormented his wife if she failed to meet his expectations at their remote island farmhouse. (Wilkie 2017)

Rather than counting incidents, the evidence in court described a state of affairs (for example the "almost cult-like" atmosphere and the use of the adverb 'regularly'). Certainly the only reported Court of Appeal decision available at the time of writing, *Conlon*, suggests that judges are taking an appropriately contextual approach to the abuse with only a passing reference to 'repeatedly or continuously' thus illustrating that, at least in this particular case, the wording is serving its purpose without (yet) giving the court any difficulties (at [26]).

8.4.4 Bringing the Power Dimension into the Courtroom

One aspect of the *Conlon* judgment that is very encouraging is the way in which the Court of Appeal now considers the power differential between the parties. This is exactly the differential that was missing from the *Protection from Harassment Act* judgements referred to earlier (*Hills, Widdows* and *Curtis*). Conlon was convicted at first instance of controlling or coercive behaviour and was sentenced to a total of four and a half years' imprisonment, four of which were for the controlling or coercive behaviour. Conlon appealed his sentence on the basis that the sentence was excessive because the judge failed to take into account the victim's behaviour towards the perpetrator. The Court of Appeal rejected the argument, and was not convinced by this attempt to reframe the abuse as a relationship dispute. Instead of considering the actions of the victim as individual responses in isolation, the Court of Appeal commented:

> The new offence targets psychological abuse in which one partner to the relationship coerces or controls the life of the other without necessarily or frequently using threats or violence. It follows, in our judgement, that the manifestations of the serious effect on the victim of such behaviour by the offender will vary from case to case. In some cases, of which this was clearly one, the victim will, on occasions, find it difficult to resist the persuasive influence of the offender and may as a result convince herself that she is the one at fault. (at [26])

The Court of Appeal thus considered the responses of the victim within the framework of coercive control, and this means that it was prepared to emphasise rather than ignore the imbalance of power between the parties. In particular, there was judicial understanding of some of the more nuanced aspects of the effects of coercive control: 'the victim will, on occasions, find it difficult to resist the persuasive influence of the offender' (at [26]). This meant that the Court of Appeal was able to find that the actions of the parties were not equivalent: 'nothing done by the complainant justified or could justify the actions or the reactions of the appellant' (at [28]).

By way of comparison, in *Curtis*, (one of the earlier *Protection from Harassment Act* judgements), Daniel Curtis was convicted at first instance of harassment on the basis of six violent incidents that occurred while he was living with Donna Brand, his then partner and victim. While there was a power imbalance between the pair, Pill LJ did not take it into account. Curtis pushed Donna (on three separate occasions, once so that she fell over and hit her head, and once so that he bruised her chest), manhandled her, and put his hands around her neck (on two separate occasions). The only violent physical contact initiated by Donna was a punch made in self-defence (Curtis had his hands around her neck). On another of the occasions, she threw some beer over him, but only after he had been angry and was shouting at her. Pill LJ acknowledged that Curtis was more at fault than Donna: 'the jury would have been entitled … to conclude that the appellant's conduct was deplorable and worse than that of Donna' (at [32]). He did not, however, go on to consider the significance of Curtis being more at fault. In other words, he did not consider that the one-sided nature of the violence indicated the existence of a power imbalance between the parties in this case. Curtis was more at fault; he was the perpetrator. Donna was less at fault, and her actions were mostly defensive. Instead, Pill LJ seemed to view the violence before him in *Curtis* 'as individual, physically aggressive responses to a relationship dispute' (Bishop 2016, p. 62). For example, Pill LJ stated that 'the spontaneous outbursts of ill-temper and bad behaviour, with aggression on both sides, ... interspersed as those outbursts were with considerable periods of affectionate life, cannot be described as such a course of conduct' (at [32]). Pill LJ's use of the phrase 'on both sides', is inappropriately suggestive of an *equal* balance of power between the parties.

In this way, s 76 could be said to have facilitated an important and progressive development, and goes some way to compensate for the difficulties around the artificial boundaries referred to above. As Stark himself said: 'the wrong identified by coercive control is the wrong of subordination. The fact that a major state has for the first time in history identified this as a wrong when committed in personal life is revolutionary in implication, however imperfect the execution' (Personal communication, 4 September 2017).

8.5 Conclusion

In many ways, s 76 has provided a progressive and innovative alternative route for the prosecution of domestic abuse in England and Wales. In particular, the way in which the power imbalance between defendant and victim is the focus of the courtroom investigation, rather than at the periphery, makes for a more meaningful assessment of the actions of the defendant and of the harm suffered by the victim. The construction of the offending behaviour as taking place 'repeatedly or continuously' has allowed the court to move away from its unhelpful tendency to 'lapse back' into an incident-specific focus that was historically a problem in the context of domestic abuse. Some difficulties remain, however. Parliament's construction of a legislative 'gap' did not allow it to give enough consideration to the behaviour (domestic abuse and coercive control) that it was trying to regulate. The analysis of s 76 shows that it reflects mistaken assumptions as to the nature of coercive control: in particular that coercive control consists exclusively of psychological or emotional abuse (and does not also include physical violence), and that there is a transactional moment of separation for a victim that can operate as a useful legal boundary. Developments since 2015 show how this could be improved upon: the *Domestic Abuse (Scotland) Act 2018* deals with both of those issues and is an example of what Evan Stark has referred to as a 'gold standard' for domestic abuse and coercive control legislation (for further discussion, see Chaps. 9 and 10 in this volume). It could point the way for further reform in England and Wales (Brooks 2018).

References

Barnett, A. (2017). 'Greater than the mere sum of its parts': Coercive control and the question of proof. *Child and Family Law Quarterly, 29*(4), 379–400.

Bishop, C. (2016). Domestic violence: The limitations of a legal response. In S. Hilda & V. Bettinson (Eds.), *Interdisciplinary perspectives on protection, prevention and intervention*. London: Palgrave Macmillan.

Bishop, C., & Bettinson, V. (2015). Is the creation of a discrete offence of coercive control necessary to combat domestic violence? *Northern Ireland Legal Quarterly, 66*(2), 179–197.

Brooks, L. (2018, February 1). Scotland set to pass "gold standard" domestic abuse law. *Guardian (online)*. Retrieved from https://www.theguardian.com/society/2018/feb/01/scotland-set-to-pass-gold-standard-domestic-abuse-law.

Buckland, R. HC Deb. (2015, January 20), *591*(172).

Bunch, C. (1990). Women's rights as human rights: Toward a re-vision of human rights. *Human Rights Quarterly, 12*(4), 486–498.

Burke, A. (2007). Domestic violence as a crime of pattern and intent: An alternative reconceptualization. *George Washington Law Review, 75*, 553–612.

Campbell, K. (1997/1998). Stalking around the main issue. *Kings College Law Journal, 8*, 128–133.

Cretney, A., & Davis, G. (1996). Prosecuting 'domestic' assault. *Criminal Law Review, 3*, 162–174.

Crown Prosecution Service. (2016). *Violence Against Women and Girls Crime Report 2015–16*. Retrieved from www.cps.gov.uk/publications/docs/cps_vawg_report_2016.pdf.

Dobash, R., & Dobash, R. (1979). *Violence against wives: A case against the patriarchy*. New York, NY: Free Press.

Douglas, H. (2015). Do we need a specific domestic violence offence? *Melbourne University Law Review, 39*(2), 434–471.

Douglas, H. (2018). Legal systems abuse and coercive control. *Criminology & Criminal Justice, 18*(1), 84–99.

Dutton, M. (1992). Understanding women's responses to domestic violence: A redefinition of battered woman syndrome. *Hofstra Law Review, 21*, 1191–1242.

Finch, E. (2001). *The criminalisation of stalking: Constructing the problem, evaluating the solution*. London: Cavendish.

Harris, J. (2000). *An evaluation of the use and effectiveness of the protection from harassment act 1997*, Home Office Research Study 203. London: Home Office.

Hester, M. (2013). Who does what to whom? Gender and domestic violence perpetrators in English police records. *European Journal of Criminology, 10*(5), 623–627.

Office, Home. (2014a). *Strengthening the law on domestic abuse—A consultation*. London: Home Office.

Office, Home. (2014b). *Strengthening the law on domestic abuse consultation—Summary of responses*. London: Home Office.

Infield, P., & Platford, G. (2000). *The law of harassment and stalking*. London: Butterworths.

Johnson, M. (1995). Patriarchal terrorism and common couple violence: Two forms of violence against women. *Journal of Marriage and the Family, 57*(2), 283–294.

Johnson, H. (1998). Rethinking survey research on violence against women. In R. Dobash & R. Dobash (Eds.), *Rethinking violence against women*. Thousand Oaks, CA: Sage.

McMahon, M., & McGorrery, P. (2016). Criminalising coercive and controlling behaviour: The next step in the prosecution of family violence? *Alternative Law Journal, 41*(2), 98–101.

Monckton-Smith, J., Szymanska, K., & Haile, S. (2017). *Exploring the relationship between stalking and homicide*. Gloucestershire: Suzy Lamplugh Trust.

Mulligan, S. (2009). Redefining domestic violence: Using the violence and control paradigm for domestic violence legislation. *Children's Legal Rights Journal, 29*, 33–43.

Povey, D., & Prime, J. (1999). *Recorded crime statistics England and Wales, April 1998–March 1999*, Home Office Statistical Bulletin 18/99. London: HM Stationery Office.

Reece, H. (2006). The end of domestic violence. *Modern Law Review, 69*(5), 770–791.

Ormerod, O., & Rees, T. (2001). Harassment: Separate incidents not linked. *Criminal Law Review*, 318–320.

Romm, C. (2018, May 8). A domestic-violence expert on Eric Schneiderman and Coercive Control. *The Cut*. Retrieved from https://www.thecut.com/2018/05/an-abuse-expert-on-schneiderman-and-coercive-control.html.

Tuerkheimer, D. (2004). Recognising and remedying the harm of battering: A call to criminalize domestic violence. *Journal of Criminal Law and Criminology, 94*(4), 970–1032.

Tuerkheimer, D. (2013). Breakups. *Yale Journal of Law and Feminism, 25,* 51–100.

Wilkie, S. (2017, October 11). Shetland man jailed for 30 years of abusing wife. *Express*. Retrieved from www.express.co.uk/news/uk/865233/Shetland-man-Robert-Simmons-jailed30-years-abusing-wife.

Youngs, J. (2015). Domestic violence and the criminal law: Reconceptualising reform. *Journal of Criminal Law, 79*(1), 55–70.

Chapter 9
The Making of the New 'Gold Standard': The *Domestic Abuse (Scotland) Act 2018*

Marsha Scott

Abstract On 1 February 2018, the Scottish Parliament unanimously voted to pass the *Domestic Abuse (Scotland) Bill 2018*, legislation that Professor Evan Stark called the new 'gold standard' for criminalising coercive control and domestic abuse. The occasion was marked by the entire body of parliamentarians in the Debating Chamber standing, turning to the public gallery, and giving an ovation to survivors and advocates sitting there. For the first time, Scotland had a specific offence defining and criminalising domestic abuse, an offence that comprehensively describes psychological abuse and places it securely in the centre of behaviours deemed criminal. This chapter outlines the notable features of this new law, describes the critical influence of key champions in the criminal and civil justice arenas, and considers the impact of an unprecedented engagement by officials with victims-survivors and their advocates in the law's development and passage.

Keywords Domestic abuse · Family violence · Coercive control · Child victim · Law reform

9.1 Introduction

On the first day of February 2018, the Scottish Parliament unanimously voted to pass the *Domestic Abuse (Scotland) Bill 2018*. The entire body of parliamentarians in the Debating Chamber then stood, turned to the public gallery and gave a standing ovation to survivors and advocates sitting there (Wilson and Hutchinson 2018). The legislation introduced what Professor Evan Stark called the new 'gold standard' for criminalising coercive control and domestic abuse (Brooks 2018); Stark and Marianne Hester have also described the new offence as constituting 'one of the most radical attempts yet to align the criminal justice response with a contemporary feminist conceptual understanding of domestic abuse as a form of

---

M. Scott (✉)
Scottish Women's Aid, Edinburgh, Scotland
e-mail: Marsha.Scott@womensaid.scot

coercive control' (Stark and Hester 2019, p. 85). For the first time, Scotland had a specific offence defining and criminalising domestic abuse, an offence codified in law that described psychological harm and placed it securely in the centre of behaviours deemed criminal. This chapter describes the notable features of the new law, the critical influence of key champions in the criminal and civil justice arenas and the impact of an unprecedented engagement by officials with victims–survivors and their advocates in this law's development and passage.

9.2 The Scottish Context

Prior to the passage of the new Act in 2018, Scotland had no specific offence of domestic abuse. Domestic abuse was prosecuted under a number of other offences, most often as a breach of the peace or threatening or abusive behaviour. The law and national policy developed in parallel, but often non-congruent, processes that allowed for different definitions of domestic abuse in national strategies, policing and prosecution.

The definition of domestic abuse in policy documents was from the beginning linked to United Nations documents (most notably, the 1993 *Declaration on the Elimination of Violence against Women),* was gendered and—unlike in Wales, Northern Ireland and England—was restricted to partners and ex-partners. For example, the following definition was developed by the Scottish Partnership on Domestic Abuse in 2000:

> Domestic abuse can be perpetrated by partners or ex-partners and can include physical abuse (assault and physical attack involving a range of behaviour), sexual abuse (acts which degrade and humiliate women and are perpetrated against their will, including rape) and mental and emotional abuse (such as threats, verbal abuse, withholding money and other types of controlling behaviour such as isolation from family or friends). Children are witness to and subjected to much of this abuse; there is a correlation between domestic abuse and the mental, physical and sexual abuse of children.

> Domestic abuse is associated with broader inequalities in society, is part of a range of behaviours constituting male abuse of power, and is linked to other forms of male violence, such as rape and child abuse. Domestic abuse occurs in all social groups, is not caused by stress, unemployment, poverty, alcohol or mental illness, nor by the women who experience the abuse. (Scottish Centre for Crime and Justice Research 2015, p. 1)

The definition is noteworthy for its recognition of a broad range of harms (physical, sexual, mental, emotional and economic), its acknowledgement that abuse is overwhelmingly perpetrated by men and its linkage of abuse to broad social inequalities. Although a similar definition was adopted by police and the Crown Office Procurator Fiscal Service (Scottish Government 2015), it would take 18 years for the criminal law to give effect to this definition.

9.3 Early Adoption of Coercive Control in Scotland

Scotland was an early adopter of Evan Stark's critique of the 'violent-incident' model of domestic violence and his paradigm of coercive control (Stark 2007). The women's sector was the first and strongest advocate for challenging the old paradigm. In April 2006, the *Women's Support Project* in Glasgow brought Stark to Scotland to present at a seminar, and in September 2007, just as Stark's (2007) book was being published, *Scottish Women's Aid* (a national service provider and policy advocacy organisation for survivors of domestic abuse) brought him to Edinburgh to speak at the organisation's annual national conference. That appearance by Professor Stark was the first of many all over Scotland in the 10 years that followed, including a 3-month stint as Leverhulme Visiting Professor at the University of Edinburgh in 2013.

Academics and practitioners alike were keenly aware that the phenomenon of 'domestic violence' as described in various laws bore little resemblance to its reality in women's and children's lives. Survivors' accounts of their experiences over the more than 40 years of the *Women's Aid* movement in Scotland provide eloquent testimony about the long-lasting trauma and harm caused by domestic abuse generally, and psychological violence specifically (see, for example, Glasgow Women's Library, n.d).

Stark's (2007) critique of existing constructions of domestic violence highlighted three 'myths' in the dogma that he claimed was obstructing progress on reducing the prevalence of abuse:

1. that domestic violence occurs as discrete incidents of physical violence (rather than as a 24/7 ongoing pattern of coercion and control that is sometimes enforced by physical violence);
2. that domestic violence is 'domestic' and occurs only in the home where a perpetrator and victim live together (whereas health and criminal justice data indicate that in many cases, perpetrators are no longer living with their partners when victims come to the attention of services, and that separation does not bring safety); and
3. that the most salient aspect of the 'violence' is physical assault (however, physical violence, when present, is most often used instrumentally to enforce the perpetrator's control, along with other acts of humiliation, coercion, degradation, and threats to children, other family members and pets; rather than only physical violence, domestic abuse is a violation of the victim's human rights, a liberty crime).

These critiques of past thinking and practices were to form the backbone of Scotland's new law.

9.3.1 Gender (a)Symmetry

While the *Women's Aid* movement in Scotland began to highlight Stark's gendered coercive control paradigm in its policy work, the gender symmetry debate raged in academia. Many academics, police and practitioners argued that domestic abuse was primarily male-perpetrated (e.g. Dobash et al. 1992) but others claimed that women were as violent as men in intimate relationships (e.g. Strauss 1999). Adoption of the new coercive control paradigm depended on a resolution of this debate, not necessarily in academia, but certainly in policy circles. The Scottish Government commissioned research (e.g. Gadd et al., 2008) and sponsored academic debates, hoping to establish a policy consensus.

Meanwhile, *Women's Aid* and other feminist campaigners were making the case for asymmetry and defending the gendering of policy in Scotland. Reframing the gender asymmetry debate was critical to progress on developing the law to match Scotland's policy documents (Lombard and Whiting 2018). In addition to Stark's work on coercive control, campaigners' arguments were supported robustly by the publication of Michael Johnson's (2008) work.

Johnson, a quantitative researcher, argued that discussions of gender symmetry in domestic abuse often conflated a number of distinct phenomena:

- intimate terrorism (involving violence and control), experienced predominantly by women and perpetrated predominantly by men;
- violent resistance, perpetrated mostly by women with mostly male victims;
- mutual violent control; and
- situational couple violence, largely gender symmetrical (Johnson 2006, 2008).

Like Stark, Johnson framed his analysis by emphasising the role of power and control in relationship violence and demonstrating that the failure to distinguish among these different phenomena produced ostensibly contradictory findings in the literature. Johnson's analysis had particular resonance in the criminal justice system, as there was a keen desire to understand the growing number of cases going through Scotland's courts. In particular, Johnson's analysis was helpful in explaining why official figures, which conflated situational couple violence (one-off incidents of violence) with intimate terrorism, had significant numbers of female perpetrators. Separating those one-off incidents from the course-of-conduct offence of intimate terrorism allowed a very different picture of offending to emerge.

Reflecting this interest, in 2015, the Crown Office Procurator Fiscal Service (COPFS, the agency with primary responsibility for criminal prosecutions in Scotland) invited Johnson to speak to attendees at its Prosecution College. Since then, references to 'situational couple violence' can be found in numerous COPFS speeches and protocols (see, e.g. COPFS 2014). Ultimately, the framing of domestic abuse as a gender-based issue was accepted and now distinctively characterises developments in Scotland (Wilson and Lombard 2018, p. 31).

9.4 The Road to a Specific Offence

Within the constitutional framework of the United Kingdom, authority for developing policy and law relating to violence against women is almost entirely devolved to the Scottish Parliament. Policing, the criminal and civil courts and the criminal justice system are distinctively Scottish institutions and have historically operated differently to the rest of the United Kingdom. In recent years, there have been multiple initiatives for dealing with domestic abuse. These include the establishment of a domestic abuse court in 2004 (Scottish Government 2007), the promotion of national training strategies in domestic abuse for police, health workers, social workers and those employed in the health, education, housing sectors as well as lawyers, members of the judiciary and court administration staff (Scottish Government 2004), the setting up of a National Domestic Abuse Taskforce within Police Scotland in 2013, and, most significantly, the development of the *Equally Safe* strategy for dealing with violence against women (Scottish Government 2015, [1.1]–[1.9]). Underpinning these developments has been the '4Ps' approach to domestic abuse: protection (legal remedies); provision (effective service delivery); prevention (strategies for stopping domestic abuse and reducing reoffending); and participation (by those who have experienced domestic abuse) (Scottish Government and Convention of Scottish Local Authorities 2009).

In the context of these developments, an appetite was growing in civil society for legislative reform, including a new specific offence. Despite Scotland's reliable cross-party consensus on violence against women policy, activists felt some reluctance in earlier years and were concerned that the process would endanger Scotland's existing definition and reignite debates about the role of gender in domestic violence that were won in the original days of the Scottish Partnership on Domestic Abuse (Scott 2006). But the need for reform became ever clearer as the new paradigm began to be accepted. In addition, evidence from a 30-year, 70-country study (Weldon 2002; Htun and Weldon 2012) was unequivocal:

> [r]egardless of national context, attempts to address violence against women under the rubric of more general laws against violence or assault have generally been unsuccessful.... Obtaining an effective response from the law enforcement bureaucracy has generally required both legal reform and training of law enforcement officials from police officers to judges. (Weldon 2002, p. 14)

Then a high-profile case put pressure on the government and criminal justice system, and the door to reform was well and truly open. In July 2012, Bill Walker, a sitting member of the Scottish Parliament, was charged with 23 counts of assault and one count of breach of the peace involving his three ex-wives and a stepdaughter.

Sheriff Katherine Mackie, sitting in the Edinburgh Sheriff Court in August 2013, found Walker guilty of all charges and sentenced him to the maximum allowable in summary court: imprisonment for 1 year. The case and, in particular, Mackie's eloquent remarks to the court, fuelled a new sense of outrage by some politicians and women's organisations that domestic abuse was treated routinely by the criminal justice system as a low-tariff crime (The Guardian 2013), that much of Walker's behaviour was not criminal under Scottish law, and that despite a criminal conviction on these charges, Walker would not even be rendered ineligible to sit in parliament (Scottish Parliamentary rules require a sentence of more than 1 year as a ground for expulsion). Walker did, though, resign 1 week after his conviction.

The Crown contended that Walker's conduct towards each of his ex-wives had four similarities: controlling behaviour, uncontrollable bursts of temper, violent conduct, and unprovoked and inexplicable assaults. Sheriff Mackie observed:

> There was evidence showing the accused to be controlling, domineering, demeaning and belittling towards the three complainers, his former wives. The evidence also showed him to be untrustworthy, disloyal and unfaithful towards others including his present wife. Whether I accepted that evidence, however abhorrent, unacceptable and abusive such behaviour might be it does not amount to a criminal offence.
>
> The complaint against the accused is not that he behaved abusively but that he committed criminal offences of assault, on 23 occasions, and on one occasion, breach of the peace. The offences are said to have occurred while in an intimate relationship with each of the complainers. (*PF v Bill Walker*, 20 September 2013)

Significantly, Sheriff Mackie also noted:

> As is ably demonstrated by this case the response to domestic abuse incidents is now radically different from that of thirty or so years ago. The circumstances of these offences, where reported to police … would not now be considered 'just a domestic'. It is now recognised that the effects of domestic abuse can be profound resulting in physical and psychological harm to those who experience it, whether directly or indirectly, and considerable cost to society at large. (*PF v Bill Walker*, 23 August 2013)

Walker was sentenced on 20 September 2013, and 1 week later, Lesley Thomson QC, the Solicitor General for Scotland, announced that COPFS had appointed Anne Marie Hicks to a newly created national post of specialist domestic abuse prosecutor. She would have responsibility for coordinating the prosecution services' response to domestic abuse cases, reviewing prosecution policies, engaging with stakeholders and increasing awareness of domestic abuse among prosecutors and police. Thomson commented:

> Anne Marie Hicks will return to an area of work that she piloted by leading the domestic abuse unit, which was set up in Glasgow in 2009, and I have asked her to review all areas of COPFS work and training in domestic abuse in consultation with partner agencies ahead of a COPFS domestic abuse conference in spring 2014.
>
> If her review indicates any changes need to be made to prosecution policy, then such changes will be prioritised. We will continue to deal with prosecution of domestic abuse by means of robust prosecution policy. (Peterkin 2013)

The following year, speaking at the annual COPFS conference, Thomson called on the Scottish Parliament to consider the creation of a bespoke offence of domestic abuse. Thompson observed that existing Scottish law focused on 'specific instances, e.g. of assault or threatening or abusive behaviour, rather than the long-term, repeated nature of much domestic abuse' (Scottish Government 2015). She also suggested that a specific offence offered an opportunity to reflect on the impact and consequences of all types of abusive behaviours, including non-violent tactics of control and abuse (Scottish Government 2015, [1.7]).

Between March and June 2015, the Scottish Government consulted on whether a specific offence would improve the ability of the justice system to respond to domestic abuse (Scottish Government 2015a). Responses were sought in relation to the adequacy of existing laws and whether a new, specific offence concerning domestic abuse should be introduced. Seventy-three submissions were received; respondents included members of advocacy and support groups, local authority, health and MAP representatives, lawyers and academics and other groups and individuals. Responses reflected strong agreement (93%) that current laws were not adequate and that a specific offence would be an improvement (96%). A majority of respondents (67%) thought that any specific offence of 'domestic abuse' should be restricted to people who are partners or ex-partners (Scottish Government 2015b). Interestingly, of the six respondents who disagreed, five were 'legal and academic respondents' (Scottish Government 2015b).

In September 2015, the First Minister announced that the Scottish Government would publish a draft of a specific offence to deal with those who commit psychological abuse and engage in coercive and controlling behaviour. During the drafting period, members of the Government's Bill Team corresponded regularly with policy experts in *Scottish Women's Aid*, who offered to test the proposed language with survivors and service users, and with *Women's Aid* staff working directly with women, children and young people experiencing domestic abuse. Focus groups were held in a number of areas of Scotland to gather survivors' expert input, and the Bill team made language changes that were especially evident in a number of sections of the Bill, such as the discussion of the effects of abuse. Survivors were particularly keen that explicit references be made to constraints on their autonomy. Section 2 of the Bill describes what constitutes abusive behaviour. This section, and the related explanatory notes are peppered with phrases from service users and advocates, including 'regulating day-to-day activities' and 'restricting freedom of action'. The explanatory note for this section is one of a number that uses language that came from consultation with survivors:

> Section 2(3)(b) provides that behaviour which has the effect of isolating the victim from friends, relatives or other sources of support can be considered to have a relevant effect. This could include, for example, controlling the victim's movements or access to their phone or other forms of communication, not allowing visits from or to the victim's friends or family, or deliberately failing to pass on messages from friends or family.

In December 2015, the draft law was released for consultation, and on 17 March 2017, Cabinet Secretary for Justice Michael Matheson, Member of the Scottish Parliament (MSP), introduced the Bill (Justice Committee of the Scottish Parliament 2017). The Justice Committee had responsibility for gathering evidence and conducted a number of public consultation sessions with various experts. In addition, a subgroup of MSPs held private sessions with survivors (who were supported by a number of victim support agencies, including *Scottish Women's Aid* and *Shakti Women's Aid*). The significant impact of these meetings with survivors was reflected in Michael Matheson reading out statements from two of them (one of whom was in the public gallery) during the final debate on the Bill. Matheson concluded debate on the Bill by noting that 'the very heart of this legislation is the voices of those women who have experienced domestic abuse' (Wilson and Hutchison 2018).

The Bill was amended as it passed through Parliament. Amendments included:

- new language to provide for extraterritorial jurisdiction to comply with the Council of Europe's *Convention on Action Against Violence Against Women and Domestic Abuse* (the *'Istanbul Convention'*), which the Scottish Government has committed to (Westminster Parliament has signed but not yet ratified this Convention);
- new elements added to the section dealing with aggravation involving children; and
- changes to the drafting regarding non-harassment orders. The original Bill included provisions requiring courts to consider making non-harassment orders when sentencing for the offence of domestic abuse. Amendments extended consideration of the making of these orders to also cover children and created a presumption in favour of making such orders.

The *Domestic Abuse (Scotland) Act 2018* was passed in February 2018. It came into force on 1 April 2019.

9.5 Notables Features of the Act

The offence of domestic abuse is distinctive. It focuses on the abuse rather than victim, examines a course of behaviour rather than a discrete incident, is grounded in human rights (autonomy, freedom from fear and coercion) and reflects what women and children have told us about their experiences of abuse.

9.5.1 Course of Behaviour

Moving away from constructing domestic abuse as an incident to a pattern of behaviours is one of the central tenets of the new offence in Scotland. The elements of the offence are contained in section 1:

1. Abusive behaviour towards partner or ex-partner

(1) A person commits an offence if—

    (a) the person ("A") engages in a course of behaviour which is abusive of A's partner or ex-partner ("B"), and

    (b) both of the further conditions are met.

(2) The further conditions are—
  (a) that a reasonable person would consider the course of behaviour to be likely to cause B to suffer physical or psychological harm,
  (b) that either—
    (i) A intends by the course of behaviour to cause B to suffer physical or psychological harm, or
    (ii) A is reckless as to whether the course of behaviour causes B to suffer physical or psychological harm.
(3) In further conditions, the references to psychological harm include fear, alarm and distress.

A course of behaviour, defined in section 10(4) of the Act, 'involves behaviour on at least two occasions'. Additionally, 'psychological harm' expressly includes fear, alarm and distress (s 1(3)).

The offence may be committed against a partner or ex-partner: 'partner' is defined in section 11 to include spouses, civil partners, parties living together as if spouses of each other and persons in an intimate relationship; an ex-partner is a person who had previously been in such a relationship. Unlike the offence of 'controlling or coercive behaviour' that was enacted in England and Wales, the Scottish offence of domestic abuse does not extend to other familial relationships (such as an adult child who abuses an elderly parent). The restricted scope of section 1 is congruent with the existing policy definitions of domestic abuse in Scotland and has been justified on the basis that abuse of partners and ex-partners has a 'different dynamic' to other forms of abuse within families (Scottish Government 2015a, [1.34]-[1.35]).

The use of a 'reasonable person' threshold in section 1(2), while not unfamiliar to Scottish courts (e.g. in stalking legislation), was innovative. So, too, was the recklessness element. The language of the Act provides that prosecution must demonstrate *either* that the defendant intended to harm the victim, or that they were 'reckless' about potential harm. These two legal constructions were especially welcome to those who were familiar with victim–survivor stories, which typically are filled with details that would lead a 'reasonable person' to understand that harm was an expected outcome of the offender's course of behaviour.

The Act also includes a detailed discussion (extensive but 'not exhaustive') of what constitutes abusive behaviour. This section of the Act reflected consultation with survivors, sometimes using their words to describe the offence.

9.5.2 Abusive Behaviour

What constitutes abusive behaviour is non-exhaustively defined in section 2.

2. What constitutes abusive behaviour

(1) Subsections (2) to (4) elaborate on section 1(1) as to A's behaviour.
(2) Behaviour which is abusive of B includes (in particular)—
   (a) behaviour directed at B that is violent, threatening or intimidating,
   (b) behaviour directed at B, at a child of B or at another person that either—
      (i) has as its purpose (or among its purposes) one or more of the relevant effects set out in subsection (3), or
      (ii) would be considered by a reasonable person to be likely to have one or more of the relevant effects set out in subsection (3).
(3) The relevant effects are of—
   (a) making B dependent on, or subordinate to, A,
   (b) isolating B from friends, relatives or other sources of support,
   (c) controlling, regulating or monitoring B's day-to-day activities,
   (d) depriving B of, or restricting B's, freedom of action,
   (e) frightening, humiliating, degrading or punishing B.
(4) In subsection (2)—
   (a) in paragraph (a), the reference to violent behaviour includes sexual violence as well as physical violence,
   (b) in paragraph (b), the reference to a child is to a person who is under 18 years of age.

It is noteworthy that 'violent' behaviour directed at B is not restricted to physical violence; it includes sexual violence (s 2(4)), as well as behaviour that has a 'relevant effect'. The *Explanatory Notes* prepared by the Scottish Government provide numerous examples of relevant abusive behaviours and effects. For example, they indicate that behaviour which makes a victim dependent on, or subordinate to, a perpetrator can be considered to have a relevant effect under section 2(3)(a) where it prevents the victim from having access to money, forces the victim to leave their job, takes charge of household decision-making to the exclusion of the victim, or treats the victim as a domestic slave (Explanatory Notes, *Domestic Abuse (Scotland) Act 2018*).

9.5.3 'Is the Behaviour Harmful?' Versus 'How Much Did She Suffer?'

Although the Act does not make the so-called victimless prosecutions possible (whereas there have already been at least two victimless prosecutions in England and Wales: Finnigan 2016; Kingsley Napley 2018), it does shift the focus from the evidence of injury experienced by the victim to evidence of perpetration. Indeed, it is not necessary for the prosecution to prove that the victim actually did suffer harm or experience any relevant effect (although such evidence may be led). Instead, the prosecution must establish that a reasonable person would consider that the course of behaviour would be *likely* to cause either physical or psychological harm to the victim (taking into account the particular characteristics of the victim).

4. Evidence of impact on the victim

(1) The commission of an offence under section 1(1) does not depend on the course of behaviour actually causing B to suffer harm of the sort mentioned in section 1(2).
(2) The operation of section 2(2)(b) does not depend on the behaviour directed at someone actually having on B any of the relevant effects set out in section 2(3).
(3) Nothing done by or mentioned in subsection (1) or (2) prevents evidence from being led in proceedings for an offence under section 1(1) about (as the case may be)—

   (a) harm actually suffered by B as a result of the course of behaviour, or
   (b) effects actually had on B of behaviour directed at someone.

Shifting the focus from the victim and onto the offending behaviour opens up the possibility for dramatically changing victims' experiences, especially in court. Notions of 'deserving victims', questions about 'why didn't she just leave', and the relentless pressure to present in court as traumatised and broken have made testifying a necessary evil at best, and a form of re-victimisation at worst. Although courts will interpret and implement these provisions in their own ways, this framing of the offence offers hope to victims and their supporters that a trial might be harder on the accused than on the victim, which Shakespeare might refer to as a 'consummation devoutly to be wished'.

9.5.4 Children Experience Domestic Abuse Rather Than Merely 'Witness' It

A significant feature of the Scottish legislation is that it re-frames the experience of children and young people involved in domestic violence, constructing them as *experiencing* the abuse rather than merely *witnessing* it. This is achieved through section 5 of the Act, which deals with 'aggravation in relation to a child'.

In a development that paralleled the increasing adoption of the new coercive control paradigm, victim advocates, children's rights organisations and researchers had begun to challenge the notion that children who are not direct targets experience domestic violence merely as 'witnesses'; that is, that the harm that a child experiences is solely a consequence of witnessing incidents of violence directed at the non-offending parent (the mother in the vast majority of cases), rather than a product of the child's own experience of control and coercion (see, e.g. Callaghan et al. 2018; Katz 2015, 2016; Morrison 2015; Morrison and Wasoff 2012; Stanley 2011).

Much research confirms the widespread exposure of children to domestic abuse as well as its adverse impact. For instance, a study by Edelson et al. (2003) reported that women who were abused by their partners reported that their children frequently saw the abuse, nearly always overheard it, were frequently themselves injured (either accidentally or when they intervened to stop the abuse) and were threatened with physical harm.

Moreover, linked to the awareness that separation does not bring safety for adult victims is the continuation of abuse through child contact arrangements. The most visible evidence of harm to children was in the context of court-ordered contact with the offending parent. *Scottish Women's Aid*, the Centre for Research on Families and Relationships at the University of Edinburgh and the office of the Commissioner for Children and Young People in Scotland (CCYPS) collaborated on numerous pieces of work in an effort to generate change.

The CCYPS commissioned two pieces of research: one investigated child contact proceedings and recommended that a common definition of domestic abuse be adopted and that service providers receive more extensive training in relation to children affected by domestic abuse and contact (Morrison and Tisdall 2013). The other project—*Power Up/Power Down*—focused specifically on how the views of children were treated in contact disputes (Mackay 2013). The study involved 27 children and young people aged between 6 and 17 years. A series of sessions explored themes of power, children's rights, making their voices heard in court, and how to improve the experience and outcomes for children affected by domestic abuse in family court actions relating to contact decisions. A system mapping exercise followed and participation work with children and young people produced a set of materials for professionals (Scottish Women's Aid, n.d.).

During the consultation process prior to the launch of the new Act, a new coalition of children's charities and women's charities was formed, and the combination was a powerful voice for children. The primary concern of this coalition was the need to address the gap between criminal and civil proceedings. The civil–criminal gap was one of the key findings of the system mapping process, and it reflected the fact that officials (in particular, sheriffs) often had no or little information about the behaviour of the offending parent when making contact decisions. Creating a status for children as co-victim with the non-offending parent offered the opportunity to ensure that abusive behaviours discussed in criminal cases where children were victims would have to be raised in linked civil cases where child contact discussions were being made.

Nevertheless, the idea that children were victims simply by living in a family where there is domestic abuse was difficult for officials to accept, and the language in the first version of the Bill reflected this:

5. Aggravation in relation to a child

(1) This subsection applies where it is, in proceedings for an offence under section 1(1)—

  (a) specified in the complaint or libelled in the indictment that the offence is aggravated by reason of involving a child and
  (b) proved that the offence is so aggravated.

(2) The offence is so aggravated if—

  (a) at any time in the commission of the offence—

   (i) A directs behaviour at a child, or
   (ii) A makes use of a child in directing behaviour at B.

  (b) a child sees or hears, or is present during, an incident of behaviour that A directs at B as part of the course of behaviour.

Ministers, Members of the Scottish Parliament and government officials were lobbied extensively to change this language, replacing it with language that provided children with co-victim status. This was apparently a step too far for the government, but a subsequent amendment was a significant improvement. The powerful coalition of children's and women's organisations negotiated some important changes to the final language of section 5, working closely with the Government's Bill Team. Section 5 of the Act now includes the following additional subsections.

5. Aggravation in relation to a child

...

(3) The offence is so aggravated if a child sees or hears, or is present during, an incident of behaviour that A directs at B as part of the course of behaviour.

(4) The offence is so aggravated if a reasonable person would consider the course of behaviour, or an incident of A's behaviour that forms part of the course of behaviour, is likely to adversely affect a child usually residing with A or B (or both).

(5) For it to be proved that the offence is so aggravated, there does not need to be evidence that a child—

  (a) has ever had any—

   (i) awareness of A's behaviour, or
   (ii) understanding of the nature of A's behaviour, or

  (b) has ever been adversely affected by A's behaviour.

A child is defined as a person under 18 years of age who is not the primary victim nor the offender (s 11). Significantly, reference to a child or young person being 'adversely affected' by an offender's behaviour includes the experiencing of fear, alarm or distress by the child (s 10). Particular procedural provisions apply as follows: evidence from a single source is sufficient to prove that the offence is aggravated (s 6) and, although proof of harm is not required, evidence may be given of a child's observations of, or feelings as to the offender's behaviour, or the child's situation arising from that behaviour (s 9). Additionally, when aggravation in relation to a child is established, the court must note this when stating and recording the conviction and must take the matter into account when imposing a sentence (s 7).

The enduring problem of re-victimisation of children via court-ordered contact processes was raised a number of times in the final debate on the Bill. The Government has committed to further addressing these concerns as part of its review of the *Children (Scotland) Act 1995* (Scot) and other legislation (Scottish Government 2018c).

9.6 Looking Ahead

On 20 March 2017, the new *Domestic Abuse Bill* was announced by First Minister Nicola Sturgeon. Cabinet Secretary for Justice Michael Matheson commented that, in his experience, development of the Bill had involved 'an unprecedented amount of engagement with stakeholders'; the First Minister replied, 'That's how the best laws are made' (personal communication, Nicola Sturgeon, First Minister). Just over 1 year later, the *Domestic Abuse (Scotland) Act 2018* passed virtually unanimously and, as mentioned, was hailed by Professor Evan Stark as 'a new gold standard'. In an interview in *The Guardian* newspaper, Stark commented:

> There is no evidence whatsoever to suggest that creating this broad offence will lead to reduced reporting or policing of simple assaults.... But the critics are right about one thing. What matters now is what happens when the first calls come in under the new law. How will the police and the courts respond to that first caller who insists 'violence wasn't the worst part'. Will she be told: 'Talk about the violence', or what we hope she'll hear: 'Yes, I know what you mean (Brooks 2018).

Mirroring Stark's concept of 'coercive control' and Johnson's 'intimate terrorism', the new law frames domestic abuse as a liberty crime, acknowledging that victims have human rights to autonomy, to live free from fear and coercion, to enjoy the space for action denied them for so long by the constraints of patriarchy and women's inequality. For the first time, domestic abuse legislation is congruent with national policy as expressed in government documents (Scottish Government 2018a). For the first time, Scotland has domestic abuse legislation that begins to operationalise what has become the mantra of the *Women's Aid* movement in Scotland—that domestic abuse is a cause and consequence of women's inequality.

The Scottish Parliament has committed the government to report its progress 3 years after commencement, as implementation of the legislation will be neither simple nor straightforward. Commencement of the Act, on April 1 2019, will require investments of time, training, money and political will across all sectors and in all areas of the country.

A number of problems remain. For example, the divide between civil and criminal cases is not addressed in this legislation. However, the language in section 5 (dealing with aggravation in relation to a child) does remove the requirement for children to witness abuse and acknowledges that a reasonable person might assume that if children are in a family where abuse occurs, they are victims. This is a positive development. The Government launched a significant consultation on the *Children (Scotland) Act 1995*, which looks specifically at provisions in existing law relating to court decisions about child contact (Scottish Government 2018c). Children's and women's charities continue to coordinate consistent messages to officials that this is a critical issue and that positive developments are expected in any forthcoming legislation.

Another problem that was not addressed in the Act was the issue of emergency orders. During the progress of the *Domestic Abuse Bill* through parliament, at the urging of *Scottish Women's Aid*, the Justice Committee considered the potential benefits of introducing emergency barring orders (EBOs). Various forms of EBOs are in place across Europe, and they are required for compliance with Article 52 of the Council of Europe's *Istanbul Convention* which requires parties to the convention to have in place:

> …measures to ensure that the competent authorities are granted the power to order, in situations of immediate danger, a perpetrator of domestic violence to vacate the residence of the victim or person at risk for a sufficient period of time and to prohibit the perpetrator from entering the residence of or contacting the victim or person at risk.

Thus, these orders empower authorities to immediately remove a suspected perpetrator of abuse from the family home, enabling victims to stay in their own homes. Women and children forced to leave their homes because of domestic abuse are the third-largest source of homelessness applications in Scotland, and robust short-term orders protecting their right to stay would reduce harm as well as serve natural justice. The Government responded to this call for amendment with a commitment to launch a consultation process in parallel with the review of the *Children (Scotland) Act 1995*, opining that the new legislation was not straightforward and that a robust consultation was needed. After meeting with *Scottish Women's Aid* to discuss potential parameters for the review and related legislation, an EBO consultation has now been launched by the Scottish Government (Scottish Government 2018b).

In summary, the policy landscape in Scotland has shifted profoundly as a consequence of the new Act. The salience of gender, the influence and expertise of survivors and advocates, and early moves to reflect children's human rights in the State's response to domestic abuse are milestones delivered by the development, debate and discourse surrounding the Act. Implementation of the Act heralds a new stage in which Scotland has the opportunity to transform institutional responses and demonstrate the difference legislation can make in the lives of the Scottish people. Watch this space!

References

Brooks, L. (2018, February 1). Scotland set to pass 'gold standard' domestic abuse law, *The Guardian*. Retrieved from https://www.theguardian.com/society/2018/feb/01/scotland-set-to-pass-gold-standard-domestic-abuse-law.

Callaghan, J. E. M., Alexander, J. H., Sixsmith, J., & Fellin, L. C. (2018). Beyond "witnessing": Children's experiences of coercive control in domestic violence and abuse. *Journal of Interpersonal Violence, 33*(10), 1551–1581.

Crown Office Procurator Fiscal Service. (2014). *Challenging Abuse Together* (COPFS Conference on Domestic Abuse, Glasgow, 8 May 2014). Retrieved from http://www.copfs.gov.uk/images/Documents/Our%20Priorities/Domestic%20abuse/Speech%20by%20PF%20Domestic%20Abuse%20at%20COPFS%20Conference%208%20May%202014.pdf.

Dobash, R. P., Dobash, R. E., Wilson, M., & Daly, M. (1992). The myth of sexual symmetry in marital violence. *Social Problems, 39*(1), 71–91.

Edelson, J. L., Mbilinyi, L. F., Beeman, S. K., & Hagemeister, A. K. (2003). How children are involved in adult domestic violence: Results from a four-city telephone survey. *Journal of Interpersonal Violence, 18*(1), 18–32.

Explanatory Notes, *Domestic Abuse (Scotland) Act 2018*.

Finnigan, L. (2016, September 9). Man, 24, is one of the first people jailed for coercive control offences using victimless prosecution, *The Telegraph*. Retrieved from https://www.telegraph.co.uk/news/2016/09/09/man-24-is-one-of-the-first-people-jailed-for-coercive-control-of/.

Htun, M., & Laurel Weldon, S. L. (2012). The civic origins of progressive policy change: Combating violence against women in global perspective, 1975–2005. *American Political Science Review, 106*(3), 548–569.

Johnson, M. P. (2008). *A typology of domestic violence: Intimate terrorism, violent resistance, and situational couple violence*. Boston, MA: Northeastern University Press.

Johnson, M. P. (2006). Conflict and control: Gender symmetry and asymmetry in domestic violence. *Violence Against Women, 12*(11), 1003–1018.

Justice Committee of the Scottish Parliament, *Domestic Abuse (Scotland) Bill*. Retrieved from https://www.parliament.scot/parliamentarybusiness/CurrentCommittees/104168.aspx.

Katz, E. (2015). *Surviving Together: Domestic Violence and Mother-Child Relationships* (PhD thesis, University of Nottingham).

Katz, E. (2016). Beyond the physical incident model: How children living with domestic violence are harmed by and resist regimes of coercive control. *Child Abuse Review, 25*(1), 46–59.

Kingsley Napley. (2018, February 22). Prison sentence following 'victimless prosecution' for controlling and coercive behaviour. Retrieved from https://www.kingsleynapley.co.uk/insights/blogs/criminal-law-blog/prison-sentence-following-victimless-prosecution-for-controlling-and-coercive-behaviour.

Lombard, N., & Whiting, N. (2018). What's in a name? The Scottish government, feminism and the gendered framing of domestic abuse. In N. Lombard (Ed.), *The Routledge handbook of gender and violence*. New York, NY: Routledge.

Mackay, K. (2013). The treatment of the views of children in private law child contact disputes where there is a history of domestic abuse: A report to Scotland's Commissioner for Children and Young People. Retrieved from https://www.cypcs.org.uk/publications/domestic-abuse.

Morrison, F. (2015). 'All over now?' The ongoing relational consequences of domestic abuse through children's contact arrangements. *Child Abuse Review, 24*(4), 274–284.

Morrison, F., & Tisdall, E. K. (2013). *Child contact proceedings for children affected by domestic abuse: A report to Scotland's Commissioner for Children and Young People*. Retrieved from https://www.cypcs.org.uk/publications/domestic-abuse.

Morrison, F., & Wasoff, F. (2012). Child contact centers and domestic abuse: Victim safety and the challenge to neutrality. *Violence against Women, 18*(6), 711–720.

Peterkin, T. (2013). Domestic abuse prosecutor for Scotland appointed. *The Scotsman* 27 September 2013. Retrieved from https://www.scotsman.com/news/politics/domestic-abuse-prosecutor-for-scotland-appointed-1-3112943.

PF v Bill Walker. (2013, August 23). Retrieved from http://www.scotland-judiciary.org.uk/8/1109/PF-v-BILL-WALKER.

PF v Bill Walker. (2013, September 20). Retrieved from http://www.scotland-judiciary.org.uk/8/1131/PF-v-BILL-WALKER.

Scott, M. (2006). *Partnership, Power and Policy: A Case Study of the Scottish Partnership on Domestic Abuse* (PhD thesis, University of Edinburgh).

Scottish Centre for Crime and Justice Research. (2015). *Violence Against Women and Girls*. Retrieved from http://www.sccjr.ac.uk/wp-content/uploads/2015/10/SCCJR-Violence-against-women-and-girls.pdf.

Scottish Government. (2004). *Domestic Abuse: A National Training Strategy*. Retrieved from https://www2.gov.scot/Publications/2004/03/18901/33132.

Scottish Government. (2007). *Evaluation of the Pilot Domestic Abuse Court*. Retrieved from https://www2.gov.scot/Publications/2007/03/28153424/3.

Scottish Government. (2015a). *Equally Safe: Reforming the Criminal Law to Address Domestic Abuse and Sexual Offences*. Retrieved from https://www2.gov.scot/Publications/2015/03/4845/4.

Scottish Government. (2015b). *Equally Safe: Reforming the Criminal Law to Address Domestic Abuse and Sexual Offences—Analysis of Consultation Responses*. Retrieved from https://www2.gov.scot/Publications/2015/03/4845/4.

Scottish Government. (2018a). *Equally Safe: Scotland's Strategy to Eradicate Violence Against Women*. Retrieved from https://www.gov.scot/publications/equally-safe-scotlands-strategy-prevent-eradicate-violence-against-women-girls/.

Scottish Government. (2018b). *Protective Orders for People at Risk of Domestic Abuse: Consultation*. Retrieved from https://www.gov.scot/publications/consultation-protective-orders-people-risk-domestic-abuse/pages/2/.

Scottish Government. (2018c). *Review of Part 1 of the Children (Scotland) Act 1995 and Creation of a Family Justice Modernisation Strategy: A Consultation*. Retrieved from https://www.gov.scot/publications/review-part-1-children-scotland-act-1995-creation-family-justice/.

Scottish Government and Convention of Scottish Local Authorities. (2009). *A Partnership Approach to Tackling Violence Against Women in Scotland. Guidance for Multi-Agency Partnerships*. Retrieved from http://www.womenssupportproject.co.uk/userfiles/file/uploads/MAP%20Guidance%2009.pdf.

Scottish Women's Aid. (n.d.). *Power Up/ Power Down: Changing the Story, Hearing Children and Young People's Voices*. Retrieved from https://womensaid.scot/project/power-up-power-down/.https://womensaid.scot/project/power-up-power-down/.

Glasgow Women's Library. (n.d.). *Speaking Out: Recalling Women's Aid in Scotland Exhibition*. Retrieved from https://womenslibrary.org.uk/discover-our-projects/speaking-out/#SpeakingOutIntro.

Stanley, N. (2011). *Children experiencing domestic violence: A research review*. Dartington: Research in Practice.

Stark, E. (2007). *Coercive control: How men entrap women in personal life*. Oxford: Oxford University Press.

Stark, E., & Hester, M. (2019). Coercive control: Update and review. *Violence Against Women, 25*(1), 81–104.

Straus, M. A. (1999). The controversy over domestic violence by women: A methodological, theoretical, and sociology of science analysis. In X. B. Arriaga & S. Oskamp (Eds.), *Violence in intimate relationships*. Thousand Oaks, CA: Sage.

The Guardian. (2013, September 20). Former MSP Bill Walker jailed for 12 months for attacks on wives, *The Guardian* (online). Retrieved from https://www.theguardian.com/politics/2013/sep/20/msp-bill-walker-jailed-domestic-abuse.

Weldon, S. L. (2002). *Protest, policy, and the problem of violence against women: A cross-national comparison*. Pittsburgh, PA: University of Pittsburgh Press.

Wilson, L., & Hutchison, C. (2018, February 2). MSPs pass Domestic Abuse Bill. *The Guardian*. Retrieved from https://www.bbc.com/news/live/uk-scotland-scotland-politics-42858902.

Part IV
A Way Forward?

Chapter 10
A Comparative Evaluation of Offences: Criminalising Abusive Behaviour in England, Wales, Scotland, Ireland and Tasmania

Vanessa Bettinson

Abstract This chapter analyses the new offences introduced in England and Wales in 2015, Scotland in 2018, Ireland in 2018 and the less recent offences in Tasmania in 2004 addressing the use of coercive control in domestic relationships. Each legislature has chosen different approaches to a shared problem and, as other jurisdictions are considering whether or how to criminalise non-physical abuse at this time, it is timely to consider which model has the greatest potential to achieve the stated objectives of these offences. I argue that the Scottish model is most promising and that rollout to other nations should be a serious consideration. This is based on Scotland having developed an offence that aligns as far as could be expected with its existing policy approaches to domestic abuse. The legislation has a focus on current or ex-partners, no requirement to show that the victim actually suffered harm, an ability to reflect the wide range of behaviours and impact that abusive behaviour can cause, and a sentencing range that adequately reflects the broad range of offending covered by these offences. In comparison, other models have shortcomings, such as greater evidential barriers for prosecution, limitation periods or a failure to take into account the different levels of severity of consequences caused by the prohibited behaviour.

Keywords Controlling or coercive behaviour · Domestic abuse · Sentencing · Comparative law

10.1 Introduction

Government consultations about how and whether to capture in criminal law non-physical harm arising from coercive and controlling behaviours have taken place in several jurisdictions (Department of Justice (NI) 2016; HM Government

V. Bettinson (✉)
School of Law, De Montfort University, Leicester, UK
e-mail: VBettinson@dmu.ac.uk

© Springer Nature Singapore Pte Ltd. 2020
M. McMahon and P. McGorrery (eds.), *Criminalising Coercive Control*,
https://doi.org/10.1007/978-981-15-0653-6_10

2018; State of Victoria 2016; Scottish Government 2016a). This chapter discusses four jurisdictions where criminal offences in this regard have been created: England and Wales, Scotland, Ireland and Tasmania. In England and Wales, s 76 of the *Serious Crime Act 2015* (E&W) ('*SCA*') makes it a criminal offence to use controlling or coercive behaviour towards an intimate partner or family member; Ireland criminalises coercive or controlling behaviour in a current or former intimate relationship under s 39 of the *Domestic Violence Act 2018* (IR) ('*DVA*'); Scotland's *Domestic Abuse (Scotland) Act 2018* (Scot) s 1 ('*DASA*') prohibits domestic abuse and Tasmania's *Family Violence Act 2004* (Tas) ss 8–9 ('*FVA*') criminalises economic abuse and emotional abuse or intimidation. In some jurisdictions, concerns that attempts to criminalise in this area will be superficial or symbolic have led to the conclusion not to legislate at this time (Douglas 2015; State of Victoria 2016).

Given the high profile of combatting domestic abuse across the world, it is appropriate to conduct a comparative analysis of these offences. This exercise should assist other jurisdictions undertaking their own consultation processes to determine how to address in the substantive criminal law psychological and other harms caused within a coercive and controlling relationship. Indeed, Northern Ireland has already consulted about this very issue and will be considering which model to adopt, or whether to explore its own path (Department of Justice (NI) 2016). This chapter provides a comparative analysis and concludes that the world should be watching how Scotland implements its domestic abuse offence (see further, Bettinson 2018). The comparative exploration analyses the elemental components of these offences and highlights the strengths of each model. It is acknowledged from the outset that substantive criminal law can only do so much. It is interpreted by people, and success in any jurisdiction must surely be based on ongoing education of the public and specialist training of court and law enforcement personnel. To that end, any jurisdiction considering reform in this area should bear in mind the salient warning of Burman and Brooks-Hay (2018, p. 78): 'Legislative change cannot on its own lead to improvements'.

10.2 Context

Other chapters in this book have well rehearsed the various forms that domestic abuse takes. Whilst criminal laws in the United Kingdom jurisdictions have traditionally looked at domestic abuse in its physical forms, they have tended to inadequately address the impact of non-physical forms of abusive behaviour and their harmful impact on the victim (Bettinson and Bishop 2015). Characterising psychological abuse as repetitive use of non-physical tactics—many of which can look to observers outside the relationship like normal interactions (Dutton and Goodman 2005; Williamson 2010; Stark 2007)—remains a key challenge when considering a model upon which to shape a criminal offence. Policy definitions of domestic abuse adopted in England, Wales and Scotland are expansive (Home Office 2013; Crown Office and Procurator Fiscal Office 2017). They include a wide range of abusive behaviours, including psychological and financial harm. The Westminster government is also currently considering whether to extend the policy definition to legislatively recognise economic abuse (HM Government 2018). Similarly, Tasmania has recognised the significance of economic abuse in the context of family violence, having criminalised it under s 8 of the *FVA*. The United Nations Committee Against Torture also suggested that Ireland needed a policy definition of domestic abuse that covered non-physical injury (United Nations Committee against Torture 2017, paras [32]–[33]). As policy definitions of domestic abuse have evolved over time, substantive criminal law has been slow to adapt, and until recently, few jurisdictions had specific domestic abuse offences.

Previously, the types of harms captured by the criminal law were limited, for the most part, to physical injuries, and there was little capacity to include the ongoing, cumulative nature of many forms of abusive behaviour within a domestic context (Bettinson and Bishop 2015; Bettinson 2016). The aim of preventing and combatting domestic abuse is now a high priority political issue in England, Wales, Scotland, Ireland and Australia (and indeed in most countries around the world). In England and Wales, a promise to draft a *Domestic Abuse Bill* was made in the 2017 Queen's Speech and a consultation to further this agenda began in March 2018 (Queen Elizabeth II 2017; HM Government 2018). In Scotland, a commitment was made to strengthen the criminal justice response to domestic abuse culminating in the passing of the *Domestic Abuse (Scotland) Bill* on 1 February 2018. Ireland's first draft of the *Domestic Violence Bill* did not include the coercive control offence, and attracted criticism from the United Nations for failing to adequately address psychological abuse; the proposed offence was subsequently introduced into the 28 November 2017 draft (United Nations Committee against Torture 2017, paras [31]–[32]). Caution has been called for in Australia regarding new criminal offences intended to capture the psychological harm of coercive control (see, e.g. Douglas 2015). Definitions of family violence tend to be broad in Australian jurisdictions (see, e.g. *Family Violence Protection Act 2008* (Vic) s 5(1)). Despite the heightened prioritising of domestic abuse and the desire to improve criminal justice responses, in particular, a degree of scepticism exists about moves towards increased criminalisation of domestic abuse. Concerns include the inability to promote access to justice for victims, the potential of implementation to have damaging consequences for victims and a raft of evidential concerns (Walklate et al. 2018; Tolmie 2018; Douglas 2018). However, these reservations cannot justify continued inaction by the criminal law towards the use of non-physical tactics that generate a psychological impact upon the victim, ultimately inhibiting their liberty and (for many) being more damaging than a single act of violence.

England, Wales and Scotland have developed separate policy approaches following devolution and consequently the criminal offences created by each jurisdiction embody different models. Legislation enacted in Ireland closely resembles the English and Welsh model, extending to former partners regardless of co-habitation, but excluding other family members. The Tasmanian offences stand out from other approaches; created prior to the inclusion of coercive control in policy dialogues, they address psychologically and economically abusive behaviours but are hampered by a statutory limitation period. These variations open up the opportunity to conduct a comparative analysis to consider which jurisdiction takes the more promising approach, and what lessons can be learnt from each model by other nations seeking to criminalise forms of psychological abuse.

The subsequent analysis considers the following features of the various offences: their *actus reus*, their *malum reus*, their *mens rea*, the protected victim/s, available defences and maximum penalties. It illustrates how the offences diverge, and argues that the Scottish approach offers a promising model of criminalisation that should influence similar debates in other legal jurisdictions. To draw some comparative reflections, elemental themes will be compared across the offences. Tables are used to illustrate further the manner in which each offence is constructed and draw out the complexities that arise in respect of the elements that need to be established to secure a conviction.

10.3 *Actus Reus*: The Prohibited Conduct

The *actus reus* of the offences describes the prohibited behaviour that leads to the victim being harmed. The definitions regarding behaviour are critical in determining how the offences will apply in practice and how new terms, unfamiliar to criminal law, will be employed. The purpose behind these novel offences is to ensure that the pattern of behaviour characteristic of coercive control is captured, rather than the focus on single incidents that are common to most offences. Table 10.1 illustrates the variations contained in the offences in England, Wales, Scotland, Ireland and Tasmania relating to prohibited behaviour and the subsequent analysis compares several features of the prohibited conduct.

10.3.1 Behaviour

Under s 76(1)(a) of the *SCA* the offence of coercive or controlling behaviour is committed where the person 'repeatedly or continuously engages in behaviour towards another that is controlling or coercive.' The prohibited behaviour is not explained within the legislation and therefore will be open to judicial interpretation. Examples of the prohibited behaviour are, though, outlined in the Home Office's (2015) *Statutory Guidance Framework*, a document required under s 77 of the *SCA*. That document reflects the cross-government policy definition of domestic violence and abuse, with controlling behaviour defined as

> a range of acts designed to make a person subordinate and/or dependent by isolating them from sources of support, exploiting their resources and capacities for personal gain, depriving them of the means needed for independence, resistance and escape and regulating their everyday behaviour. (Home Office 2013, p. 1)

Table 10.1 The *actus reus* of family violence offences in various jurisdictions

Jurisdiction	Frequency	Behaviour	Explanation of behaviour	Directed at	Timeframe
England and Wales *Serious Crime Act 2015* (E&W) s 76	Repeatedly or continuously	Controlling or coercive	Policy guidance	Victim only	Post-enactment: No limitation
Scotland *Domestic Abuse (Scotland) Act 2018* (Scot) s 1	Course of behaviour	Abusive	Legislation: s 2 Violence (sexual or physical), threatening or intimidating behaviour	Victim, child under 18 or another person	Post-enactment: No limitation
Ireland *Domestic Violence Act 2018* (IR) s 39	Persistently	Controlling or coercive	Not defined	Victim only	Post-enactment: No limitation
Tasmania *Family Violence Act 2004* (Tas) s 8	Course of conduct	Coerce to relinquish control over assets or income; dispose of property; prevent participation over household expenditure decisions; withhold (or threaten to) child maintenance support	Legislation: ss 8 (a)–(e)	Victim only	Limitation period applies: 12 months after the last action that made up the course of conduct
Tasmania *Family Violence Act 2004* (Tas) s 9	Course of conduct	Likely to control or intimidate, cause mental harm, apprehension or fear	Legislation: 'course of conduct'	Victim only	Limitation period applies: 12 months after the last action that made up the course of conduct

Coercive behaviour is defined as

> an act or pattern of acts of assault, threats, humiliation and intimidation or other abuse that is used to harm, punish, or frighten their victim. (Home Office 2013, p. 1)

The behaviours may include activities which, on their own, are non-criminal, such as gestures or a look. Coercive and controlling behaviours generally do not fit within other offences in England and Wales, as these are limited in their ability to criminalise cumulative psychological conduct that causes psychological harm. In Ireland, s 39 of the *DVA* is very similar to the English and Welsh model, in that it also requires the prosecution authorities to prove that the defendant used controlling or coercive behaviour. The legislation does not expand upon the terms 'controlling or coercive,' and *Women's Aid* noted that guidance would have been helpful to avoid ambiguities in the application of the offence (Women's Aid (Ireland) 2017, p. 9). Clarity would have been particularly welcome given the novelty of the terms and in order to explicitly include non-physical conduct. The political intention for the offence to cover psychological abuse is evident from Deputy Minister for Justice and Equality Charles Flanagan's statement on the *Final Stage Report*:

> [t]he new offence sends a clear and consistent message that non-violent control in an intimate relationship is criminal and will be treated as such. (Dáil Éireann 2018)

The Irish offence was enacted on 2 January 2019 and it is too soon to evaluate whether in practice psychological abuse could alone form the basis of the coercive control offence. There are several cases, however, that have been reported in the media in England and Wales, where the s 76 offence has been in force since December 2015. Generally, these cases contain a combination of physical and psychological violence, indicating that prosecutors are very cautious about charging in cases solely based upon psychological tactics. Equally, the dearth of cases based on psychological behaviours alone could be accounted for by a lack of community and police awareness about the criminalisation of non-physical abuse. Paul Playle's conviction following a jury trial does, however, stand out as an exception to this. He was a husband who stalked his wife online by sending messages that he pretended were from her previous ex-partner, and then comforted her as she became increasingly distressed and reclusive (BBC News 2018). This conviction offers promise for the future application of this offence to non-physical forms of abuse, and suggests that greater encouragement should be given to prosecution authorities to bring cases that are based on psychological behaviours.

In contrast, Scotland has chosen to prohibit behaviour described as 'abusive', rather than controlling or coercive, under s 1 of the *DASA*. The provision prohibits persons from 'engag[ing] in a course of behaviour which is abusive of their partner or ex-partner'. The key term 'abusive' is expanded upon in s 2 of the *DASA* and has been carefully crafted to detail, in a non-exhaustive manner, the many forms abuse can take. Physical violence is explicitly stated to include sexual violence under s 2 (4)(a), and no hierarchy is created between physical, sexual and psychological forms of abuse. Without the domestic abuse offence, the complainant's narrative of ongoing abuse was not relevant to the prosecution's case where the focus was placed upon isolated incidents to establish the elements of the non-fatal or sexual offences available. Now, all these forms of abuse can be considered part of the behaviour used to control the victim. In addition, if a serious sexual or non-fatal offence occurred the perpetrator can also be charged separately on the indictment for that offence (Scottish Government 2016b, p. 7). In other jurisdictions, sexual violence is not explicitly stated as a prohibited behaviour.

An early effort to address behaviours that cause psychological suffering and economic abuse was made in Tasmania, Australia under the *FVA*. Section 8 prohibits economic abuse and details the many forms which can occur within a marriage or partnership. While the prohibited conduct shows sensitivity towards the experiences of many female partners, it has been noted that many of the cited behaviours overlap with the broader range of conduct prohibited under s 9 (which prohibited any course of conduct likely to control or intimidate, cause mental harm, apprehension or fear: McMachon and McGorrery 2016a, pp. 10, 18–19).

10.3.2 Frequency

In England and Wales, the behaviour must be carried out repeatedly or continuously, whilst in Ireland the offence refers to persistent behaviour. Neither jurisdiction provides clarity about the meaning of these terms in the legislation itself, although the statutory guidance indicates that the prosecution must provide evidence of a *pattern* of coercive and controlling behaviour (Home Office 2015, p. 5). Courts in England and Wales have found the prohibited behaviour to be evidenced over a relatively short period of time. For example, the media reported the case of Lee Coleman. He is reported to have subjected the victim to domestic abuse throughout their 12-year relationship; however, much of this behaviour predated the enactment of the s 76 offence. The case in court, therefore, concentrated only upon a 1-week period where he subjected his partner to a combination of physical violence and psychological tactics (Swindon Advertiser 2016). Coleman had not wanted his partner to take up a tenancy of a local pub. He used name-calling, telling her that she was useless, and when she left the family home he threatened to set fire to it, prompting her to return. Asleep in her children's bedroom, he smothered her with a pillow with the intention of scaring her. Afterwards, he took her car keys, bank cards and emptied their joint bank account before he went to work. The sentencing judge noted that in this short space of time Coleman had undertaken 'a campaign of coercive and controlling behaviour to intimidate her and make her toe the line or leave you' (Wilts and Gloucestershire Standard 2016). This case demonstrates how s 76 of the *SCA* can apply over a short timeframe, and given that conviction followed a jury trial, indicates that juries are willing to accept that controlling behaviour can be criminal even where it seemed to occur over a relatively short period of time.

The approaches of England, Wales and Ireland in regard to the frequency of the prohibited behaviour differ significantly from Scotland and Tasmania; the latter two jurisdictions adopt what might appear to be similar terms to each other: a 'course of behaviour' and a 'course of conduct.' Although they appear alike, however, these phrases are interpreted differently. In respect of the offence created by s 9 of the *FVA* (Tasmania), a course of conduct is expressly defined to include 'limiting the freedom of movement of a person's spouse or partner by means of threats of intimidation'. McMahon and McGorrery (2016a, p. 8) comment that this is an interesting definition as it relates to the prohibited conduct itself without reference to temporal matters. For example, in *Howe v S* [2013] the magistrate found, in *obiter dicta* comments, as follows:

> It seems to me that if the threat or act of intimidation had the effect of limiting the freedom of movement of a person, ... that a single act of threat or intimidation could, in those circumstances, amount to a 'course of conduct' and hence amount to an offence contrary to that section. (*Howe v S* [2013] at [22])

As a result, even a single incident can constitute a 'course of conduct' under s 9 of the *FVA*. This reasoning would also be consistent with the approach under the s 8 offence, which suggests the course of conduct required for the offence of economic abuse can consist of '*one* or more of' the actions listed in ss 8(a)–(e). In contrast, Scotland's course of behaviour model is expected to require conduct occurring on at least two or more occasions (although this has not been defined within the Act), and there appears to be no temporal limitations between each incident (this view was held by a number of stakeholders during consultation on the Scottish offence: Scottish Government 2016b, p. 16–17). Prior to the introduction of the domestic abuse offence in Scotland, a pattern of behaviour that led to increasing levels of psychological harm by an abuser was not reflected in the available offences, which typically focused on single incidents. For example, the *Criminal Justice and Licensing (Scotland) Act 2010* (Scot) ('*CJLSA*') s 38 prohibits non-physical ('threatening or abusive') behaviour that is likely to cause a person fear or alarm, which may consist of 'a single act' or 'a course of conduct', and goes some way to criminalising behaviour that is typical of domestic abuse cases (though the legislation is silent about what is meant by the term 'abusive'). Section 39 of that Act then addresses stalking and adopts a course of conduct model where behaviour actually causes the victim to feel fear or alarm 'on at least two occasions'. Unlike s 38, the abusive, prohibited conduct for the stalking offence is listed in s 39(6). Whilst some recognition is given to the cumulative effect of the behaviour in a course of conduct model, this differs somewhat from a *pattern of behaviour* which, as explained by other authors in this collection, encompasses more than just a collection of isolated incidents. For instance, the new domestic abuse offence in s 1 of the *DASA* creates something different and distinctive from the offences contained in the *CJLSA* by extending to 'a course of behaviour.' Under the new domestic abuse provision, the behaviour must be abusive and can reflect higher levels of severity than that covered by both the ss 38 and 39 offences, because it includes sexual or physical violence, as well as threatening or intimidating behaviour. Noteworthy is Burman and Brooks-Hay's (2018) argument that there is a degree of overlap between the offences which renders the new domestic abuse offence unnecessary. They suggest that whilst an offence that permits the listing of both physically violent and other (non-violent) abusive behaviour together within a single charge, might 'better reflect the experience of victims... [the] very wide scope and the wide range of behaviours potentially risks over-criminalisation'. (Burman and Brooks-Hay 2018, p. 77). However, a bespoke offence that addresses all forms of domestic abuse and the varying degrees of severity that can result from them is necessary, in that it avoids 'inappropriate shoe-horning of such conduct into stalking offences' (McMahon and McGorrery 2016b, p. 101). What would be desirable is a reconsideration of the theoretical framework underpinning the criminal law and a restructuring of all offences seeking to reduce the overlapping of offences.

10.3.3 Target of the Behaviour

The target of the behaviour in the majority of models is the primary victim of the abuse, which ranges from partners to ex-partners and family members (an overview of who constitutes a 'victim' in each jurisdiction is provided in Part IV below). In comparison, the Scottish and Tasmanian offences appear to at least acknowledge that a victim can be coerced or controlled by behaviours directed at others. For example, the Scottish model is sensitive to the way children under 18 can be used to exert psychological harm towards their abused parent (*DASA* s 2(4)(b)). The Tasmanian s 8 offence also recognises how a partner can generate non-physical harm against a parent by specifically prohibiting the withholding of child maintenance support or disposal of property owned by an affected child. The Tasmanian approach is, though, considerably narrower than the Scottish inclusion and arguably the broader approach is more suitable in cases involving coercive control where credible threats and psychological tools adopted by the perpetrator are widely variable, being designed for the specific vulnerabilities of their victim.

10.3.4 Timeframe

The Tasmanian offences differ from the other jurisdictions in terms of the timeframe in which the prohibited behaviour occurs. Restrictions in England, Wales, Ireland and Scotland are that the conduct occurs after the offences were enacted, and this also applies in Tasmania. However, whilst ahead of their time (entering into force on 30 March 2005) McMahon and McGorrery (2016a, p. 11) have noted that ss 8 and 9 of the *FVA* have had limited effect with less than 10 convictions within the first decade of their enactment. They argue that the statutory limitation period relating to the prohibited behaviours of the offence has restricted the number of convictions (they also accord the lack of convictions to the requirement that the behaviours must be deemed unreasonable, as discussed below). Initially, a prosecution could not be brought after 6 months of the last act alleged to have constituted part of the 'course of conduct' of the offence; this has since been extended to 12 months since October 2015 (McMahon and McGorrery 2016a, p. 11). Limitation periods are certainly a complication in already complex cases. They reduce the ability of courts to appreciate the pattern of coercive or controlling behaviour that occurs over the course of a relationship. By excluding aspects of the conduct, the full extent of the victims' experience will be obscured in the courtroom.

10.4 *Malum Reus*: The Impact of the Behaviour

The *malum reus* (or prohibited harm) of the respective offences are structured to capture a range of effects caused by a perpetrator of coercive control. Once again, each jurisdiction has articulated this aspect of the offence differently, but they share the central premise that the behaviour affects the victim psychologically, either exclusively or in addition to physical harm. The Scottish and Tasmanian offences provide the prosecution with an easier task than in England, Wales and Ireland by not requiring proof that the conduct has caused the psychological harm to the victim. Table 10.2 depicts the differences between the offences and the aspects relevant to the impact they have upon the victim.

As the this table illustrates, the impact of the behaviour is described differently in various jurisdictions. Under s 76 of the *SCA* the behaviour may have a 'serious effect' on the victim in two ways (s 76(1)(c)). The first limb is expressly associated with potential physical violence, whilst the second is associated with broader

Table 10.2 The *malum reus* of family violence offences in the various jurisdictions

Jurisdiction	Impact	Proof of impact
England and Wales *Serious Crime Act 2015* (E&W) ss 76 (1)(c), (4)	'Serious effect', which includes causing the victim to fear violence will be used against them on two or more occasions, and/or causing the victim serious alarm or distress which has a substantial adverse effect on their usual day-to-day activities	Must prove that harm occurred
Scotland *Domestic Abuse (Scotland) Act 2018* (Scot) ss 1 (2)(b)(i), (3), 4(1)	physical or psychological harm, including fear, alarm or distress	Need not prove that harm occurred
Ireland *Domestic Violence Act 2018* (IR) ss 39(1)(b), (2)	'Serious effect', which includes causing the victim to fear violence will be used against them or to experience serious alarm or distress that has a substantial adverse impact on their usual day-to-day activities	Must prove harm occurred
Tasmania *Family Violence Act 2004* (Tas) s 8	Unreasonable control or intimidation, mental harm, apprehension or fear	Need not prove that harm occurred
Tasmania *Family Violence Act 2004* (Tas) s 9	Unreasonable control or intimidation, mental harm, apprehension or fear	Need not prove that harm occurred

psychological impacts on the victim. The Irish legislation has adopted the same language, although it does not require that the fear of violence occur on two or more occasions under the first limb (*DVA* s 39(2)). In Scotland, the impact of the behaviour has been included within the legislation in a more detailed manner. The abusive behaviour by the perpetrator must be 'violent, threatening or intimidating' (*DASA* s 2(2)(a)), or alternatively, the behaviour would affect the victim by, for example, making them dependent on, or subordinate to the perpetrator or isolating them from friends or family among other listed activities (ss 2(3)(a)–(e)). Whilst this is quite specific and detailed, Burman and Brooks-Hay (2018) argue that further judicial interpretation is highly likely. This detailing of abusive behaviour within the statute stands in stark contrast to s 9 of the *FVA* where 'emotional abuse' is referred to in the heading to the section but is not included within the provision itself. Instead, the term mental harm is used and it has been suggested that emotions such as 'distress, grief, fear or anger' will not suffice unless they lead to psychological harm (McMahon and McGorrery 2016a, p. 16). Section 1 of the *DASA* in Scotland, in providing legislative detail of the type of harms experienced by victims, helpfully raises awareness in the courtroom about this issue. The specific listing of the type of prohibited behaviour and the impact it has makes them both more visible, enabling victims to identify the harmful behaviour and provides increased certainty in the law to potential perpetrators by stating more clearly what amounts to criminal behaviour and avoiding overcriminalisation.

10.4.1 Proof of Impact

Interestingly, the jurisdictions diverge in respect of the *malum reus* element concerning the impact of the harm to the victim. The English, Welsh and Irish models' approach towards harm is not a preventative one, as each jurisdiction requires the prosecution to establish that the victim has experienced the specified harm. The threshold for the harm has been set high as well, as the effect upon the victim in both models must be a serious one; where serious alarm or distress is caused, a substantial adverse impact on the victim's day-to-day activities is also required. These requirements in the respective jurisdictions therefore create significant evidential obstacles for prosecutions, having the effect of raising the threshold for prosecution, potentially leaving victims to be unheard and delegitimised should no charges be brought (impacting upon the likelihood the victim will report future abuses). Further, the higher threshold could lead to a lower number of successful prosecutions, which if reported by the media could also lower victim confidence in the police/justice system to handle family violence.

The Scottish and Tasmanian offences, on the other hand, have greater preventative capacity. Under s 1 of the *DASA*, the abusive behaviour must have as its *purpose*, or must be considered to have as its purpose by a reasonable person, any of the relevant effects listed in s 2(3)(a)-(e). There is no requirement that the victim actually experienced the behaviour as harmful to themselves. Burman and

Brooks-Hay (2018, p. 74) contend, however, that the reality of the courtroom will make it necessary to ask the victim about the harm they suffered. Likewise, for the Tasmanian offences, the economic abuse or course of conduct embarked upon must be with the purpose of causing the stated harms to the victim. With so few convictions, it is difficult to conclude whether this has meant victims have not been expected to show the actual harm they experienced.

In jurisdictions that have opted to develop an offence that does not require evidence of actual harm to the victim, the focus of the prosecution will be on the behaviours themselves, as well as the state of mind of the perpetrator. This is preferable to centring on factors such as the victim's mental state or why the victim remained in an abusive relationship.

10.5 *Mens Rea*: The Mental Element

The state of mind of an offender at the time they perform the prohibited act is a central element to any criminal offence (other than strict or absolute liability offences). *Mens rea* terms reflect the culpability and blameworthiness of the offender. Subjective approaches are associated with higher degrees of blame than objective ones, and consequently garner greater penalties. The difficulty with subjective approaches is that they tend to be harder to prove. Table 10.3 compares the various *mens rea* requirements of the offences.

Table 10.3 The *mens rea* of family violence offences in the various jurisdictions

Jurisdiction	*Mens rea* requirement
England and Wales *Serious Crime Act 2015* (E&W) s 76(1)(d)	The defendant must know, or ought to know, that the behaviour will have a serious effect on the victim (subjective or objective)
Scotland *Domestic Abuse (Scotland) Act 2018* (Scot) ss 1(2)(a)–(b)	A reasonable person would consider the course of behaviour to be likely to cause the victim to suffer physical or psychological harm, *and* either (i) the defendant intended the behaviour to cause the victim such harm, or (ii) the defendant was reckless as to whether the behaviour would cause the victim such harm (objective and subjective)
Ireland *Domestic Violence Act 2018* (IR) s 39(1)(c)	The defendant must knowingly engage in the behaviour, and a reasonable person would consider the behaviour likely to have a serious effect on the victim (subjective and objective)
Tasmania *Family Violence Act 2004* (Tas) s 8	The defendant must intend to unreasonably control or intimidate the victim, or to cause the victim mental harm, apprehension or fear (subjective only)
Tasmania *Family Violence Act 2004* (Tas) s 9	The defendant must know, or ought to know, that the behaviour is likely to unreasonably control or intimidate the victim, or to cause the victim mental harm, apprehension or fear (subjective or objective)

To be found guilty under s 76 of the *SCA* the prosecution must establish, inter alia, that the defendant either had knowledge that the behaviour would have a serious effect on the victim or that they ought to have had knowledge of this (*SCA* s 76(1)(d)). Knowledge is not deemed to be as blameworthy a state of mind as intention; Simester et al. (2013, p. 149) explain that knowledge differs from intention as it does not require the defendant to think a 'relevant circumstance exists with provable certainty...it is sufficient that the defendant accepts, or assumes, and has no serious doubt, at the time he acts, that the circumstance is present'. Where the objective state of mind would apply, s 76(5) of the *SCA* clarifies that this is to be judged from the perspective of 'a reasonable person in possession of the same information'. The *mens rea* requirement chosen for s 76 therefore reflects a relatively low threshold of culpability to prove the offence, which could be a reason why a relatively low maximum penalty was set (Bettinson and Bishop 2015).

In Ireland, the *mens rea* requirement for the s 39(1) *DVA* offence differs from the English and Welsh model because it requires both subjective and objective *mens rea* elements (as opposed to one or the other). The meaning of 'knowingly' has not been defined in the *DVA*, which is unfortunate because it implies that the prosecution must prove what the defendant understood his behaviour to be abusive. Given that the terms 'coercive' and 'controlling' are also not defined in the legislation, it allows defendants to argue that they did not understand what coercive control was, or that they were not employing it within their intimate relationships. A successful educative effect of introducing the offence should, however, make such arguments less persuasive. During consultation on the draft Bill, Women's Aid Ireland raised a concern about the clarity of the *mens rea* term 'knowingly', asking whether it was necessary that the person appreciates the consequences of their actions (Women's Aid (Ireland) 2017). In the context of harassment offences, Finch (2002, p. 710) points out that the impact of the behaviour is 'no less harmful because it is unintentional'. No revision was made in respect of this point, the Act retained the same wording as the Bill. The prosecution also has an additional *mens rea* requirement to satisfy, as a reasonable person must consider the prohibited behaviour likely to have a serious effect on the victim. Educating the public will be essential for the Irish offence to have some degree of success, as it will be in any jurisdiction with an objective *mens rea* element. The failure to provide definitions for key terms in the offence is particularly unfortunate in this regard. Although s 9 *FVA* adopts the term 'knowingly' as its mens rea requirement in common with England, Wales and Ireland, the s 8 Tasmanian offence differs. That provision requires a defendant to intend their actions, thereby adopting a wholly subjective approach. This is problematical where defendants suggest that they believed that their behaviour fell within the range of normal interactions within an intimate relationship.

It is contended that Scotland has the more considered approach to the *mens rea* requirement of this kind of offence. The *mens rea* for s 1 of the *DASA* consists of two parts, an objective limb, followed by a subjective one. This range of *mens rea* requirements (reasonable person test plus intention or recklessness) justifies a sentencing range that can be tailored to the individual circumstances of the case. Under this model, it must first be established that the behaviour would be considered by a reasonable person to cause the victim physical or psychological harm. Defendants' claimed unawareness about the effect their behaviour would have on the victim is irrelevant at this part of the assessment. Once this aspect has been established, the prosecution must then also prove that either the defendant intended to cause the victim to suffer such harm, or was reckless as to it. In cases where the defendant suggests that they did not realise that their conduct would harm the victim, they may still be caught by the recklessness element, which in Scottish criminal law is interpreted to be either subjectively reckless, where a person takes an unjustified risk of which they were aware, or objectively reckless, where the person takes an unjustified risk of which they were either aware or ought to have been aware of (see Ferguson and McDiarmid 2014, p. 168).

10.6 The Victim

There is no unanimous position about who can be a victim of non-physical harm in a domestic setting. Table 10.4 shows the different range of victims for each offence.

The Tasmanian and Scottish offences are the narrowest in scope, applying only to current or former spousal or partner relationships. An alternative charge for behaviour that causes physical or mental harm or an apprehension or fearfulness outside the relationship is the offence of stalking under s 192 of the *Criminal Code Act 1924* (Tas). It seems that this offence covers the elements of s 9 of the *FVA*, regardless of the relationships status between the defendant and victim (McMahon and McGorrery 2016a, pp. 21–22). This is unfortunate as s 9 makes the behaviour in an ongoing relationship visible, whereas the power dynamics that occur in a coercive and controlling relationship are lost in the generic anti-stalking legislation. Also of narrow application is the Scottish offence, which can be committed against

Table 10.4 The victim of family violence offences in the various jurisdictions

Jurisdiction	Victim
England and Wales *Serious Crime Act 2015* (E&W) ss 76(1)(b), (2)	The defendant and the victim are personally connected, which includes being in an intimate relationship, or living together and either (i) being members of the same family or (ii) having previously been in an intimate relationship
Scotland *Domestic Abuse (Scotland) Act 2018* (Scot) ss 1	The defendant and the victim are partners or ex-partners
Ireland *Domestic Violence Act 2018* (IR) s 39(4)(a)	The victim may be the defendant's spouse, civil partner or someone with whom they were or are in an intimate relationship
Tasmania *Family Violence Act 2004* (Tas) s 8	The defendant and the victim are current or former spouses or partners
Tasmania *Family Violence Act 2004* (Tas) s 9	The defendant and the victim are current or former spouses or partners

a partner or ex-partner. The meaning of 'partner' or 'ex-partner' is a spouse or civil partner, where the parties live together as if spouses, or in an intimate personal relationship with each other (*DASA* s 10(2)(a)–(c)). The Irish legislation adopts the same approach as the Scottish legislation. The range of victims is widest under the English and Welsh offence, where the victim can be either an intimate partner *or a family member*. The s 76 *SCA* offence is committed where the parties 'are personally connected' which, as explained above, is satisfied when the two parties are either in an intimate relationship, or when they live together and are members of the same family, or live together and have previously been in an intimate personal relationship with each other.

Cairns (2017, pp. 264–265) notes that the Scottish offence—and presumably the argument can be extended to include the Irish offence—seeks 'to separate abuse between partners and former partners, and abuse between other family members', implying 'that the harm of domestic abuse arises from the relationship between the parties', whereas the 'scope of domesticity' is wider under s 76. Cairns argues that further debate is needed to justify placing abusive behaviours in relationships of partners or ex-partners above other forms of family abuse and queries whether there is sufficient difference between abuse taking place in this context compared to other family relationships. In its favour, the Scottish approach has aligned with the existing policy definition of domestic abuse, potentially avoiding confusion and delays in its application (Crown Office and Procurator Fiscal Office 2017). On the other hand, victims of abusive behaviours by other family members are vulnerable and their experiences should not be any less visible to the criminal law. Section 76 of the *SCA* recognises this by extending to all family members, with some caveats. For example, members of a family must be living together, providing no protection to the adult child who continues to care for their parent after leaving home. Children aged under 16 experiencing coercive and controlling behaviours by their parents also cannot be victims of the offence (*SCA* s 76(3)). It is contended that a single offence will struggle to raise the visibility of all forms of family violence, with each raising complex issues about power and control within the dynamics of the family. The Scottish and Irish approach of concentrating on intimate partner violence within a domestic abuse offence would seem sensible at this time. A coherent and considered criminal law framework is needed to address distinct forms of familial abuse, which would be in line with Ashworth's view of fair labelling and ensuring that the law is not excessive (Ashworth 2008).

A significant limitation of the s 76 offence concerns relationships that have ended. Section 76(2) extends only to former intimate partners where they continue to live together. This peculiarity is the result of a desire to plug a gap in the existing legislation, rather than to create a carefully designed framework of criminal offences in this area. Once the relationship ends in England and Wales, the expectation is that the offences under the *Protection from Harassment Act 1997* (UK) will apply to behaviour that amounts to a course of conduct that causes harassment (s 2), stalking (s 2A) or puts a person in fear of violence (s 4) (Home Office 2015). Although this provides a degree of protection at what is a particularly dangerous time for victim-survivors of domestic abuse, it creates confusion in the criminal law about what abusive behaviour is and wrongly focuses on the location of the harm rather than the relationship it takes place within (Bettinson 2016).

10.7 Defences

Most of the jurisdictions with these new offences provide legislative defences. Sections 8 and 9 of the *FVA* in Tasmania allow a defendant to escape liability where it can be established that their behaviour was not unreasonable; for this reason, McMahon and McGorrery (2016a, p. 8) note that these provisions seem to allow for *reasonably* controlling or intimidating behaviour and question what would amount to such conduct. Similar conclusions can be drawn when considering the defences available for the offences in England, Wales and Scotland. Under s 76 (8) of the *SCA* a defendant will not be guilty where they believe the coercive or controlling behaviour is in the best interests of the victim, and in all the circumstances the behaviour was reasonable. Notably, this only extends to behaviour that caused the victim to be seriously alarmed or distressed and had a substantial adverse effect on their daily activities, and does not apply in circumstances where the relevant behaviour caused the victim to experience fear that violence would be used against them on two or more occasions (s 76(10)). Without any appeal cases on this point, the inhibiting effect of this defence on prosecutorial decisions to bring charges cannot yet be determined. It has, however, been suggested that the defence is for the most part redundant as the *malum reus* requires the defendant to cause a substantial adverse effect to the victim (Bettinson 2016, p. 174). Behaviour that is thought to be in the best interests of the victim, *and* which is reasonable, would rarely have such a negative effect on the victim.

Section 5 of the *DASA* contains the Scottish defence, which does not refer to a notion that the defendant was acting in the best interests of the victim. Instead, it applies where the defendant can show that the course of behaviour was reasonable in the particular circumstances. What amounts to reasonable will need to be subject to judicial scrutiny and will be based on individual circumstances. Therefore, concerns raised by McMahon and McGorrery (2016a, p. 15) about how to determine norms or standards of reasonableness could extend to both s 76 of the *SCA* and s 1 of the *DASA*. In Ireland, the offence of coercive control introduced by s 39 (1) of the *DVA* does not have a discrete defence; however, the defendant must knowingly use controlling or coercive behaviour persistently. This potentially allows arguments to be presented by the defendant that they believed their behaviour to be loving and caring rather than controlling. Presented as an element of the offence (as it is in s 9 of the *FVA*), though, it is likely to be more problematic to the prosecution's case than the defences for s 76 of the *SCA* and s 1 of the *DASA*.

10.8 Maximum Penalties

Standing on its own, the offence of controlling or coercive behaviour carries a maximum penalty of 5 years' imprisonment, whether it occurs in England, Wales or Ireland (*SCA* s 76(11)(a); *DVA* s 39(3)(b)). This sentence is significantly lower than the maximum life imprisonment penalty available for the most serious non-fatal offences in each jurisdiction: causing grievous bodily harm contrary to s 18 of the *Offences Against the Person Act 1861* (UK) and causing serious harm contrary to s 4 of the *Non-Fatal Offences Against the Person Act 1997* (IR). The types of cases involving coercive and controlling behaviours will vary in the use of behaviours, the degree of harm caused and the culpability involved. This spectrum is not reflected within these offences. However, prosecutors may also decide to add further charges to an indictment where there is evidence of sexual or physical assault. This occurred in the case of *R v Conlon* [2018] (at [31]). The appellant based his challenge against a 4-year sentence for a s 76 conviction on the ground that it was manifestly excessive. He had controlled many aspects of the complainant's life, including dictating what she could wear and how she could style her hair, and vetting who she could speak to by checking her phone each day. On one occasion, which formed the basis of a conviction under s 47 of the *Offences Against the Person Act 1861* (UK), he punched her several times in the face after he saw her speak to another man. In addition to receiving a sentence of 4 years imprisonment for the s 76 offence, he was given a concurrent sentence of 16 months for the assault and a consecutive sentence of 6 months for two counts of perverting the course of justice, earned as a result of attempting to encourage the complainant to change her evidence. The sentencing judge held that the sentence imposed for controlling or coercive behaviour was 'aggravated by the assault occasioning actual bodily harm' (at [22]), which raises the potential that the offender was twice punished for the same act (double punishment). It isn't clear whether the Court of Appeal agreed with that approach, but they certainly didn't seem to repudiate it.

The Tasmanian offences offer lower maximum penalties (2 years' imprisonment for both offences). In contrast, the Scottish offence has the ability to take into account the severity of the behaviour and the harm it causes, with commensurate degrees of censure, having a maximum penalty of 14 years' imprisonment (*DASA* s 8(b)).

10.9 Conclusion

Time will tell whether these efforts to criminalise abusive behaviours have been successful through the number of convictions they achieve and the increased awareness among the public regarding them. The comparative analysis provided here allows other jurisdictions to develop their own models based on what are suggested to be the ideal components of each offence. The *actus reus* has the role of describing the prohibited behaviour as a pattern, and Scotland's s 1 *DASA's* use of the terminology 'course of behaviour' aligns most accurately to the patterns of behaviour that form coercive control (Stark 2007). In addition, s 1 favours the term 'abusive' over coercive control, which could prove to be more enduring by encapsulating behaviours associated with family violence in the future. All the offences considered in this chapter rightly acknowledge the harm to the victim of family violence can extend beyond the physical. In fact, domestic abuse can involve either physical, psychological, sexual or economic abuse, or a combination of each, and understanding the role of sexual violence in domestic abuse is a relatively underexplored area of research (as is the role of economic abuse). That sexual violence can and does form part of a pattern of behaviour is clearly stated in the terms of the Scottish offence, making this form of coercive control as equally visible as physical and psychological violence. No hierarchy is created by the Scottish legislation thereby placing physical, sexual and psychological violence on an equal footing in respect of domestic abuse and arguably makes the Scottish offence a superior model out of the jurisdictions considered here. A further factor for jurisdictions to consider, as England and Wales are currently in the process of doing, is whether economic abuse should be expressly included as a criminalised form of non-physical domestic abuse (HM Government 2019).

Another appropriate component of the actus reus for an offence aimed at criminalising abusive behaviour is illustrated by the operation of the Scottish and Tasmanian offences. Neither requires a causal link between the harm and the behaviour. This approach focuses attention onto the behaviour rather than the mental state of the victim-complainant. In contrast, the offences in England and Wales and Ireland require that the relevant behaviour has an impact on victims. Proving the causal link is particularly onerous on the prosecutor, who must demonstrate that the victim experienced 'serious' alarm or distress which has a 'substantial adverse' effect on them. This threshold places a significant burden on the prosecuting authority to prove these offences and could deter, or at least limit, their use.

Having compared the range of *mens rea* elements of each offence analysed, it has been suggested that Scotland could have the most appropriate model. Unlike the predominantly subjective approaches of its counterparts, s 1 *DASA* makes it much more difficult for a defendant to be acquitted on the basis that they did not appreciate that their behaviour would cause the prohibited harm. However, the breadth of the *mens rea* raises another issue which is linked to the penalties available for the offence. For this reason, it is debatable whether the Scottish or English and Welsh approach is preferable in terms of the maximum penalty for the offences. On the one hand, the maximum penalty of 14 years in Scotland allows judicial officers sufficient scope to capture the broad range of behaviours these offences are directed towards. On the other hand, it also means that offenders convicted of 'low-level' controlling or coercive behaviour are convicted of the same offence as those committing more heinous and prolonged forms of abuse. This could suggest that the most appropriate approach could in fact be a hierarchy of offences and maximum penalties, rather than a one-size-fits-all approach.

There was some diversity in who can be a 'victim' under the various offences, including current intimate partners, former intimate partners or the more generic 'family members'. The Scottish and Irish legislations have what is perhaps the most appropriate approach, because they extend it to abusers who continue to adopt a pattern of prohibited behaviour after the relationship has ended. Beyond the intimate partner context, including all family members within the terms of the same offence may be problematical at this time. Further research and understanding about the way abusive behaviours manifest and how the dynamics of power and control interact with abuse are required in this area to determine whether a model aimed at intimate partner violence should be extended to all family relationships.

Other nations should give careful consideration to their criminal law frameworks when addressing abusive behaviours. Each of the jurisdictions considered has created a progressive offence that conveys a broad range of culpable behaviours associated with coercive control and psychological abuse. However, there is only so much a single offence can be expected to do, and further consideration should be given to developing a typology of abusive behaviours in substantive criminal law.

References

Ashworth, A. (2008). Conceptions of overcriminalization. *Ohio State Journal of Criminal Law, 5*(2), 407–425.

BBC News. (2018, January 24). Paul Playle jailed for stalking wife for two years. Retrieved from https://www.bbc.co.uk/news/uk-england-sussex-42805203.

Bettinson, V. (2016). Criminalising coercive control in domestic violence cases: Should Scotland follow the path of England and Wales? *Criminal Law Review, 3*, 165–180.

Bettinson, V. (2018, February 12). Vanessa Bettinson: Scotland gives hope to world's domestic abuse victims. *The Scotsman*. Retrieved from https://www.scotsman.com/news/opinion/vanessa-bettinson-scotland-gives-hope-to-world-s-domestic-abuse-victims-1-4687367.

Bettinson, V., & Bishop, C. (2015). Is the creation of a discrete offence of coercive control necessary to combat domestic violence? *Northern Ireland Legal Quarterly, 66*(2), 179–197.

Burman, M., & Brooks-Hay, O. (2018). Aligning policy and law? The creation of a domestic abuse offence incorporating coercive control. *Criminology and Criminal Justice, 18*(1), 67–83.

Cairns, I. C. M. (2017). What counts as a 'domestic'? Family relationships and the proposed criminalisation of domestic abuse in Scotland. *Edinburgh Law Review, 21*(2), 262–268.

Crown Office and Procurator Fiscal Office. (2017). *Joint Protocol between Police Scotland and Crown Office and Procurator Fiscal Service*. Retrieved from http://www.scotland.police.uk/access-to-information/policies-and-procedures/partnership-agreements/.

Dáil Éireann debate. (2018) *Domestic Violence Bill 2017 [Seanad]: Report and Final Stages*. Retrieved from https://www.oireachtas.ie/en/debates/debate/dail/2018-04-25/30/.

Department of Justice (NI). (2016). *Domestic Abuse Offence and Domestic Violence Disclosure Scheme: A Consultation*. Retrieved from https://www.justice-ni.gov.uk/consultations/domestic-abuse-offence-and-domestic-violence-disclosure-scheme.

Douglas, H. (2015). Do we need a specific domestic violence offence? *Melbourne University Law Review, 39*(2), 434–471.

Douglas, H. (2018). Do we need an offence of coercive control? *Precedent, 144*, 18–21.

Dutton, M., & Goodman, L. (2005). Coercion in intimate partner violence: Toward a new conceptualization. *Sex Roles, 52*(11–12), 743–756.

Ferguson, P. R., & McDiarmid, C. (2014). *Scots criminal law: A critical analysis* (2nd ed.). Edinburgh: Edinburgh University Press.

Finch, E. (2002). Stalking the perfect stalking law: An evaluation of the efficacy of the *Protection from Harassment Act 1997*. *Criminal Law Review*, 703–719.

HM Government. (2018). *Transforming the Response to Domestic Abuse: Government Consultation*. Retrieved from https://consult.justice.gov.uk/homeoffice-moj/domestic-abuse-consultation/.

HM Government. (2019). *Transforming the Response to Domestic Abuse: Consultation Response and Draft Bill*. Retrieved from https://www.gov.uk/government/publications/domestic-abuse-consultation-response-and-draft-bill.

Home Office. (2013). *Circular 003/2013: New government domestic violence and abuse definition*. Retrieved from https://www.gov.uk/government/publications/new-government-domestic-violence-and-abuse-definition.

Home Office. (2015). *Controlling or Coercive Behaviour in an Intimate or Family Relationship: Statutory Guidance Framework*. Retrieved from https://www.gov.uk/government/publications/statutory-guidance-framework-controlling-or-coercive-behaviour-in-an-intimate-or-family-relationship.

McMahon, M., & McGorrery, P. (2016a). Criminalising emotional abuse, intimidation and economic abuse in the context of family violence: The Tasmanian experience. *University of Tasmania Law Review, 35*(2), 1–22.

McMahon, M., & McGorrery, P. (2016b). Criminalising controlling and coercive behaviour: The next step in the prosecution of family violence? *Alternative Law Journal, 41*(2), 98–101.

Queen Elizabeth II. (2017). *Queen's Speech 2017*. Retrieved from https://www.gov.uk/government/speeches/queens-speech-2017.

Scottish Government. (2016a). *The Creation of A Specific Offence of Domestic Abuse—Proposed Associated Reforms to Criminal Procedure*. Retrieved from https://www.gov.scot/Publications/2016/10/3259.

Scottish Government. (2016b). *Criminal Offence of Domestic Abuse Analysis of Consultation Responses*. Retrieved from https://www.gov.scot/Publications/2016/09/4616.

Simester, A. P., Spencer, J. R., Stark, F., Sullivan, G. R., & Virgo, G. J. (2013). *Simester and Sullivan's criminal law theory and doctrine* (5th ed.). Oxford: Bloomsbury Publishing.

Stark, E. (2007). *Coercive control: How men entrap women in personal life*. Oxford: Oxford University Press.

State of Victoria. (2016). *Royal Commission into Family Violence: Report and Recommendations Vol III*. Retrieved from http://www.rcfv.com.au/Report-Recommendations.

Swindon Advertiser. (2016, July 20). Workmates 'stunned' to hear man had tried to smother woman in her sleep. Retrieved from http://www.swindonadvertiser.co.uk/news/14628801.Workmates__stunned__to_hear_man_had_tried_to_smother_woman_in_her_sleep/.

Tolmie, J. (2018). Coercive control: To criminalize or not to criminalize? *Criminology and Criminal Justice, 18*(1), 50–66.

United Nations Committee Against Torture. (2017) *Concluding observations on the second periodic report of Ireland*. Retrieved from https://tbinternet.ohchr.org/Treaties/CAT/Shared%20Documents/IRL/INT_CAT_COC_IRL_28491_E.pdf.

Walklate, S., Fitz-Gibbon, K., & McCulloch, J. (2018). Is more law the answer? Seeking justice for victims of intimate partner violence through the reform of legal categories. *Criminology and Criminal Justice, 18*(1), 115–131.

Williamson, E. (2010). Living in the world of the domestic violence perpetrator: Negotiating the unreality of coercive control. *Violence Against Women, 16*(12), 1412–1423.

Wilts and Gloucestershire Standard. (2016, July 21). *Controlling south Cerney man who threatened to smother partner to death is jailed for three years*. Retrieved from https://www.wiltsglosstandard.co.uk/news/14633717.controlling-south-cerney-man-who-threatened-to-smother-partner-to-death-is-jailed-for-three-years/.

Women's Aid (Ireland). (2017). *Women's Aid Submission on the Domestic Violence Bill 2007*. Retrieved from https://www.womensaid.ie/about/policy/publications/womens-aid-submission-on-the-domestic-violence-bill-2017-december-2017-updated/.

Legislation

Crimes Act 1958 (Vic)
Criminal Code Act 1924 (Tas)
Criminal Justice and Licensing (Scotland) Act 2010 (Scot)
Domestic Abuse (Scotland) Act 2018 (Scot)
Domestic Violence Act 2018 (IR)
Family Violence Act 2004 (Tas)
Non-Fatal Offences Against the Person Act 1997 (IR)
Offences Against the Person Act 1861 (UK)
Protection from Harassment Act 1997 (UK)
Serious Crime Act 2015 (E&W)

Cases

Howe v S [2013] TASMC 33
R v Conlon [2018] 1 Cr App R (S) 38

Chapter 11
Coercive Control as the Context for Intimate Partner Violence: The Challenge for the Legal System

Jane Wangmann

Abstract The last 30 years have seen considerable change in the legal landscape to better address the harm of intimate partner violence (IPV), including the introduction of stalking and intimidation offences, as well as civil protection orders, yet many gaps and issues remain. The creation of an offence that seeks to capture the harm of coercive control is presented as one way in which to fill some of the gaps between the experience of IPV and the way the criminal law has traditionally conceived of this harm. In this chapter, I raise questions about whether such an offence will achieve its aims if attention is not also paid to the practice and implementation of current (and new) laws. In particular, I discuss the dominance of the incident framework not only in terms of criminal law responses, but also in terms of those responses designed to better address the pattern of IPV, namely, civil protection orders. A key concern of this chapter is the conceptual gap that emerges between the intentions of law reform and the practice or implementation of that law. In so doing, I draw on recent cautions voiced by Julia Tolmie (2018a) and Sandra Walklate and colleagues (2018). I argue that an understanding of coercive control is necessary for all legal engagements that seek to address the harm of IPV, and that if attention was centred on whether there should be a discrete offence it may distract from the need to simultaneously do more work to ensure that a deeper understanding of coercive control informs all areas of legal practice.

Keywords Intimate partner violence · Coercive control · Civil protection order · Criminal law

J. Wangmann (✉)
Faculty of Law, University of Technology Sydney, NSW, Australia
e-mail: Jane.Wangmann@uts.edu.au

11.1 Introduction

The response of the criminal justice system to intimate partner violence (IPV) has been the subject of extensive criticism on multiple fronts—from what acts and behaviours the law defines as criminal, to the practice and implementation of the law. Many of these criticisms centre on the tendency of the criminal law to focus on primarily physical or visible forms of violence, and the reliance on an incident framework when such acts are criminalised. This, however, is not the way in which IPV is experienced; rather than being an incident, or even a series of incidents, IPV is a patterned and repeated form of behaviour(s) exerted to coerce and control the victim. It also involves far more than physical or visible forms of violence; it includes emotional or psychological abuse, financial abuse and other controlling behaviours. As a result, the traditional criminal law response has left unrecognised and unaddressed multiple other forms of abuse that are experienced as part of IPV, 'bear[ing] little resemblance' to the lived experience of IPV (Tuerkheimer 2004, p. 959). Critically, the focus on incidents of 'violence' has also meant that any appreciation of, let alone response to, the context in which those acts and behaviours operate has been absent from criminal justice responses. This effectively 'decontextualizes' IPV and 'conceals the reality of an ongoing pattern of conduct occurring within a relationship characterized by power and control' (Tuerkheimer 2004, pp. 960–961).

As a result of this disconnect, a number of scholars (e.g. Stark 2007; Tuerkheimer 2004; Burke 2007) and more recently some legislatures have sought to construct a criminal offence that better captures both the non-physical forms of violence and abuse as well as the patterned and repetitive nature of IPV. In England and Wales, this offence seeks to criminalise 'controlling or coercive behaviour in an intimate relationship' which is constructed as continuous or repeated behaviour that coerces or controls another person where that behaviour has a 'serious effect' on the victim, and the alleged perpetrator of the behaviour knew, or ought to have known, that their behaviour would have this effect (*Serious Crimes Act 2015* (E&W) s 76). Ireland also introduced an 'offence of coercive control' which has similarities to the English and Welsh offence requiring that the coercive or controlling behaviour has a 'serious effect' on the victim and that a 'reasonable person' would consider it likely that the behaviour would have that effect (*Domestic Abuse Act 2018* (IR) s 39). In Scotland, the offence is one of 'domestic abuse'; defined as a 'course of behaviour' which is abusive to the victim, where a 'reasonable person would consider the course of behaviour is likely to cause' the victim 'to suffer physical or psychological harm' (*Domestic Abuse (Scotland) Act 2018* (Scot) s 1). These offences are designed to fill some of the gaps between the lived experience of IPV and the traditional response of the criminal law, and as such potentially represent a significant positive change.

In this chapter, I raise questions about whether the introduction of such offences will be as effective as desired if attention is not also paid to the practice and implementation of current (and new) laws. This is essentially an argument about the continuing problems of practice and implementation that has 'dogged' much feminist engagement with law reform around IPV and other harms experienced predominantly by women (Hunter 2008, p. 6). In her work on civil protection orders and family law proceedings, Rosemary Hunter (2008, pp. 6–8) canvassed some of the reasons why feminist law reform efforts encounter implementation problems. These include: the nature of legal culture(s), the process of 'translation' of the harms women experience into 'existing legal forms and concepts' and the way in which feminist claims may be 'co-opted to serve other interests' (see also Hunter 2006, pp. 737–739; Smart 1986; Thornton 1991; Graycar and Morgan 2005). In this chapter, I explore the conceptual gap that emerges between the intentions of law reform and the practice or implementation of that law through a discussion of the dominance of the incident framework not only in terms of criminal law responses, but also in terms of those responses designed to better address IPV, namely, civil protection orders. I draw on recent cautions voiced by Julia Tolmie (2018a) and Sandra Walklate and colleagues (2018) who collectively highlight the continuing problems with implementation of existing offences, as well as the particular challenges for implementation of these new offences, and the potential risks or unintended consequences that might flow from the creation of such new offences.

In the first part of this chapter, I canvas the reasons why there have been moves to create a discrete offence that better captures the harm of IPV. I briefly discuss some of the literature which has emphasised the broader contextual nature of IPV; particularly work by Evan Stark (2007) in which he has argued that the domestic violence movement has stalled as a result of its focus on violence and not coercive control. I then turn to a discussion of the implementation gap that continues to be an issue of concern in law reform around IPV. Here I present a case study on civil protection orders where despite the promise of capturing the *patterned* nature of IPV, *incidents* continue to dominate (Wangmann 2012; Hunter 2008). In the final section, I turn to potential problems and unintended consequences that might arise with the implementation of the newly created offences in England/Wales, Scotland and Ireland. I raise cautions about whether centring efforts on a discrete offence may distract from the extent to which a deeper understanding of coercive control is necessary for all legal responses including adequate implementation of the new offences. Here I draw on developments in family law and civil protection orders, as well as the criminal law, to emphasise the extent to which an understanding of coercive control is required at all levels—in legislation, practice and procedure, and responses to victims and perpetrators more generally.

11.2 Criminalising Coercive Control

One of the key arguments in favour of introducing a dedicated offence of IPV is that such offences fill an important gap in the existing criminal law, which to a large extent remains focused on incidents of largely physical or visible forms of violence (Bettinson and Bishop 2015, p. 185). These new offences represent potentially positive developments in how the criminal law responds to IPV. For example, in describing the new Scottish offence, Michele Burman (2018, p. 45) stated that it 'carries with it the aspiration of facilitating a criminal justice response that is less incident-based and more appreciative of the ongoing patterns of behaviour which characterise abuse'. There are questions, however, about whether the newly created offences can achieve this, as well as a more fundamental question about whether the problems with the criminal law's response to IPV 'are deeper and more extensive than simply the fragmentation of long-standing patterns of harm into individualised transactions' (Tolmie 2018a, p. 51).

The recent debate and action on criminalising coercive control across different jurisdictions have been linked to the influential work of Evan Stark. Stark (2007, p. 10) seeks to 'reframe' IPV from a focus on one-off violent events, to one that recognises the 'multidimensionality of oppression in [the] personal life' of women, that is, coercive control. Stark (2007, p. 5) explains that coercive control is 'ongoing and its perpetrators use various means to hurt, humiliate, intimidate, exploit, isolate, and dominate their victims', that victims are 'frequently deprived of money, food, access to communication or transportation, and other survival resources even as they are cut off from family, friends, and other supports', and that 'coercive control is personalized, extends through social space as well as over time'. Stark's understanding and articulation of coercive control is explicitly gendered: 'it relies on women's vulnerability *as women* due to sexual inequality' (p. 5, emphasis in original) and recognises that 'the main means used to establish control is the microregulation of everyday behaviors associated with stereotypic female roles, such as how women dress, cook, clean, socialize, care for their children, or perform sexually' (p. 5).

It is important to recognise, as Stark (2007, p. 11) also does, that this understanding of IPV as 'coercive control, 'power and control' or 'entrapment' is not new; the 'use of the phrase "coercive control" stretches back to …the 1970s' (Rathus 2013, p. 377) in the work of Rebecca and Russell Dobash where they argued that 'violence in the family should be understood primarily as coercive control' (Dobash and Dobash 1979, p. 15). Susan Schechter (1982, p. 224) described battering as a way to 'maintain or establish control' and drew connections to women's position in the family and society more broadly. Similarly, other scholars and practitioners have used the phrase 'power and control' to describe the way IPV functions (Pence and Paymar 1993); the power and control wheel (and its various iterations) developed as part of the Domestic Abuse Intervention Project (Duluth, USA) remains an effective illustration of the nature of IPV and how it functions (see https://www.theduluthmodel.org/wheels/). In another way James Ptacek (1999, p. 10) has used the concept of 'social entrapment' to emphasise 'the inescapably social dimension of women's vulnerability to men's violence, women's experience of violence, and women's abilities to resist and escape'. What is fundamental to all of this theoretical work is that this understanding of control came from the accounts provided by women themselves.

11.2.1 Traditional Emphasis on Physical or Visible Forms of Violence

Stark's articulation of coercive control illustrates the disjuncture between the criminal law's traditional emphasis on incidents of physical or visible forms of violence, and the other forms of abuse that women experience as part of the ongoing, repeated and cumulative experience of IPV.

The initial emphasis on physical violence in the translation of IPV into 'legal claims' might be seen as a 'strategic' one, legitimising 'the notion that women were subjects of abuse and that physical battering was something serious and unique that happened to women' (Schneider 2000, p. 65). However, as Elizabeth Schneider emphasises, 'feminists did not intend to limit the concept of abuse to solely physical harm' and these moves to translate women's experiences into something that could be actioned by law was 'premised on an understanding of coercive behaviour and power and control...rather than "number of hits"' (2000, p. 65).

Over time the criminal law has continued to develop, often in response to feminist-informed critique to create new offences that better capture some of the non-physical forms of violence and abuse experienced as part of IPV. The creation of the new offences in England/Wales, Ireland and Scotland represents the most recent attempts in this area, but there have been other significant and often innovative changes in the area of criminal law (and indeed other legal responses to IPV) to take account of these criticisms; these have included the creation of some course of conduct offences (such as stalking), aggravated forms of existing offences where they have been perpetrated in a domestic or family relationship, the flagging of offences as domestic or family violence offences and the creation of offences (in a small number of jurisdictions) that capture economic or emotional abuse (ALRC and NSWLRC 2010, [13.10]).

The criminalisation of stalking is the most notable and widespread of these developments. Criminalised in England and Wales by the *Protection From Harassment Act 1997* (UK), in Scotland by the common law and the *Criminal Justice and Licensing (Scotland) Act 2010*, and in various jurisdictions in Australia from 1993, stalking offences are arguably capable of capturing a wide range of behaviours that women complain about as part of IPV. The extent to which this is possible has, of course, been determined by the practice and interpretation of the law. For example, in England and Wales, there has been some particularly narrow interpretations of the offences of stalking and harassment (Bettinson and Bishop 2015, pp. 187–190) where the court has found it difficult to recognise the behaviour complained about as a 'course of conduct' if it took place in an ongoing relationship in which there were periods of 'affection' between the victim and the alleged offender (Bettinson and Bishop 2015, p. 188). Australian scholars have also debated to what extent stalking, harassment and intimidation offences can adequately address forms of non-physical IPV. On the one hand, Marilyn McMahon and Paul McGorrery (Chap. 5) highlight the limitations of these offences to address non-physical forms of IPV between current intimate partners; however, other scholars have pointed to the flexibility of these provisions to capture some forms of behaviour (see Douglas and Burdon 2018, who argue that the recording and monitoring of a victim by a perpetrator using a smartphone would fit within the various Australian stalking offences). The scope of these provisions depends on their construction and implementation. For example, in New South Wales (NSW), Australia, the offence is one of 'stalking *or* intimidation' (*Crimes (Domestic and Personal Violence) Act 2007* (NSW) s 13(1), emphasis added). The inclusion of intimidation defined as 'conduct amounting to harassment or molestation of the person' and 'any conduct that causes a reasonable apprehension of injury … or of violence or damage to any person or property' (*Crimes (Domestic and Personal Violence) Act 2007* (NSW) s 7) extends the reach of the provision beyond typical stalking behaviours. The legislation further provides that 'for the purpose of determining whether a person's conduct amounts to intimidation, a court may have regard to any pattern of violence … in the person's behaviour' (s 7(2)).

Other jurisdictions, such as Tasmania, have gone substantially further and introduced offences of emotional and economic abuse (*Family Violence Act 2004* (Tas) ss 8–9; see Barwick et al. Chap. 7). This approach in Tasmania is distinctive; whilst other jurisdictions may include economic and emotional abuse as a possible ground for seeking a civil protection order, Tasmania is the only Australian jurisdiction to have 'taken the road of criminalisation' (Murray and Powell 2011, p. 112). While the emotional abuse offence is described as such in the heading to the provision, it in fact seeks to address a 'course of conduct' that is likely to control, intimidate, cause the victim mental harm or to be fearful. In this way, this offence represents an early example of the more expansive offences recently introduced in England/Wales, Scotland and Ireland. The Tasmanian offences have been criticised in terms of their scope and evidential difficulties (urbis 2008, pp. 11–12; Douglas 2015, p. 457; McMahon and McGorrery 2016, pp. 7–9, 13–22). There have been very few prosecutions (discussed below).

Another key development in criminal law practice has been the ability in some jurisdictions to flag offences as domestic violence related. For instance, in NSW offences that are perpetrated in a domestic violence context are flagged as such (*Crimes (Domestic and Personal Violence) Act 2007* (NSW) s 12). This can be useful in determining bail, and in stalking offences to determine whether a person's behaviour amounts to a pattern, amongst other matters. This flagging also enables us to see the wide range of offence categories that are used in cases of IPV, not all of which involve physical and visible forms of violence (see, e.g. Ringland and Fitzgerald 2010, p. 2). In this way, this administrative measure facilitates the construction of a more complete picture of IPV beyond what might be the presenting incident/charge currently before the court.

i. Incident framework

The traditional incident frame of the criminal law runs counter to the patterned, repetitive experience of IPV and has a number of consequences for the adequacy of the response to this harm. It means that while a perpetrator may have used violence and abuse on multiple previous occasions, as well as multiple forms of violence and abuse in a given event, that person may only be charged with offences that address a single form of behaviour or act of violence (although they may of course face multiple individual charges that respond to different forms of violence used in that event). As Tolmie (2018a, p. 51) has emphasised, the focus on incidents means that behaviours that form part of IPV are 'stripped of much of its overall architecture—those aspects of the pattern of abuse that are psychological and financial, for example, along with the motivations of the abuser and the cumulative effect on the victim'. This, in turn, enables the incident to be portrayed as one-off, isolated, out-of-character and minor, where such a 'decontextualized examination of disaggregated incidents can leave a case in shreds' (Hunter 2008, p. 41). Not only does the traditional frame of the criminal law cast IPV in this way, this also tends to be the way in which violent men describe their acts of violence that have come to the attention of the law (Kelly and Westmarland 2016, p. 116).

The new offences in England/Wales, Scotland and Ireland seek to address this 'fleeting snapshot' (Hirschel and Buzawa 2002, p. 1457), through the creation of an offence that requires more than one form of violence and abuse over time—the law in England and Wales refers to the coercive or controlling behaviour being used 'repeatedly or continuously' (*Serious Crime Act 2015* (E&W), s 76(1)(a)); in Scotland, the provision requires a 'course of behaviour' (*Domestic Abuse (Scotland) Act 2018*, s 1(1)(a)); and in Ireland, reference is made to the behaviour being 'persistently engage[d] in' (*Domestic Abuse Act 2018* (IR) s 39(1)). A key question will be whether these new offences manage to shift the gaze from an incident frame to a contextual one; these are fundamentally different.

Given the dominance of incident framework in criminal law, there is a risk that rather than looking contextually, the offence will be practised as an 'additive' one, where incidents are simply added together (Tolmie 2018a, p. 59). This has been seen in other 'course of conduct' offences, such as stalking, where individual incidents are examined and proven to determine whether they 'add up to' a course of conduct (Bettinson and Bishop 2015, p. 189). As Kelly and Westmarland (2016, p. 114) have emphasised, there is a fundamental difference between considering an 'ongoing pattern of behaviour' compared to 'one, two, or three isolated "incidents"'. A contextual frame pays attention to the fact that acts and behaviours only have the 'potential' to be part of IPV, that it is through the way those acts and behaviours interact and give meaning to each other, within the relationship and its history, that such acts attain their meaning for the victim and the perpetrator (Cavanagh et al. 2001, pp. 698–699). While Bettinson and Bishop (2015, p. 191) argue that the decision not to use 'course of conduct' in England and Wales might assist in a shift away from assessing individual incidents, it is difficult to see how this will eventuate given references to 'repeatedly', and to 'acts' in the policy definitions of controlling and coercive behaviour (Home Office 2015, p. 3).

There is also tension between recognising an ongoing form of behaviour (coercive control) and enabling it to be evidenced by a series of acts and behaviours as a singular offence. This implies a time-bound approach to these offences, whereas coercive control, by its very nature, extends beyond the acts and behaviours that might be packaged together to prove the offence; it is ongoing and embedded 'without clear beginning or end, nonetheless has a demonstrable impact that is cumulative over time and across social space on … victims whose lives and liberties become severely constrained' (Stark and Hester 2019, p. 96). This links to the problem identified by Sandra Walklate and colleagues (2018) about the inherent difficulty in translating a clinical concept into a legal one.

It is also important to consider that the criminal law is not confined to how particular offences are defined in law, but is also shaped by its practice and procedure. One area in which there has been progress is in terms of the admission, in some contexts, of relationship evidence. The admission of this type of evidence can be very useful to place a single assault that would otherwise appear to be 'out of the blue' as '[]explicable' (*Roach v The Queen* (2011) 242 CLR 610, [42]). *Roach* demonstrates the potential for this kind of evidence. This case concerned a single charge of assault occasioning actual bodily harm in Queensland in which the trial judge admitted evidence of previous uncharged assaults pursuant to *Evidence Act 1977* (Qld) s 132B, 'on the basis that, without it, the jury would be faced with a seemingly inexplicable or fanciful incident' (*Roach* at [19]). The potential for relationship evidence to add much needed context to support individual charges is further illustrated in the NSW case of *Pasoski v R* [2014] NSWCCA 309, in which the defendant had been charged with physical and sexual assaults and the relationship evidence that was admitted related to behaviours that were controlling (for example, limiting the victims contact with friends and family, checking up on her at work and telling her 'what to wear and how to do her hair and makeup') (*Pasoski* at [12]).

While it is still the single incident that is the focus of the trial, *Roach* and *Pasoski* demonstrate how relationship evidence can be useful to add the context needed in the successful prosecution of individual IPV offences. However, other cases and research point to the fact that the use of this evidence is not necessarily widespread and is variable and inconsistent. For example, in *R v Grant* (2016) 262 A Crim R 348, a Northern Territory case, a distinction was drawn between those acts that were similar to the charged acts (that is, uncharged physical assaults) and those that were not (verbal abuse and threats) where the latter forms of behaviour were not admissible as relationship evidence being 'too far removed from the matter at issue in this case' (*Grant* at [59]). In Victoria, a study of intimate partner homicides perpetrated by men between 2005 and 2014 found that 'a history of family violence is not always fully recognised in homicide prosecutions' for a 'variety of reasons' including that the police may not have collected the evidence, it may have been deemed inadmissible, or it may have been removed as a result of a plea negotiation (McKenzie et al. 2016, pp. 74–75). McKenzie and colleagues further note that '[m]isunderstandings about the nature, causes, dynamics and impact of family violence may also influence what evidence is considered relevant in a homicide prosecution' (McKenzie et al. 2016, p. 75).

11.3 A Gap in Legislation or a Gap in Implementation?

It is important to ask whether the gap that is sought to be filled by the creation of a dedicated IPV offence is purely a legislative gap, or whether it is also, and more fundamentally, an implementation gap. As noted above, the 'implementation problem' has been a critical one for feminist-engaged law reform. A key concern in any move to criminalise coercive control is whether the creation of a new offence simply leaves unchallenged the more complex and ingrained problems associated with implementation and practice.

Lessons might be learnt from the implementation of civil protection order legislation in Australia—a legal response designed to address many of the same gaps in the traditional criminal law response that the new offences seek to fill.

11.3.1 *Other Measures that Have Been Designed to Address the Limitations of the Criminal Law: Civil Protection Orders*

Civil protection order schemes were introduced across multiple jurisdictions in order to address some of the limitations of the criminal law discussed above. Such schemes tend to possess a range of progressive elements that provide scope to better capture the 'lived experience' of IPV, such as the broad range of behaviour that might ground an order, the consideration in some jurisdictions about how acts and behaviours function (for example, to cause fear), the lower standard of proof, the focus on future protection and in some jurisdictions the inclusion of an objects clause or preamble which recognises the gendered nature of IPV.

The various Australian state and territory legislation that provides for the making of such orders generally recognise a wide range of behaviours within their respective definitions of domestic or family violence. For example, in Tasmania, family violence is defined as including 'threats, coercion, intimidation or verbal abuse', 'economic abuse' or 'emotional abuse or intimidation' (*Family Violence Act 2004* (Tas) s 7); and in Queensland domestic violence is defined as including behaviour that is 'emotionally or psychologically abusive; 'economically abusive'; 'coercive', or in 'any other way controls or dominates' the person seeking protection and causes that person to be fearful for their 'safety or wellbeing' or that of any other person (*Domestic and Family Violence Protection Act 2012* (Qld) s 8).

Unlike the incident frame of the criminal law, the complaint for a civil protection order enables an applicant to include a wide range of information about acts and behaviours perpetrated over time. This means that it is possible to detail events that might otherwise be construed as minor or not warranting the attention of the law; however, when seen together reveal a patterned and cumulative experience able to be comprehended as IPV warranting the making of an order.

Despite this promise, questions have been raised about whether the civil protection order system has been successful in moving away from incidents (Hunter 2008; Wangmann 2012). A study of cross applications in civil protection order proceedings in NSW found that the incident framework continued to dominate (Wangmann 2012). Many of the complaint narratives examined in that study focused on a single incident (which may have involved multiple forms of violence and abuse). Perhaps more concerning was that incidents continued to be prominent in the way in which some professionals, particularly police officers explained their practice. As part of this study, semi-structured interviews were conducted with 27 professionals working in the civil protection order system (police officers, police prosecutors, lawyers, women's support workers and magistrates). While many of the professionals articulated a well-developed understanding of IPV when asked generally about how they defined IPV—for example, referring to context, power, control and gender—this understanding tended to dissipate, particularly for police officers, when asked more practice-based questions about scenarios in which both parties were alleged to have used violence against each other (dual events) (Wangmann 2012, pp. 709–710). Dual events present particular challenges for the legal system in terms of determining who is the person that requires the protection of the law—if an incident frame is taken, and not a contextual one, it runs the risk that when women use violence in the context of their victimisation this is treated as equivalent to the predominant perpetrator's use of violence. An incident framework enables delineation between one incident and another where the actors change position. This shifting approach is illustrated in this comment made by a police officer:

> [W]e had a situation where a DV incident took place over a fairly short period of time,… where the victim in one assault [the woman] went inside and the incident moved inside and then the victim became the offender … by assaulting the previous defendant. So the victim outside had moved inside and became the defendant. …. You've got two assaults in that time frame, we got telephone interim orders for both parties and we ended up charging both … for the two separate assaults. (Wangmann 2012, pp. 710–711)

Hunter (2008) also found a resort to incidents in her study of civil protection orders in Victoria. Hunter found that magistrates 'encouraged by the terms of the legislation…tended to see violence in terms of isolated, decontextualized "incidents" rather than as a pattern of coercive behaviour' (2008, p. 111). As a result, lawyers representing victims 'noted that magistrates were looking for a recent incident, the most current acts or threats, in order to grant an order, rather than wanting to hear about the history of violence in the relationship' (2008, p. 111).

While many single incidents detailed in an application will be sufficient to support the making of a civil protection order, the absence of information about other acts and behaviours perpetrated over time means that the patterned and cumulative environment of IPV is not conveyed. This 'connective framework' may be particularly critical where the incident that led to the application was of a more minor nature (Wangmann 2012, p. 707), where applications have been made by both parties, or where the legislation requires a likelihood of repetition in order to grant an order (Hunter 2008, p. 111). In addition, the content of the application and the order (if made) may have flow-on effects for other legal proceedings such as family law, where the adequacy of those narratives may play an important role in the weight given to those orders, and any assessment about whether the violence and abuse has relevance to the making of parenting and financial orders following separation. As is the case with criminal offences, the 'spotlight' on single incidents allows the defendant in a protection order proceeding to raise 'counter stories...that suggest that the behaviour was uncharacteristic' (Wangmann 2012, p. 707) or explicable:

> This may be a particular problem if the incident took place at separation. For example, there are well-worn stories about the devastation experienced on the failure of the relationship, or the pain of still being in love with the woman, which are often deployed to conceal stories of control. The documentation of multiple incidents can prevent such stories of thwarted romance from taking a dominant role in the interpretation of events. (Wangmann 2012, p. 707, citations omitted)

As a result, it appears that a legal process that was designed to be more responsive to the harm of IPV has tended to reproduce its incident-based constraints. This reveals a great deal about the practice of law in this intersecting criminal/civil space around the harm of IPV and is suggestive of greater and more profound challenges about how to move away from the dominance of incidents than can be addressed by simply creating a new offence (Wangmann 2012, p. 719).

11.3.2 Problems with Practice and Implementation Remain

The most recent Australian inquiries into domestic and family violence have generally avoided the attraction of simply creating new criminal offences (although notably a dedicated strangulation offence was created in Queensland) and instead sought to target practice. For example, in deciding against recommending a dedicated domestic violence, the Special Taskforce on Domestic and Family Violence in Queensland noted that:

> ...the difficulties with prosecuting domestic and family violence offences relate more to problems with evidence gathering, witness cooperation, police practice and court processes. It is these elements which have undermined the effective use of existing Criminal Code provisions. The Taskforce was particularly concerned that simply creating a dedicated offence of domestic and family violence would not alleviate these barriers. Enacting a new offence specifically for domestic and family violence that faced the same evidentiary and process issues, would still not achieve the goal of protecting victims or increasing accountability of perpetrators. (2015, pp. 14–15)

Similarly, the Victorian Royal Commission into Family Violence noted that '[w]hatever laws we have will only be as effective as those who enforce, prosecute and apply them. Improving these practices, through education, training and embedding best practice and family violence specialisation in the courts, is likely to be more effective than simply creating new offences...' (RCFV 2016b, p. 189). The RCFV further noted that '[s]imply changing the laws by carving out a specific response for family violence is not likely to address those underlying deficiencies' (RCFV 2016b, p. 228).

While it is too early to make evaluative assessments of the coercive control offence introduced in England and Wales in December 2015 (the Irish and Scottish offences commenced operation in 2019), some of the early information points to the continuation of the same concerns about practice that have been long-standing in efforts to get the criminal law to respond better to IPV. For example, there appears to be 'patchy' implementation across England and Wales with some police forces laying very few charges since the offence was introduced (McClenaghan and Boutard 2017; Walklate et al. 2018, p. 118), and there has been a lack of dedicated training for police with only 8 of the 43 police forces having been provided with training about the new offence 2 years after its introduction (Travis 2017). Johnson and Barlow (2018) also uncovered critical gaps in practice—with low levels of charging, even lower levels of decisions to prosecute, 'missed opportunities for using' the new offence, and that calls to police about coercive control were 'given a lower priority' than other domestic abuse-related crimes by 'call handlers'. In this context, Walklate and colleagues have asked whether 'general frontline police officers can, and should be expected to understand the complexities of coercive control as a form of abuse' (2018, p. 121). The centrality of this question is confirmed in a recent report by Her Majesty's Inspectorate of Constabulary and Fire & Rescue Services (2017) on the 'police response to domestic abuse' which found that an 'understanding of victim/perpetrator dynamics (techniques of coercive and controlling behaviours)' remained the top competency identified as 'requiring improvement among frontline officers and specialist officers/investigators' by 'domestic violence practitioners' (p. 28).

Similar problems have been seen in Tasmania, Australia, where two potentially innovative criminal offences came into force in 2005: 'emotional and psychological abuse' and 'economic abuse'. There have been few prosecutions of these offences. Karryne Barwick and colleagues (Chap. 7) detail that by the end of 2017, some 12 years after the offences commenced operation, only 73 charges have been finalised; involving 34 guilty pleas, 6 charges proven by the court, 2 dismissals and 31 withdrawals. These Tasmanian offences are perhaps the most troubling given how long they have been available, and hence are perhaps indicative of more deep-seated problems with the use of the criminal law.

Whilst training about the new offence is obviously critical, the need for training and education of key professionals working in the legal system is a more far-reaching one. The extent of repetition of recommendations that call for further education and training of professionals working within the criminal justice system, and the legal system more broadly, points to greater challenges with the adequacy of responses to IPV than can be satisfied through the implementation of a single offence and training about that offence. For example, recommendations about the need for further education of police, lawyers and judicial officers were made in some of the earliest Australian inquiries (see, e.g. NSW Task Force on Domestic Violence 1981, pp. 75–77, 79–80, 83–85; Law Reform Commission (ACT) 1986, rec 21) and have continued through to the most recent (see, e.g. RCFV 2016a, p. 57, pp. 102–104; Special Taskforce on Domestic and Family Violence in Queensland 2015, pp. 36–38, 43; ALRC and NSWLRC 2010, pp. 1465, 1471, 1477, 1521). Whilst some of these recommendations are specific, relating to particular legislative provisions and procedures, a number are directed at a more conceptual level (see, e.g. Special Taskforce on Domestic and Family Violence in Queensland 2015, rec 138, p. 43). The repetition of recommendations that are directed at this conceptual level suggests that an education package targeted at the new offence may miss the opportunity of influencing more substantive change in responses to IPV (including in relation to the implementation of any dedicated offence). It is here where I suggest Stark's work (2007) is potentially more transformative. While Stark does propose the creation of a criminal offence of coercive control (2007, p. 365), this is only part of his strategising to change the way in which we conceive of and respond to IPV. Stark notes that while many professionals have already adopted a definition that recognises coercive control, practice remains focused on violence; 'documenting individual acts without identifying their political context or consequence, once again depicting the bars without grasping that they are part of a cage' (2007, p. 366). While creating a new offence may assist in moving the legal system in a more responsive direction, unless an understanding of coercive control is extended across all areas and levels, for example, understanding how victims may respond to the violence and abuse they experience, how safety is considered at all levels—then any positive change might be more circumscribed than is hoped for. James Ptacek's work (1999, p. 174) on social entrapment is also important here as he draws attention to the role of institutions in maintaining, facilitating and replicating social entrapment.

11.3.3 Particular Challenges for the New Offences

In addition to general issues related to practice and implementation in this area, there are particular implementation concerns associated with the offences in England/Wales, Scotland and Ireland. Tolmie has argued 'the successful implementation of such an offence may require a complexity of analysis that the criminal justice system is not currently equipped to provide and will require significant reforms in practice and thinking' (Tolmie 2018a, p. 50). It is this challenge of implementation that needs to be addressed in any consideration of whether to amend the law—it is both a challenge of whether the law achieves what it set out to achieve, and also whether it may have unintended consequences.

How these offences are interpreted within the court system when they are prosecuted will be critical. For instance, given the relative absence of prosecutions in Tasmania, there are few reported decisions that reveal anything about how these offences are understood (see Douglas 2015, pp. 457–458; McMahon and McGorrery 2016, pp. 11–13). As yet there are no reported decisions from England and Wales about the interpretation of this new offence, however, some questions about potential difficulties have been raised by scholars following the passage of the legislation. A key concern will be how the terms 'coerce' and 'control' will be understood by the courts—these terms are not defined in the legislation; however, there is statutory guidance (Home Office 2015). Particular concern has focused on the gendered nature of coercive control and that some behaviours may be misconstrued as normal, or as 'signs of affection…because the behaviours engaged in through a desire to control may merge with acceptable and desirable expressions of love and concern' (Bishop and Bettinson 2018, p. 9. See also Tolmie 2018a, pp. 55–56). Not only may it be difficult to identify coercive control given that it deliberately utilises gendered norms of accepted behaviour, many instances of coercive control may also play out in a more 'covert' manner which results in the woman containing herself in order to manage the perpetrator's violent behaviour. This may mean that 'less and less physical violence and other punishing behaviour is needed to ensure compliance' on the part of the victim (Bettinson and Bishop 2015, p. 184). The difficulty in differentiation may create problems of both under- and over-policing—on the one hand, a great deal of controlling behaviour may not be identified as such by the police or judicial officers because it is difficult to differentiate what is 'normal', or within an 'acceptable' range of relationship behaviour, at the same time, there is the possibility that the new offences may capture behaviours that the offence was not designed to address (see arguments raised in submissions to Justice Committee, Comataidh a' Cheartais (Scotland) (2017) [46], [47]–[58]; see also Burman 2018, p. 45).

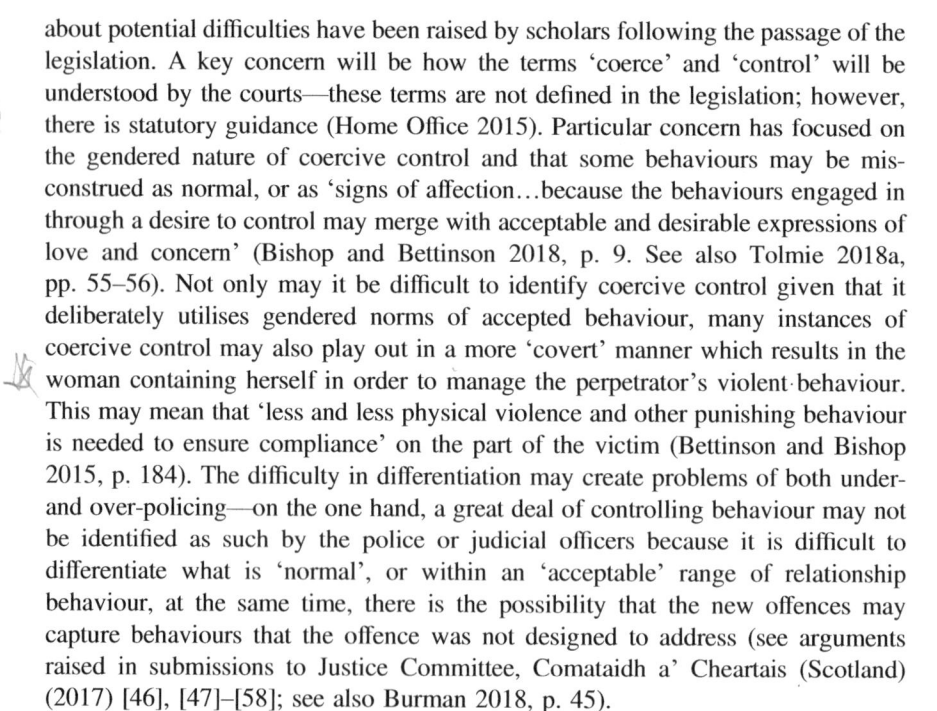

This type of difficulty of being able to identify coercive control from gendered behaviours that might be 'normalised and reinforced at a societal level' (Bishop and Bettinson 2018, p. 9) can be seen in a recent decision in another legal domain that also addresses IPV; family law. In the Australian decision of *Ackerman & Ackerman* [2013] FMCAfam 109, which concerned parenting arrangements and property division following the breakdown of the relationship, the mother alleged that the father was controlling: a 'domestic tyrant' (at [20]), that he had isolated her from family and friends, limited her work time, 'required her to meet oppressively high standards in terms of the performance of housework responsibilities' (at [20]), was intimidating, monitored her movements, and stalked her after separation. Echoing Michael Johnson's work on typologies (2008), the father sought to characterise his behaviour as 'situational couple violence' and not 'coercive control' (at [25]). The *Family Law Act 1975* (Cth) defines family violence (the term used in that legislation) as 'violent, threatening or other behaviour by a person that coerces or controls a member of the person's family… or causes the family member to be fearful' (s 4AB). The federal magistrate determined that the mother's allegations 'fell well short of violent or threatening behaviour. They may be criticised as sexist or insensitive, but, in my view…they are not, family violence' (at [155]). The federal magistrate described the father as an 'unabashed traditionalist where marriage is concerned' (at [128]).

This case perhaps represents a particular risk of the language of coercive control in the Australian context, where the work of Michael Johnson on typologies of IPV has proved attractive in some quarters, particularly family law (see the FCA &

FCCA 2016, pp. 8–9). Johnson (2008) has, over time, identified five different types of IPV based on the presence or absence of control: coercive controlling violence, violent resistance, situational couple violence, separation-instigated violence and mutual violent control. While it is important to understand and investigate the heterogeneity of violence within intimate relationships, there are also a number of risks with the articulation of typologies particularly within law (see Wangmann 2016; Rathus 2013; Meier 2017). The use of the term 'coercive control' within legislation (particularly without definition) may risk it being seen as reflecting typologies rather than the broader feminist understandings of the lived experience of IPV.

11.4 Unintended Outcomes

One of the clear lessons arising from experience in the area of feminist-informed law reform is the need to consider any risks or unintended consequences that might flow from an otherwise well-intentioned change to the law. A range of possible risks associated with the new offences have been canvassed by other scholars (see Tolmie 2018a; Walklate et al. 2018; Burman and Brooks-Hay 2018). In this chapter, I seek to draw attention to two key concerns: minimisation and unintended consequences.

11.4.1 Minimisation of Some Levels of Control

Tolmie has drawn attention to the risk of minimisation where only the most 'overt' cases of coercive control or only those where there is also evidence of physical violence will be prosecuted (Tolmie 2018a, pp. 59–60). This risk is arguably embedded in the drafting of the offence in England and Wales where the alleged behaviour needs to have had 'a serious effect' on the victim defined as causing the victim to 'fear, on at least two occasions, that violence will be used against' them or that causes the victim 'serious alarm or distress which has a substantial adverse effect on [the victim's] usual day-to-day activities' (*Serious Crime Act 2015* (E&W) s 76(4)). While this threshold was clearly directed at limiting the reach of the offence, it raises the problem with 'definitional' decisions and whether the offence as drafted fits the lived experience of IPV. If the focus on physical violence meant that IPV was portrayed as 'extraordinary' rather than as a commonplace event in the lives of many women (Schneider 2000, pp. 66–67; Mahoney 1991, pp. 2–3), the way in which the coercive control offence is currently drafted in England and Wales may facilitate a similar characterisation. That is to say that women's 'everyday' experiences (Kelly and Westmarland 2016, p. 114) may remain outside the reach of the English and Welsh offence due to this threshold. Significantly, Scotland did not adopt the same threshold approach in its offence of domestic abuse instead focusing on the alleged offender requiring that a 'reasonable person would consider that the course of behaviour [that is the subject of the charge] to be likely to cause [the victim] to suffer physical or psychological harm' (*Domestic Abuse (Scotland) Act 2018* s 1(2)(a); see Burman 2018, p. 44).

The requirement that the behaviour has a 'serious effect' on the victim in England/Wales and Ireland may unduly turn the focus on the victim—How did she respond? How did she react?—rather than on the accused's behaviour. This risk is evidenced in a recent English case (Armstrong 2018) in which the man who was accused of verbally abusing his former partner (for example, telling her to 'fuck off' and calling her a 'slag' and spitting in her face) was acquitted. While the judge found that the man's behaviour was 'disgraceful', the judge was not of the view that it had had a 'serious effect' on the victim who was described as 'too "strong and capable" to be under his control' (Armstrong 2018). This requirement of 'serious effect' raises questions about whether judicial officers are adequately equipped to make this assessment and the risk that they may draw on stereotypical notions about who is a victim, and how victims might behave and respond to the violence and abuse that they experience—one can still be 'strong and capable' yet experience coercive control that has had a serious effect on one's life.

11.4.1.1 The Absence of a Gendered Understanding May Risk Women Being Identified as Offenders

As noted above, there is a risk that the new offences will merely direct the legal system to consider multiple incidents and deem them to 'add up' to coercive control, rather than to consider the cumulative, interrelated way in which acts and behaviours give meaning to each other to create the context of control over time. If incidents continue to define how the offence is interpreted this may pose risks to women being identified as perpetrators of coercive control, particularly if there is a failure to articulate the gendered nature of this harm (Burman and Brooks-Hay 2018, p. 76; Walklate et al. 2018, pp. 122–123).

In this context, scholars have pointed to the unintended increase in women arrested for domestic violence on their own or in dual contexts following the introduction of mandatory or pro-arrest policing policies (Hirschel and Buzawa 2002). Research that explored the reasons for this increase found that many of these women were being arrested for using violence in the context of their own victimisation (Melton and Sillito 2012; Miller 2001). To address this problem, many jurisdictions (particularly in the USA) introduced policies to assist the police to identify who is primary or predominant aggressor in the relationship (Hirschel and Buzawa 2012). The impact of these policies has been mixed (see Hirschel and Buzawa 2012, p. 179; Hirschel and Deveau 2017, p. 1172) which has raised questions about whether the nuance these policies require of the police is possible within a system that emphasises incidents (Hirschel and Buzawa 2002, pp. 1456-1458)—a concern that echoes the complexity that is being asked of police in the context of the new offences introduced in England/Wales, Scotland and

Ireland. This has led some commentators to express concerns about women being charged under these new offences (see Tolmie 2018a; Walklate et al. 2018; Burman and Brooks-Hay 2018).

Consideration also needs to be given to how a new offence of this kind might impact on women who have intersecting needs and experiences regarding IPV, and encounter different service responses. This has two key facets—the first concerns the extent to which the woman (whether it is because of her race, cultural background, sexuality, economic status and so on alone or in combination) is able to articulate what she has experienced as coercive or controlling in a form able to be recognised by law, and the second concerns whether some women, particularly those who may be more likely to fight back verbally and physically for a range of reasons including past poor responses from the police, might end up being targeted by the offence. The second concern picks up the unintended consequence outlined above that some women may find themselves charged with this offence.

The risk of misidentifying female victims as the primary aggressor is particularly acute in the Aboriginal and Torres Strait Islander (ATSI) community. The Australian Law Reform Commission (ALRC) recently inquired into the high incarceration rates of ATSI peoples in Australia (ALRC 2017). That report drew attention to the 'poor police responses' encountered by ATSI women experiencing family violence, including that some police may emphasise the woman's criminality rather than her victimisation (ALRC 2017, [11.69]). The report noted increasing concern about the criminalisation of Indigenous women through the failure of the police to identify who is the primary aggressor in a relationship, the police charging women for breaches of protection orders, and noted that ATSI women are 'more likely than their non-Indigenous counterparts to be charged and imprisoned for "acts intended to cause injury" — where in some cases resorting to violence may be seen as the only feasible means of defending themselves and their children against a violent partner' (ALRC 2017, [11.72]). A recent study in Queensland has raised further concern about the way in which the protection order system is becoming an entry point to the criminal justice system for ATSI people, particularly women, where ATSI people are over-represented as applicants and respondents, as persons charged and convicted of contravening a protection order, and in receiving a sentence of imprisonment for that contravention (Douglas and Fitzgerald 2018).

11.5 More Than just a Discrete Offence

In this final section, I want to explore further what I consider to be the greater challenge posed by Stark's work. While the creation of a discrete offence might for some women enable behaviours previously unrecognised to be addressed through a criminal charge, an understanding of coercive control as the defining feature of IPV across all legal domains and practice may arguably be more transformative. Tolmie (2018a) made a similar argument in relation to the need for understandings of coercive control to extend across all aspects of the criminal law:

> ...many of the conceptual and evidentiary challenges presented by the concept of coercive control should be addressed in respect of all IPV offending. This means that the traditional interpersonal violence offending in the context of IPV must be understood in the context of the wider patterns of harm in which it occurs and evidence on such patterns should be routinely presented at trial. (Tolmie 2018a, p. 63)

While it is possible that the creation of a discrete offence may perform an important educative function about the nature of coercive control that may extend across legal areas, there is a risk that the creation of this offence may be interpreted as *the site* to recognise this harm. In this way, coercive control might become *the offence* rather than being the 'overriding framework' (Kelly and Westmarland 2016, p. 114) for understanding the lived experience of IPV. Untethering other criminal offences from the context of coercive control may undermine the extent to which an understanding of coercive control is seen as important to how those offences are prosecuted, presented and determined. Mary Ann Dutton and Lisa Goodman (2005) in their work on conceptualising coercive control have also drawn attention to how an understanding of coercive control can assist more broadly in the legal arena—in criminal law where women may use violence in response to her victimisation (particularly for battered women who kill, see Sheehy 2018), and to understand the context and seriousness of what might otherwise be presented as an isolated incident:

> In the legal arena, this more refined conceptualization of coercion in relationships with IPV might assist prosecutors and defense attorneys to explain more adequately both victim and perpetrator behaviour in physical and sexual assault cases involving intimate partners. Legal professionals might be able to understand more thoroughly the pattern of abuse within which specific violent acts take place; and therefore be able to make more informed decisions about perpetrator dispositions and victim safety. (Dutton and Goodman 2005, p. 754)

I have already argued how the admission of relationship evidence, which is able to reveal the situated context of an otherwise isolated incident, can be important to the successful prosecution of a case. Attention was drawn to how an understanding of coercive control introduced through relationship evidence can be critical to countering arguments that an assault, for example, was fanciful or uncharacteristic behaviour on the part of the accused. The admission of this evidence, however, is variable and inconsistent. An understanding of coercive control can also transform other areas of practice, such as sentencing. Julie Tolmie (2018b) has detailed how the incident-based approach of the criminal law in New Zealand (as is the case in many other jurisdictions) leaves victim safety absent from consideration at sentencing. This is significant given the ongoing nature of IPV, and often the ongoing relationship, marks it as distinctive from other criminal offences. If admitted, relationship evidence can also play an important role in sentencing in countering the view of the incident as one-off and isolated. The focus on victim safety is an important one as it requires us to pay attention to something that is distinctly different for IPV compared to acts of violence perpetrated between strangers. As Tolmie (2018b, p. 202, emphasis in original) points out this is not necessarily about incarceration or '*longer* sentences' but rather 'sentences that are *crafted differently*'.

This is particularly important given the over-incarceration of Indigenous peoples (Tolmie 2018b, p. 202; see also discussion above). Understanding victim safety will be particularly critical in the prosecution of any dedicated offence, given what various IPV death review processes have documented in terms of the presence of control in their case examinations (see, e.g. NSWDVDRT 2017, p. 2).

Discussions about the recognition of coercive control in criminal law responses must also be considered in the context of developments and responses in other legal domains. IPV (like other harms) is not addressed by a single area of law alone—indeed, many women find themselves navigating responses to the harms that they experience across family law, child protection, civil protection orders, crimes compensation and the criminal law (including as defendants). Understandings of coercive control are also critical to practice in these multiple domains. This is particularly important given how few victims of IPV turn to the criminal law for assistance (Cox 2016, p. 105). Increasing attention has been paid to the way in which legal responses are fragmented, and the way in which the same woman with the same harm is positioned differently across these domains (Hester 2011; Stubbs and Wangmann 2015). In Australia, this fragmentation is not only doctrinal, but is also facilitated by the federal structure in which legal responsibilities are divided between the federal government, the states and territories. The focus on criminal law and whether it should criminalise coercive control tends to ignore the fact that coercive control is already recognised in some areas of Australian law. Many of the Australian states and territories have articulated broad definitions of IPV within their civil protection order legislation which recognises a wide range of violent and abusive behaviours that might ground the making of such an order, and since 2012 the Australian *Family Law Act 1975* (Cth) has also defined 'family violence' as acts and behaviours that coerce or control a person or cause them to be fearful. These developments are important as they remind us that legal responses to IPV are not singular, and that the criminal law represents only part of the response to IPV.

These positive developments in other legal domains also remind us that despite legislative recognition, implementation continues to require attention (see discussion of civil protection orders above). In the context of family law in Australia, a recent evaluation of the 2012 changes to the *Family Law Act 1975* (Cth) which included the new expansive definition of family violence (amongst other amendments) again draws attention to the limits of legislative change. Rae Kaspiew and colleagues (2015) found that while post-reform cases included more allegations about a wider range of acts and behaviours that might comprise family violence, and that this had resulted in some positive shifts away from orders of shared parental responsibility, it had, however, had a 'negligible' impact on orders about care time in the cases that were fully litigated (p. 66). While it is important to acknowledge that family law decisions represent a complex interplay of a wide range of competing factors (alcohol and other drugs, mental health issues and parenting capacity) in addition to, or in combination with, family violence the apparent lack of traction in limiting care time raises questions about the extent to which the broader understanding of family violence is being put into action—that is to say, if the court finds that there is family violence, then what? It also draws attention to other issues such as the evidentiary hurdle to establish family violence in family law cases if the court is to take it into account. Similar questions were raised in British Columbia, Canada following the introduction in that province of a more comprehensive definition of family violence under the *Family Law Act* (Boyd and Lindy 2016). In their study of case law following the introduction of this new definition, Susan Boyd and Ruben Lindy found that:

> Our review of the case law … reveals that a number of problematic assumptions about family violence remain. Even if family violence is established under the broad definition … many decisions tend towards an assumption that shared parental responsibility, and even parenting time, is an appropriate arrangement or goal. The consequences of being abused or being exposed to abuse appear to be too often underestimated. (Boyd and Lindy 2016, p. 136)

This may seem unconnected to questions about whether and how the criminal law should recognise coercive control—however, what this family law research reveals is issues around the depth of understanding that is generated from legislative change, and the need for an understanding of coercive control to permeate practice, procedure and outcomes across multiple legal domains. That is to say if we understand that IPV is more than physical violence, that it is about a patterned repeated use of intimidation, violence and control then what does it mean for how we practice law(s) that seeks to respond to this harm.

11.6 Conclusion

Efforts to get the criminal law to better respond to the harm of IPV are to be welcomed—and there is much that is significant in these recent moves to design a criminal offence that seeks to better capture the lived experience of IPV. The new offences introduced in England/Wales, Ireland and Scotland do represent positive steps; however, there are also a number of cautionary lessons that can be learnt from the experience with feminist-informed efforts designed to move the law in a more responsive direction in regard to IPV. This chapter has emphasised the need to keep a clear focus on the more ingrained long-standing problems with the practice of law in response to IPV; by leaving these factors unaddressed, the new offences run the possibility of failing to live up to their promise. While it is too early to make evaluative assessments of the offence of 'controlling or coercive behaviour' introduced in England and Wales in December 2015 (and the offences in Ireland and Scotland only commenced operation in 2019)—some of the early information points to the continuation of the same concerns about the practice of law that have been long-standing in efforts to get the criminal law to respond better to the harm(s) of IPV. If these new offences are to be effective in better reflecting the harm of IPV, efforts also need to ensure that an understanding of coercive control extends beyond the new offence. While it might be argued that training of police and other legal professionals around the new offences will be useful (and they will), an understanding of coercive control needs to extend to the way in which all offences that are perpetrated in intimate relationships are responded to, as well as how the harm of IPV is responded to by other areas of law that are also of critical importance to women.

Walklate and colleagues in their critical commentary on the creation of offences to capture coercive control ask 'whether more law is the answer?' (2018; see also Padfield 2016, p. 151)—certainly it appears that there are enough cautionary tales to suggest that simply legislating a new offence will not achieve a great deal if it is done in the absence of changing the practice of law in addressing IPV. While Stark does seek to 'criminalise coercive control' (Stark 2007, p. 23) how this might be achieved is also multi-pronged—it should not be merely seen in terms of whether there is a 'law on the books' but rather how all the laws that respond to IPV understand and recognise coercive control in implementation and practice.

References

Armstrong, J. (2018, November 22). Violent boyfriend cleared after judge says partner is 'too strong' to be a victim. *Mirror Online* (UK). Retrieved from https://www.mirror.co.uk/news/uk-news/violent-boyfriend-cleared-after-judge-13629612.

Australian Law Reform Commission. (2017). *Pathways to Justice—Inquiry into the Incarceration Rate of Aboriginal and Torres Strait Islander Peoples*, ALRC Report No 133.

Australian Law Reform Commission and NSW Law Reform Commission. (2010). *Family Violence—A National Legal Response*, ALRC Report No 114, NSWLRC Report No 128.

Bettinson, V., & Bishop, C. (2015). Is the creation of a discrete offence of coercive control necessary to combat domestic violence? *Northern Ireland Legal Quarterly, 66*(2), 179–197.

Bishop, C., & Bettinson, V. (2018). Evidencing domestic violence, including behaviour that falls under the new offence of 'controlling and coercive behaviour. *International Journal of Evidence & Proof, 22*(1), 3–29.

Boyd, S., & Lindy, R. (2016). Violence against women and the B.C. Family Law Act: Early jurisprudence. *Canadian Family Law Quarterly, 35*(2), 101–138.

Burke, A. (2007). Domestic violence as a crime of pattern and intent: An alternative reconceptualization. *George Washington Law Review, 75*(3), 552–612.

Burman, M. (2018). Domestic abuse: A continuing challenge for criminal justice. In O. Brooks-Hay, M. Burman, & C. McFeely (Eds.), *Domestic abuse: Contemporary perspectives and innovative practices*. Edinburgh: Dunedin Academic Press.

Burman, M., & Brooks-Hay, O. (2018). Aligning policy and law? The creation of a domestic abuse offence incorporating coercive control. *Criminology & Criminal Justice, 18*(1), 67–83.

Cavanagh, K., Dobash, R., Dobash, R., & Lewis, R. (2001). 'Remedial work': Men's strategic responses to their violence against intimate female partners. *Sociology, 35*(3), 695–714.

Cox, P. (2016). *Violence against women: Additional analysis of the Australian bureau of statistics' personal safety survey, 2012*. Sydney, NSW: ANROWS.

Dobash, R. E., & Dobash, R. (1979). *Violence Against Wives: A Case Against the Patriarchy*. New York, NY: Free Press.

Douglas, H. (2015). Do we need a specific domestic violence offence? *Melbourne University Law Review, 39*(2), 434–471.

Douglas, H., & Burdon, M. (2018). Legal responses to non-consensual smartphone recordings in the context of domestic and family violence. *University of New South Wales Law Journal, 41*(1), 157–184.

Douglas, H., & Fitzgerald, R. (2018). The domestic violence protection order system as entry to the criminal justice system for Aboriginal and Torres +Strait Islander people. *International Journal for Crime, Justice and Social Democracy, 7*(3), 51–57.

Dutton, M. A., & Goodman, L. (2005). Coercion in intimate partner violence: Toward a new conceptualization. *Sex Roles, 52*(11/12), 743–756.

Family Court of Australia and the Federal Circuit Court of Australia. (2016). *Family Violence Best Practice Principles* (4th ed).

Graycar, R., & Morgan, J. (2005). Law reform: What's in it for women? *Windsor Yearbook of Access to Justice, 23*(2), 393–419.

Her Majesty's Inspectorate of Constabulary and Fire & Rescue Services. (2017). *A progress report on the police response to domestic abuse*. London: HMICFRS.

Hester, M. (2011). The three planet model: Towards an understanding of contradictions in approaches to women and children's safety on contexts of domestic violence. *British Journal of Social Work, 41*(5), 837–853.

Office, Home. (2015). *Controlling or coercive behaviour in an intimate or family relationship: Statutory guidance framework*. London: Home Office.

Hirschel, D., & Buzawa, E. (2002). Understanding the context of dual arrest with directions for future Research. *Violence Against Women, 8*(12), 1449–1473.

Hirschel, D., & Deveau, L. (2017). The impact of primary aggressor laws on single versus dual arrest in incidents of intimate partner violence. *Violence Against Women, 23*(1), 1155–1176.

Hunter, R. (2008). *Domestic violence law reform and women's experiences in court: The implementation of feminist reforms in civil proceedings*. Amherst, NY: Cambria Press.

Hunter, R. (2006). Narratives of domestic violence. *Sydney Law Review, 28*(4), 733–776.

Johnson, M. (2008). *A typology of domestic violence: Intimate terrorism, violent resistance, and situational couple violence*. Lebanon, NH: Northeastern University Press.

Johnson, K., & Barlow, C. (2018, February 15). Researching police responses to coercive control. *N8 Policing Research Partnership*. Retrieved from https://n8prp.org.uk/researching-police-responses-to-coercive-control/.

Justice Committee, Comataidh a' Cheartais, The Scottish Parliament Pàrlamaid na h-Alba. (2017). *Stage 1 Report on the Domestic Abuse (Scotland) Bill*. Edinburgh: Scottish Parliament Corporate Body.

Kaspiew, R., Carson, R., Qu, L., Horsfall, B., Tayton, S., Moore, S., Coulson, M., & Dunstan, J. (2015). *Court Outcomes Project* (Evaluation of the 2012 Family Violence Amendments). Melbourne: Australian Institute of Family Studies.

Kelly, L., & Westmarland, N. (2016). Naming and defining 'domestic violence: Lessons from research with violent men. *Feminist Review, 112*(1), 113–127.

Mahoney, M. (1991). Legal images of battered women: Redefining the issues of separation. *Michigan Law Review, 90*(1), 1–94.

Law Reform Commission (ACT). (1986). *Domestic Violence*. Report No. 30. Canberra: Australian Government Publishing Service.

McClenaghan M., & Boutard, C. (2017, November 24). Questions raised over patchy take-up of domestic violence law. *The Bureau of Investigative Journalism*. Retrieved from https://www.thebureauinvestigates.com/stories/2017-11-24/coercive-control-concerns.

McKenzie, M., Kirkwood, D., Tyson, D., & Naylor, B. (2016). *Out of Character? Legal Responses to intimate partner homicides by men in Victoria 2005-2014*. Discussion Paper. Melbourne, VIC: Domestic Violence Resource Centre Victoria.

McMahon, M., & McGorrery, P. (2016). Criminalising emotional abuse, intimidation and economic abuse in the context of family violence: The Tasmanian experience. *University of Tasmania Law Review, 35*(2), 1–22.

Meier, J. (2017). Dangerous liaisons: A domestic violence typology in custody litigation. *Rutgers University Law Review, 70*(1), 115–174.

Melton, H., & Sillito, C. (2012). The role of gender in officially reported intimate partner violence. *Journal of Interpersonal Violence, 27*(6), 1090–1111.

Miller, S. (2001). The paradox of women arrested for domestic violence: Criminal justice professionals and service providers respond. *Violence Against Women, 7*(12), 1339–1376.

Murray, S., & Powell, A. (2011). *Domestic violence: Australian public policy*. Melbourne, VIC: Australian Scholarly.

NSW Domestic Violence Death Review Team. (2017). *Report 2015–2017*. Sydney, NSW: DVDRT.

NSW Task Force on Domestic Violence. (1981). *Report of the New South Wales Task Force on Domestic Violence to Honourable NK Wran QC, MP Premier of NSW*. Sydney, NSW: Women's Coordination Unit.

Padfield, N. (2016). Editorial: Controlling or coercive behaviour in an intimate or family relationship. *Criminal Law Review, 3*, 149–151.

Pence, E., & Paymar, M. (1993). *Education groups for men who batter: The duluth model*. New York, NY: Springer.

Ptacek, J. (1999). *Battered women in the courtroom: The power of judicial responses*. Boston, MA: Northeastern University Press.

Rathus, Z. (2013). Shifting language and meanings between social science and the law: Defining family violence. *University of New South Wales Law Journal, 36*(2), 359–389.

Royal Commission into Family Violence (Victoria). (2016a). *Summary and recommendations*. Melbourne, VIC: Royal Commission into Family Violence Victoria.

Royal Commission into Family Violence (Victoria). (2016b). Report and recommendations: Vol III. Melbourne, VIC: Royal Commission into Family Violence.

Ringland, C., & Fitzgerald, J. (2010). Factors which influence the sentencing of domestic violence offenders. *Crime and Justice Statistics Bureau Brief*, Issue Paper No. 38. Sydney, NSW: Bureau of Crime Statistics and Research.

Schechter, S. (1982). *Women and male violence: The visions and struggles of the battered women's movement*. London: Pluto Press.

Schneider, E. (2000). *Battered women and feminist lawmaking*. New Haven, NJ: Yale University Press.

Sheehy, E. (2018). Expert evidence on coercive control in support of self-defence: The trial of Teresa Craig. *Criminology & Criminal Justice, 18*(1), 100–114.

Smart, C. (1986). Feminism and law: Some problems of analysis and strategy. *International Journal of the Sociology of Law, 14*(2), 109–123.

Special Taskforce on Domestic and Family Violence in Queensland. (2015). *Not now, not ever: Putting an end to domestic and family violence in queensland*. Brisbane, QLD: Special Taskforce on Domestic and Family Violence in Queensland.

Stark, E. (2007). *Coercive control: How men entrap women in personal life*. Oxford: Oxford University Press.

Stark, E., & Hester, M. (2019). Coercive control: Update and review. *Violence Against Women, 25*(1), 81–104.

Stubbs, J., & Wangmann, J. (2015). Competing conceptions of victims of domestic violence within legal processes. In D. Wilson & S. Ross (Eds.), *Crime, Victims and Policy: International Contexts, Local Experiences*. Palgrave Macmillan: Bassingstoke.

Thornton, M. (1991). Feminism and the contradictions of law reform. *International Journal of the Sociology of Law, 19*(4), 453–474.

Tolmie, J. (2018a). Coercive control: To criminalize or not to criminalize? *Criminology & Criminal Justice, 18*(1), 50–66.

Tolmie, J. (2018b). Considering victim safety when sentencing intimate partner violence offenders. In K. Fitz-Gibbon, S. Walklate, J. McCulloch, & J. Maher (Eds.), *Intimate partner violence, risk and security: Securing women's lives in a global world*. Oxon: Routledge.

Travis, A. (2017, December 29). Police 'not equipped' to enforce new domestic violence laws. *The Guardian* (online). Retrieved from https://www.theguardian.com/uk-news/2017/dec/29/police-not-equipped-to-enforce-new-domestic-abuse-laws.

Tuerkheimer, D. (2004). Recognizing and remedying the harm of battering: A call to criminalize domestic violence. *Journal of Criminal Law & Criminology, 94*(4), 959–1031.

Urbis Keys Young. (2008). *Review of the family violence act 2004*. Hobart: Anglicare Tasmania.
Walklate, S., Fitz-Gibbon, K., & McCulloch, J. (2018). Is more law the answer? Seeking justice for victims of intimate partner violence through the reform of legal categories. *Criminology & Criminal Justice, 18*(1), 115–131.
Wangmann, J. (2012). Incidents v context: How does the NSW protection order system understand intimate partner violence? *Sydney Law Review, 34*(4), 695–719.
Wangmann, J. (2016). Different types of intimate partner violence—What do family law decisions reveal? *Australian Journal of Family Law, 30*(2), 77–111.

Chapter 12
Alternative Constructions of a Family Violence Offence

Heather Douglas

Abstract The crime of torture was introduced into the *Queensland Criminal Code* in 1997. While initially this crime was introduced to respond to a gap in the criminal justice response to child abuse, it has since been used on many occasions in response to cases involving domestic and family violence. This chapter tracks the introduction of the crime of torture into Queensland law and reviews case law and sentencing data to show how it has been applied in the context of domestic and family violence. In the context of increased recognition of the serious impact of non-physical forms of family violence, it shows how the crime of torture can be applied to cases of domestic and family violence that do not involve physical abuse. Drawing on case studies, the chapter also identifies shortcomings of the offence and explores the possibility of the introduction of a less serious version of the offence.

Keywords Torture · Cruelty · Family violence · Non-physical abuse

12.1 Introduction

The crime of torture was introduced into the *Queensland Criminal Code (Criminal Code Act 1899* (Qld) sch 1 ('QCC') s 320A in 1997. While initially, the crime of torture was instituted to respond to a gap in the criminal justice response to child abuse, it has since been applied on many occasions in response to cases involving domestic and family violence (DFV). This chapter tracks the introduction of the crime of torture into Queensland law and reviews case law and sentencing data to show how it has been applied in the context of DFV. The chapter considers some of the definitional and procedural limitations of the torture crime and highlights the potential applicability of the crime of torture to cases of DFV that involve coercive and controlling behaviours but do not involve physical abuse. Research has drawn

---

H. Douglas (✉)
TC Beirne School of Law, University of Queensland, QLD, Australia
e-mail: h.douglas@law.uq.edu.au

© Springer Nature Singapore Pte Ltd. 2020
M. McMahon and P. McGorrery (eds.), *Criminalising Coercive Control*,
https://doi.org/10.1007/978-981-15-0653-6_12

attention to the significant effects of non-physical forms of family violence. For example, scholars have identified that psychological abuse (Sackett and Saunders 1999) and financial abuse (Kutin et al. 2017) perpetrated within an intimate partner relationship contribute to depression, low self-esteem and stress. In light of the perceived need to recognise the serious impacts of non-physical forms of family violence, a number of jurisdictions beyond Australia, including Canada (Sheehy 2018) and the United States (Tetlow 2016) have looked to the private crime of torture as a possible approach. Drawing on women's experiences of DFV, the chapter presents several case studies to illustrate women's experience of coercive control in the context of DFV and highlights the limitations of the torture offence, identifying a gap in the Queensland criminal justice response to coercive and controlling behaviours. The chapter builds on earlier arguments for the introduction of less serious version of the torture offence, referred to as 'cruelty', and explains why this would be a positive development. The chapter outlines the distinctive features of the offences of torture and cruelty as compared to the United Kingdom offence of coercive control (*Serious Crime Act 2015* (E&W) s 76), and briefly to the Scottish offence of abusive behaviour (*Domestic Abuse (Scotland) Act 2018*). It concludes by recommending that criminalisation of DFV— through the introduction of the offence of torture, and less serious offence of cruelty—be considered in Australian jurisdictions.

12.2 Torture in Queensland

12.2.1 Background to the Offence

In 1996, Shane Paul Griffin violently assaulted his stepson, a child who was only five years old (*R v Griffin* [1998] 1 Qd R 659). Griffin was charged with assault (QCC s 335). The prosecution case was that Griffin became frustrated with his stepson because he was misbehaving and that he punished the child by inflicting electric shocks on him. The shocks were around 600 volts and were delivered from a hand-cranked, hand-held generator. At that time, such machines were used to test the wiring for insulation. The offence came to the attention of police because a family friend, who had seen Griffin tie the victim down, reported it to them (Oberhardt 1996). According to the prosecution evidence, Griffin had taped the child's arms and hands to restrain him, then sat on the child's back and administered the shock via wires attached to the boy's legs. While reasonable force was then allowed for domestic discipline and is still allowed in Queensland (see QCC s 280), the prosecution case was that the force used was not reasonable. A jury convicted Griffin and the sentencing judge, Healy DCJ, ordered him to serve one year of imprisonment, the maximum sentence available at that time. Media reports identified that Judge Healy said he would have imposed a higher penalty but for the fact that he was constrained by law (Oberhardt 1997). After administering the punishment, Griffin told the child he had been obliged to do it and maintained throughout the trial that 'he never did anything the boy didn't deserve' (Oberhardt 1996). There was no evidence of physical injury or adverse effects on the child's mental health. In the circumstances, this meant that more serious charges with higher penalties, for example assault occasioning actual bodily harm (QCC s 339) or grievous bodily harm (QCC s 317), were not able to be pursued by the prosecution.

Griffin's initial sentence of one year's imprisonment was reduced on appeal to six months' imprisonment. While Australia signed the *Convention against Torture and Other Cruel, Inhuman or Degrading Treatment or Punishment* in 1985, it was not ratified until 1989 (United Nations Treaty Collection 2018). Chief Justice Macrossan and Derrington J alluded to the language associated with international definitions of torture in their discussion of the offending behaviour:

> At the centre of civilised living, there is a need for regulation and control and those in the position of parents are not to be regarded as having a totally free hand to adopt and administer whatever form of unusual or eccentric punishment they might choose. Concepts similar to those which might be adopted from another context like the notion of "cruel and unusual punishment" can be appealed amongst other relevant factors in determining a proper penalty. The need for deterrence against the tendency of persons to act in any similar fashion on other occasions is a relevant consideration. (*Griffin* at 662)

However, in considering the sentence, Macrossan CJ and Derrington J were also influenced by the fact that Griffin was a first-time offender and they found that this justified the reduced penalty. In contrast, Byrne J found that it was open to the sentencing judge to conclude that the offence was in the worst category of assaults and he would not have reduced the sentence.

12.2.2 Introduction of the Offence of Torture in Queensland

In 1997, after the Griffin trial but prior to the hearing of the Griffin appeal, the Queensland Parliament introduced the crime of torture:
Criminal Code 1899 (Qld) s 320A

(1) A person who tortures another person commits a crime.
    Maximum penalty- 14 years imprisonment.
(2) In this section—
    pain or suffering includes physical, mental, psychological or emotional pain or suffering, whether temporary or permanent.
    torture means the intentional infliction of severe pain or suffering on a person by an act or series of acts done on 1 or more than 1 occasion.

Characterised by an act or series of acts that result in the infliction of serious pain or suffering on the victim, the offence attracts a significant maximum penalty of 14 years' imprisonment. The offence is an indictable offence that must be heard in the District Court before a jury. In commenting on the introduction of the offence, Member of Parliament (MP) Naomi Wilson emphasised that the introduction of the offence was a direct response to the 'torture' in the Griffin case. She said:

> The creation of this offence was considered appropriate after the case of Shane Paul Griffin who was recently convicted of assault after torturing his stepson with an electric cattle prod (sic). The only charge available was assault, and the judge sentenced Griffin to one year's imprisonment—the maximum—although it was noteworthy that he said Griffin deserved more. [This Bill] introduced a new section of torture which may cover similar cases to Griffin's in the future … .(Wilson 1997, p. 528)

Given its origins in the *Griffin* case, it is not surprising that the focus of the *Criminal Law Amendment Bill* 1996 (Qld) ('the Bill'), that introduced the offence of torture, was on protecting children. The Bill included a number of other changes underlining this focus. For example, it also replaced the crime of desertion of children with a crime of 'cruelty to children under 16', which includes desertion as well as acts of omission and failing to provide the child with adequate food, clothing, medical treatment, accommodation or care in certain circumstances (QCC s 364). The maximum penalty at the time that offence was introduced was five years' imprisonment. Notably, when introduced this charge (QCC s 364) required 'pain and suffering' to result to the child, mirroring the language of the torture charge, but this was later changed to 'harm' and the maximum penalty was increased to seven years in the *Criminal Code and Other Acts Amendment Act 2008* (Qld) s 64. Frank Carroll MP emphasised the Bill's focus, and the apparent connection between the torture and cruelty offences, in his comments to Parliament. He said: 'children are further protected by the introduction of tough new penalties for a new crime called torture and by broadening the definition of cruelty' (Carroll 1997, p. 606).

12.2.3 The Application of Torture to Domestic and Family Violence

In 2000, the Queensland Taskforce on Women and the Criminal Code ('The Taskforce') was required to report and make recommendations to the relevant Minister on the operation of the *Criminal Code* as it impacts on women. The Taskforce acknowledged the potential usefulness of the offence of torture in the context of DFV. The Taskforce (2000, p. 77) identified that criminal offences generally focus on separate events and this focus masks the reality of the situation of many battered women. The Taskforce (2000, p. 77) also noted that as at the year 2000, all cases where the offence of torture had been charged involved victims who were children, but suggested that as a course of conduct offence, 'the offence of torture in section 320A seems to describe many of the types of domestic violence with which women live.' It also recommended that in order to increase the application of the torture charge to offences committed in the context of DFV, it might be appropriate to include an example to demonstrate how the offence could be used in that setting (Taskforce 2000, p. 81). Parliament did not take up this recommendation.

A 2003 examination of the application of the torture charge in DFV cases showed that the charge was beginning to be used in response to cases involving DFV where the victims were adult women and intimate partners of the offender (Douglas 2003). However, this 2003 study also showed that there were some matters where the elements of the offence of torture appeared to be present but were still resulting in lower level assault prosecutions (Douglas 2003, p. 91). Figures available from the Queensland Sentencing Advisory Council ('QSAC') (2018) identify that from 1 July 2005 to 30 June 2017 there were 154 torture offences successfully prosecuted, involving 134 individual offenders. Eleven of these offences were identified as involving a 'domestic violence offender', however such identifications have only been available since 2015 (see *Criminal Law (Domestic Violence) Amendment Bill* 2015 (Qld) cl 18; *Penalties and Sentences Act 1992* (Qld) s 12A) so this is likely to be a significant 'undercounting' of torture cases involving DFV. Underlying the serious nature of the offence of torture, of the 154 torture offences successfully prosecuted, most were finalised in the District Court (n = 137) and resulted in a sentence of imprisonment (n = 147) (QSAC 2018). Further, reflecting the seriousness of the offence, the average number of months of imprisonment ordered to be served for the crime of torture in the period was quite high, 59.1 months (close to five years) (QSAC 2018). Notably 123 of the 154 (80%) successfully prosecuted cases of torture involved a male offender (pointing to its gendered nature), and there were 63 charges of breach of protection order (*Domestic and Family Violence Protection Act 2012* (Qld) s 177) charged alongside a torture offence (QSAC 2018). The statistics do not disclose the gender of the victim or how many individual breach charges were associated with a single torture charge. Nevertheless, these figures do suggest that a significant number of torture cases are associated with DFV.

Unfortunately, only a small proportion of cases of torture are publicly reported on case databases. In her recent review of cases publicly available on the Austlii case database, Sheehy (2018) identified only 56 published cases involving torture in Queensland from 1999 to 2017. Of these, Sheehy identified that 12 cases (21%) involved women as victims of torture perpetrated by a male partner or former male partner. As I have argued elsewhere, some of the published torture cases do demonstrate that the torture offence is potentially appropriate for DFV cases as it can capture the 'ongoing nature of abuse and the emotional impact of the degradation the victim experienced' (Douglas 2015, p. 454). Some recent cases involving successful prosecutions of torture in the context of DFV are outlined below. These case examples demonstrate the potential breadth of coercive and controlling behaviours that might underpin a torture charge.

In *R v Ellis* [2018] QCA 70 ('*Ellis*'), Mitchel Ellis pleaded guilty to three offences including torture (QCC s 320A), assault occasioning actual bodily harm (QCC s 339) and malicious act with intent (QCC s 317). He received a sentence of 6.5 years' imprisonment for the torture offence and unsuccessfully appealed the sentence. Ellis had been in a relationship with the female victim for two months, and believing she had been unfaithful to him, became extremely jealous. Over a period of four hours, Ellis engaged in a number of physically violent and demeaning acts towards the victim. Some of the physically violent acts included slapping her on the face as she sat on the toilet, striking her with a towel, demanding she get into a cupboard, heating a towel over a flame threatening to burn her vagina and glue it shut and heating a butter knife telling her he would put it on her eyelids so she wouldn't have any eyes (*Ellis* at [5]). At sentencing, the judge took into account that throughout the ordeal 'the applicant also verbally taunted the complainant, was domineering and, when his demands were not met, became angrier' (*Ellis* at [15]). In dismissing the appeal against sentence, Philippides JA highlighted the prolonged and brutal nature of the offending. Her Honour said:

> Although the offending concerned a single episode, it involved the protracted perpetration of violence of a callous and brutal nature calculated to inflict physical and mental torture. The violence was inflicted in the complainant's house where she was entitled to be safe and protected and in the context of the applicant's irrational jealousy after the complainant ended their relationship. In addition, the conviction for domestic violence offences was required to be treated by the Court as an aggravating factor. (*Ellis* at [25])

In *R v Peirson* [2006] QCA 251 ('*Peirson*') the offender was convicted of two charges of breaching a protection order (*Domestic and Family Violence Protection Act 2012* (Qld) s 177), deprivation of liberty (QCC s 355) and torture. The torture took place over the period of an hour. The victim and offender had a 16-month-old son and the victim was pregnant with their second child. The conduct that formed the basis of the torture charge consisted of the offender's threats to kill the victim and her baby, he also punched, hit and stabbed the victim, and kept her captive for over an hour. There was a history of DFV. In sentencing Peirson, the judge described his conduct as 'extremely brutal, cowardly, directed towards a defenceless and pregnant ... woman, including threats to her life, humiliating to her...' (*Peirson* at [18]). The Court of Appeal refused to adjust the three-year sentence for torture. Justice Cullinane stated that 'the seriousness of the conduct involved in the offence of torture here cannot be underestimated. It has to be viewed against a history of breaching DFV protection orders and the fact that he was on bail for such an offence when this offence was committed' (*Peirson* at [30]).

While the torture took place over a period of hours in the cases of *Ellis* and *Peirson*, some DFV torture cases are charged in relation to behaviours that take place over a longer time period. For example, HAC was charged and found guilty of four counts of assault causing actual bodily harm (QCC s 339), seven counts of rape (QCC s 348) and one count of torture against his wife (*R v HAC* [2006] QCA 291) ('*HAC*'). He appealed unsuccessfully against the conviction of torture on the basis that the trial judge's directions to the jury were incorrect. Importantly the evidence in the case included physical assaults but also that, over a six-month period, HAC had made his wife:

… eat chillies, making her eat spiders and cockroaches if any were found, administering karate chops to her neck, and preventing her children from calling her "Mum" or expressing affection to her. … forcing [her] to sleep outside and toilet outside; urinating on her; making her drink his urine; hosing her because she had urine on her; forcing her to clean the house late at night; to search for the garden objects, and the like (*HAC* at [53]).

After HAC went to stay at a friend's place telling his wife that he would kill her on his return, she took an overdose of tablets, wanting to deny HAC the satisfaction of killing her. She awoke after the overdose in hospital. The victim testified that at the time she felt that she was worthless, because she was not 'even a mum anymore', because 'the kids couldn't even call me mum. I was just a thing' (*HAC* at [35]). In agreeing that no substantial miscarriage of justice had occurred, Holmes JA stated that HAC had 'committed a variety of painful and degrading abuses on his wife, with… the underlying intention to humiliate her' (*HAC* at [64]). After further submissions, the sentence for torture was subsequently reduced from ten years to seven and a half years (*HAC* at [11]). In resentencing the offender, Jerrard J described his behaviour as 'brutal, controlling, and deplorable', observing that the 'debasing conduct engaged in towards his wife over six months shows a lower level of violence but a higher degree of control over another person who was relentlessly abused' than other cases (*HAC* at [5], [8]).

Several other successfully prosecuted cases of torture inflicted in the context of ongoing DFV were reported in the news-press. For example, one man was convicted of torture of his ex-partner, as a result of abuse over a two-year period (NewsMail 2017). The behaviour underlying the torture charge included beating the victim, dousing her in petrol, placing a noose around her neck, tying her up and leaving her in a cupboard. The victim was also locked in the bedroom away from her children on Christmas day. The prosecutor was reported to say that the accused had 'significant power over her…. It's a shocking example of domestic violence over protracted time' (NewsMail 2017). In this case, the offender was sentenced to eight years' imprisonment. In another case reported in the news press, the offender had abused his partner over a three-year period (Branco 2018). Incidents of abuse included zip-tying her to a tree and trying to light her on fire, and on another occasion, duct taping her to a chair and cutting her hair off. In this case, the accused was sentenced to nine years' imprisonment with the judge commenting that the offending was 'gruelling', brutal' and 'sadistic' (Branco 2018).

The Queensland cases dealing with torture in the context of DFV attract similar descriptive language. The offenders' behaviour was often described as 'degrading', 'humiliating', 'demeaning', 'controlling', 'brutal' and 'protracted'. In his explanation of why coercive control should be opposed, Stark (2007, pp. 368–369) explains that people should be treated as ends in themselves 'as autonomous centers of freedom whose dignity and worth deserve the fullest possible support. Violations of liberty are the central moral wrong in coercive control, regardless of whether violence is their means'. The prosecuted cases of torture outlined here provide examples of coercive and controlling behaviour that attacks the victim's dignity and liberty. While the perpetrators in the cases considered all used physical violence as at least part of their means to control the victim and to undermine her dignity and liberty, the cases also highlight non-violent, degrading and humiliating acts perpetrated by offenders in the course of torture. These examples suggest the possibility that the crime of torture can be used as a response to coercive control, even in circumstances where physical violence is not used.

12.2.4 Limitations of Torture in Cases Involving Domestic and Family Violence

A number of published cases have highlighted difficulties associated with the successful prosecution of the torture charge in Queensland that may be especially problematic in the context of DFV. Some cases have identified the difficulty in proving intention under the provision. For example, one offender was charged with a number of offences, including four counts of torture (*R v LM* [2004] QCA 192 ('*LM*')). The prosecution alleged that LM had done things to her four children in order to create symptoms of illness, resulting in unnecessary medical procedures. At trial, she was convicted of two counts of torture and acquitted of the other two. She appealed against the torture convictions. On the question of proving intention, McMurdo P observed that 'it is purely a matter for the jury to decide the question of appellant's past intentions' and 'ordinary people will … often be puzzled at the extent of human depravity revealed in the criminal courts' (*LM* at [64]). Later McMurdo P observed:

> To establish the offence of torture the prosecution must prove that the accused person intentionally inflicted severe pain or suffering on the complainant by at least one act…To convict the appellant, the jury must have been unanimously agreed beyond a reasonable doubt that she did at least one of the particularised acts intending to inflict severe pain or suffering. (*LM* at [94])

The difficulty in directing a jury on intention in relation to torture charges was also emphasised in the case of *R v Ping* [2005] QCA 472 ('*Ping*'). In the initial trial, the judge had directed the jury on intention, stating:

> An intention resides in the consciousness of a person… If it is to be proved … it's proved by a process of inference or deduction from surrounding circumstances, for instance, what the person did, *what a person of ordinary knowledge and common sense would realise, would follow or flow from what they did*… (*Ping* at [36]) (emphasis added)

The Court of Appeal in *Ping* found that the italicised part of the passage extracted above was misleading. It found that the jury should have been told that the Crown had to prove, beyond a reasonable doubt, that the appellant had 'an actual subjective intention' that his acts would inflict 'severe pain and suffering on the victim (*Ping* at [38]). It would not be sufficient to prove that suffering is the consequence of the acts and that the acts were deliberate (*Ping* at [27]).

Another issue that has been raised is double jeopardy both in relation to charges, (including delimiting the relevant 'series of acts' for prosecuting torture) and in sentencing. In *R v Burns* [1999] QCA 189 ('*Burns 1*') the Crown alleged that Burns strangled his wife with his belt, threatened to kill her, tied her up, raped her and punched her numerous times over the course of two hours. He was charged with torture, assault occasioning actual bodily harm (QCC s 339) and two counts of rape. He pleaded guilty to the charge of assault occasioning actual bodily harm, and the charges of torture and rape were dealt with at trial where he was found guilty. He was sentenced to serve concurrent sentences on the rape and torture charges, with no sentence for the assault charge 'as the acts relied on to constitute that offence were comprehended in the offence of torture' (*Burns 1* at [1]). On appeal, the two rape and torture convictions were set aside and a new trial was ordered on those offences (*Burns 1*). Relevant to the context of this chapter, at the second trial Burns claimed that he had a defence to the torture charge in double jeopardy (QCC s 17) on the basis that the charge of torture overlapped with the assault charge to which he already pleaded guilty (*R v Burns* [2000] QCA 201 ('*Burns 2*')). The jury was directed on double jeopardy but determined that Burns was guilty of torture and he was sentenced. It is impossible to look into the reasons for the jury's decision to convict. It may have determined that if they did not convict Burns of torture he would go unpunished. Certainly double jeopardy appears to be a real issue in this case and it is questionable whether sentencing sufficiently deals with the concern.

There has also been a discussion about the meaning of 'series' in s 320A of the QCC. In *R v M* [2003] QCA 380, the offender was found not guilty of two counts of common assault but found guilty of one count of torture and one count of assault occasioning bodily harm in relation to abuse of his partner's young child. Similar to *R v Burns* [2000] QCA 201, double jeopardy concerns were reflected in sentencing and he was sentenced to eight years' imprisonment for torture, but not further punished for the other offence because it was based on the same behaviour as the torture charge. However the offender appealed the conviction on the basis that 'the torture charge was duplicitous' because 'the particulars relied upon by the prosecution could not be said to form one series of acts.' He argued that there had been two breaks in time when he did not see the child victim and, in those periods, he was not violent towards him. McMurdo P observed that the offender had remained in telephone contact (up to a dozen times a day) with the child during the breaks in physical contact. In any event, McMurdo P was not persuaded that the torture charge's date range (between 8 November 2000 and 12 September 2001) was so broad as to put the offender's chance of a fair trial at risk. Thus, even when there are breaks in the abuse, there can still be a 'series' for the purpose of the torture charge. Such breaks are not unusual in relationships involving DFV, and periods of calm in the relationship are often used by the abuser as part of his controlling tactics (Stark 2007, p. 5).

In summary, Queensland case law highlights some limitations with the Queensland torture offence that may have particular implications for its application in some cases involving DFV. For a start, the intention is difficult to prove. The courts have identified that, in order to convict, the jury must be satisfied beyond a reasonable doubt that the accused had a subjective intention when deliberately carrying out the acts underlying the torture charge, that those acts would inflict severe pain and suffering on the victim (*Ping* at [38]). This may be particularly difficult to prove in some cases involving DFV where there is usually no witnesses to the events other than the victim.

Further, in all published decisions that involve a successfully prosecuted charge of torture, other charges were also prosecuted alongside the torture charge. Most commonly, the concurrent charge involved an assault causing physical injury (e.g. *HAC*, *Burns*, *R v Latsamyvong* [2017] QCA 174). Notably, in many cases, torture charges appear to be initially charged but later withdrawn (e.g. *R v Samad* [2012] QCA 63; *R v Murphy* [2017] QCA 267). This may result from the concern with double jeopardy as well as the difficulties associated with proving the requisite intention for torture. The concurrent charging of torture with charges that involve physical violence shows that physical violence towards the victim is usually alleged as part of the behaviour underlying a charge of torture. Torture is defined as the 'intentional infliction of severe pain or suffering by an act or series of acts' and the pain or suffering may be 'physical, mental, psychological or emotional' (QCC s 320A). Saying words intentionally to inflict severe pain or suffering to a victim would not be sufficient to underpin a charge of torture. But the definition shows that torture could conceivably involve acts that are not physically directed towards the body of the victim, yet are intended to inflict severe psychological pain or suffering on the victim. However, without a direct physical assault on the victim, it may be difficult to demonstrate that the resulting pain or suffering is 'severe'. This may be another limitation of the torture charge, especially given, as I explore in the next section, that many women who experience DFV do not necessarily experience physical abuse.

12.3 The 'Worst' Forms of Abuse

In this section, I present some brief case studies drawn from interviews conducted with women who have experienced DFV to consider the forms of DFV they reported to be most harmful to their sense of freedom and dignity. Throughout 2014 to 2017, I interviewed 65 women up to three times each about their experience with DFV and how they engaged with the legal system in response. At the second interview, I asked women to identify the most difficult abusive behaviours to deal with. Of the 59 women who answered this question, 41 (83%) identified emotional or psychological abuse as the most difficult abuse they dealt with over the course of their relationship. The women made many comments about their experiences of the harmful effects of coercive and controlling behaviours, many of which did not involve physical violence.[1] Five brief case studies are outlined below.

---

[1] Pseudonyms are used when referring to the participants' comments to protect their anonymity. Thanks to the women who shared their stories for this research and to Dr. Jennifer Bell for research assistance. This work was supported by the Australian Research Council's Future Fellowship scheme (project number FT140100796). For more information about this study see: <https://law.uq.edu.au/research/our-research/using-law-and-leaving-domestic-violence-project/using-law-and-leaving-domestic-violence>.

12.3.1 Case Studies

Milly: Milly said that, for her, the emotional abuse was the worst. She described her partner as manipulative, verbally aggressive and controlling. She described how, as the relationship progressed, she came to believe that everything that went wrong in the relationship was her fault:

> With the manipulation, everything would end up being my fault and then he'd just hammer that in verbally, over and over and over again. Your fault this, your fault that, you did this, you did that.... It was my fault that he ended up having to get angry.

Although Milly earned an income, her abusive partner controlled the finances. She says that she quickly understood what she was 'allowed' to spend money on. I interviewed her after leaving the relationship. She said, 'I conformed really quickly, which is disappointing when I think of it now.'

Lahleh: Lahleh had migrated to Australia only a couple of years before meeting her partner. She reported that her partner demanded that she stay in the house with the curtains closed. He made threats to harm her if she tried to leave, and if she tried to reason with him he would become angry and throw and break dishes. She said:

> The things he said were worse than hitting.... He always told me stories about a woman— man and wife, their door of the car opened, she fell out when they were driving. One time he sharpened a knife in the kitchen and ... he was cutting and he said, 'this knife cuts beef like tofu'—he looks towards to me and did the move...

The 'move' was a slicing motion. Lahleh reported that she felt extremely intimidated by this behaviour.

Lisa: Lisa said that the abuse began gradually:

> It didn't become clear to me until we were really isolated. First, it was he didn't like my male friends, which I had a lot of because I worked in the car industry. Yeah, he didn't like me having any contact with my male friends, whether it be phone calls, texts or visits, yet he still maintained relationships with females.

There were many arguments. On one occasion, when she was 24 weeks pregnant, Lisa asked her partner to come home. She said '[h]e was angry. When he came home ... he got his phone and smashed it in front of me.' After the baby was born, they moved to an isolated place four hours' drive from the next major town. This was ostensibly for his job. She received no money from him and tried to live on the Family Allowance welfare benefit. Her only contacts were on *Facebook* and he monitored this. He would regularly ask her to have sex and she usually submitted because the one time she refused, he 'punched a hole in the wall next to my head where I had been standing.' When I asked what aspects of the abuse were the worst, she said:

> I think the mental. I think that's what has taken its toll on me. How can I put it? I think—it's not just what he did to me, it's the fact that ... I don't have faith in my judgment anymore, I'm not open to relationships anymore, I'm closed down. Does that make sense?

Jane: Jane explained that her partner used to break things that were important to her: 'I'm angry with you so I'm ripping up your violin exam paper—certificate. I'm angry with you, I'm going to break your squash racquet.' She described herself as becoming 'worn down'. In retrospect, Jane could see she experienced a high level of emotional abuse in the relationship. She would sometimes have a coffee with a friend and her husband would call her on the phone incessantly while she was in the cafe. She would see his number flash on her screen and she would—

> get the flooding of ... the fear flood, yeah, where your whole body just kind of ... I knew that he'd be angry. Why aren't you doing this or that? Because I was the handmaiden.

When Jane eventually separated from her partner, she applied for a property settlement through the Family Court (a federal court in Australia). Jane employed a private solicitor to assist her. Jane reported that her partner continued to abuse her through the legal system after separation. He frustrated efforts to reach a settlement; he kept her in mediation for many hours without any intention to settle and emailed her lawyer frequently. All of these behaviours significantly increased her legal costs and extended her engagement with the legal system.

Felicity: Felicity described her relationship with her partner as extremely controlling. She said her ex-partner used rages, 'silent treatment', threats of harm and isolation to control her. Felicity was a committed Christian and her partner made many comments about the negative things God would say about her behaviour. On one occasion he 'yanked' the crucifix she was wearing from her neck. During the relationship, her partner also alienated her from her sister and parents. He became angry at Felicity whenever they called or visited, and eventually, they stopped coming. During another outburst he threw her belongings onto the lawn and ripped up her personal papers in front of her. He said on one occasion 'I would put a $2.50 bullet through your brain but ... that's overcapitalising on you.' Towards the end of the relationship, Felicity would lock herself and the children in the bedroom to feel safe. When I asked Felicity what was the worst aspect of the abuse she had experienced she said:

> Emotional and psychological abuse. I will always remember it. It made me doubt myself and question myself and continually justify what you are doing and why you are doing it and cover myself.

12.3.2 Falling Short of Torture

Bettinson and Bishop (2015, p. 184) have observed that victims of domestic abuse and coercive control often internalise the rules of the relationship and begin to automatically perform as the perpetrator requires. Ultimately, less and less physical violence or threats are required to ensure the victim's compliance. Eventually, the victim is controlled through a range of signs and signals not understood by those outside the relationship. The case studies outlined in this section provide examples of patterns of coercive and controlling behaviour that do not include direct physical violence or physical harm. Nevertheless, from the women's perspectives, the various controlling tactics and behaviours of abusers had significant impacts on each woman's ability to exercise her freedom and autonomy. Despite their effectiveness, the behaviours described in the case studies, individually or as part of a pattern, generally fall short of satisfying the elements of any criminal offences currently available in Queensland, including torture. Notably, some of the facts outlined in the case studies may be sufficient to underpin a charge of financial or emotional abuse under Tasmanian legislation, see *Family Violence Act 2004* (Tas) ss 8 and 9 (see Chap. 7 in this collection). Furthermore, an offence of coercive control similar to the *Serious Crime Act 2015* (E&W) s 76 (see also Chaps. 8 and 10 in this collection) may also be applicable in these examples. In most of the case studies it is likely to be difficult for the prosecution to prove, beyond a reasonable doubt, that the perpetrator 'intentionally inflicted' pain or suffering on the victim under the torture provision. Furthermore, it may also be difficult to prove that the harm suffered by the women in these case studies reaches the threshold of 'severe' pain or suffering required under the torture provision.

12.4 Introducing a New Offence: Cruelty

The analysis of published cases in Part II of this chapter demonstrated that the crime of torture in Queensland is often successfully prosecuted in cases involving DFV. Torture may be an appropriate charge in response to DFV behaviour when it is possible to prove that the abuser intended to inflict (and did indeed inflict) severe pain or suffering on the victim by carrying out an act or series of acts (QCC s 320A). The successfully prosecuted charges of torture show more than 'apparently random tantrums' of a spouse with a 'nasty disposition'; rather they suggest an underlying purpose of control and/or punishment (see Tetlow 2016, p. 188). For many women who experience DFV (recall the case studies explored in Part III of this chapter), there may be no direct physical violence (or at least no recent physical violence) and the requisite intent and a 'severe' level of harm may be difficult to prove. In Queensland, there is no other offence available that reflects the ongoing coercive and controlling pattern of behaviour of DFV identified by the case studies outlined previously. There is, therefore, potentially a gap in the QCC.

In determining whether it is appropriate to criminalise behaviour Husak (2008, p. 120) prescribes four requirements: the behaviour must cause (or risk causing) a non-trivial harm; hardship and stigma should be reserved for conduct that is wrongful; punishment must be deserved; and the prosecution should have the burden of proof (see also Chap. 6). The case studies outlined earlier, and previous research (e.g. Stark 2007), demonstrate there is harm caused by coercive controlling behaviours, even when there is no physical injury. Below I restate a suggestion that I have made elsewhere, that a crime of cruelty should be introduced to the QCC which would operate as a less serious form of the crime of torture (Douglas 2015).

12.4.1 Constructing a Crime of Cruelty in Queensland

As noted earlier, the Queensland Parliament introduced the crime of torture as a response to child abuse in 1996. At the same time, the Queensland Parliament introduced an offence of 'cruelty to children under 16' (QCC s 364). Thus, cruelty is a familiar language in the QCC and this familiarity helps to support and justify its use in the context outlined here. The Oxford Dictionary defines cruelty as 'behaviour which causes pain or suffering to a person … (with) indifference to or pleasure in causing pain and suffering'. The word cruelty may be an appropriate word to name many of the coercive and controlling patterns of behaviour associated with DFV that result in harm, but where the harm is less serious (or does not meet the 'severe' harm required under the torture offence). I suggest the crime of cruelty may be constructed. A more detailed discussion of this suggestion can be found in Douglas (2015), briefly though, I suggest the offence would be constructed as follows:

s 320B. Cruelty

(1) A person who commits cruelty to another person commits a crime.
    Maximum penalty — 5 years imprisonment.
(2) If the person commits cruelty to a person in a relevant relationship the offender is liable to imprisonment for 7 years.
(3) In this section—
    cruelty means the infliction of pain or suffering on a person by an act or series of acts done on 1 or more than 1 occasion.
    pain or suffering includes physical, mental, psychological or emotional pain or suffering, whether temporary or permanent.
    relevant relationship means a relevant relationship under the *Domestic and Family Violence Protection Act 2012* (Qld) s 13.

Like torture, the crime of cruelty would encompass a series of acts that individually may not fit the definition of existing criminal offences, but which as a series of actions may be understood as cruelty. The proposed cruelty offence would require that pain and suffering are inflicted, but unlike the torture offence, the pain and suffering would not need to be severe. Any pain and suffering would be sufficient; the types of acts, and the level of pain and suffering inflicted, would be relevant to sentencing outcomes. Finally, the crime of cruelty would be a crime of general intent, similar to assault in Queensland (QCC s 335). The prosecution would have to prove that the accused intended to do the acts the subject of the charge but would not need to prove the accused intended harm. The element of intent for cruelty would be less difficult for the prosecution to prove, compared with the specific intent (that the accused intended to inflict serious pain or suffering to the victim) associated with the more serious crime of torture (QCC s320A). However, to successfully prosecute cruelty the prosecution would need to prove a connection between the acts and the pain and suffering of the victim (i.e. causation).

The crime would be applicable to cases involving DFV but may be applicable in other circumstances as well. However, if committed in the context of DFV a higher maximum penalty for the offence would be available and a higher sentence would likely be imposed to account for the aggravating feature of the offending occurring in that context (see, e.g., *Penalties and Sentences Act 1992* (Qld) s 9(10A)). This would demonstrate the seriousness of cruelty when perpetrated in the context of DFV. Generally, the crime of cruelty would be finalised in the lower courts with an option for the charge to be transferred to the higher courts if a higher sentence was deemed appropriate (Douglas et al. 2017, pp. 118–120).

12.5 Conclusions

The crimes of torture and cruelty outlined in this chapter are similar to the United Kingdom offence of coercive control (*Serious Crime Act 2015* (E&W) s 76) and the Scottish offence of domestic abuse (*Domestic Abuse (Scotland) Act 2018*), analysed in detail in Chaps. 8 and 10 of this collection, in that they can recognise the patterns of violence inherent in family violence and in particular the non-physical forms it often takes. However, torture and cruelty differ from the offences of coercive control and domestic abuse in important ways. First, and perhaps most significantly, the names or labels of the offences are different. As others have argued (Ashworth 2009, p. 78; Chalmers and Leverick 2008, pp. 227–228) labels should be simple and descriptive and should reflect the nature and magnitude of the wrongdoing. The terms 'torture' and 'cruelty' are well-understood in criminal law (at least in Queensland, Australia) and reflect the harm experienced by the victim. The naming of DFV offences as torture and cruelty may, as Sheehy (2018, p. 226) suggests, best identify the harm for women and overcome 'the discourses of banalisation, mutualisation and justification that plague' violence against women. In contrast 'coercive control' is a complex terminology, not necessarily well-understood by the general public and relies on the concept being successfully translated from clinical practice to criminal law (Walklate et al. 2018, p. 117). In contrast the Scottish offence titled 'abusive behaviour', while clear risks minimising the seriousness of the harm experienced. In the United Kingdom context, research suggests that police have found the offence difficult to interpret and that implementation of the offence has been slow (Wiener 2017). Notably, the UK offences of coercive control and domestic abuse are complex and longwinded compared to the comparative simplicity of the torture and proposed cruelty offences. Furthermore, the UK offence of coercive control requires that the perpetrator's behaviour must have a 'serious effect' on the victim (*Serious Crime Act 2015* (E&W) ss 76(1), (4)) and this is defined to mean either that the behaviour causes the victim to fear violence on at least two occasions, or to cause the victim serious alarm or distress having a 'substantial adverse effect' on their everyday activities. In comparison, the torture offence requires that the prosecution prove the perpetrator caused 'severe pain or suffering' of any kind to the victim, and the proposed cruelty offence requires the prosecution prove the perpetrator caused 'pain or suffering' to the victim. Torture and cruelty do not require proof that the victim was fearful. Fear may be difficult to demonstrate. For example, some women who have been traumatised over a long time (either because of DFV or other experiences), or who do not fit stereotypes of battered women, may not be fearful; they may present as emotionally unengaged or indeed they may appear angry (Allimant and Ostaplej-Platkowski 2011). While torture requires proof of serious pain and suffering (similar to the UK offence requirement of 'substantial adverse effect'), the proposed lower level offence of cruelty simply requires pain or suffering. Furthermore, the offences of torture and cruelty do not require that the prosecution prove the perpetrator and victim were in a specific relationship unless, in the case of cruelty, they are pursuing a higher maximum sentence. These aspects of the offence of cruelty make it less complex for prosecutors to prove.

As this chapter shows, the crime of torture has been successfully prosecuted in a number of serious cases of DFV in Queensland, Australia. While to date, Queensland is the only Australian state that has introduced a crime of torture, as Sheehy (2018, p. 254) identifies, at least 13 other jurisdictions have criminalised private torture throughout the world, including three American states (Alabama, California and Michigan), and the countries of Austria, Belgium, Brazil, Bulgaria, France, Germany, Malta, Rwanda, Slovenia and Spain.

Torture is recognised as a form of human rights abuse (United Nations 1984). Stark's (2007) definition of DFV as coercive control identifies its main harms as 'political' and reflect 'the deprivation of rights and resources that are critical to personhood and citizenship' (Stark 2007, p. 5; see also, Davidson 2019, forthcoming). It is appropriate then, that DFV is named as torture where its harms are serious. The Queensland crime of torture applied to the context of DFV aptly captures the ongoing pattern of abusive behaviours underlying DFV, and the deprivation of personhood experienced by the victim and intended by the abuser (Douglas 2003, p. 454). Meanwhile the proposed related offence of cruelty captures the ongoing pattern of abusive behaviours underlying DFV but is available in those contexts where the resulting harm may be less serious and where intention to cause pain and suffering may not be able to be proved. While adjustments will need to be made to aspects of the offences to ensure they are appropriate to other Australian jurisdictions, it is suggested that crimes of torture and cruelty may adequately fill a gap in the criminal response to DFV. As Tetlow (2016, p. 250; see also Marcus 1994) claims in her argument for the introduction of a charge of torture as a response to DFV in the USA:

> Identifying domestic violence as torture gives us a name for the scope of the terror batterers inflict. It reveals domestic violence as a pattern of accumulated cruelty, with searing psychological scars often worse than the physical pain.

References

Allimant, A., & Ostapiej-Piatkowski, B. (2011). *Supporting Women from CALD Backgrounds who are Victim/Survivors of Sexual Abuse*, ACSSA Wrap No 9. Melbourne: Australian Centre for the Study of Sexual Assault. Retrieved from https://aifs.gov.au/sites/default/files/publication-documents/w9.pdf.

Ashworth, A. (2009). *Principles of criminal law* (6th ed.). Oxford: Oxford University Press.

Bettinson, V., & Bishop, C. (2015). Is the creation of a discrete offence of coercive control necessary to combat domestic violence? *Northern Ireland Legal Quarterly, 66*(2), 179–197.

Branco, J. (2018, January 24). Nine years jail for man who hit pregnant partner with a hammer. *Brisbane Times*. Retrieved from https://www.brisbanetimes.com.au/national/queensland/nine-years-jail-for-man-who-hit-pregnant-partner-with-a-hammer-20180124-p4yyu9.html.

Chalmers, J., & Leverick, F. (2008). Fair labelling in criminal law. *Modern Law Review, 71*(2), 217–246.

Davidson, N. (2019, forthcoming). The feminist expansion of the prohibition of torture: Towards a post-liberal international human rights law? *Cornell International Law Journal*, 1–30.

Douglas, H. (2003). Crime in the intimate sphere: Prosecutions of intimate partner violence. *Newcastle Law Review, 7*(2), 79–100.

Douglas, H. (2015). Do we need a specific domestic violence offence? *Melbourne University Law Review, 39*(2), 434–471.

Douglas, H., Barrett, M., & Higgins, E. (2017). *Criminal process in Queensland*. Sydney, NSW: Thomson Reuters.

Husak, D. (2008). *Overcriminalisation*. Oxford: Oxford University Press.

Kutin, J., Russell, R., & Reid, M. (2017). Economic abuse between intimate partners in Australia: prevalence, health status, disability and financial stress. *Australian and New Zealand Journal of Public Health, 41*(3), 269–274.

NewsMail. (2017, December 11). Torture felt like being in car crash, says victim. *NewsMail*. Retrived from https://www.news-mail.com.au/news/torture-felt-like-being-in-car-crash-says-victim/3287228/.

Oberhardt, M. (1997, May 14). Jail term cut for tot assault. *Courier Mail*.

Oberhardt, M. (1996, November 5). Stepdad 'zapped' boy, 5. *Courier Mail*.

QSAC: Queensland Sentencing Advisory Council. (2018). 'Torture Statistics'.

Queensland, *Parliamentary Debates*, Legislative Assembly, 19 March 1997 (Frank Carroll).

Queensland, *Parliamentary Debates*, Legislative Assembly, 18 March 1997 (Naomi Wilson).

Queensland Taskforce on Women and the Criminal Code. (2000). *Report of the Taskforce on Women and the Criminal Code*. Retrieved from http://www.justice.qld.gov.au/__data/assets/pdf_file/0017/463022/report-of-the-taskforce-on-organised-crime-legislation.pdf.

Sackett, L., & Saunders, D. (1999). The impact of different forms of psychological abuse on battered women. *Violence and Victims, 14*(1), 105–117.

Sheehy, L. (2018). Criminalising private torture as feminist strategy: Thinking through the implications. In K. Fitz-Gibbon, S. Walklate, J. McCulloch, & J. Maher (Eds.), *Intimate partner violence, risk and security: Securing women's lives in a global world*. London: Routledge.

Stark, E. (2007). *Coercive control: How men entrap women in personal life*. Oxford: Oxford University Press.

Tetlow, T. (2016). Criminalizing 'private' torture. *William and Mary Law Review, 58*, 183–250.

United Nations, Office of the High Commissioner for Human Rights. (1984). *Convention Against Torture and other Cruel, Inhuman or Degrading Treatment or Punishment*. Retrieved from https://www.ohchr.org/EN/ProfessionalInterest/Pages/Cat.aspx.

United Nations Treaty Collection. (2018). *Status of Treaties: Convention against Torture and Other Cruel, Inhuman or Degrading Treatment or Punishment*. Retrieved from https://treaties.un.org/Pages/ViewDetails.aspx?src=IND&mtdsg_no=IV-9&chapter=4&clang=_en.

Walklate, S., Fitz-Gibbon, K., & McCulloch, J. (2018). Is more law the answer? Seeking justice for victims of intimate partner violence through reform of legal categories. *Criminology & Criminal Justice, 18*(1), 115–131.

Wiener, C. (2017). What is 'invisible in plain sight': Policing coercive control. *Howard Journal of Crime and Justice, 56*(4), 500–515.

Legislation

Criminal Code and Other Acts Amendment Act 2008 (Qld)
Criminal Law (Domestic Violence) Amendment Bill 2015 (Qld)
Criminal Law Amendment Bill 1996 (Qld)
Domestic and Family Violence Protection Act 2012 (Qld)
Domestic Abuse (Scotland) Act 2018
Family Violence Act 2004 (Tas)
Penalties and Sentences Act 1992 (Qld)
Serious Crime Act 2015 (E&W)

Cases

R v Burns [1999] QCA 189 (28 May 1999)
R v Burns [2000] QCA 201 (30 May 2000)
R v Ellis [2018] QCA 70 (17 April 2018)
R v Griffin [1997] QCA 115
R v HAC [2006] QCA 291 (11 August 2016)
R v Latsamyvong [2017] QCA 174 (18 August 2017)
R v LM [2004] QCA 192 (4 June 2004)
R v M [2003] QCA 380 (1 September 2003)
R v Murphy [2017] QCA 267 (8 November 2017)
R v Peirson [2006] QCA 251 (14 July 2006)
R v Ping [2005] QCA 472 (16 December 2005)
R v Samad [2012] QCA 63 (23 March 2012)

Printed in Great Britain
by Amazon